America's Best Day Hiking Series

Hiking PENNSYLVANIA

MIKE BLEECH

Human Kinetics

D1295039

Library of Congress Cataloging-in-Publication Data

Bleech, Mike, 1949-
    Hiking Pennsylvania / Mike Bleech.
        p. cm.
    ISBN 0-7360-0166-2
    1. Hiking--Pennsylvania--Guidebooks. 2. Pennsylvania--Guidebooks. I. Title.

    GV199.42.P4 B45 2000

    917.4804'44--dc21

                                                        00-025312

ISBN: 0-7360-0166-2

Acquisitions Editor: Patricia Sammann
Managing Editor: Coree Schutter
Assistant Editors: Judy Park, Anne Cole, Amy Kraus, and John Wentworth
Copyeditor: Barbara Walsh
Graphic Designer: Robert Reuther
Graphic Artist: Francine Hamerski
Photo Editor: Clark Brooks
Cover Designer: Jack W. Davis
Photographer (cover): Bruce Coleman © Phil Degginger/Bruce Coleman, Inc.
Photographer (interior): Jeri Bleech
Illustrator: Tim Shedelbower
Printer: Versa Press

Information for maps on pages 4, 6, 10, 12, 16, 20, 24, 28, 32, 36, 40, 44, 48, 52, 56, 62, 66, 68, 72, 76, 80, 84, 88, 92, 96, 100, 104, 108, 112, 116, 120, 124, 128, 132, 136, 140, 144, 150, 156, 160, 164, 166, 170, 174, 178, 180, 184, 188, 192, 196, 200, 204, 206, 210 was supplied by the Pennsylvania Bureau of State Parks; page 146—adapted from the Gettysburg Convention and Visitors' Bureau; page 154—adapted from Community Care Foundation.

On the cover: Pine Creek in the Grand Canyon of Pennsylvania

Human Kinetics books are available at special discounts for bulk purchase. Special editions or book excerpts can also be created to specification. For details, contact the Special Sales Manager at Human Kinetics.

Printed in the United States of America   10 9 8 7 6 5 4 3 2 1

Human Kinetics
Web site: http://www.humankinetics.com/

United States: Human Kinetics
P.O. Box 5076
Champaign, IL 61825-5076
1-800-747-4457
e-mail: humank@hkusa.com

Canada: Human Kinetics
475 Devonshire Road Unit 100
Windsor, ON N8Y 2L5
1-800-465-7301 (in Canada only)
e-mail: humank@hkcanada.com

Europe: Human Kinetics, P.O. Box IW14
Leeds LS16 6TR, United Kingdom
+44 (0)113-278 1708
e-mail: humank@hkeurope.com

Australia: Human Kinetics
57A Price Avenue
Lower Mitcham, South Australia 5062
(08) 82771555
e-mail: liahka@senet.com.au

New Zealand: Human Kinetics
P.O. Box 105-231, Auckland Central
09-523-3462
e-mail: humank@hknewz.com

This book is dedicated to my mother, Audrey Bleech, who did not wait for the schools to teach me to read; to my wife, Jeri Bleech, who hiked many of the trails and contributed in many more ways; and to my old pal, Bill Anderson, who fed S. Kitty while Jeri and I were away from home.

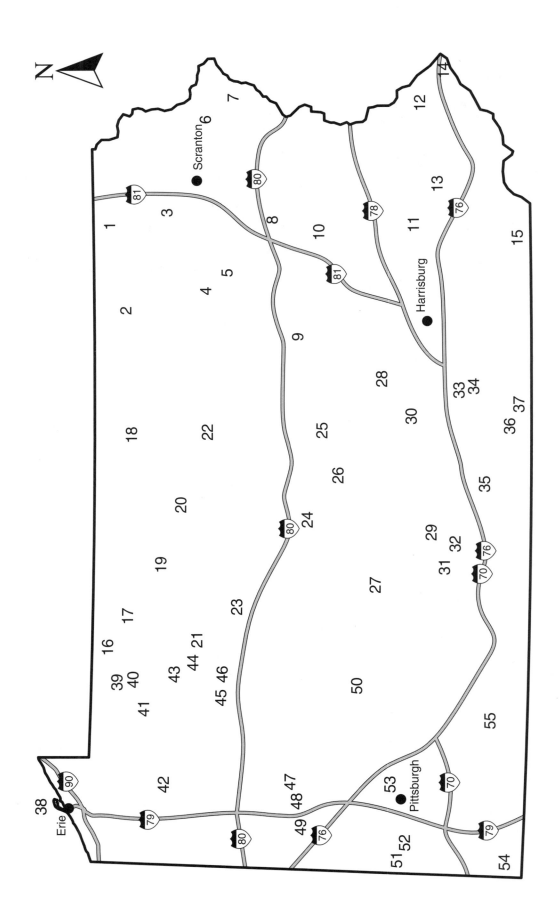

Contents

How to Use This Book

Hiking is an antidote to modern life. It gives the body some much-needed (and enjoyable) exercise, and it gives the mind both rest and stimulation. It even lifts the spirit to connect again with this earth that we're a part of but seldom have time to think about. With the America's Best Day Hiking Series, we hope to provide you with an incentive to start or continue hiking, for the pleasure and the challenge of it.

Each book in the series offers information on more than 100 of the most interesting and scenic trails in a particular state, as well as notes about recreational, historical, and sightseeing destinations located near the trails. The assortment of trails ranges from short, easy hikes for occasional hikers and families with young children to longer, more rugged ones for the experienced trailblazer. None of the trails takes more than a day to hike, although some trails may be linked together to create a hike of several days.

The trails in *Hiking Pennsylvania* are divided into three main areas—East, Central, and West. Divider pages signal the beginning of each new area, and those pages include information on the local topography, major rivers and lakes, flora and fauna, weather, and best features of the area.

The innovative format is designed to make exploring new parks and trails easy. Information on each park or other nature area always appears on a right-hand page. It begins with the park's name and a small state map that shows the park's general location. Bulleted highlights then point out the trails' most interesting features. A description of the park's history and terrain comes next, with practical information on how to get to the park and the park's hours, available facilities, permits and rules, and the address and phone number of a contact who can give you more information. The section entitled "Other Areas of Interest" briefly mentions nearby parks and recreational opportunities, with phone numbers to call for more information.

After the general information follows a selected list of trails in the park. The length and difficulty of hiking each is given, along with a brief description of its terrain. The difficulty rating, shown by boot icons, ranges from one (the easiest) to five (the most difficult).

On the other side of the page is a full-sized map of the park. Our book's larger format allows us to provide clear, readable maps that are easy to follow.

easiest 👢 👢 👢 👢 👢 most difficult
　　　　1　2　3　4　5

The next right- and left-hand pages are usually descriptions of the two best hikes in that park, along with a trail map at the bottom of each page (a few parks have only one hike, with just one map that primarily shows the trail). Each hike begins with information on the length and difficulty of the trail, and the estimated time to walk it, plus cautions to help you avoid possible annoyances or problems. The description of the trail provides more than directions; it's a guided tour of what you will see as you hike along. The scenery, wildlife, and history of the trail are all brought to life. Points of interest along the trail are numbered in brackets within the text, and those numbers are shown on the trail map to guide you. The approximate distance from the trailhead to each point of interest is given.

The park descriptions, maps, and trails are all kept as a unit within an even number of pages. Parks for which only one trail is highlighted take up only two pages; those with the regular two trails cover four pages. We've perforated the book's pages so you can remove them if you like, or you can copy them for your personal use. If you carry the pages with you as you hike, you might want to use a plastic sleeve to protect them from the elements. You also can make notes on these pages to remind you of your favorite parts of the park or trail.

If you want to find a park or trail quickly, use the trail finder that appears on the next pages. It gives essential information about each highlighted trail in the book, including the trail's length, difficulty, special features, and park facilities.

We hope the books in the America's Best Day Hiking Series inspire you to get out and enjoy a wide range of outdoor experiences. We've tried to find interesting trails from all parts of each state. Some are unexpected treasures—places you'd never dream exist in the state. Some may be favorites that you've already hiked and recommended to friends. But whether you live in a city or in the country, are away vacationing or are at home, some of these trails will be near you. Find one you like, strap on your hiking boots, and go!

Trail Finder

KEY

RV camping   tent camping   swimming   canoeing

fishing   boating   picnicking   biking

Trail Sites and Trails	Park Facilities	Miles	Trail Difficulty Rating	Hills	Escarpment	Forest	Lake	Wetlands	Overlook	River/Stream	Page #
1 Salt Spring State Park	fishing, picnicking										
Fall Brook Trail		.6	5 boots	✓		✓		✓	✓	✓	4
2 Mt. Pisgah State Park	swimming, canoeing, fishing, boating, picnicking										
Mill Stream Nature Trail		1	3 boots	✓		✓	✓	✓	✓	✓	7
Oh! Susanna Trail		2	2 boots	✓		✓	✓		✓	✓	8
3 Lackawanna State Park	RV camping, fishing, tent camping, swimming, canoeing, boating, picnicking										
Turkey Hill Trail		1.5	3 boots	✓		✓				✓	10
4 Worlds End State Park	canoeing, fishing, picnicking, tent camping, RV camping										
High Rock Trail		.9	6 boots	✓	✓	✓			✓	✓	13
Canyon Vista Trail		3.6	5 boots	✓		✓			✓	✓	14
5 Ricketts Glen State Park	tent camping, RV camping, boating, canoeing, fishing, picnicking, biking										
Falls Trail		3.1	6 boots	✓	✓	✓		✓	✓	✓	17
Grand View Trail		1.9	3 boots	✓		✓			✓		18
6 Promised Land State Park	All facilities										
Little Falls Trail		.8	2 boots	✓		✓				✓	21
Conservation Island Nature Trail		1.1	2 boots	✓		✓	✓	✓			22
7 Delaware Water Gap National Recreation Area	canoeing, boating										
George W. Childs Recreation Site	picnicking	.85	4 boots	✓	✓	✓			✓	✓	25
Dingmans Falls Trail	swimming, fishing	.74	1 boot	✓		✓		✓		✓	26
8 Hickory Run State Park	tent camping, RV camping										
Hawk Falls Trail	picnicking	1.2	3 boots	✓	✓	✓				✓	29
Shades of Death Trail	swimming, fishing	1.9	3 boots	✓		✓	✓			✓	30

Continued ☞

Continued 🖝

#	Trail Sites and Trails	Park Facilities	Miles	Trail Difficulty Rating	Hills	Escarpment	Forest	Lake	Wetlands	Overlook	River/Stream	Page #
19	**Sizerville State Park**	(icons)										
	Nady Hollow Trail		1.63	4 boots	✓		✓				✓	73
	Bottom Lands Trail		.9	2 boots	✓		✓		✓		✓	74
20	**Ole Bull State Park**	(icons)										
	Castle Vista Trail		.5	3 boots	✓	✓	✓			✓	✓	77
	Beaver Haven Nature Trail		1.1	1 boot			✓		✓		✓	78
21	**Allegheny National Forest— Elk County**	(icons)										
	Little Drummer Historical Pathway		3.4	2 boots	✓		✓	✓	✓		✓	81
	Elk Loop		1	2 boots	✓		✓					82
22	**Little Pine State Park**	(icons)										
	Panther Run/Love Run Trails/Love Run Road		2.8	5 boots	✓		✓			✓	✓	85
	Carsontown Trail		1.1	2 boots			✓		✓		✓	86
23	**Parker Dam State Park**	(icons)										
	Beaver Dam Trail		2.8	2 boots	✓		✓	✓	✓		✓	89
	Souders Trail		1	2 boots	✓		✓				✓	90
24	**Black Moshannon State Park**	All facilities										
	Star Mill Trail		1.95	2 boots			✓	✓	✓			93
	Bog Trail		.47	1 boot			✓	✓	✓			94
25	**Reeds Gap State Park**	(icons)										
	Blue Jay Trail		1.45	3 boots	✓		✓				✓	97
	Interpretive Trail		1	2 boots	✓		✓				✓	98
26	**Greenwood Furnace State Park**	(icons)										
	Greenwood Trail		.6	3 boots	✓		✓					101
	A Walk Through Historic Greenwood Furnace		1.8	2 boots					✓			102
27	**Canoe Creek State Park**	(icons)										
	Limestone Trail		1.21	3 boots	✓		✓				✓	105
	Marsh Trail		.9	2 boots			✓	✓	✓			106

Continued ☞

Continued ☞

x

Trail Sites and Trails	Park Facilities	Miles	Trail Difficulty Rating	Hills	Escarpment	Forest	Lake	Wetlands	Overlook	River/Stream	Page #
37 Gettysburg											
The Gettysburg National Cemetery		.6	🥾								145
Downtown Gettysburg Walking Tour		1.5	🥾								146
38 Presque Isle State Park											
Gull Point Trail		1.9	🥾			✓	✓	✓			151
Sidewalk/Dead Pond Trails		3.7	🥾			✓	✓	✓			152
39 Warren											
Crescent Park Tree Walk		.7	🥾							✓	154
40 Chapman State Park	All facilities										
Penny Run Trail		1.5	🥾🥾🥾	✓		✓		✓		✓	157
Nature Trail		1	🥾🥾			✓	✓	✓		✓	158
41 Allegheny National Forest— Warren County	All facilities										
Hearts Content Scenic Area Interpretive Trail		1.1	🥾🥾	✓		✓				✓	161
Tanbark Trail		9	🥾🥾🥾🥾	✓		✓		✓		✓	162
42 Erie National Wildlife Refuge											
Tsuga Nature Trail		1.2	🥾🥾	✓		✓	✓	✓		✓	164
43 Allegheny National Forest— Beaver Meadows Recreation Area											
Salmon Creek Loop		1.7	🥾🥾	✓		✓	✓	✓		✓	167
Seldom Seen Trail		1.7	🥾🥾	✓		✓		✓		✓	168
44 Buzzard Swamp											
Buzzard Swamp Trail		3.5	🥾🥾	✓		✓	✓	✓		✓	171
Songbird Sojourn Interpretive Trail		1.6	🥾🥾	✓		✓		✓		✓	172
45 Cook Forest State Park											
Seneca Trail		.92	🥾🥾🥾🥾🥾	✓	✓	✓		✓	✓	✓	175
Longfellow Trail		1.83	🥾🥾🥾🥾	✓		✓				✓	176

Continued ☞

#	Trail Sites and Trails	Park Facilities	Miles	Trail Difficulty Rating	Hills	Prairie/Grass	Forest	Lake	Wetlands	Overlook	River/Stream	Page #
46	**Clear Creek State Park**	(icons)										
	River Trail		.9	2 boots	✓		✓				✓	178
47	**Jennings Environmental Education Center**	(icons)										
	Blazing Star Prairie Self-Guided Trail		.6	2 boots	✓		✓				✓	181
	Woodwhisper Trail		.36	1 boot			✓			✓		182
48	**Moraine State Park**	(icons)										
	Wyggeston Trail Loop		1.6	2 boots	✓		✓					185
	Sunken Garden Trail		1.6	1 boot			✓	✓		✓	✓	186
49	**McConnell's Mill State Park**	(icons)										
	Kildoo Trail		2.1	3 boots	✓	✓	✓				✓	189
	Hell's Hollow Trail		1	2 boots	✓	✓	✓				✓	190
50	**Yellow Creek State Park**	(icons)										
	Laurel Run Trail		.77	2 boots			✓	✓	✓		✓	193
	Ridge Top Trail		2.3	3 boots	✓		✓				✓	194
51	**Raccoon Creek State Park**	(icons)										
	Mineral Springs Trail		1.5	3 boots	✓		✓				✓	197
	Valley Trail		2.4	3 boots	✓		✓	✓			✓	198
52	**Wildflower Reserve— Raccoon Creek State Park**											
	Jennings/Deer/Old Wagon Road Trails		.5	2 boots	✓		✓					201
	Audubon Trail		1.1	3 boots	✓		✓			✓		202
53	**Point State Park**											
	Fort Pitt		.8	1 boot							✓	204
54	**Ryerson Station State Park**	(icons)										
	Pine Box Trail		2	4 boots	✓		✓				✓	207
	Deer Trail		.8	2 boots	✓		✓					208
55	**Ohiopyle State Park**	(icons)										
	Ferncliff Trail		1.9	3 boots	✓		✓				✓	211
	Mitchell Trail		2.3	2 boots	✓		✓					212

Terrain/Landscape

East

More densely populated than the rest of the state, the eastern third of Pennsylvania extends from the Delaware River west to, and past in the extreme north and south, the Susquehanna River, and from the New York border south to the Maryland and Delaware borders.

Topography

Pennsylvania's eastern third exhibits the greatest changes in topography, from sea level at the Delaware River estuary to Appalachian Mountain ridges.

The northern-tier counties are a part of the Appalachian Plateau, which was scoured by Ice Age glaciers, leaving the land more rolling than the north-central region. The Pocono Plateau is on the southeastern tip of this feature, in small parts of Lackawanna, Wayne, Pike, Monroe, Carbon, and Luzerne counties. It is not as large an area as developers and tourism promotion agencies would have you believe. The heavily forested Allegheny Plateau, more commonly called the Allegheny Highlands, extends into southwestern Bradford County, most of Sullivan County, and southwest Wyoming County. It was not glaciated and exhibits more rugged terrain.

Long Appalachian Mountain ridges and valleys slice through the east-central region. Ridges are steep and rocky. Valleys are broad and rolling. Though elevations above 2,000 feet exist in but a few places, changes in elevation are some of the greatest in the state, especially where the Delaware and Susquehanna Rivers and their major tributaries cut through the mountains.

The southeast corner of the state drops to the gently rolling coastal piedmont, to a narrow strip of flat coastal plain, and finally to sea level along the lower Delaware River. Though just a small portion of the state, this is its richest farmland; in this area is the famous Pennsylvania Dutch region. This is also the most densely populated and highly developed part of the state.

Major Rivers and Lakes

Most Americans are familiar with the famous painting of George Washington crossing the ice-choked Delaware River from Pennsylvania into New Jersey. To a great extent, eastern Pennsylvania lies between the Delaware and the broad Susquehanna River. The Delaware still flows freely where it forms the eastern border with New York and New Jersey. Major tributaries in Pennsylvania are the Lackawaxen, the Lehigh, and the Schuylkill Rivers. The Susquehanna has been dammed in several places in the southeast, primarily for the purpose of generating electric power. The west and north branches meet at Northumberland to form one of America's great rivers, the main tributary of Chesapeake Bay.

There are no large natural lakes in Pennsylvania; however, the Pocono region is dotted with small lakes and ponds. Lake Wallenpaupack, a popular tourist destination along the border of Wayne County and Pike County, is the largest human-made reservoir in the northeast.

Common Plant Life

Most of the forest, like most forest elsewhere in Pennsylvania, consists of hardwoods mixed with eastern hemlock, some white pine, and numerous pine plantations, which are often red pine. The hardwoods include primarily oak, maple, hickory, poplar, and beech. Mountain laurel and rhododendron are scattered through the forest, sometimes in dense patches. On the Pocono Plateau, trees of more northerly forests may be found, including tamarack and red spruce. This region also has more wetlands than most of the state. Bogs and the shores of shallow lakes are covered with pickerelweed, water lilies, and a multitude of aquatic plants.

Forestland is becoming increasingly scarce south of Interstate Route 78 because of agriculture and suburban sprawl. What little remains in the piedmont and coastal plain is composed of trees that are characteristic of more southerly forests. You might find persimmon, river birch, or post oak.

Common Birds and Animals

Wildlife in general is more abundant north of I-78, between Harrisburg and Easton. White-tailed deer can be seen on most evening drives and along most trails. Black bears are abundant but far more reclusive, as are bobcats, which are far more numerous than most people realize. Gray squirrels are found wherever mast-producing trees grow. Fox squirrels tend to be locally abundant along some of the major waterways. Raccoons, mink, and beavers are a common sight along the shorelines of streams and lakes. A trap and transfer program has met with some success in restoring otters to the Pocono Plateau.

The checkerboard mix of woodlots and fields in various stages of cultivation and reclamation by nature provide habitat for a huge variety of birds. More than 200 species have been identified in some state parks.

South of I-78, deer are still fairly numerous on what little land is not yet developed. Wildlife is being squeezed out by suburban sprawl. One notable exception is along the lower Susquehanna River, where numerous waterbirds and raptors thrive. This is the only part of the state where you are likely to see the great egret, snowy egret, cattle egret, black-crowned night heron, or yellow-crowned night heron. Another exception is along the lower Delaware River, which is an important stopover for waterfowl along the Atlantic Flyway.

Climate

Average summer high temperatures vary from the high 70s in the Pocono region to the high 80s in the extreme southeastern tip. Average winter lows are in the mid-teens in the north and the mid-20s along the southern border.

Average annual rainfall is about 50 inches in the Pocono Plateau. Other areas vary, down to 38 inches along the lower Susquehanna River. Snow cover tends to be the norm during winter north of Interstate Route 80, but it is the exception in southern-tier counties.

Best Features

- Delaware River
- Delaware Water Gap
- Delaware River Estuary
- Pocono Plateau
- Susquehanna River
- Lehigh Gorge
- Appalachian Mountains
- Ricketts Glen

1. Salt Spring State Park

- Gaze at towering ancient hemlock trees.
- Listen to the sounds of a cascading stream.
- Enjoy the relative solitude of this lightly used park.

Area Information

Salt Spring State Park has three outstanding features, the first, and least, of which is its namesake, a salt spring that is in the picnicking area. Efforts to mine the salt during the 19th century proved unprofitable. Far more imposing is a stand of virgin hemlock trees, some 600 to 700 years old. The third major feature is Fall Brook, which tumbles down a steep, narrow valley. Visit this park during the rainy spring season to get the full effect of a series of three waterfalls.

Directions: Take Pennsylvania Route 29 to Franklin Forks and turn west on Salt Spring Road. Turn left at the sign to the park after about 1 mile.

Hours Open: Day-use areas are open from 8:00 A.M. to sunset.

Facilities: There is a picnic area and adjacent rest rooms. Silver Creek is stocked with trout.

Permits and Rules: Fires and disposal of hot coals are permitted only in provided facilities. Pets must be leashed and controlled at all times. Alcoholic beverages are prohibited.

Further Information: Salt Spring State Park, c/o Lackawanna State Park, RR 1, Box 230, Dalton, PA 18414-9785; phone 717-945-3239.

Park Trails

Hemlock Trail 🥾—.1 mile—This trail is an alternate route for a section of Fall Brook Trail. It passes Penny Rock, a popular place to sit and listen to the waterfalls.

Woodland Trail 🥾🥾🥾—.9 mile—Get a better look at the ancient hemlock.

Fall Brook Trail 👢👢👢👢👢

Distance Round-Trip: .6 mile

Estimated Hiking Time: 40 minutes

Caution: Part of this trail is along the edge of a deep gorge. Numerous roots and rocks make footing treacherous. If you prefer to climb the gentler part of the trail and descend the steepest part, walk the trail in reverse of these directions.

Trail Directions: From the parking area behind an old farmhouse, walk across the dirt road and across a footbridge to the head of this short, spectacular trail [1]. Almost immediately, the trail begins a very steep climb along the edge of a narrow gorge. Listen to the song of Fall Brook as it rolls and tumbles below. With each step you will encounter roots or rocks. But these obstructions form natural steps; without them, the climb might be impossible.

The hardest part of the climb is past where the trail follows the gorge out to a small point at about .2 mi. Here you come to the first and highest of three small waterfalls [2]. The next two waterfalls come in quick succession. Pause in this area, find a comfortable seat, lean back, keep quiet, and listen to the waterfalls. They have a soothing quality. Following the exact course of the trail is difficult in this area because it is not marked, and people have worn several alternate courses into the ground. But if you remember to keep the gorge to your right, you will get to where you should be going. The temptation to get off the trail for a better view of the waterfalls will be great. If you do, be very cautious.

At about .23 mi. the trail makes a very sharp turn to the left [3]. You will probably miss this turn and continue uphill until steps lead down to the bottom of the gorge, which is not nearly as deep at this point. You might want to explore this area and get a look at the falls from a different angle. Be careful, though, of slippery rocks. Then, as you double back up the steps and back down the trail, that turn you missed will be easier to locate.

Even if you cannot follow the actual trail, all you have to do is keep moving downhill with the gorge to your left. However, if you can keep on this part of the trail, it provides much easier walking than the first half. You might even want to wander off the trail or divert onto Woodland Trail or Hemlock Trail to examine some of the huge hemlocks. These trails are not clearly marked, and you will probably not even notice them.

The descent becomes steeper at about .4 mi. [4] and turns to the right. An alternate trail cuts directly downhill to the left at .5 mi. [5], toward the picnic area that is now in sight. A crude bench has been constructed here.

The trail ends at the bottom of the hill, near Silver Creek, at the lower end of the picnic area, after slightly more than .5 mi. A wooden trailhead marker is also at this end of the trail [6]. Walk through the picnic area to return to the trailhead and footbridge to complete the .6-mi. loop [1].

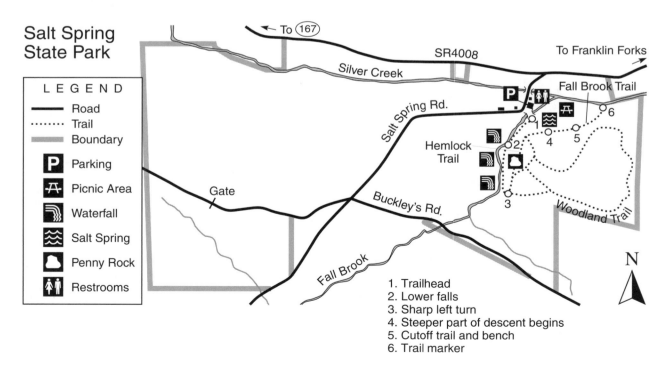

Salt Spring State Park

LEGEND
— Road
····· Trail
▬ Boundary
🅿 Parking
🛉 Picnic Area
🌊 Waterfall
≋ Salt Spring
⬭ Penny Rock
🚻 Restrooms

To 167
SR4008
To Franklin Forks
Silver Creek
Fall Brook Trail
Salt Spring Rd.
Hemlock Trail
Gate
Buckley's Rd.
Fall Brook
Woodland Trail
N

1. Trailhead
2. Lower falls
3. Sharp left turn
4. Steeper part of descent begins
5. Cutoff trail and bench
6. Trail marker

2. Mt. Pisgah State Park

- Fish for bass and panfish at Stephen Foster Lake.
- Swim in a large pool.
- Relax in the serenity of the Endless Mountains.
- Learn about nature at the environmental center.

Area Information

The region known as the Endless Mountains appears hilly, much like most of Pennsylvania. The landscape is a mix of farms and forest, with relatively sparse human settlement. But in contrast to the rest of the Appalachian Plateau, of which it is part, glaciers ground through during the Ice Age. Mt. Pisgah State Park was created out of land that had been cleared early in the 19th century for farming. History buffs should visit a restored family cemetery and the environmental education center that is dedicated to early settlers.

Stephen Foster Lake, named for the great composer who once resided in the area, was created by a dam on Mill Creek as the centerpiece of this park. The lake covers 75 acres. It is home to largemouth bass, chain pickerel, yellow perch, crappies, and bluegills. Only nonpowered and electric-powered boats are allowed.

Directions: From U.S. Route 6 at West Burlington, follow the signs 2.6 miles north on Pisgah Road, then right onto State Park Road to the edge of the park.

Hours Open: The park is open year-round. Day-use areas are open from 8:00 A.M. to sunset. The swimming pool is open between 11:00 A.M. and 7:00 P.M. from Memorial Day weekend to Labor Day.

Facilities: A 5,675-square-foot swimming pool and an environmental education center highlight facilities, which also include boat launching and mooring, boat rentals, restrooms, a children's playground, a picnic area, two pavilions, a bathhouse, and a food concession.

Permits and Rules: Recreational activity is limited to locations where physical improvements or signs designate the appropriate use. Swimming is not allowed in the lake. Fires are permitted only in provided facilities. Dispose of all charcoal in special barrels located in the picnic area. Alcoholic beverages are not allowed. Boats must have either a launch permit, which is available at the park office; a park mooring permit; or a current Pennsylvania Fish and Boat Commission registration.

Further Information: Mt. Pisgah State Park, Department of Environmental Resources, RD 3, Box 362, Troy, PA 16947; phone 717-297-2734.

Other Areas of Interest

French Azilum, a settlement of French refugees established in 1793, is south of Towanda. For information on local attractions, contact Endless Mountains Visitor's Bureau, 712 Route 6 East, Tunkhannock, PA 18657; phone 800-769-8999.

Mt. Pisgah State Park

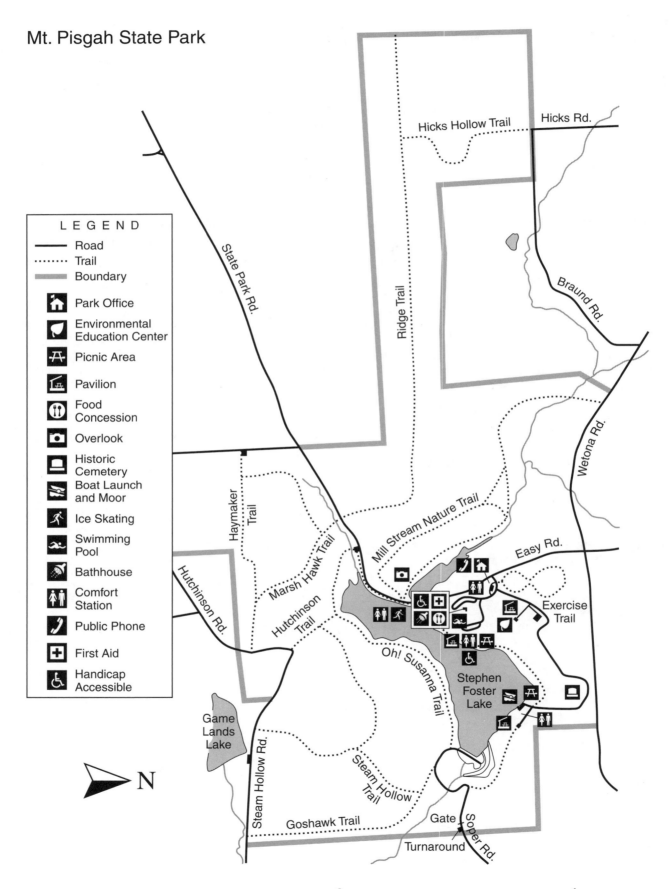

LEGEND
- Road
- Trail
- Boundary
- Park Office
- Environmental Education Center
- Picnic Area
- Pavilion
- Food Concession
- Overlook
- Historic Cemetery
- Boat Launch and Moor
- Ice Skating
- Swimming Pool
- Bathhouse
- Comfort Station
- Public Phone
- First Aid
- Handicap Accessible

Hicks Hollow Trail

Hicks Rd.

Braund Rd.

State Park Rd.

Ridge Trail

Wetona Rd.

Mill Stream Nature Trail

Easy Rd.

Exercise Trail

Haymaker Trail

Marsh Hawk Trail

Hutchinson Rd.

Hutchinson Trail

Oh! Susanna Trail

Stephen Foster Lake

Game Lands Lake

Steam Hollow Rd.

Steam Hollow Trail

Goshawk Trail

Gate

Turnaround

Soper Rd.

N

Mill Stream Nature Trail 🥾🥾🥾

Distance Round-Trip: 1 mile

Estimated Hiking Time: .75 hour

Caution: This trail is generally wide and smooth with gentle slopes. A steep drop near the end of the trail can come as a surprise.

Trail Directions: A sign and small parking area off State Park Road, at the south side of a bridge over a narrow bay off Stephen Foster Lake, mark the head **[1]** of Mill Stream Nature Trail. Pick up a trail guide. From here the trail follows the bay to its marshy head and along the small stream that feeds it, then climbs a hill and follows a forested ridge to complete the loop.

The trail begins with a gentle climb under the shade of thick hemlocks. At .1 mi. **[2]**, the trail has dropped closer to water level. You are at the cattail-lined head of the bay. Rest on a wooden bench and watch carefully for wildlife. We spotted mallards, wood ducks, and a pied-billed grebe. If you are quiet and stealthy, you might see muskrats or even a mink. On the other side of the trail, the forest begins to change from hemlock to birch, maple, and beech.

Continuing, the trail follows the small stream that flows into the bay. At .3 mi. **[3]**, the marsh and brush at the head of the bay give way to a meadow. The trail begins to climb again. It turns left away from the meadow at .4 mi. **[4]**, becoming steeper. To the right is a plantation of pines and a small opening. Watch for deer in this area. Do not get confused by a couple of trails that peel off to the right. Pine Tree Trail intersects on the right at .5 mi. **[5]**, as Mill Stream Nature Trail makes a sharp left turn. Appropriately, there are several pines near this intersection.

Red oak and hickory become important forest components where the trail completes its left turn. More roots and rocks interfere with footing in this part of the trail. At .7 mi., another bench **[6]** offers a

chance to rest and look for a completely different wildlife community than you might have seen at the first bench. Look for squirrels, turkeys, and deer feeding on acorns. The forest has become more open, allowing longer viewing. Several large trees grow in this area, including a gnarly old maple.

A trail that does not appear on the map intersects from the right at .74 mi. **[7]**. Mill Stream Nature Trail turns sharply left and passes under the limbs of a white oak. At about head height, this oak branches in four directions. A short distance later, the trail goes through a series of turns, then begins to descend toward the trailhead. Part of this decline is so steep that it is out of character with the rest of the trail. Footing can be slippery on loose gravel. Be careful you do not slide down the hill on the seat of your pants. You arrive back at the trailhead **[1]** after covering 1 mi.

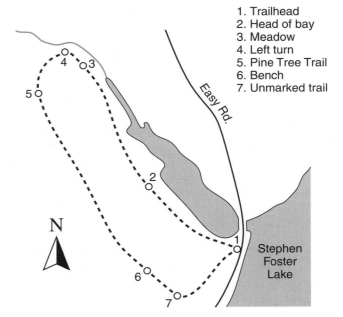

1. Trailhead
2. Head of bay
3. Meadow
4. Left turn
5. Pine Tree Trail
6. Bench
7. Unmarked trail

Oh! Susanna Trail 👢👢

Distance Round-Trip: 2 miles

Estimated Hiking Time: 1.25–1.5 hours

Caution: Bring sunscreen for unshaded areas on the second half of this hike.

Trail Directions: Several spots could be used as the starting point for this relaxing stroll around Stephen Foster Lake. The trail is named for one of the popular songs penned by the famous composer Stephen Foster. We started by the fishing area adjacent to State Park Road near the eastern end of the lake. A sign by the restrooms marks the trailhead **[1]**.

Beginning on a boardwalk, Oh! Susanna Trail follows State Park Road southwest for .1 mi. before turning abruptly left **[2]**. A wooden bridge keeps your feet dry over a small creek, then the trail begins a brief, moderate climb before dropping back toward the lake. The trail is smooth, level, and well marked with yellow paint blazes on trees. In the moist soil near the lake, hemlocks are the dominant tree, mixed with maples, birch, white pine, and oaks. Uphill, oaks are more common. Keep a sharp eye out for deer, turkeys, and other wildlife.

From a footbridge **[3]** at .4 mi., you can see the fishing area where this hike began almost directly across the lake. There are some beautiful mature hemlocks in this area. Hutchinson Trail **[4]** intersects on the right at .5 mi. I believe Hutchinson Trail is incorrectly positioned on the state park map. A sign here correctly shows Oh! Susanna Trail going to the left.

Steam Hollow Trail, which is not shown as intersecting Oh! Susanna Trail on the state park map, does intersect on the right at .7 mi. **[5]**. Following the state park map, you would believe that you had somehow wandered onto Goshawk Trail and are headed south out of the park. Do not worry, that has not happened. Stay left and you will continue on Oh! Susanna Trail toward the dam that creates Stephen Foster Lake. You will frequently see the lake through the trees on your left, which would not be the case if you had gotten onto Goshawk Trail. Just past this intersection is a patch of black birch to the right, their white bark providing vivid contrast to the green leaves of the surrounding forest.

Stop to rest on a bench **[6]** at .9 mi. Watch for wildlife up the steep hillside. As you continue, you can see the boat launch and a pavilion across the lake, and only a few steps farther the trail meets a maintenance road at the breast of the dam. Walk to the right on this road, which bends left, passing the head of Goshawk Trail, across Mill Creek just below the dam, and back up a steep incline on the other side.

In a horseshoe bend at the top of the steepest part of the incline, a sign directs Oh! Susanna Trail to exit the road to the left **[7]**. You have now passed the apex of the trail loop at 1.1 mi. From here, the trail crosses mostly open and developed areas.

The next leg of the trail climbs over a hillside meadow with a beautiful view of the lake. If you prefer the sun to the shade on the first half of the hike, you might stop for a while at a bench. Note the various stages of forest succession along the upper edge of the meadow.

After passing a pavilion, Oh! Susanna Trail crosses a blacktop road **[8]** at 1.3 mi. If you are lucky, you might, in season, be able to pick a few red raspberries where the trail passes through a wood patch.

You encounter another trailhead marker at the far end of these woods **[9]**. Continue across a footbridge, between the picnic area and the swimming pool. Ahead you will see the fishing area where you started. This last leg completes a total hike of 2 mi. **[1]**.

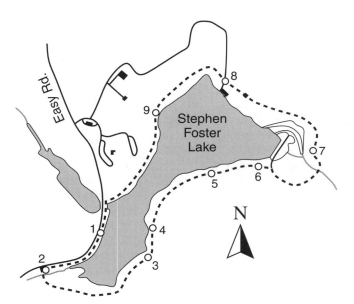

1. Trailhead at fishing area
2. Left turn
3. Footbridge
4. Hutchinson Trail
5. Steam Hollow Trail
6. Bench
7. Leave road
8. Cross blacktop road
9. Trailhead marker

3. Lackawanna State Park

- Observe different stages of forest development on land that was once farmed but is now reverting to a natural state.
- Fish for trophy bass in Lackawanna Lake.
- Enjoy outdoor activities year-round.

Area Information

Lackawanna is one of Pennsylvania's newer state parks, opened in 1972. As in most of Pennsylvania, the terrain has the appearance of rolling hills. The park is very close to the southern terminus of Ice Age glaciers along the northwest edge of the Appalachian Mountains. Most areas of the park that have not been developed are forested. However, the area was previously cleared for timber and farming. The forest you see now is in various stages of regrowth.

The centerpiece of the park is 198-acre Lackawanna Lake, a popular place for fishing, swimming, and boating. Fishing is managed under special big bass program regulations, which allow anglers to harvest four bass at least 15 inches in length per day during bass season. Trout, walleye, muskellunge, and panfish also have been stocked. Gasoline-powered boat motors are not allowed.

Directions: Take Exit 60 from Interstate Route 81 and drive 3 miles west on Pennsylvania Route 524.

Hours Open: The park is open year-round. Campgrounds are open from the second Friday in April until the third Sunday in October. Day-use areas are open from 8:00 A.M. to sunset. A swimming pool is open between 11:00 A.M. and 7:00 P.M. from Memorial Day weekend to Labor Day.

Facilities: Within the park you can find drinking water, restrooms, showers, campsites for tents and trailers, a swimming pool, a children's play area, picnic areas, and boats for rent.

Permits and Rules: Park only in designated areas. Pets must be leashed and under control. No pets are allowed in overnight camping areas. Only nonpowered and electric-powered boats are allowed on the lake. Boats must have a state park launch permit, a state park mooring permit, or a current Pennsylvania boat registration.

Further Information: Department of Conservation and Natural Resources, Lackawanna State Park, RR 1, Box 230, Dalton, PA 18414-9785; phone 717-563-9995.

Other Areas of Interest

See the largest glacial pothole on Earth at **Archbald Pothole State Park.** For more information phone Lackawanna State Park, 717-563-9995.

Park Trails

Snowflake Trail and Frost Hollow Trail 👢👢👢— 2 miles—These two trails form a loop along the hillside at the west end of Lackawanna Lake.

Turkey Hill Trail 👢👢👢

Distance Round-Trip: 1.5 miles

Estimated Hiking Time: 1 hour

Caution: Prepare for mud and a potentially wet stream crossing in rainy weather. The trail crosses a major road twice. The decline toward the end of the loop is very steep. A footbridge at the bottom of this decline might be missing planks.

Trail Directions: Turkey Hill Trail takes you on a journey back through time, from a modern highway to the remnants of early settlement and into a forest very similar to the primeval Pennsylvania forest.

A narrow blacktop road opposite the Lackawanna State Park sign where Pennsylvania Route 407 enters the park from the south leads to the trailhead. Park at the end of this road, near the lake. There are portable toilets here. Facing the lake, the trail begins to your right **[1]**.

After only .07 mi., the trail crosses Route 407 **[2]**. Be cautious of traffic here. A few yards past the road you will see a Turkey Hill Trail sign and begin a moderate climb. The trail splits at .14 mi. **[3]**. This is where the trail loops together. Take the right trail and continue a moderate climb. Ignore another trail that enters from the left.

One of the outstanding features of this trail is the maze of old stone fences along the hillside. You will cross the first of these at .21 mi. **[4]**. The trail makes a tight turn to the left after crossing a stone fence at

.36 mi. **[5]**. You are now past the steepest part of the ascent. You can see the highest part of the hill to your right. As the trail follows the side of the hill, notice the older trees, including hickory, maple, and birch, and also large wild grapevine. While following the trail is easy without trail blazes, here we saw the first yellow diamond trail blaze. Ignore a couple of trails that drop to the left while passing through an opening in the forest **[6]** at .57 mi.

Rain could make it difficult to cross a natural drainage ditch **[7]** at .64 mi. Abington Trail, for horseback riding, enters from the right at .71 mi. **[8]**. These trails run together until a small hilltop forest opening at .93 mi. **[9]**. Take the left fork to stay on Turkey Hill Trail, which at this point turns sharply to the left to complete the loop.

If you have been waiting for the perfect place to stop for a break, a flat boulder **[10]** at 1.14 mi. on the edge of a long, steep drop is a beautiful spot to watch for wildlife, and you can get glimpses of the lake through the trees.

Just past the boulder, the trail passes through a hemlock stand, a sign of moister soil. If you're hiking in hot, humid weather, you'll appreciate the cooler air under the hemlock canopy.

Shortly past the hemlocks, you cross another old stone fence and begin a very steep descent **[11]** at 1.25 mi. There is a wooden footbridge at the bottom of the slope **[12]** at 1.31 mi. Watch for missing planks. From here you are within sight of the completed loop **[3]**, where you turn right and return to the trailhead **[1]**. Be careful when crossing the road **[2]**.

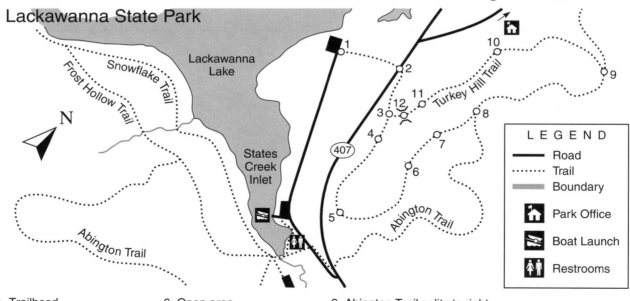

1. Trailhead
2. PA Route 407
3. Trail forks
4. First old stone fence
5. Trail turns left
6. Open area
7. Drainage ditch
8. Intersection with Abington Trail
9. Abington Trail splits to right
10. Flat boulder
11. Steep decline
12. Footbridge

4. Worlds End State Park

- Stand on panoramic vistas overlooking Loyalsock Creek Gorge.
- Ride thundering white water.
- Hike on some of the toughest short trails in the state.

Area Information

The first road through this area was built high on the steep ridges, making people feel as if they were at the end of the world. You will know that feeling when you hike the park trails. Worlds End is one of Pennsylvania's premier state parks, preserving one of the state's natural gems, the Loyalsock Creek Gorge. High overlooks provide breathtaking views of the gorge. Land was acquired during the early 1930s. Most park facilities were built by the CCC from 1934 to 1941.

White-water boating is one of the more popular activities at this park. Because stream flow fluctuates, inquire at park headquarters before coming for this purpose. Open canoes are not suitable for this treacherous journey.

Directions: The park is located near the middle of Sullivan County. Pennsylvania Route 154 between Forksville and U.S. Route 220 passes through the park.

Hours Open: Day-use areas are open from 8:00 A.M. to sunset. The swimming area is open Memorial Day weekend through Labor Day from 11:00 A.M. to 7:00 P.M.

Facilities: Visitors can stay in one of 19 rustic cabins, a tent and trailer campground, or a group tent camping site. Swimming is permitted in a small dam on Loyalsock Creek. Loyalsock Creek is stocked with trout for anglers. There are numerous picnic tables and four picnic pavilions. A food concession, open from Memorial Day weekend until Labor Day, is located near park headquarters.

Permits and Rules: Alcoholic beverages are prohibited. Outdoor activities are restricted to areas where physical improvements or postings designate the appropriate purpose.

Further Information: Department of Conservation and Natural Resources, Worlds End State Park, P.O. Box 62, Forksville, PA 18616-0062; phone 717-924-3287.

Other Areas of Interest

A large portion of the land around Worlds End State Park belongs to the **Wyoming State Forest.** For further information, write to District Forester's Office, RR 2, Box 47, Bloomsburg, PA 17815; phone 717-837-4255.

For information about events in the area, phone the **Endless Mountains Vacation Bureau,** phone 800-769-8999.

Park Trails

Butternut Run Trail 👢👢👢—2.5 miles—Easier than other park trails, this passes Butternut Run Falls.

Double Run Nature Trail 👢👢👢—1.2 miles—Climb a moderate slope up West Branch Double Run, past Cottonwood Falls.

Link Trail 👢👢👢👢—8.5 miles—This trail connects several other trails.

Worlds End Trail 👢👢👢👢👢—3.25 miles—This rough trail begins at park headquarters and goes to the Loyalsock Trail.

Worlds End State Park

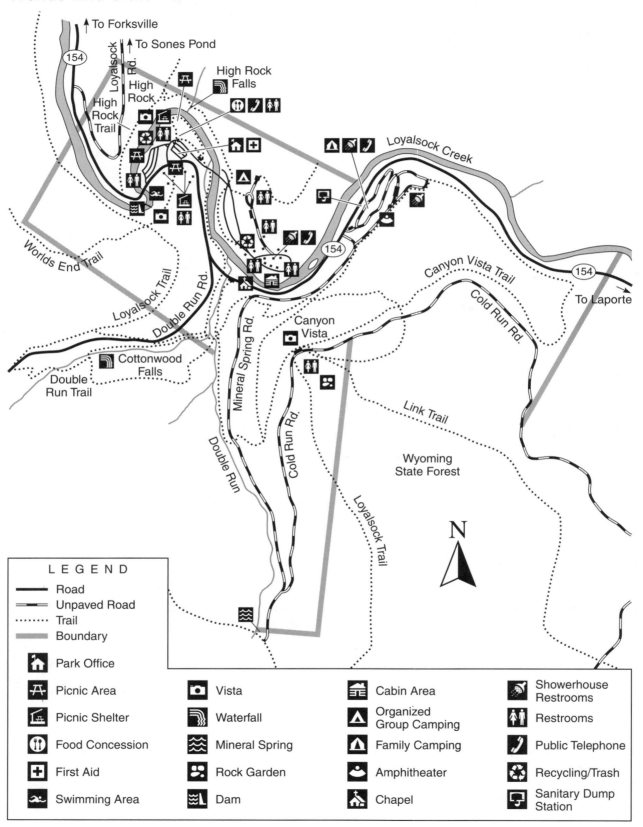

To Forksville
To Sones Pond

High Rock Falls
High Rock
High Rock Trail
Loyalsock Rd.

Loyalsock Creek

Worlds End Trail

Loyalsock Trail

Double Run Rd.

Cottonwood Falls

Double Run Trail

Double Run

Mineral Spring Rd.

Cold Run Rd.

Canyon Vista

Canyon Vista Trail

Cold Run Rd.

Link Trail

Loyalsock Trail

To Laporte

Wyoming State Forest

N

LEGEND
— Road
═ Unpaved Road
⋯ Trail
▬ Boundary

Park Office
Picnic Area
Picnic Shelter
Food Concession
First Aid
Swimming Area

Vista
Waterfall
Mineral Spring
Rock Garden
Dam

Cabin Area
Organized Group Camping
Family Camping
Amphitheater
Chapel

Showerhouse Restrooms
Restrooms
Public Telephone
Recycling/Trash
Sanitary Dump Station

High Rock Trail 👢👢👢👢👢

Distance Round-Trip: .9 mile

Estimated Hiking Time: 1 hour

Caution: The most difficult trail in the park, High Rock Trail traverses very steep terrain and boulder fields. In some places, one step off the trail could lead to a deadly fall. Do not attempt it unless you are in good physical condition and wearing hiking boots with ankle support and good traction.

Trail Directions: According to the park map, this trail begins at park headquarters. However, a better trailhead is off the road that goes from park headquarters to the cabin area, just across the bridge over Loyalsock Creek and to the left into a small parking area. You will see two trail signs as you enter this parking area, one for Butternut Trail and the other for High Rock Trail **[1]**.

High Rock Trail begins with a short climb, then turns left along the hillside following Loyalsock Creek downstream. The trail is narrow and rocky with a lot of protruding roots. You will see three different trail blazes—round yellow, round red with the letters LT in yellow, and rectangular yellow/red/yellow. The round yellow blazes are for High Rock Trail.

The trail rises moderately until you reach a boulder field at .2 mi. **[2]**. To the right, the hillside is very steep. Boulders will be the rule for most of the remainder of this trail. From the start of this boulder field, the course levels and drops gently before dropping quickly to High Rock Run (.3 mi.) **[3]**.

Once across this small run, you face a long and very steep climb through a boulder field. This will test your physical conditioning. Watch the round yellow trail blazes carefully because signs of the trail are indistinct over the boulders. As you reach each blaze, look ahead for the next one. The worst of the climb is past when you reach some large rock outcrops, after you have covered a total distance of .5 mi. **[4]**, about 850 feet from the start of the climb.

You go into a gentle decline before reaching High Rock Vista about 275 feet farther along (.55 mi.) **[5]**.

Below is an imposing view of a horseshoe bend in Loyalsock Creek. The main park facilities are mostly unseen in the finger of land inside the horseshoe.

A sign indicates the meeting of High Rock Trail and Loyalsock Trail just past the vista. Do not be concerned if this does not match the park map. Just continue to follow the round yellow blazes. You will be dropping toward the bottom of the gorge for the remainder of this hike. Be cautious at all times. The gorge drops almost vertically immediately to the left of the trail until you get near the bottom.

As you approach the bottom of the gorge, you will see a bridge over Loyalsock Creek. The trail turns abruptly right when the bridge is clearly visible, drops steeply, then turns left to the end of the trail at Pennsylvania Route 154 (.9 mi.) **[6]**. Watch for traffic. There is a pull-off immediately across the road. Just upstream you can see the swimming area.

1. Trailhead
2. Boulder field
3. High Rock Run
4. End climb
5. High Rock Vista
6. PA Route 154

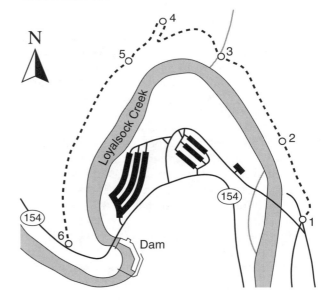

Canyon Vista Trail 👢👢👢👢👢

Distance Round-Trip: 3.6 miles

Estimated Hiking Time: 2.75 hours

Caution: Some sections are very steep. Hiking is not advised in wet weather. Thick berry briars crowd long stretches of the trail. Watch for stinging insects when these bushes are in bloom. When the berries are ripe, make noise as you walk to warn black bears of your approach. Do not wear shorts. Watch for steep ledges. Do not attempt this trail unless you are in good physical condition and wearing good hiking boots.

Trail Directions: From Pennsylvania Route 154, turn onto Mineral Spring Road, adjacent to the family camping area. The head of Canyon Vista Trail **[1]** is just a short distance up this road at the end of a campground loop. Note that you may not turn left onto this road. A sign marks the trailhead. There is no parking area. You will have to locate a pull-off nearby.

The zenith of this loop is at Canyon Vista, a splendid overlook of the Loyalsock Creek Gorge. Rock Garden, a beautiful rock outcrop, is adjacent to the vista. To make this a much easier trail, you might prefer to start there and hike only about half of the trail down to the trailhead, or to the family camping area.

From the trailhead **[1]**, you begin a steep, narrow trail. The ground slopes steeply to the right toward Mineral Spring Road. Gravel, twigs, and rocks provide poor footing. Follow blue blazes, which in this area come in three forms—blue diamonds and round can lids in two different shades of blue. Link Trail intersects after .3 mi. **[2]**. Go straight through this intersection through relatively open forest. Watch for rock ledges on your right that offer a beautiful view.

You encounter Link Trail again at a T (.9 mi.) **[3]**. Turn left, following the blue blazes. There are also yellow can lids with red X's marking Link Trail, which follows the same route to Canyon Vista. The trail is steep until you are close to the vista, which you reach after walking 1.2 mi. **[4]**. There are picnic tables, a wood fence along the vista, and a parking area here. Across a road, you will see a sign marking Rock Garden, where there are restrooms.

Past the vista, the trail follows the contour of the ridge, near the top, mostly through thick berry briars. The slope to the left is very steep, but the undergrowth is so thick you can see only a little of it. Just after dropping over the side of the hill, Link Trail is intersected again at 1.7 mi. **[5]**. Turn left at this intersection for a few steps, then turn right, following the blue blazes through an intermittent streambed, then up again into the briars.

You encounter a rock outcrop soon after leaving the briars. Feel the air get cooler. The first outcrop forms a perfect bench (2.2 mi.) **[6]**. Have a seat and feel how cool the rock is. This is one of the more pleasant sections of the trail, where it winds around, between, and beneath the outcrop formations.

The steepest part of the trail **[7]** starts 2.4 mi. from the trailhead. For the next 1,300 feet the trail is a real toe cruncher. Footing is slippery. At the bottom, the trail turns sharply left, going into a mild slope that ends at the family camping loop (3.2 mi.) **[8]**. Turn left on the loop and follow the blue blazes back to the trailhead (3.6 mi.) **[1]**.

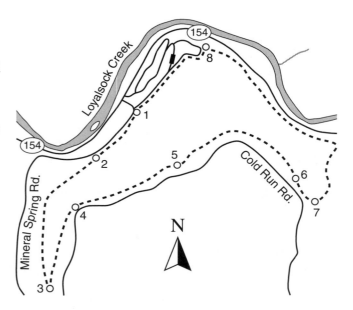

1. Trailhead	5. Link Trail
2. Link Trail	6. Rock bench
3. Link Trail	7. Steep drop
4. Canyon Vista	8. Family camping loop

5. Ricketts Glen State Park

- Hike the most beautiful short trail in Pennsylvania.
- Listen to a thundering 94-foot waterfall.
- Fish for warm-water fish at Lake Jean and for trout at Mountain Springs Lake.
- Beat the summer heat in mountain gorges.

Area Information

One of the most scenic areas in the state, Ricketts Glen was approved as a national park during the 1930s. That plan was derailed by World War II, but in 1944 it opened as a state park. Today, covering 13,050 acres, it is one of Pennsylvania's largest state parks. Ricketts Glen State Park, named for a Civil War hero who once owned the land, provides numerous opportunities for outdoor activities. Boating in nonpowered or electric-powered boats, boat rentals, swimming, and fishing for panfish and warm-water game fish are available in 245-acre Lake Jean. You can fish for trout at 40-acre Mountain Springs Lake, a Pennsylvania Fish and Boat Commission lake that adjoins the southeast corner of the park.

The heart of the park is a series of 22 spectacular waterfalls along Kitchen Creek and its two main branches through Ganoga Glen and Glen Leigh. The highest is 94-foot Ganoga Falls. Some of the towering hemlock and white pine trees in these steep gorges are ancient. Some fallen trees were determined to be 900 years old. The glens area has been designated as a national natural landmark.

Directions: The entrance to the park, near the borders of Luzerne, Sullivan, and Columbia counties, is off Pennsylvania Route 487 between Red Rock and Dushore. If you tow a heavy trailer, you should approach from the north to avoid a very steep hill between Red Rock and the park.

Hours Open: Day-use areas are open from 8:00 A.M. to sunset. The park is open year-round. The swimming beach is open between 11:00 A.M. and 7:00 P.M. from Memorial Day weekend through Labor Day unless posted otherwise. The family camping area is open year-round; however, hot showers and flush toilets are available only from mid-April through mid-October.

Facilities: The tent and trailer family camping area has a sanitary dump station. Some trails are designated for equestrian and snowmobile use. Family cabins are available for rent.

Permits and Rules: Outdoor recreational activities are restricted to locations where physical improvements or posting designates the appropriate use. Trash and litter must be placed in containers provided for this purpose, and only litter accumulated during use of the park may be placed there.

Further Information: Department of Conservation and Natural Resources, Ricketts Glen State Park, RR 2, Box 130, Benton, PA 17814-8900; phone 717-477-5675.

Park Trails

Mountain Springs Trail 👢👢👢—4 miles—This multiuse trail runs from the family cabin area to Mountain Spring Lake.

Cherry Run Trail 👢👢👢—4.6 miles—Another multiuse trail, Cherry Run Trail takes you from Mountain Springs Trail to a Fish and Boat Commission road, then to Mountain Spring Lake to form a loop with Mountain Springs Trail.

Old Bulldozer Road Trail 👢👢👢—2.9 miles—This trail connects the parking area near the bottom of Falls Trail with Mountain Springs Trail.

Old Beaver Dam Road Trail/Ganoga View Trail 👢👢👢—4 miles—These trails form a loop from the parking area at the head of Falls Trail with a spur to Ganoga Falls.

Bear Walk Trail 👢👢—1 mile—An easy trail, this roughly parallels the park road between park headquarters and the family cabin area.

Beach Trail 👢👢—.8 mile—Another easy trail, this connects the family cabin area to the family camping area, following the south shore of Lake Jean.

Evergreen Trail 👢👢👢—1 mile—This trail begins at the parking area across Pennsylvania Route 118 from the bottom of Falls Trail, passes 36-foot Adams Falls, then loops around Boston Run.

Ricketts Glen State Park

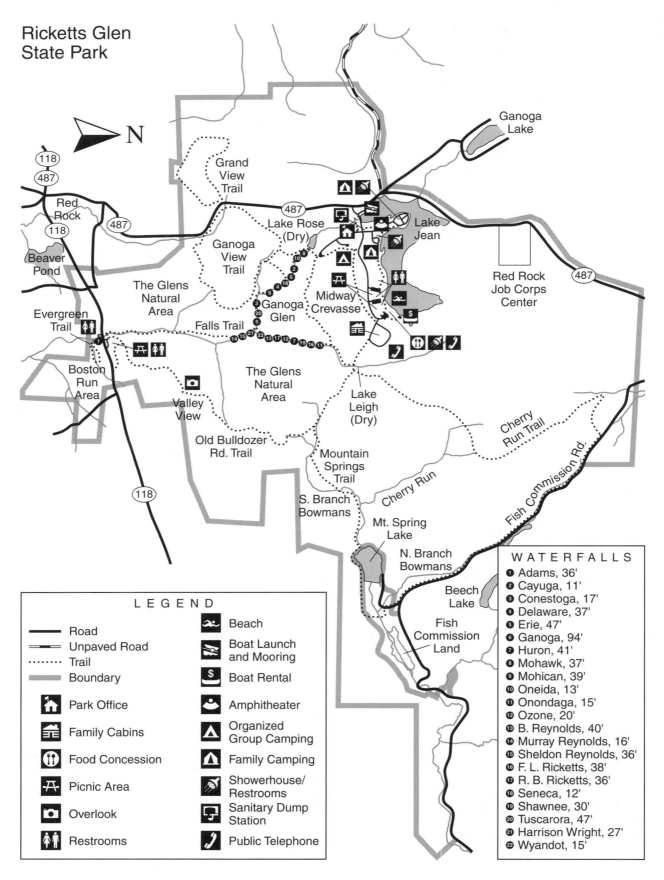

LEGEND

—— Road	![] Beach
—— Unpaved Road	![] Boat Launch and Mooring
···· Trail	![] Boat Rental
▬▬ Boundary	![] Amphitheater
🏠 Park Office	![] Organized Group Camping
Family Cabins	![] Family Camping
Food Concession	![] Showerhouse/Restrooms
Picnic Area	![] Sanitary Dump Station
Overlook	![] Public Telephone
Restrooms	

WATERFALLS

1. Adams, 36'
2. Cayuga, 11'
3. Conestoga, 17'
4. Delaware, 37'
5. Erie, 47'
6. Ganoga, 94'
7. Huron, 41'
8. Mohawk, 37'
9. Mohican, 39'
10. Oneida, 13'
11. Onondaga, 15'
12. Ozone, 20'
13. B. Reynolds, 40'
14. Murray Reynolds, 16'
15. Sheldon Reynolds, 36'
16. F. L. Ricketts, 38'
17. R. B. Ricketts, 36'
18. Seneca, 12'
19. Shawnee, 30'
20. Tuscarora, 47'
21. Harrison Wright, 27'
22. Wyandot, 15'

Falls Trail

Distance One-Way: 3.1 miles

Estimated Hiking Time: 2 hours

Caution: Do not attempt this trail unless you are in good physical condition and are wearing hiking boots with good traction. The trail is very steep and slippery. In many places there are high ledges next to the trail. Stay on the trail.

Trail Directions: Coming in the main park road from Pennsylvania Route 487, turn right immediately after passing park headquarters. This road becomes dirt and leads to a parking area at the head of Falls Trail near Rose Lake. Falls Trail is a Y-shaped set of trails connected across the top by Highland Trail. This hike will begin at the upper trailhead near Lake Rose, pass through Ganoga Glen, and continue down Kitchen Creek to Pennsylvania Route 118, passing 14 of the 22 named falls, including the three highest ones.

The trailhead at the lower end of the parking area is marked by three signs **[1]**. Immediately past these signs you descend a short set of stone steps and walk into a beautiful hemlock stand. The trail splits after less than .2 mi. **[2]**. Signs mark Highland Trail to the left and Ganoga Glen to the right. The right fork continues a gentle descent until you cross a footbridge and arrive at the next fork (.3 mi.) **[3]**. Old Beaver Dam Road Trail forks right. Take the left fork on Falls Trail. Though this trail is not blazed, you will have no trouble following it because from this point on it closely follows the creek until you pass Murray Reynolds Falls, the third major falls past Waters Meet.

The trail begins to get more difficult just before reaching the first major falls, Mohawk Falls (.4 mi.) **[4]**, which plunges 37 feet. Steps constructed of natural stone drop to the base of the falls, starting your journey through a long, narrow gorge. Oneida Falls and Cayuga Falls, just 13 feet and 11 feet, slip by before you reach towering Ganoga Falls (.7 mi.) **[5]**. You will recognize this waterfall as you approach a guard fence that begins along the top of the falls and runs along the trail as it rises around a high ledge. The best view is farther along the trail, after it descends to the base of the 94-foot falls.

After passing modest 12-foot Seneca Falls, 37-foot Delaware Falls, and 39-foot Mohican Falls, you cross a wooden footbridge over a small tributary **[6]** at about the 1-mi. mark, just below the base of Mohican Falls. A crude bench and chair offer a brief rest.

Next comes 17-foot Conestoga Falls, then Tuscarora Falls, where the water falls vertically through most of the 47-foot drop. Another 47-foot drop, Erie Falls, is next, just before you arrive at Waters Meet (1.4 mi.) **[7]**. Here, where the Glen Leigh segment of the trail forks left across a footbridge, are benches, trail signs, a map of the Falls Trail system, and a plaque designating the glens area a registered national natural landmark. You can still see Erie Falls, and if you look up Glen Leigh you will see 15-foot Wyandot Falls and a footbridge above it.

Continue downstream toward Route 118. Harrison Wright Falls, at 27 feet, is not one of the highest falls, but it is one of the most beautiful. Next, the channel narrows before plunging 36 feet over Sheldon Reynolds Falls. Finally, 16-foot Murray Reynolds Falls is the last of this series of waterfalls, 1.8 mi. from the trailhead **[8]**.

Falls Trail angles away from the creek past Murray Reynolds Falls, then drops back to the creek and over a footbridge (2.3 mi.) **[9]**. The remainder of the trail is gentle, following the creek across two more footbridges, to Pennsylvania Route 118 **[10]** for a total distance of 3.1 mi. There are two parking areas, one on each side of the highway.

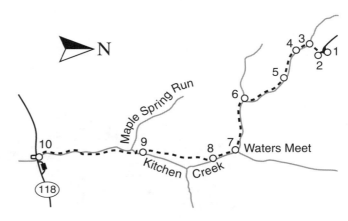

1. Trailhead	6. Footbridge
2. Highland Trail fork	7. Waters Meet
3. Old Beaver Dam	8. Murray
Road Trail	Reynolds Falls
4. Mohawk Falls	9. Footbridge
5. Ganoga Falls	10. PA Route 118

Grand View Trail 🥾🥾🥾

Distance Round-Trip: 1.9 miles

Estimated Hiking Time: 1 hour

Caution: This trail begins and ends on dirt roads that provide very easy walking. The middle section is much rougher and narrower and has more inclines and declines.

Trail Directions: Starting at park headquarters, drive out the main park road to Pennsylvania Route 487 and turn left. After about 1.4 mi. of fairly straight road, the highway makes a sharp left turn. If you go straight instead of turning with the highway, you enter a gated dirt road. Do not block this road with your vehicle. There is a pull-off adjacent to it. The gate on that dirt road is your trailhead **[1]**. From here you take a leisurely walk through three counties and encounter a spectacular panoramic view.

Walking is easy as you start the trail on this dirt road. You are surrounded by hardwood forest and mountain laurel. The forest floor is dominated by ferns. As in much of Pennsylvania, you see mainly ferns on the ground because they are one of the few plants that white-tailed deer do not eat. You arrive at a sign marking Grand View **[2]** after walking almost .6 mi. A panorama reveals itself through the trees. At this point, the trail is approaching the top of the mountain. Continue on to the top of the mountain and the fire tower (.7 mi.) **[3]**, where the view opens so you can see nearly 360 degrees. Luzerne County is to the south and east, Columbia County to the southwest, and Sullivan County to the north.

After seeing the great view from the base of the fire tower, you can turn around and return to the trailhead from here, making this a very easy hike. Or you can continue the loop. The next segment of the trail, narrower, steeper, and rocky now, will be visible at the back side of the clearing around the fire tower. After walking about 270 feet past the fire tower, you arrive at two signs. The one that reads "Trail to Rte. 487" points back the way you came. The other, which reads "Trail," points to your trail. Blue blazes will help lead the way to a T **[4]** at close to 1.3 mi. Here again are two signs. One points to Grand View, back the way you came. The other points to the right, to Route 487. Turn right here onto another dirt road. Soon after passing a gate, turn left at a T to complete the loop (1.9 mi.) **[1]**.

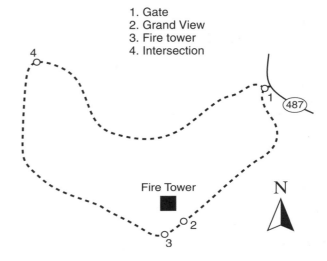

1. Gate
2. Grand View
3. Fire tower
4. Intersection

6. Promised Land State Park

- Bike on an extensive trail system.
- Relax in a quiet area of the Poconos.
- Explore habitat that, within Pennsylvania, is unique to the Poconos.

Area Information

This land was promised to the Shakers, a religious group perhaps best known for its furniture. They found the ground too rocky for farming and left. Since then, the land has been referred to sarcastically as the Promised Land. After clear-cutting and forest fires, the state acquired the land in 1902. It opened as a park in 1905. Several of the park facilities were constructed by the CCC during the 1930s. The CCC also planted many trees.

Promised Land State Park covers about 3,000 acres. Within its borders are 422-acre Promised Land Lake, 173-acre Lower Lake, and a few small streams. Promised Land Lake provides fishing for bass, pickerel, muskellunge, catfish, and panfish. Lower Lake and the streams provide fine trout fishing. The park is surrounded by 12,350 acres of Delaware State Forest.

Directions: Take Exit 7 off Interstate Route 84 south onto Pennsylvania Route 390, or onto Route 390 north from Canadensis. The park office is on Route 390 near the southern border of the park.

Hours Open: The park is open year-round. Day-use areas are open from 8:00 A.M. to sunset. Pickerel Point Campground is open year-round, except access is not guaranteed during severe winter storms. Swimming areas are open from Memorial Day weekend through Labor Day, from 11:00 A.M. to 7:00 P.M. at the main beach and during posted hours on weekends at Pickerel Point.

Facilities: The park has 487 campsites for tents or trailers, rental cabins, bike trails connected with bike trails in Delaware State Forest, two swimming beaches, picnic tables, fishing, boating, and boat rentals.

Permits and Rules: Boats must display either a state park launch permit, a state park mooring permit, or a Pennsylvania Fish and Boat Commission registration. Children at beaches must be accompanied and supervised by a responsible adult at all times. Alcoholic beverages are prohibited. Bicycles are allowed only on designated trails.

Further Information: Department of Conservation and Natural Resources, Promised Land State Park, RR 1, Box 96, Greentown, PA 18426; phone 717-676-3428.

Other Areas of Interest

Delaware State Forest has trails for hiking, biking, and snowmobiling. It includes Bruce Lake Natural Area, which has two lakes, wetlands, and unusual plants. Write to Department of Conservation and Natural Resources, Bureau of Forestry, District 9 Office, HC 1 Box 96A, Swiftwater, PA 18370-9723; phone 717-895-4000.

Park Trails

1800 Trail —1 mile—See numerous hardwood tree species and connect with Rock Oak Ridge Trail to form a loop.

Snow Shanty Trail —1 mile—See the remains of an abandoned beaver dam.

Whittaker Trail —1.5 miles—Hike through rhododendron, mountain laurel, and low bush blueberry and see a glacial depression.

Burley Inlet Trail —3.5 miles—Hike from park headquarters to Deerfield Campground.

Rock Oak Ridge Trail —3.5 miles—Use this trail as a link from Pines Campground to Bruce Lake Natural Area trails.

Lower Lake Trail —1.5 miles—Pass through the Rhododendron Area.

Promised Land State Park

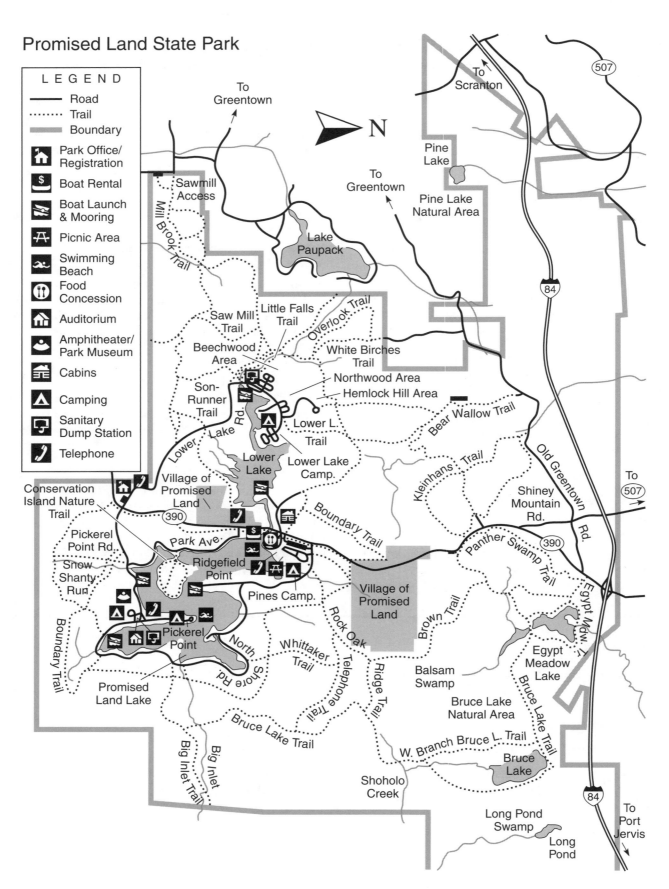

LEGEND
- —— Road
- ...... Trail
- ▓▓ Boundary
- 🏠 Park Office/ Registration
- $ Boat Rental
- 🚤 Boat Launch & Mooring
- ⛱ Picnic Area
- 🏊 Swimming Beach
- 🍴 Food Concession
- 🏛 Auditorium
- 🎭 Amphitheater/ Park Museum
- 🏚 Cabins
- ⛺ Camping
- 🚽 Sanitary Dump Station
- ☎ Telephone

To Greentown

To Scranton

507

Pine Lake

To Greentown

Pine Lake Natural Area

Lake Paupack

Sawmill Access

Mill Brook Trail

I-84

Little Falls Trail

Saw Mill Trail

Overlook Trail

White Birches Trail

Beechwood Area

Northwood Area

Hemlock Hill Area

Son- Runner Trail

Lower L. Trail

Bear Wallow Trail

Lower Lake

Lower Lake Camp.

Kleinhans Trail

Old Greentown Rd.

To 507

Shiney Mountain Rd.

Village of Promised Land

Conservation Island Nature Trail

390

Boundary Trail

Pickerel Point Rd.

Park Ave.

Village of Promised Land

Panther Swamp Trail

390

Egypt Mdw. Rd.

Snow Shanty Run

Ridgefield Point

Pines Camp.

Rock Oak

Brown Trail

Egypt Meadow Lake

Boundary Trail

Pickerel Point

North Shore Rd.

Whittaker Trail

Telephone Trail

Ridge Trail

Balsam Swamp

Bruce Lake Natural Area

Bruce Lake Trail

Promised Land Lake

Bruce Lake Trail

W. Branch Bruce L. Trail

Bruce Lake

Big Inlet Trail

Big Inlet

Shoholo Creek

Long Pond Swamp

Long Pond

I-84

To Port Jervis

Little Falls Trail 👢👢

Distance Round-Trip: .8 mile

Estimated Hiking Time: .5 hour

Caution: Parts of the trail might be under water when creek flow is high. Numerous rocks and roots protrude through the trail. The return trip is a steady though gradual climb.

Trail Directions: From Pennsylvania Route 390, turn onto Lower Lake Road at park headquarters. The trailhead is on the north side of the Lower Lake dam **[1].** There is a small parking area on the lake side of the road just around a curve from the trailhead. A sign marking the trailhead is on the opposite side of the road. From the road, you must cross a human-made drainage ditch to reach the sign. The sign points to the right, but go straight ahead down alongside East Branch Wallenpaupack Creek. After a brief drop, the trail eases into a gentler decline, following the course of the creek. It is a simple matter to follow the blue blazes from here to a series of three lovely waterfalls.

The trail is surrounded on the sides by rhododendron and above by hemlock. Notice how much cooler and less humid the air is here than it was at the trailhead. Walk quietly and you should see numerous gray squirrels and possibly a few white-tailed deer. Mallards may be feeding in the nutrient-rich creek.

At .3 mi., you come to a small but pretty waterfall **[2],** about 2 feet high. This is the first of a series of three falls in quick succession. If you are a trout angler, the beautiful pool below the falls will be tempting. Narrow beams of sunlight sparkle off the tea-colored water.

Continue downstream about 250 feet to the middle waterfall, a narrow chute leading to a 5-foot vertical drop and another scenic pool. Walk down a short set of wooden steps to the lower waterfall, a narrow 45-degree cascade that drops about 12 feet. At this point you might think that the name Little Falls Trail is a bit understated. Rock outcrops become more prominent here. Walk past the lower waterfall on the rock outcrop. Here under the hemlocks is a perfect place to enjoy a pack lunch. The rock forms a natural bench. Below you is the stream, which has cut a narrow channel through the bedrock. Watch reflected sunlight dance on the vertical rock that lines both sides of the pool below the lower waterfall. Upstream you can see both the middle and lower waterfalls. Make this the end of the trail (.4 mi.) **[3].** Below, the trail is much less interesting. Return the way you came for a total round trip of almost .8 mi. **[1].**

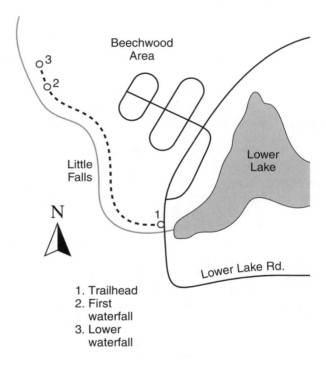

1. Trailhead
2. First
   waterfall
3. Lower
   waterfall

Conservation Island Nature Trail 👢👢

Distance Round-Trip: 1.1 miles

Estimated Hiking Time: 40 minutes

Caution: The interpretive portion of Conservation Island Nature Trail is in a poor state. Interpretive brochures are not available, many of the numbered interpretive posts are missing, and trail signs are a bit confusing. But the trail is on a small island where you should not get lost. If you do, follow the shore-line in either direction and you will come to the bridge by the trailhead.

Trail Directions: The access drive to Conservation Island is off Park Avenue between Pennsylvania Route 390 and Pickerel Point Road. From the park office, cross Route 390 onto Pickerel Point Road and drive north about .7 mi. to a sign that indicates a right turn to Conservation Island. There is a parking area at the end of this drive. The trailhead is by a gate at the end of the parking area **[1]**. You might want to bring a field guide to trees and shrubs along for this hike, and binoculars to watch wildlife.

Walk around the gate and across a bridge to Conservation Island. To your left is a long view down Promised Land Lake. To your right is a small, shallow bay. Just across the bridge, the trail forks. A sign indicates Nature Trail to the right, through overhanging rhododendron. You will be returning on the other fork.

This section of the trail is a service road that is also used as a bike trail that circles the outer edge of the island. You leave it after just .05 mile **[2]**, turning left at a sign through the middle of the island on a foot trail. Notice a blue rectangular blaze on this sign. You will follow blue blazes along the nature trail.

Several numbered posts are positioned along this trail. These are interpretive stations. Finding some of these posts is difficult, and several are missing. At post #2, notice the ferns that cover the forest floor. Examine a rotting tree at post #4 to see how it contributes to the forest community. The larger holes in it were probably made by the pileated woodpecker, the largest woodpecker in the state.

Look at the large red oak tree by post #6. You have probably seen at least one gray squirrel by this point. Because the surrounding lake moderates weather, oaks and other nut-bearing trees tend to produce nuts more reliably than at higher elevations and away from water.

You will see black cherry trees by post #9. This is close to the highest and driest land on the island. Observe how the forest changes from the lower ground along the edge of the island to the higher ground near the center of the island. As you walk over the higher ground past post #10, there are more exposed boulders; then at post #11, you reach a bedrock outcrop. You can see an effect of the deer population in this area by identifying the maple trees. The larger ones are red maples, the shorter ones are striped maples. Deer do not care for striped maple, so it can grow. But the deer browse red maple so heavily that they prevent it from regenerating.

The trail curves to the right as it drops over the side of the high ground. To your right is a very pretty rock outcrop. Then, at .4 mi., you reach a T **[3]**, rejoining the bike trail by turning left along the edge of the lake.

A sign points toward Nature Trail to the right at .8 mi. **[4]** by a particularly large hemlock tree, leaving the bike trail once again. Here, closer to the lake, there are more coniferous trees, like the red pine at post #31. After rejoining the bike trail with a right turn, you complete the loop (1.07 mi.) **[2]**. Turn right here, across the bridge and back to the gate at the end of the parking area **[1]**, after hiking almost 1.1 miles.

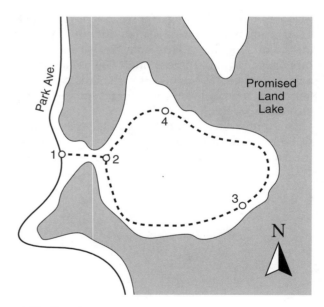

1. Trailhead
2. Leave road
3. T
4. Right turn

7. Delaware Water Gap National Recreation Area

- Float through the Water Gap on the Delaware River.
- Fish for American shad during their annual migration from the Atlantic Ocean.
- Visit numerous waterfalls.
- Swim in cool waters.

Area Information

The Delaware River is one of the last free-flowing rivers in the United States, and it provides 10 percent of the U.S. population with drinking water. It flows 37 miles through the Delaware Water Gap, an area designated as a National Wild and Scenic River. The southern end of the Water Gap is the river's course through Kittatinny Mountain, a part of the Appalachian Mountains. The Appalachian Trail enters Pennsylvania here, near 1,463-foot Mount Minsi.

The Delaware Water Gap National Recreation Area includes both sides of the river, New Jersey and Pennsylvania. On the Pennsylvania side, the steep slopes are the eastern side of the Pocono Plateau. Several streams cascade over sheer bedrock. During the 19th century, this was a popular resort area with large hotels. It was also an important area for early industry because the streams that plunge down the steep slopes provided power to turn waterwheels. Today, it is still popular for sightseeing, boating, and fishing. During May and June, huge migrations of American shad from the Atlantic Ocean swim up the Delaware River to spawn, providing outstanding sport fishing.

Directions: U.S. Route 209 passes through the national recreation area between Milford and Interstate Route 84 on the northern end to Stroudsburg and Interstate Route 80 at the southern end.

Hours Open: Delaware Water Gap National Recreation Area is open year-round. All recreation sites are for day use only.

Facilities: Campsites for tents and RVs are available at Dingmans Campground, near Dingmans Ferry. Boat access sites are located at several places along the Delaware River. Bicycles are allowed on several roads. There are two beaches with bathhouses, and several picnic areas.

Permits and Rules: Metal detectors may not be used in the national recreation area. Bicycles are not allowed on gated roads.

Further Information: Superintendent, Delaware Water Gap National Recreation Area, Bushkill, PA 18324-9999; phone 717-588-2451.

Other Areas of Interest

The **Pocono Environmental Education Center** offers study programs in a residential environment. It is located within the Delaware Water Gap National Recreation Area. Write to PEEC, RD 2, Box 1010, Dingmans Ferry, PA 18328-9614.

Park Trails

Appalachian Trail (to Mt. Minsi) 🥾🥾🥾🥾—2 miles—Hike from the Lake Lenape parking area to spectacular views of the Delaware Water Gap, climbing 1,060 feet.

Mt. Minsi Fire Road 🥾🥾🥾—1.5 miles—Use this with the Appalachian Trail to form a 4-mile loop to Mt. Minsi. The climb is 1,060 feet in elevation.

Table Rock Spur 🥾🥾🥾—.5 mile—This spur off the Appalachian Trail takes you to a spectacular view of the Delaware Water Gap.

Delaware Water Gap

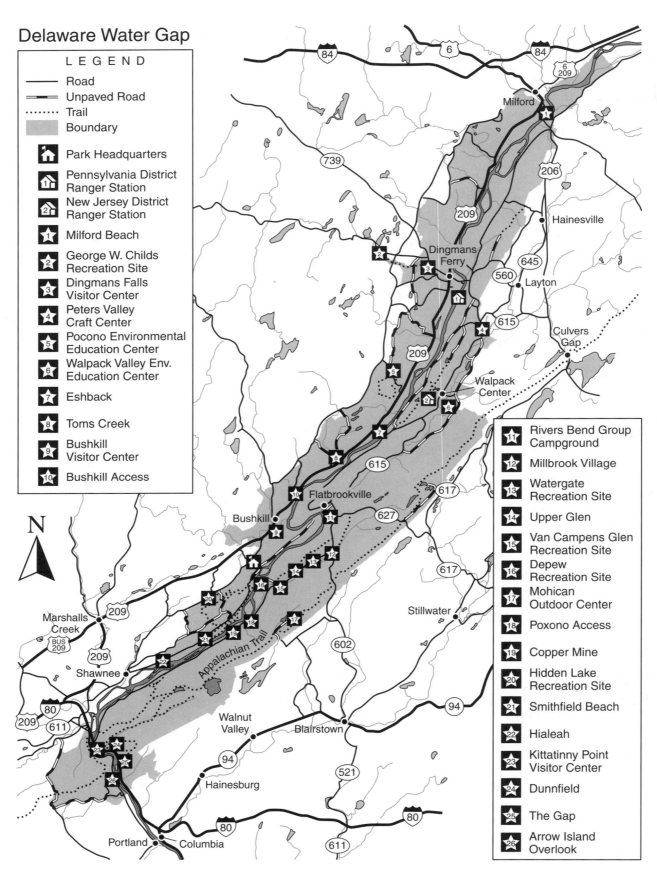

LEGEND

— Road

═ Unpaved Road

⋯⋯ Trail

▓ Boundary

🏠 Park Headquarters

🏠 Pennsylvania District Ranger Station

🏠 New Jersey District Ranger Station

⭐1 Milford Beach

⭐2 George W. Childs Recreation Site

⭐3 Dingmans Falls Visitor Center

⭐4 Peters Valley Craft Center

⭐5 Pocono Environmental Education Center

⭐6 Walpack Valley Env. Education Center

⭐7 Eshback

⭐8 Toms Creek

⭐9 Bushkill Visitor Center

⭐10 Bushkill Access

⭐11 Rivers Bend Group Campground

⭐12 Millbrook Village

⭐13 Watergate Recreation Site

⭐14 Upper Glen

⭐15 Van Campens Glen Recreation Site

⭐16 Depew Recreation Site

⭐17 Mohican Outdoor Center

⭐18 Poxono Access

⭐19 Copper Mine

⭐20 Hidden Lake Recreation Site

⭐21 Smithfield Beach

⭐22 Hialeah

⭐23 Kittatinny Point Visitor Center

⭐24 Dunnfield

⭐25 The Gap

⭐26 Arrow Island Overlook

N

George W. Childs Recreation Site 👢👢👢👢

Distance Round-Trip: .85 mile

Estimated Hiking Time: 40 minutes

Caution: Most of this trail is either downhill or uphill, with many steep steps. In places, the trail is close to cliffs.

Trail Directions: From U.S. Route 209 at Dingmans Ferry, turn west onto Pennsylvania Route 739, then turn left onto Silver Lake Road and follow the signs to a left turn into the George W. Childs Recreation Site. Immediately after crossing a small bridge, turn left into a parking area. The trailhead is at the end of the parking area, near the restrooms. Signs here include a map of the area **[1]**.

Almost immediately after beginning the hike, turn left across a footbridge, then turn right down along Dingmans Creek. Several picnic tables here are also accessible from a parking lot off Silver Lake Road. From here, the trail follows the creek past three beautiful waterfalls, crosses the creek, and returns on the opposite side, the side where you began. Between the footbridge at the start of the trail and the lowest footbridge are four more footbridges. You can cross any of them to shorten the loop, or just walk onto them for different views of the waterfalls.

You reach the top of Factory Falls **[2]** after .15 mi. An old stone structure to your left is the remains of a wooden mill, built in 1825, which was operated by a waterwheel. Past the mill, you begin descending steps past the falls and a pavilion that provides an excellent view of Factory Falls.

Down more steps, you come to an overlook by Fulmer Falls (.2 mi.) **[3]**. This overlook is past the crest of the waterfall, so close you can almost reach out and touch it. Look at the moss and lichens on the rock around the falls. This biological community is supported by mist and spray from the falls. The trail follows a ledge around the waterfall. There is a guard fence, but watch children if you bring them on this hike.

The trail continues down sets of steps to the head of Deer Leap Falls (.4 mi.) **[4]**. A footbridge crosses the creek right at the top of the falls. This offers an interesting vantage point. Past the waterfall, the trail rises to get around the pool below the falls, then descends down more steps to the lower footbridge (.5 mi.) **[5]**. You get the best view of Deer Leap Falls before crossing the footbridge. Note signs here that designate this section of Dingmans Creek as a special "delayed harvest artificial lures only" area.

The lower footbridge is the halfway point of this hike. From here, it's all uphill back to the trailhead. You begin climbing immediately, first up stone steps, then up a moderate slope. You will see the same sights as you saw on the way down but from a different perspective. You are past the upper falls and the worst of the climb when you arrive at a small, flat peninsula where there are picnic tables and a water pump (.7 mi.) **[6]**. This is the perfect place to eat a pack lunch. The air is cool under the shade of hemlocks. It is much quieter than the picnic areas on the other side of the creek, and you have a good appetite after hiking the steep trail. Then there is the cold, clear water from the pump. It tastes wonderful after the climb.

Go straight through an intersection just past the water pump. You will see a footbridge to the right. The straight route does not look like much of a trail until you step through a notch in rocks on the far side of the intersection. Then the trail becomes clear. Continue to the trailhead **[1]** for a total loop of .85 mi.

1. Trailhead
2. Factory Falls
3. Fulmer Falls
4. Deer Leap Falls
5. Lower footbridge
6. Water pump

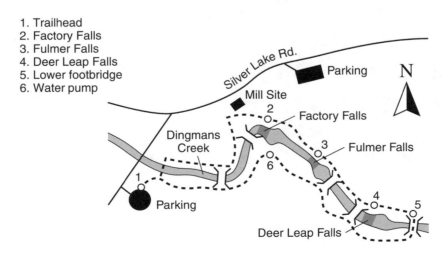

Dingmans Falls Trail 🥾

Distance Round-Trip: .74 mile

Estimated Hiking Time: .5 hour

Caution: This trail is a wheelchair-accessible board-walk. However, it has a slight incline. Stay on the boardwalk to avoid damaging the fragile ecosystem.

Trail Directions: From U.S. Route 209 just south of Dingmans Ferry, turn west onto Johnny Bee Road, then turn right after about a half mile at the sign to Dingmans Falls. Be careful on this road. In places it is barely wide enough for two cars to pass. There is a parking area and a visitors center at the end of this road. The trailhead **[1]**, which is marked by a sign, is at the edge of the parking area between the visitors center and the restrooms.

The trail is a raised boardwalk with rails on both sides. Just onto the trail, you cross a footbridge over Dingmans Creek, then the trail bends left and over a small tributary. To your right, just .07 mi. from the trailhead, is Silver Thread Falls **[2]**. Feel the rush of

cool air coming through this narrow cut in the sheer bedrock. Though the water volume over this falls is not great, it is splendid, splashing 80 feet.

The boardwalk is surrounded by rhododendron, hemlock, and sugar maple. During early July when the rhododendron blossoms, this is like walking through a huge flower garden. The trail swings back across Dingmans Creek on a second footbridge at .18 mi. **[3]**. A bench at the upper side of this bridge is a fine place to relax and enjoy the serenity of this quiet gorge.

After a mild incline, you pass a left fork in the trail that is blocked by a cable, then a stairway to a view-ing platform at the top of the waterfall. You arrive at Dingmans Falls **[4]** after a distance from the trailhead of .37 mi. This imposing waterfall drops several feet from its crest onto a narrow shale ledge, drops several feet again, then tumbles over a stair-step-like drop to a tea-colored pool 130 feet below the top. Please do not throw coins into this pool. The color is caused by tannic acid from hemlocks, the same acid Native Americans and early settlers used for tanning animal hides and for medicinal purposes.

Return the way you came for a total distance back to the trailhead **[1]** of .74 mi.

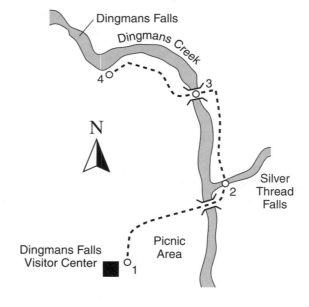

1. Trailhead
2. Silver Thread Falls
3. Second footbridge
4. Dingmans Falls

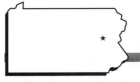

8. Hickory Run State Park

- See the largest boulder field of its kind in the Appalachians.
- Enjoy exceptional trout fishing.
- Journey back in time by touring historic remains.

Area Information

One of Pennsylvania's largest state parks, Hickory Run covers 15,500 acres. Before the Civil War, this area was known as the "Shades of Death" because it was shrouded by a dense forest of white pine and hemlock. Several lumber camps and villages were constructed, and the forest was cut by 1880. Today, the forest is mature again, but it consists of more hardwoods. Some remnants of the logging mills remain along Hickory Run and Sand Spring Run. The park administration area includes three buildings that were part of the village of Hickory Run.

The National Park Service acquired the land and with the help of the WPA built the Hickory Run Recreation Demonstration Area during the 1930s. This was given to the Commonwealth of Pennsylvania in 1945 and became a state park. A boulder field, unusual in its flatness, that was created at the southern terminus of an Ice Age glacier is the largest of its kind in the eastern United States. It measures about 400 feet by 1,800 feet and is a national natural landmark.

Directions: Take Exit 41 from Interstate Route 80 and drive east 6 miles on Pennsylvania Route 534. From the Northeast Turnpike Extension, take Exit 35 and drive 3 miles west on Pennsylvania Route 940, then turn right onto Route 534 for 6 miles to the park.

Hours Open: The park is open year-round. Swimming is permitted from 11:00 A.M. to 7:00 P.M. at the Sand Springs Day Use Area. Day-use areas are open from 8:00 A.M. to sunset.

Facilities: Trails are available for hiking, snowmobiling, and cross-country skiing. The park has a swimming beach, a family camping area, a group camping area, a sanitary dump station, a swimming beach, a picnic pavilion, and numerous picnic tables.

Permits and Rules: Alcoholic beverages are prohibited. Pets are not allowed in the family campground. Outdoor recreational activity is limited to locations where physical improvements or signs designate the appropriate use. Fires and disposal of hot coals are permitted only in provided facilities.

Further Information: Department of Conservation and Natural Resources, Hickory Run State Park, RR 1, Box 81, White Haven, PA 18661-9712; phone 717-443-0400.

Other Areas of Interest

Lehigh Gorge State Park offers a 25-mile hiking and biking trail and white-water boating. Write to Department of Conservation and Natural Resources, Lehigh Gorge State Park, c/o Hickory Run State Park, RR 1, Box 81, White Haven, PA 18661; phone 717-443-0400.

Park Trails

Orchard Trail 👢👢—1 mile—Walk to the Mud Run Natural Area from the organized tent camping area.

Boulder Field Trail 👢👢👢—3.5 miles—See the largest boulder field of its kind in the eastern United States.

Pine Hill Trail 👢👢👢—3.8 miles—Get a good view of Lehigh Gorge State Park and connect with Fire Line Trail.

Self-Guiding Nature Trail 👢👢—.5 mile—This short loop begins and ends at the main beach parking lot.

Fire Line Trail 👢👢👢👢—2.3 miles—From a parking area off Route 534 near the eastern border of the park, walk along the Lehigh Gorge.

Hickory Run State Park

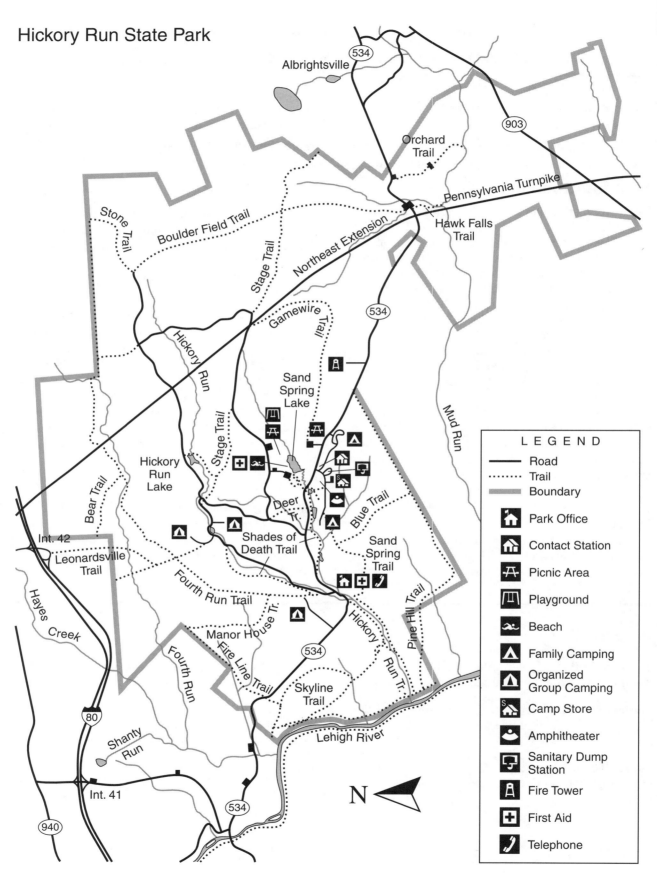

Hawk Falls Trail 👢👢👢

Distance Round-Trip: 1.2 miles

Estimated Hiking Time: .75 hour

Caution: You must cross a stream over stepping stones. If you get off the trail near the crest of Hawk Falls, there are sheer rock ledges. Rocks and roots protrude through the trail in most areas.

Trail Directions: The trailhead **[1]** is off Pennsylvania Route 534 near the eastern end of Hickory Run Park, about 4.5 miles from the park office, just east of the Northeast Turnpike Extension overpass. There are parking areas on both sides of the road—on the north side for Boulder Trail and on the south side for Hawk Falls Trail. A kiosk by the parking area might appear to mark the trailhead, and several renegade trails start from the parking area. However, the actual trailhead is marked by a sign along Route 534 toward the overpass, by a gap in the guardrails. This trail is wide, easily recognizable, and marked by rectangular yellow blazes. Just past the guardrails, boulders have been placed across the trail to deny access by vehicles.

Rhododendrons and mature forest crowd the trail. You begin descending a moderate slope almost immediately, following Hawk Run downstream. At .18 mi. you pass an interesting rock outcrop **[2]**. See how the roots of hemlock trees hug the rock. Soon you reach the level of the creek and cross it over stepping stones (.24 mi.) **[3]**. Be careful. The stones may roll or tip under your feet. The opposite creek bank is steep and slippery.

Across the creek, you pass another interesting rock outcrop on your left. The trail is nearly level here. As you begin to hear the falls, you will pass several false trails where people have taken detours to see the top of the falls. Some lead to precarious ledges. Continue on the correct trail by following the yellow blazes. Past the crest of the falls the trail dips, turns to the right down a moderate slope, then turns sharply right at a double yellow blaze on a large white pine. A patch of myrtle, an exotic plant, indicates that a building or home once stood nearby.

Take a short exit from the trail here, straight ahead to Mud Run. Here you can see a structure made of natural stone, the remnants of an old bridge. The trail you have been following to this point was once a wagon road. This stream is Mud Run, which has delayed harvest regulations in this area. Watch for trout rising to the surface to feed on insects.

From this sharp right turn, walk downstream along Mud Run. Turn right where Hawk Run flows into Mud Run, through rhododendrons so thick the trail forms a tunnel. Look down Mud Run and you can see the Northeast Turnpike Extension overpass high above. The sound of the falls becomes louder, then you break out of the rhododendron into the perfect view of Hawk Falls (.6 mi.) **[4]**, which plunges 25 feet. Framed on either side by sheer rock, it begins through a narrow channel at the crest, falls vertically onto a ledge, then falls again over a broader crest into a beautiful pool.

As you gaze at the falls, you may see a pewee fly from its perch on limbs overhanging the pool to catch a flying insect, or common yellowthroats hopping through the rhododendron. This is an excellent trail for bird watching.

Return the way you came for a round trip of nearly 1.2 mi.

1. Trailhead
2. Rock outcrop
3. Ford stream
4. Hawk Falls

Shades of Death Trail 👢👢👢

Distance Round-Trip: 1.9 miles

Estimated Hiking Time: 40 minutes

Caution: Parts of this trail pass over rocky footing and along steep slopes. You might get your feet wet crossing spring seeps.

Trail Directions: Take Pennsylvania Route 534 east about .3 mi. from park headquarters to a sign that marks the trailhead [1]. Small parking areas are located both above and below the trailhead. You can also park near park headquarters.

As an alternative you can hike this trail in the opposite direction, walking downhill, starting near Dam #5 off Route 534, about 1.2 mi. east of park headquarters. Park in the amphitheater area, then walk back down Route 534, across Sand Spring Run, then left over the guardrails. There is a service road on the opposite side of the road. Be very cautious of traffic. There is no berm beside the road, so you have to walk along the road's edge.

From the lower trailhead [1], you descend a moderate slope, cross a short footbridge over a tiny stream, and go down a set of steps to face Sand Spring Run where it rushes down a smooth bedrock chute. The trail will follow up this stream past several small waterfalls and through narrow gaps in the bedrock. It is regarded as the prettiest trail in the park. Watch for yellow trail blazes.

After passing a crumbling stone foundation, the narrow trail climbs to the top of Stametz Dam (.15 mi.) [2]. Pause here to gaze at the reflections of hemlock and rhododendron on the calm pool. This pool is stocked with trout.

Ignore the steps that go uphill to the left and continue along the edge of the pool, back into forest, then through rhododendron that surrounds the trail. A sharp left turn takes you through a narrow crevasse in a rock outcrop (.4 mi.) [3]. At the top of this crevasse, you cross a rock pile, angling to the right, where the trail would be difficult to follow if not for the yellow trail blazes.

Once over the rock pile, the trail returns to the edge of Sand Spring Run. The valley bottom is very narrow, just wide enough for the stream. The trail follows the edge of a steep slope through rhododen-

dron and hemlock. Higher up the slope you will be able to spot white oak and chestnut oak. The trail forks by a set of steps. Steps that fork right are a short spur to a rock outcrop right on the edge of the stream. Look for a human-made rock structure in this area. A little farther along, turn left and climb another set of wooden steps to a road. At the top of the steps is a Shades of Death trail sign (.6 mi.) [4].

At the sign, turn right along the road until you reach the narrow end of a field on your left. Make a short climb to the field and follow the lower edge of the field to the CCC Dam (.7 mi.) [5]. Large white pines in this area were probably seedlings when the area was logged during the 19th century. Red and white bobbers hanging from lower limbs prove that this small impoundment is a favorite trout fishing hole.

Continuing past the CCC Dam, the trail follows what is apparently an old road. As it ascends the hill, look to your right to see a stone structure that was built to constrict stream flow, perhaps for a waterwheel to power a mill. You come to an intersection with Beach Trail [6], which turns left, at .9 mi. You could complete this as a one-way hike by walking up Beach Trail less than 200 feet to Route 534, where there is a small pull-off large enough for two small cars. Or you can continue ahead to Dam #5 [7] after walking slightly less than 1 mi. This is an old wood-and-rock structure.

From here, return the way you came for a round-trip of 1.9 mi.

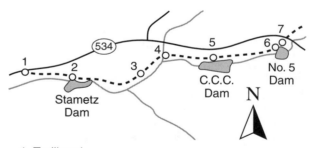

1. Trailhead
2. Stametz Dam
3. Crevasse
4. Shades of Death sign
5. CCC Dam
6. Beach Trail
7. Dam #5

9. Shikellamy State Park

- Test your fishing skills on smallmouth bass, walleyes, muskellunge, and crappies.
- Dine at a full-menu restaurant.
- View the start of the broad Susquehanna River from an island and from atop cliffs.

Area Information

Shikellamy State Park straddles the confluence of the West Branch Susquehanna River and the North Branch Susquehanna River, the beginning of one of America's great rivers and the major tributary of Chesapeake Bay. This part of the river is actually a human-made impoundment, Lake Augusta. On a typical summer day the lake is abuzz with pleasure boats and anglers. Fishing is good for walleyes, catfish, muskellunge, crappies, and especially smallmouth bass.

This park honors Shikellamy, who was a chief of the Iroquois during the first half of the 18th century. It is an unusual park in several ways. The first part of the park to open, in 1960, was the 78-acre Blue Hill section on the west side of the Susquehanna River in Union County. The 53.5-acre section on the southern tip of Packers Island in Northumberland County opened a dozen years later.

The Blue Hill section provides panoramic views from atop river bluffs. It is relatively undeveloped. Deer and other wildlife thrive in a mix of mature hardwood forest and scrub forest. The Packers Island section has the appearance of a city park, with beautiful flower gardens, manicured picnic areas, boat docks, a restaurant, and a fuel dock. Yet it is a good study of a river-bottom forest, with trees identified by signs.

Directions: The Blue Hill section of Shikellamy State Park is north of Shamokin Dam on U.S. Route 11, then left on County Line Road. The entrance to the Packers Island section is off Pennsylvania Route 147 between Northumberland and Sunbury.

Hours Open: The park is open from 8:00 A.M. to sunset.

Facilities: A picnic area, restrooms, a playground, and scenic overlooks are located in the Blue Hill section. Packers Island features a restaurant with a fine view of the river, many picnic tables, bike trails, boat docks, a fuel dock, boat rentals, and a boat launch ramp.

Permits and Rules: Do not feed wildlife. Alcoholic beverages are prohibited. Boats must have either a state park launching permit, a state park mooring permit, or a current Pennsylvania Fish and Boat Commission registration. Fires and the disposal of hot coals are restricted to provided facilities. Trash and litter must be placed in containers provided for this purpose; disposal is limited to items accumulated during the use of the park. Pets must be leashed and controlled at all times.

Further Information: Department of Conservation and Natural Resources, Shikellamy State Park, Bridge Avenue, Sunbury, PA 17801-1005; phone 570-988-5557.

Other Areas of Interest

For information about the surrounding area, contact **Northumberland County Tourist Agency,** 609 Market Street, Sunbury, PA 17801, phone 717-988-4295; or **Susquehanna Valley Visitors Bureau,** RR 3, 219 D Hafer Road, Lewisburg, PA 17837, phone 717-524-7234.

Park Trails

Dry Hollow Trail 👢👢—.1 mile—This trail connects the picnic loop with Deer Trail.

Oak Ridge Trail 👢👢—.16 mile—Watch for squirrels and deer along this link between the picnic loop and the deer trail.

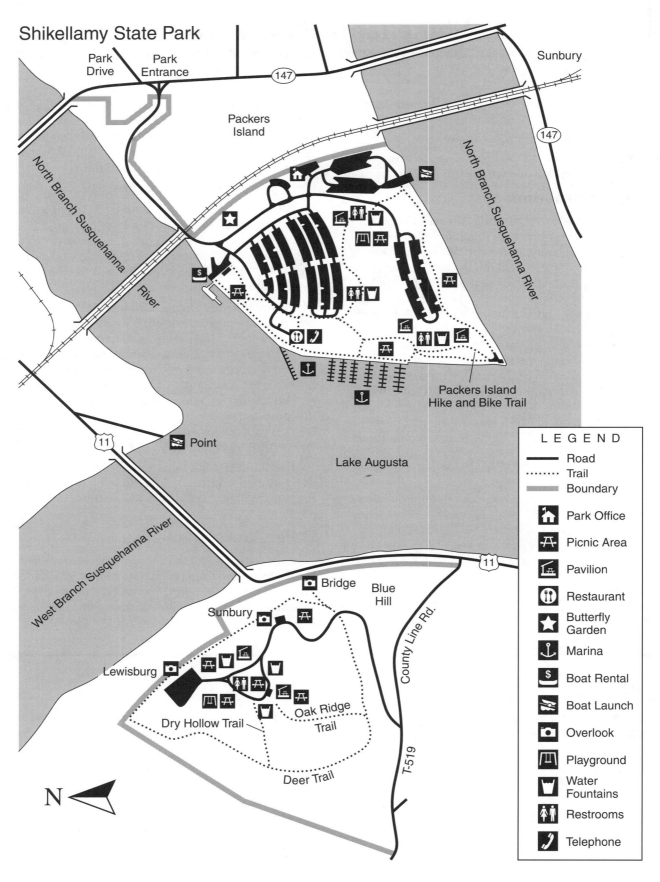

Shikellamy State Park

Park Drive

Park Entrance

Sunbury

147

Packers Island

North Branch Susquehanna River

North Branch Susquehanna River

147

Packers Island Hike and Bike Trail

11

Point

Lake Augusta

West Branch Susquehanna River

11

Bridge

Blue Hill

Sunbury

County Line Rd.

Lewisburg

Oak Ridge Trail

Dry Hollow Trail

Deer Trail

T-519

N

LEGEND
- —— Road
- ······· Trail
- ▬▬ Boundary
- 🏠 Park Office
- 🛆 Picnic Area
- Pavilion
- 🍴 Restaurant
- ★ Butterfly Garden
- ⚓ Marina
- $ Boat Rental
- Boat Launch
- 📷 Overlook
- Playground
- Water Fountains
- 🚻 Restrooms
- ☎ Telephone

32

Packers Island Trail 🥾

Distance Round-Trip: .69 mile

Estimated Hiking Time: 20 minutes

Caution: You will cross one road where you must watch for cars. Be alert for bicycles all along the trail.

Trail Directions: As you enter the Packers Island section of the park, better known locally as the marina, take the second left turn and drive to the farthest corner of the farthest parking area, the corner toward the river. Walk to the paved hike-and-bike trail at the end of this parking area. This is the trailhead **[1].** Restrooms are situated close to this corner of the parking area. Note that there is another, smaller parking area even farther toward the bottom of the island. However, the first left turn in the park is the most direct route to it.

The restaurant and the union of the West Branch Susquehanna River with the northern channel of the North Branch Susquehanna River around Packers Island are behind your back, and the boat mooring area is to your right when you begin walking. Go straight at a fork just 50 feet past the trailhead. Look at the vertical river bluffs across the river. That is the Blue Hill section of Shikellamy State Park.

You will pass at least a couple of plastic bag dispensers on this trail. Can you guess what they are for without reading the signs? A lot of people walk dogs here.

While this area certainly is not a pristine river-bottom forest, the trees are typical of this type of habitat. Several trees alongside the trail wear identification signs. Try to identify the trees while you walk, then check your identification against the signs. Some of the trees you will see are silver maple, slippery elm, white ash, river birch, red mulberry, ailanthus altissima, and sweet cherry. The latter two are exotics from Asia.

Very little underbrush obstructs your view along this trail. The only potentially confusing trail forks are really not a problem because you can see where they go and where you should be going. Ignore right forks toward a trail closer to the river unless you choose to use them as alternate routes. It really doesn't matter since, as long as you walk downriver, they all arrive at Point Sitting Area (.2 mi.) **[2].** This is the extreme lower tip of Packers Island, where the southern channel of the North Branch flows into Lake Augusta. Have a seat on one of the four benches. Watching a river flow is very soothing, almost hypnotic.

Turn right when you walk off Point Sitting Area (it would have been a left turn if you had not walked onto the sitting area platform), walking up the south channel of the North Branch. Look at the buoys in the water where the trail angles away from the water. They regulate boat speed, which helps make this section quiet. High walls across the water hold back floodwaters.

Turn left just before reaching the boat launch ramp (.47 mi.) **[3].** Watch for cars when you cross a road (.5 mi.) **[4],** then go up a slight incline. Past the restrooms, the trail bends left and goes into a mild decline and back to the trailhead (.69 mi.) **[1].**

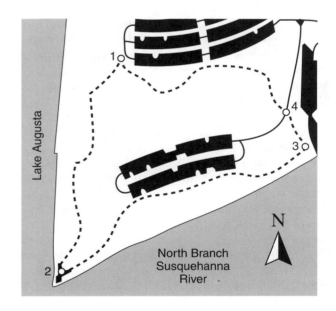

1. Trailhead
2. Point Sitting Area
3. Boat launch ramp
4. Road

Deer Trail 👢👢👢

Distance Round-Trip: 1 mile

Estimated Hiking Time: .5 hour

Caution: There are sheer drops in the area around the overlooks. Watch for cars when you cross the park road.

Trail Directions: Driving north from Shamokin Dam on Route 11, turn left onto County Line Road, then turn right into Shikellamy State Park. Drive to the large parking area at the end of the road, by the Lewisburg overlook. Use this overlook as the trailhead **[1]**. You can see far up the West Branch Susquehanna River to Lewisburg, about 6 miles to the north. This river eventually swings westward, where it drains the southern Allegheny Highlands. Here near its mouth it is reasonably healthy. Fishing is excellent upriver toward Williamsport. But above Lock Haven, it is virtually dead, a result of acidic drainage from the coal mining region in its headwaters. During the 19th century great rafts of white pine floated down this river and on to the Atlantic coast.

Facing the river, turn left on Deer Trail, past the end of the parking area and into hardwood forest. Trees are generally different from the island habitat across the river in the Packers Island section of the park but are more typical of the surrounding area. Look for oak, maple, and hickory. Turn sharply left less than .1 mi. from the overlook **[2]** for a nice diversion from the river-bluff overlooks that are the primary attractions of this section of the park. Keep a sharp eye for gray squirrels and deer.

This is a very small park, so any confusion over where you should be headed is not going to get you into trouble, as long as you stay away from the sheer river bluffs. Dry Hollow Trail forks left at .3 mi. **[3]**. It can be used to shorten this loop, as can Oak Ridge Trail, which forks left at .5 mi. **[4]**. Stop between these forks, the most secluded portion of the park, to enjoy the woods. This is a fine place to watch birds, especially during migration periods, and to scan the hillside for deer.

Watch for cars when you cross the park road (.68 mi.) **[5]**. Just past the road, take a spur trail down to the bridge overlook (.7 mi.) **[6]**. Look across Lake Augusta and up the North Branch Susquehanna River. Above this point, it has an S-shaped course to its headwaters in New York and the northeast corner of Pennsylvania.

Return to Deer Trail and turn right to the Sunbury overlook (.8 mi.) **[7]**. This provides a good view up the North Branch and of the river community of Sunbury. Continue to the Lewisburg overlook to complete the 1-mi. loop **[1]**.

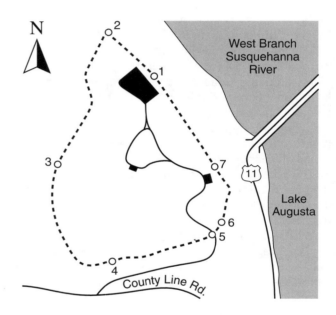

1. Trailhead
2. Sharp left
3. Dry Hollow Trail
4. Oak Ridge Trail
5. Park road
6. Bridge overlook
7. Sunbury overlook

10. Tuscarora State Park

- Tour the famous anthracite coal region.
- Fish, swim, and boat on a quiet lake.
- Come during winter for ice skating, ice fishing, and sledding.

Area Information

The finest coal in the world, anthracite, or hard coal, has been mined for many years in the area around Tuscarora State Park. But this secluded valley was spared. The virgin forest was cut and less-steep places were put to the plow, but at least the soil was not ripped away. Today, this area, known locally as Locust Valley, is a maturing second-growth forest. Farmland and a golf course surround the park.

A dam was built in 1960 in cooperation with the U.S. Soil Conservation Service for flood prevention and for recreation. The impoundment, Tuscarora Lake, provides a beautiful swimming beach, a wildlife habitat, and a place for quiet boating. Anglers catch muskellunge, bass, yellow perch, catfish, sunfish, pickerel, and trout.

While camping is not allowed at Tuscarora State Park, Locust Lake State Park, which is administered along with Tuscarora, is just a short drive to the west over country roads. It is primarily a family camping area, with 282 campsites.

Directions: Turn south at Barnesville, which is on Pennsylvania Route 54 between Interstate Route 81 and Pennsylvania Route 309. Turn left at the T to the park entrance or right to park headquarters.

Hours Open: The park has only day-use facilities, which are open from 8:00 A.M. to sunset, except that the boat launch is open and fishing is allowed 24 hours per day. The park is open year-round. The beach is open between 11:00 A.M. and 7:00 P.M. from Memorial Day weekend to Labor Day.

Facilities: Tuscarora State Park is primarily a day-use park. It has swimming in a lake, fishing, boating, boat rentals, picnic tables, restrooms, a shower house by the beach, and a food concession. There is also a flying field for radio-controlled airplanes.

Permits and Rules: Alcoholic beverages are prohibited. Boats must have either a state park launching permit, a state park mooring permit, or a current Pennsylvania Fish and Boat Commission registration. Outdoor recreational activities are restricted to locations where signs or physical improvements designate the appropriate use. Fires and the disposal of hot coals are restricted to provided facilities. Trash and litter must be placed in containers provided for this purpose, and disposal is limited to items accumulated during the use of the park. Pets must be leashed and controlled at all times, and they are not allowed at the swimming area.

Further Information: Department of Conservation and Natural Resources, Tuscarora State Park, RD 1, Box 1051, Barnesville, PA 18214-9603; phone 717-467-2404.

Other Areas of Interest

Locust Lake State Park, just a short drive from Tuscarora State Park, is complementary. It is designed primarily for family camping, which Tuscarora does not offer. It also has fine trails. Contact Locust Lake State Park through Tuscarora State Park.

Park Trails

Laurel Trail Loop 🥾—.4 mile—Loop off Log Trail through mountain laurel.

Locust Mountain Trail 🥾—.4 mile—This spur trail off Crow Trail leads to a reforestation area.

Tuscarora State Park

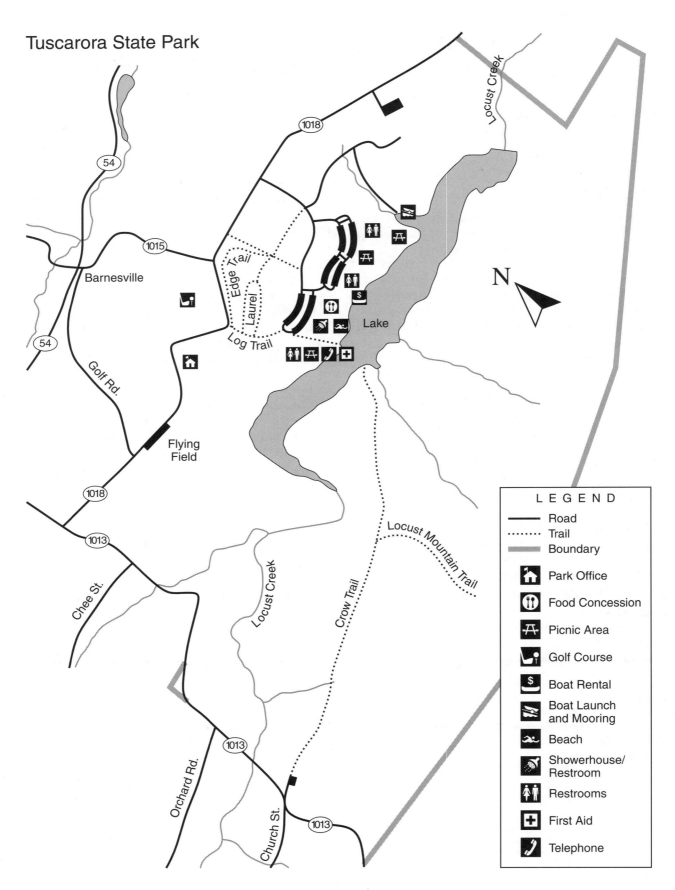

LEGEND

———	Road
········	Trail
▓▓▓	Boundary
🏠	Park Office
🍴	Food Concession
⛱	Picnic Area
⛳	Golf Course
$	Boat Rental
🚤	Boat Launch and Mooring
🏊	Beach
🚿	Showerhouse/Restroom
🚻	Restrooms
➕	First Aid
☎	Telephone

Crow Trail

Distance Round-Trip: 2.7 miles

Estimated Hiking Time: 1.5 hours

Caution: There are no trail signs or trail blazes. Wear bright orange clothing during hunting season.

Trail Directions: Crow Trail is a very pleasant stroll through dense forest and overgrown fields to the undeveloped edge of Tuscarora Lake. Starting at park headquarters, drive west on Pennsylvania Route 1018 to Pennsylvania Route 1013 and turn left. Go past two right turns, then turn left onto a gravel road just before the third right turn. No sign marks this gravel road. Turn right just before a gate into a small parking area. The gate is the head of Crow Trail **[1]**. A huge white oak is at the left side of the gate, and mature hemlocks are along the right side of the trail.

The trail is wide, actually a continuation of the access road, but overgrown with grass because it is only occasionally used by official vehicles. Just 885 feet into the trail you cross a right-of-way. Examine the deep ruts made by ATVs. Farther along, you pass through overgrown fields. This is a great place to see wildlife, especially deer or black bears that come here during fall to feed on apples. Any wildlife you see will probably be either in a field or crossing the trail. In the forest, rhododendron and mountain laurel are so thick in most places that you cannot see anywhere else. You will have to use your ears to identify sounds. Learn the difference between the thud of deer hooves and the shuffling of squirrels.

In some places, rhododendron and mountain laurel grow side by side. Study the differences between these two similar species, particularly leaf size. Rhododendron tends to be taller, and its leaves curl under slightly. Also along this trail, try to identify at least six different coniferous trees. The best variety is found on the edges of the fields. Try to identify at least four oak species and at least two birch species.

Locust Mountain Trail forks right .9 mi. from the trailhead **[2]**. Take a detour up this fork into a field where you'll see plastic tubes that have been driven into the ground. Can you guess their purpose?

Continuing on Crow Trail, curve right and drop downhill toward Tuscarora Lake, about 500 feet past Locust Mountain Trail. You begin getting glimpses of the lake from the lower end of another overgrown field. Notice how the trail is eroded down to bare rocks on the steeper slope. Crow Trail ends right at the edge of Tuscarora Lake (1.4 mi.) **[3]**. Pause here for a pack lunch or something to drink, and absorb the scenery. Canada geese are probably on the water or on the far shore. You can see the swimming beach across the lake and the dam far to the right.

Return to the trailhead the way you came **[1]** for a total hike of 2.7 mi.

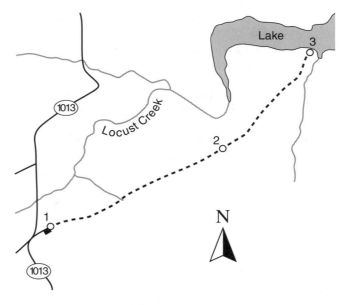

1. Trailhead
2. Locust Mountain Trail
3. Tuscarora Lake

Log and Edge Trails

Distance Round-Trip: 1 mile

Estimated Hiking Time: .5 hour

Caution: There is no actual trail to complete this loop; however, it's a simple matter to follow power lines. Wear bright orange clothes during hunting season. Log Trail borders an area that is open to hunting.

Trail Directions: Log Trail, Edge Trail, and a power line right-of-way provide a short loop through a quiet hardwood forest and along the edge of a cultivated field on top of a ridge where you get a good view of the area. It is a perfect hike for a picnic while you're waiting for the food to cook. Afterward, you can cool off with a dip in the lake. Drive down the park entrance road and turn right into the first day-use area parking lot. There are two levels in this parking lot. The trailhead for Log Trail is at the far end of this parking lot, in the middle of the short drive that connects the two levels **[1].** It is not marked by a sign or trail blazes, but the trail is obvious.

As you begin walking uphill, notice that mountain laurel bushes and rhododendron bushes grow side by side. The forest is dominated by red maple, white oak, chestnut oak, and red oak mixed with hemlock and white pine. You will also find sassafras, an unusual tree that has leaves of three different shapes. Some are oval with slightly pointed tips, some are shaped like mittens, and some have a small lobe in either side of a larger lobe. Native Americans and early settlers used sassafras roots to make a delicious tea that, according to some people, has medicinal uses. Some people still make it. But do not pick it here. It is illegal to damage or remove any plant from state park land.

The trail is grassy where it is fairly level but eroded to gravel on steeper slopes. Laurel Loop Trail forks left in two places separated by about 400 feet as you get close to the top of the hill. There are no signs at these forks. You can see a paved road straight ahead on the flat top of the hill, and a fence at the edge of a golf course across the road. Turn right onto Edge Trail just before a gate (.3 mi.) **[2].**

At the start, Edge Trail is gravel. Trees here, mostly oak, are among the largest on this loop. You walk along the edge of the park, beside the road, then turn right along the edge of a cultivated field (.4 mi.) **[3].** Look ahead and left for a good view of the anthracite coal region terrain. A long valley stretches into the distance, and beyond that a long ridge. Look for signs of coal power along the horizon of the ridge. Hawthorne and other brush on the edge of the field make this a good area for wildlife. Edges are generally good places to see wildlife because they often provide different foods than the forest or field. Watch for ruffed grouse and listen for the drumming noise they make when they flush into the air. This is also a likely place to see songbirds, such as indigo buntings, that are different from those you saw in the forest.

Walk along the edge of the field to the power lines (.7 mi.) **[4],** then turn right. To the right, in the woods, are a couple of picnic tables and the crumbling remains of an old stone fence.

Follow the power line right-of-way downhill past a large blue water tank (.8 mi.) **[5].** Thick brush will prevent you from walking directly under the power lines, so walk to the right in the woods until you reach the tank. There is no actual trail through this area until you pass the water tank, then the right of way goes down a steep slope to the parking area where you began this hike (.9 mi.) **[6].** Turn right to return to the trailhead (1 mi.) **[1].**

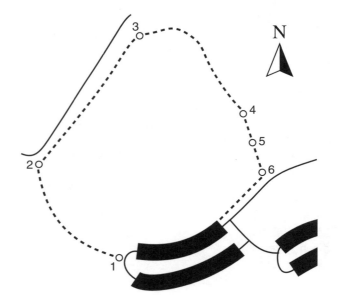

1. Trailhead
2. Edge Trail
3. Field
4. Power lines
5. Water tank
6. Parking area

11. Nolde Forest Environmental Education Center

- Explore one of the first managed forests in America.
- Find the witch on top of the Nolde Mansion.
- Search for signs of the 19th-century iron and forest industries.
- Learn what the lone pine is.

Area Information

Nolde Forest Environmental Education Center was established in one of the first planned forests in America. As in most of Pennsylvania, the forest seen by the early European invaders was completely cut for lumber or to fuel the iron furnaces, where iron was extracted from ore during the 19th century. Remains of several iron furnaces are still evident in the area. One of these consumed 46 acres of forest for fuel each year. The wood was converted to charcoal in hearths. Hearth remains can be seen along some trails. Look for bits of charcoal and discolored soil.

Jacob Nolde, a wealthy Reading businessman, bought the land shortly after 1900. According to legend, Nolde saw a lone pine tree and decided that if a pine could grow there, so could other trees. With commercial use in mind, he began planting trees in 1907, when the American forestry movement was just beginning. Nolde received national recognition for his forestry efforts just three years later. A German immigrant himself, Nolde hired a German forester in 1912 to create a forest in the image of Germany's Black Forest.

Jacob Nolde's son, Hans, build a Tudor-style mansion here in 1926. It alone is worth a visit. Check out the witch-and-bat weather vane and the children's entrance. The mansion is now used as office and library for the center.

After Hans Nolde died in 1965, the Commonwealth of Pennsylvania purchased Nolde Forest. In 1970, it became the first environmental education center operated by the Bureau of State Parks with help from federal grants and the Berks County Intermediate Unit. Students and teachers at all levels use the park's numerous educational programs. The center is "dedicated to helping people develop a sound environmental ethic."

Though managed by the Bureau of State Parks, Nolde Forest offers no recreational activities. The only activities allowed other than educational programs are hiking and watching or photographing wildlife. This is an excellent place for bird watching. Look for unusual trees such as Scotch pine, red pine, Norway spruce, Douglas fir, and Japanese larch. This forest did not sprout naturally; it was planted.

Directions: The center is located on Pennsylvania Route 625, also called New Holland Road, about 3 miles south of Reading.

Hours Open: The park is open year-round from 8:00 A.M. to sunset. The Mansion Area closes at 4:00 P.M.

Facilities: There are no recreational facilities at Nolde Forest Environmental Education Center.

Permits and Rules: Bicycles, swimming, and alcoholic beverages are not allowed. Pets must be leashed at all times.

Further Information: Nolde Forest Environmental Education Center, 2910 New Holland Road, Reading, PA 19607; phone 610-775-1411.

Other Areas of Interest

For information about the area, contact **Reading and Berks County Visitors Bureau,** 352 Penn Street, Reading, PA 19602-1010; phone 610-375-4085 or 800-443-6610.

Park Trails

Middle Road 🥾🥾—.7 mile—View coniferous plantations from a fire road.

Chestnut Trail 🥾🥾—.4 mile—This trail connects the Mansion Area with Kissinger Road.

Laurel Path 🥾🥾🥾—.5 mile—Walk the crest of a hill from the Mansion Area to Cabin Hollow Road.

Cabin Hollow Road 🥾🥾🥾—.65 mile—This trail connects Boulevard Trail with Middle Road.

Nolde Forest Environmental Education Center

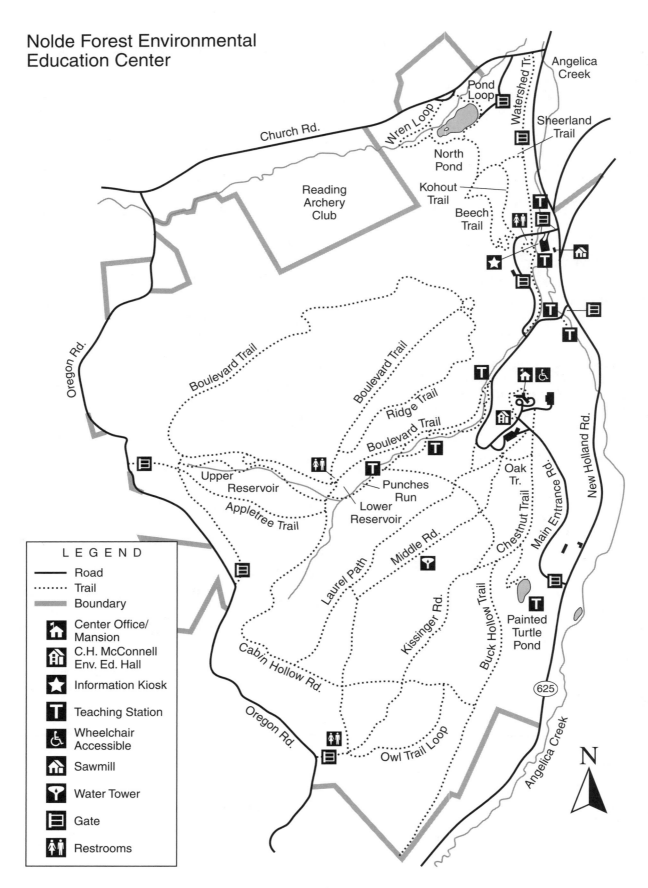

LEGEND

— Road
⋯⋯ Trail
▬ Boundary

🏠 Center Office/ Mansion
🏚 C.H. McConnell Env. Ed. Hall
★ Information Kiosk
T Teaching Station
♿ Wheelchair Accessible
🏠 Sawmill
Y Water Tower
☰ Gate
🚻 Restrooms

Boulevard Trail 🥾🥾🥾

Distance Round-Trip: 2.7 miles

Estimated Hiking Time: 1.5 hours

Caution: This trail is very steep just before it reaches its highest elevation.

Trail Directions: Drive in Main Entrance Road and turn left into the parking area by the C.H. McConnell Environmental Education Hall. The first drive to the parking area is a one-way exit. Go to the T and turn left, then turn left again into the upper end of the parking area. Use the kiosk at the upper end of this parking area as your trailhead **[1]**. This kiosk contains park brochures and a map of the park.

Walk out the entrance to the parking area and turn left on the paved road, passing the "road closed" sign. This road turns downhill, passing a stone wall. Turn left at a kiosk and two benches. This is the actual trailhead for Boulevard Trail (.2 mi.) **[2]**. Walk uphill, crossing a bridge, on a gravel road. Watershed Trail forks left before the bridge. It can be used as an alternate route for the lower section of Boulevard Trail.

Boulevard Trail climbs about 400 feet in elevation up the valley of Punches Run, starting through a deciduous forest. Kissinger Road forks left at .4 mi. **[3]**. Cabin Hollow Road forks left a few paces before Boulevard Trail splits (.6 mile) **[4]**. There are restrooms, a water fountain, and picnic tables by this split, which is the loop portion of Boulevard Trail. The water fountain does not work; the restrooms do. Pause here and look for a very unusual small tree. This had been an American chestnut forest before it was cut for iron furnace fuel. Though chestnut blight has all but eliminated the American chestnut, the tree still tries to grow. Small American chestnut trees can still be found, but they will almost certainly be killed by the blight before they can mature.

Take the left, or straight, fork of the trail. You enter a coniferous forest past the restrooms, still continuing to climb. After a series of switchbacks up the steepest part of the trail, Sprauge Trail forks left (.9 mi.) **[5]**. From here, Boulevard Trail curves right, over the top of the hill, cresting in deciduous woods (1.2 mi.) **[6]**. Enjoy the next 350 feet of level trail and the soothing breeze. If there is any wind at all, this is where you will feel it. Watch for red raspberry bushes along the trail.

At 1.7 mi., where Boulevard Trail makes a hairpin turn to the right, you can see a rock outcrop to the left **[7]**. Take a few minutes to enjoy it, but be careful. After a comfortable descent, with conifers on the right and hardwoods on the left, you arrive at the restrooms to complete the loop portion of Boulevard Trail (2.2 mi.) **[4]**. Turn left and retrace your route to the trailhead for a total hike of 2.75 mi., or you can take an alternate route back.

As an alternate route, walk down Boulevard Trail from the restrooms to the intersection with Kissinger Road (2.3 mi.) **[3]** and turn right. Cross a wooden footbridge and pass the end of an unmarked trail. This is the end of Watershed Trail. Continue uphill on Kissinger Road to a sharp left turn (2.4 mi.) **[8]**. Only Kissinger Trail is marked at this turn. The road that goes straight is not marked. Stay on Kissinger Trail to the next intersection (2.5 mi.) **[9]** and turn off Kissinger Trail to the left. You will encounter a couple more intersections before you reach the parking area kiosk, but you can see the parking area by the time you reach them. The total distance using this return option is 2.7 mi. **[1]**.

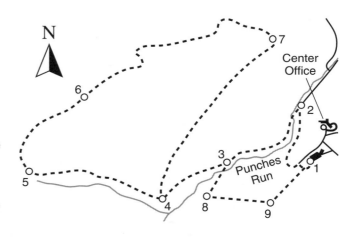

1. Parking area kiosk
2. Trailhead kiosk
3. Kissinger Road
4. Boulevard Trail splits
5. Sprauge Trail
6. Hill crest
7. Rock outcrop
8. Kissinger left
9. Left off Kissinger

Watershed Trails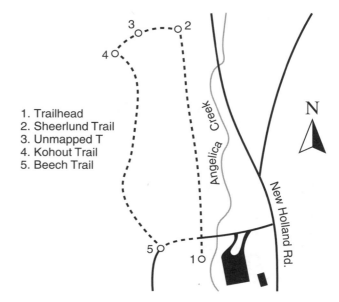

Distance Round-Trip: .53 mile

Estimated Hiking Time: .5 hour

Caution: This trail is very steep in short sections. In places it is very narrow and nearly overgrown with brush.

Trail Directions: Turn into the Sawmill Parking Area from Route 625, also called New Holland Road. Use the kiosk by the entrance to the parking area as your trailhead **[1]**. Walk out of the parking lot and turn left across the bridge. Immediately after crossing the bridge, only 100 feet from the kiosk, turn right onto Watershed Trail. This intersection is marked by a sign, and there are restrooms to the left.

Watershed Trail follows Angelica Creek downstream. Examine a human-made structure on the creek bank below the bridge. Can you figure out its purpose?

Tall spruce and hemlock trees shade the trail as it gently descends to the valley floor. Try to spot a sycamore tree along the creek bank before the trail bends away from the creek to the intersection of Sheerlund Trail (.18 mi.) **[2]**. Turn left onto this narrow trail, which is crowded by thick underbrush, up a moderately steep slope. The woods are a mix of deciduous and coniferous.

Turn left at an unmapped T (.27 mi.) **[3]**. As you continue up this steep portion of the hike, look at the posts that have been laid at an angle across the trail. Can you guess their purpose? It is directly related to the purpose of the human-made device on the creek bank near the start of this hike.

Turn left onto Kohout Trail at the next intersection (.29 mi.) **[4]**, beginning a fairly level stretch along the hillside. William G. Kohout was the German-born, Austrian-trained forester hired by Jacob Nolde to help plant this forest. Though this was a planned forest, you will see that some native vegetation, like the wild grape in this area, has become reestablished.

After the trail bends right, around the end of the hill, you begin a gentle descent to the end of Kohout Trail at Beech Trail (.48 mi.) **[5]**. You can see the restrooms and the entrance to the parking area to the left. Turn left on this road and return to the trailhead (.53 mi.) **[1]**.

1. Trailhead
2. Sheerlund Trail
3. Unmapped T
4. Kohout Trail
5. Beech Trail

12. Tyler State Park

- Hike in a setting that is more pastoral than in most state parks.
- Bike on 10.5 miles of trails, or ride horses over 9 miles.
- Fish for bass and sunfish, and watch wildlife on Neshaminy Creek.

Area Information

Tyler State Park is more pastoral than most Pennsylvania state parks, a mix of cultivated fields and woodlots. It was farmed by the Tyler family, who had one of the finest Ayrshire dairy herds in the county as well as poultry, sheep, pigs, and horses. Several old stone farm dwellings, some dating to the early 18th century, still stand in the park. Some are still in use. The park opened in 1974, yet about 25 percent of the land is still under cultivation through leases, continuing three centuries of tradition.

Neshaminy Creek divides the park. The west side of the creek is a maze of trails. Most are bike, hike, and equestrian trails combined, and in addition they are used by official park vehicles and farm vehicles. The east side of the creek is more highly developed for day-use activities such as picnicking and games. The creek itself is a rich habitat for wildlife such as ducks, geese, muskrats, and raccoons.

Directions: The park is bordered on the south by Pennsylvania Route 332 between Newtown and Richboro. From the Pennsylvania Turnpike, use Exit 27 and follow Route 332 east, or use Exit 28 and follow U.S. Route 1 north to Interstate Route 95, then drive west on the four-lane bypass around Newtown. There are several entrances to the park. The easiest way to reach the trailhead is to use the Swamp Road entry from the Newtown bypass.

Hours Open: The park is open year-round from 8:00 A.M. to sunset.

Facilities: Tyler State Park has several picnic areas, playgrounds, equestrian trails, bike trails, hike trails, canoe rental, and warm-water fishing.

Permits and Rules: Alcoholic beverages are prohibited. Boats must have either a state park launching permit, a state park mooring permit, or a current Pennsylvania Fish and Boat Commission registration. Outdoor recreational activities are restricted to locations where signs or physical improvements designate the appropriate use. Fires and the disposal of hot coals are restricted to provided facilities. Trash and litter must be placed in containers provided for this purpose, and disposal is limited to items accumulated during the use of the park. Pets must be leashed and controlled at all times.

Further Information: Department of Conservation and Natural Resources, Tyler State Park, 101 Swamp Road, Newtown, PA 18940-1151; phone 215-968-2021.

Other Areas of Interest

For more information about the surrounding area, contact **Bucks County Tourist Commission, Inc.,** 152 Swamp Road, Doylestown, PA 18901; phone 215-345-4552.

Delaware Canal State Park has a 60-mile trail that follows the only remaining continuously intact canal from the great towpath canal-building era of the early 19th century. Write to Department of Conservation and Natural Resources, Delaware Canal State Park, 11 Lodi Road, Upper Black Eddy, PA 18972; phone 610-982-5560.

Park Trails

Hay Barn Grass Trail 👢—.38 mile—This trail connects No. 1 Lane with Dairy Hill Trail.

College Park Trail 👢—.4 mile—This trail connects No. 1 Lane with Dairy Hill Trail.

Mill Trail 👢👢—.6 mile—This connects Mill Dairy Trail with Stable Nature Area Trail.

Woodfield Trail 👢👢—.5 mile—This trail combines with a section of Mill Dairy Trail as an exercise trail.

White Pine Trail 👢👢—.4 mile—This trail can be used to form a loop with Dairy Hill Trail.

Tyler State Park

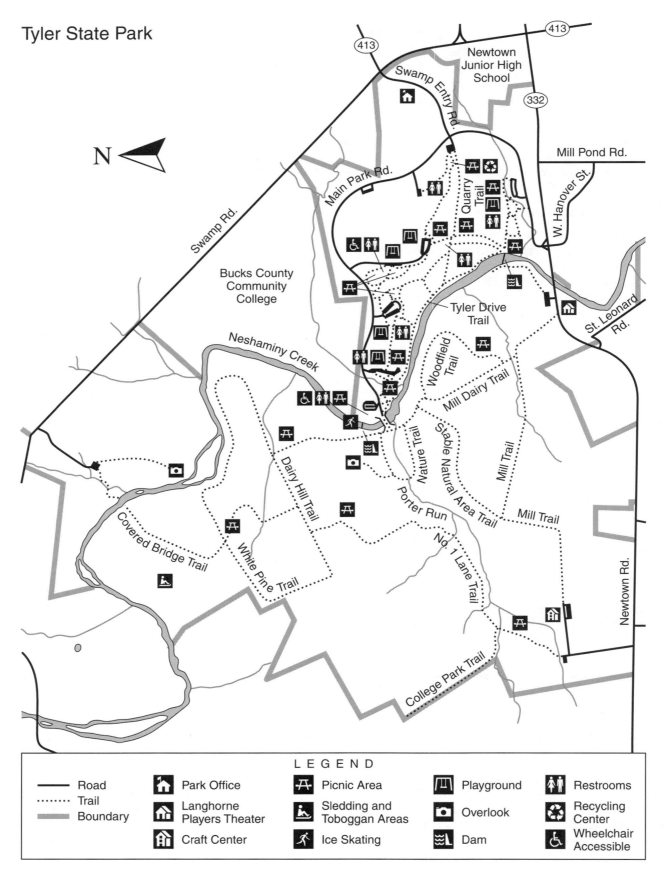

N

Swamp Rd.

413

Newtown Junior High School

413

332

Mill Pond Rd.

Swamp Entry Rd.

Main Park Rd.

W. Hanover St.

Bucks County Community College

Quarry Trail

Tyler Drive Trail

St. Leonard Rd.

Neshaminy Creek

Woodfield Trail

Mill Dairy Trail

Mill Trail

Dairy Hill Trail

Nature Trail

Stable Natural Area Trail

Mill Trail

Covered Bridge Trail

White Pine Trail

Porter Run

No. 1 Lane Trail

Newtown Rd.

College Park Trail

L E G E N D

—— Road	Park Office	Picnic Area	Playground	Restrooms
···· Trail	Langhorne Players Theater	Sledding and Toboggan Areas	Overlook	Recycling Center
▬▬ Boundary	Craft Center	Ice Skating	Dam	Wheelchair Accessible

Mill Dairy Trails 👢👢

Distance Round-Trip: 3.35 miles

Estimated Hiking Time: 1.75 hours

Caution: There are signs at intersections; however, there are many intersections along this hike, so you must be alert. Watch for bicycles, horses, and vehicles on these trails.

Trail Directions: Follow Main Park Road from either Route 332 or Swamp Road to the boathouse area at the edge of Neshaminy Creek. Park in the boathouse parking lot and walk across the creek on the causeway, just downstream from Neshaminy Weir Dam. The trailhead is just across the causeway on Mill Dairy Trail **[1]**, where you turn right. You will walk on well-marked paved trails throughout this route.

The Thompson Dairy House, which you pass on your right, was built in 1775. Enjoy the view from the outside because it is not open to the public. Following an easy climb, cross a bridge and hit a T and a stop sign (.4 mi.) **[2]**. This is Dairy Hill Trail. Turn left and continue to climb past Covered Bridge Trail, which forks right at .6 mi. **[3]**, to No. 1 Lane Trail (.7 mi.) **[4]**, where you turn left toward two white barns. Walk between the barns and a two-story white house.

After you cross a bridge, there is a picnic table and a water fountain on the left (.8 mi.) **[5]**. Let the water run for a couple of minutes and it will get cool. You are now on top of the hill. The remainder of the trail is quite level, or downhill. Gaze around the horizon at the checkerboard of fields and woodlots. Far to the left you can see houses, tanks, and towers. If there is a breeze, this is where you will feel it best.

You should see numerous birdhouses on poles in open areas along this route. These are intended for eastern bluebirds, though other birds also use them. Naturally occurring hollow nesting trees are scarce. Human-made houses like these have been very successful in increasing the population of this beautiful bird.

You reenter the woods before passing Hay Barn Grass Trail (1.3 mi.) **[6]**, which forks acutely right. This is a very relaxing portion of the hike as you wind through the woods and by old buildings. Do not fight the temptation to sit on one of the stone bridges. Look at the yellow poles set in College Park Trail (1.7 mi.) **[7]**. They are obviously there to prevent vehicles from using the trail. A sign also warns that horses are not allowed on that trail. There is a small waterfall, when there is enough water in the stream, above a bridge just past the intersection.

After leaving the woods, passing another old house on the left and crossing a bridge, turn left onto Stable Mill Trail (2 mi.) **[8]**. This is a much wider paved trail that is open to motor vehicles past the Pennsylvania Guild of Craftsmen building, where the trail narrows, to a house. Yellow pipes block vehicles from going farther.

Turn left onto Natural Area Trail (2.6 mi.) **[9]**, leaving cultivated fields behind and reentering woods. This starts your descent back toward the trailhead. Natural Area Trail ends at a T with Mill Dairy Trail (3.2 mi.) **[10]**. Across a split-rail fence is a nice view of Neshaminy Creek. Turn left and follow Mill Dairy Trail back to the trailhead by the causeway (3.35 mi.) **[1]**.

1. Trailhead
2. Dairy Hill Trail
3. Covered Bridge Trail
4. No. 1 Lane Trail
5. Water fountain
6. Hay Barn Grass Trail
7. College Park Trail
8. Stable Mill Trail
9. Natural Area Trail
10. Mill Dairy Trail

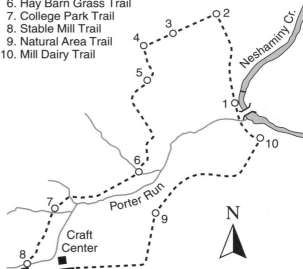

Nature Trail 👢👢👢

Distance Round-Trip: .64 mile

Estimated Hiking Time: .5 hour

Caution: Numerous unmarked spur trails make it difficult to follow Nature Trail. Brush and briars crowd the narrow trail in several places. Roots and rocks interfere with footing on most of the trail. There is a steep climb past the stream crossing.

Trail Directions: Drive to the boathouse parking area. Walk across Neshaminy Creek on the causeway. The first half of this causeway is higher to allow canoes to pass. Go through the T with Mill Dairy Trail angling left to a dirt trail. A sign that reads "Nature Trail START" is posted at the trailhead **[1]**. Nature Trail is not to the right of the causeway, as indicated on the park map.

A sign at the trailhead instructs that horses and bicycles should not use dirt trails, to minimize wear. But watch for them nonetheless. You will probably see bike tracks, at least, on the trail.

Nature Trail starts immediately uphill into a hardwood forest, following the valley of a small tributary stream, Porter Run. Several numbered wood posts in various stages of decay are situated along this trail. Interpretive brochures to accompany these posts are no longer available. Now the main significance of the posts is to reassure you that you are on Nature Trail. There are so many unmarked spur trails that are just as wide as Nature Trail that staying on Nature Trail is difficult, especially on the uphill section of the loop. This is typical of heavily used parks. This hike will be a test of your ability to use distance and landmarks to follow a trail.

This is still a good nature study even without an interpretive brochure. Carry field guides and try to identify trees, birds, or whatever interests you. Examine the straight trunks of tulip trees, the blotchy bark of sycamore, the shaggy bark of hickory, the craggy bark of oak, and the smooth bark of beech. See if the red raspberries along the way are ripe. Look for signs of wildlife. Try to identify and locate birds by their songs. Watch across the narrow valley for a large rock outcrop.

A spur trail cuts right, up the steep hillside, to a scenic overlook about .14 mi. from the trailhead **[2]**. It is a pleasant diversion, but you could encounter difficulty staying on the trail to the overlook and returning to Nature Trail because you encounter so many other spur trails.

The odds that you are actually on Nature Trail when you get to the top of the loop are minimal, but the only really important thing here is finding the stream crossing (.3 mi.) **[3]**, which is just a couple of hops over the creek on stones. The best way to identify the crossing is to first identify where the trail climbs the opposite side of the valley. Get above the rock outcrop to the first place where a trail looks practical, then look for the trail. Do not attempt a dangerous climb. There is no chance of your getting lost because you can follow the valley back to the trailhead.

After scrambling up the steep hillside, the trail begins a steady decline toward the trailhead. Do not stray off the trail while you pass over the top of the rock outcrop (.45 mi.) **[4]**. There are dangerous drops. The last yards of Nature Trail are steep and rocky. Turn left when you come to a T with a paved trail (.52 mi.) **[5]**, and return to the trailhead near the causeway (.64 mi.) **[1]**.

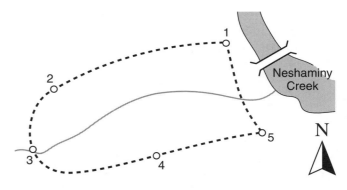

1. Trailhead
2. Overlook
3. Stream crossing
4. Rock outcrop
5. Paved T

13. French Creek State Park

- Wander through one of the largest forests remaining in southeastern Pennsylvania.
- Fish in two small lakes, one for trout, the other for trophy bass.
- Play disc golf on two woodland courses.
- Learn the art of orienteering in what some consider the orienteering capital of North America.
- Swim at a guarded pool.

Area Information

French Creek State Park is especially valuable because it preserves a large forest habitat in the overdeveloped southeastern corner of Pennsylvania. The park covers 7,339 acres. This is critical not only for animals that live here year-round, but also for migrating neotropical songbirds that both breed here and use the area during migrations. The lack of unbroken forest is a serious threat to these songbirds.

The beautiful hardwood forest that stands here now is a far cry from the one that existed before the industrial revolution hit the area. Hopewell Furnace National Historic Site, which is managed by the National Park Service, borders French Creek State Park. Hopewell Furnace produced iron from 1771 to 1883. Charcoal was used to fuel the furnace. To make charcoal, the entire forest, which was primarily American chestnut, was cut repeatedly.

French Creek State Park was created in 1946 when the land, except for Hopewell Furnace National Historic Site, was transferred to the Commonwealth of Pennsylvania. Today, the park is the nearest large public forest to the Philadelphia area.

Fishing is high on the list of outdoor activities. Hopewell Lake, 63 acres, is managed by the Pennsylvania Fish and Boat Commission with big bass regulations that promote trophy largemouth bass fishing. Scotts Run Lake, 21 acres, is stocked regularly with trout. Only nonpowered or electric-powered boats are allowed on these lakes. Boats can be rented at the Hopewell Lake swimming pool complex.

More than 30 miles of trail interconnect through the park, making hikes of almost any length possible.

Directions: The park is located southeast of Reading. Pennsylvania Route 345, between Pennsylvania Route 724 and Pennsylvania Route 23, passes through the park.

Hours Open: The park is open year-round from 8:00 A.M. to sunset.

Facilities: Campsites for tents and RVs, a swimming pool, nonpowered and electric-powered boating, numerous picnic areas, fishing, biking, orienteering, and other recreational activities are available in the park.

Permits and Rules: Alcoholic beverages are prohibited. Boats must have either a state park launching permit, a state park mooring permit, or a current Pennsylvania Fish and Boat Commission registration. Outdoor recreational activities are restricted to locations where signs or physical improvements designate the appropriate use. Fires and the disposal of hot coals are restricted to provided facilities. Trash and litter must be placed in containers provided for this purpose, and disposal is limited to items accumulated during the use of the park. Pets must be leashed and controlled at all times and are not allowed at the swimming area or in overnight camping facilities. Motorized vehicles are not allowed on any park trails. Swimming is not allowed in the lakes. Camping is permitted only in established campgrounds.

Further Information: French Creek State Park, 843 Park Road, Elverson, PA 19520-9523; phone 610-582-9680.

Park Trails

Boone Trail 🥾🥾🥾—6 miles—This is a loop that connects all of the major attractions in the park.

Turtle Trail 🥾🥾🥾—3.6 miles—Loop through the western portion on this trail.

Mill Creek Trail 🥾🥾🥾🥾—6 miles—Probably the most challenging trail in the park, this takes you through the relatively secluded eastern section.

Buzzards Trail 🥾🥾—1.7 miles—This connects Mill Creek Trail with Hopewell Furnace National Historic Site.

Kalmia Trail 🥾🥾🥾—1 mile—Use this trail as an alternate route on Six Penny Trail. It passes through mountain laurel and mature hardwoods.

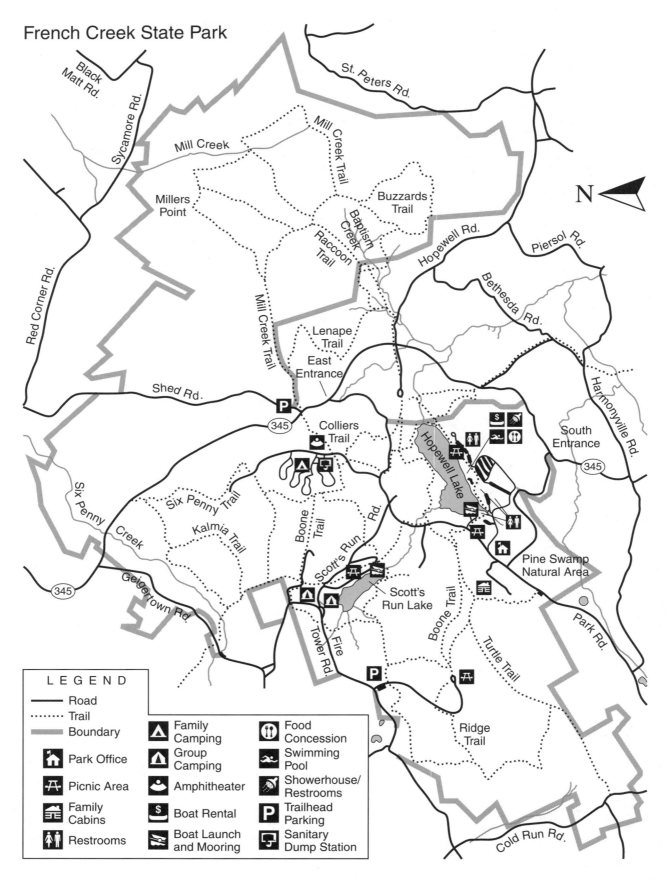

French Creek State Park

Black Matt Rd.

St. Peters Rd.

Sycamore Rd.

Mill Creek

Mill Creek Trail

Millers Point

Buzzards Trail

Baptism Creek

Raccoon Trail

Hopewell Rd.

Piersol Rd.

Red Corner Rd.

Bethesda Rd.

Mill Creek Trail

Lenape Trail

East Entrance

Harmonyville Rd.

Shed Rd.

P

345

Colliers Trail

Hopewell Lake

South Entrance

345

Six Penny Creek

Six Penny Trail

Kalmia Trail

Boone Trail

Scott's Run Rd.

Pine Swamp Natural Area

Park Rd.

345

Geigertown Rd.

Scott's Run Lake

Boone Trail

Turtle Trail

Tower Rd.

Fire Rd.

P

Ridge Trail

Cold Run Rd.

LEGEND
- —— Road
- ⋯⋯ Trail
- ━━ Boundary
- 🏠 Park Office
- 🏕 Picnic Area
- 🏚 Family Cabins
- 🚻 Restrooms
- ⛺ Family Camping
- ⛺ Group Camping
- 🎭 Amphitheater
- 💲 Boat Rental
- 🚤 Boat Launch and Mooring
- 🍴 Food Concession
- 🏊 Swimming Pool
- 🚿 Showerhouse/ Restrooms
- P Trailhead Parking
- 🚽 Sanitary Dump Station

48

Six Penny Trail 👢👢👢

Distance Round-Trip: 3.6 miles

Estimated Hiking Time: 2 hours

Caution: There are numerous roots and rocks in the steeper parts of this trail. Wear bright orange clothing during hunting season.

Trail Directions: Drive on Park Road to the east entrance and turn left on Route 345. Drive about 1.5 mi. to a gate on the left side of the road. A sign on this gate says "Road Closed No Parking." There is just enough room to pull off the road and park on either side of this gate. There is no sign here marking this as Six Penny Trail, but this is the best trailhead **[1]**.

Follow the old road past the gate to a T (.1 mi.) **[2]**, where you can see orange rectangle trail blazes on trees in both directions. Six Penny Trail is a loop. You will return to this point. Take the right fork. Following this dirt trail is easy, as it begins a gentle climb through maturing second-growth timber.

The trail begins dropping before you come to the first trail sign (.4 mi.) **[3]**, which reads "'6¢ Trail." Examine the sandstone conglomerate among the many rocks and boulders on the forest floor. Do you know the significance of this sandstone? Here is a clue: it is a sedimentary rock. Where have you seen material like this, but not in rock form?

Turn left when you reach a T (.5 mi.) **[4]**. The trail follows a gravel road away from the picnic area, then returns to a dirt trail that passes to the left of a building foundation. You will also see a small, dried-up reservoir past the foundation and farther to the right.

The boulder-strewn stretch of trail through the Six Penny Creek valley is very scenic. Have a seat on a rock and listen to vireos singing in the treetops and chipmunks chattering on the ground. This is not the place to hurry.

Turn left when you reach the intersection with Horseshoe Trail (1.3 mi.) **[5]**. There is no sign to mark this intersection; however, you will see orange trail blazes for Six Penny Trail, yellow trail blazes for Horseshoe Trail, and a yellow horseshoe nailed to a tree when you turn left.

Begin climbing from the intersection. Kalmia Trail forks left during the steepest part of the climb (1.34 mi.) **[6]**. You can use this as a shortcut back to your trailhead, following purple trail blazes, then turning right when it returns to Six Penny Trail.

Continuing on Six Penny Trail, notice the stone water diversions across the trail. Without them, the trail would soon become a rocky ditch. The trail begins to level off at the edge of private land (1.4 mi.) **[7]**. This is marked on the right by no trespassing signs, a single-wire fence, and a piece of yellow railroad track set in the ground as a post.

Six Penny Trail forks left away from Horseshoe Trail on top of the hill (1.6 mi.) **[8]**. Watch for the double orange blaze that marks this turn. Some climbing remains, but it is mild and the trail is smooth. This is the most secluded part of the trail. Pick a log and sit. Try to get a glimpse of deer browsing or warblers flitting through the brush. Listen to blue jays and crows in the trees.

A spur trail forks right to the camping area (2.3 mi.) **[9]**. There is no sign, but it is marked by orange trail blazes with green stripes. You will probably hear the sounds of children playing. Continue straight with the plain orange blazes. Cross a gravel road (2.4 mi.) **[10]**. This is another good place to look for ripe berries. About 500 feet past the gravel road, Six Penny Trail turns left at an unmapped intersection. After meandering alongside the gravel road, you curve right near a large blue tank (2.8 mi.) **[11]** and begin the descent to complete the loop (3.5 mi.) **[2]**, then turn right to the trailhead (3.6 mi.) **[1]**.

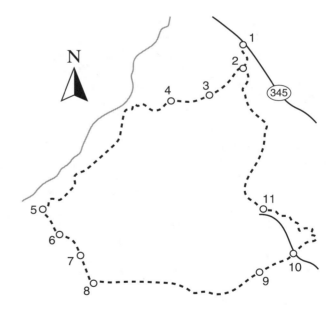

1. Trailhead
2. Loop T
3. 6¢ Trail
4. Left at T
5. Horseshoe Trail
6. Kalmia Trail
7. Private land
8. Leave Horseshoe Trail
9. Camping spur
10. Gravel road
11. Blue tank

Lenape/Colliers Trails

Distance Round-Trip: 3.6 miles

Estimated Hiking Time: 2.5 hours

Caution: Watch for motor vehicles when crossing roads. This trail is littered with roots and rocks in some places. You must pay a fee at Hopewell Furnace National Historic Site. This fee varies with the different programs.

Trail Directions: Use the east entrance from Route 345, and drive Park Road about .8 mi. to the campground entrance, which is well marked. Turn into the campground. Use the kiosk by the campground contact station as your trailhead [1].

This hike combines sections of two trails that take you on a journey in time through maturing hardwood forests to an iron furnace that began operation during the 18th century. The area was covered by a chestnut forest prior to the operation of Hopewell Furnace. But the forest was cut to produce the charcoal that fueled the iron furnace. A second-growth hardwood forest has reclaimed the land in French Creek State Park. But at Hopewell Furnace National Historic Site, you can see an iron furnace operate much as it did 200 years ago.

Lenape Trail starts down a moderately steep grade from the trailhead through hardwood forest to Route 345 (.4 mi.) [2], where it intersects with Shed Road. Traffic is sometimes heavy on this highway, so be very careful when crossing. Walk across Route 345 and a few paces down Shed Road to a gated road on your right. This is Mill Creek Trail and Lenape Trail, which you follow until Lenape Trail leaves the road grade (.7 mi.) [3].

Lenape Trail winds generally downhill past an intersection with Raccoon Trail (1.8 mi.) [4] to a gravel road (1.9 mi.) [5], where you turn right to Hopewell Road (2 mi.) [6]. Turn right on this paved road and watch for vehicle traffic, especially when you cross Route 345 (2.2 mi.) [7]. Once across Route 345, you are on the access road to Hopewell Furnace (2.8 mi.) [8].

Certainly you will want to get off the trail here to take a glimpse into Pennsylvania history. After going through the visitor center, where you pay a small fee, you enter the finest example of an early American iron plantation. One of Pennsylvania's most important furnace operations, it produced pig iron and iron castings from 1771 to 1883. During the American Revolution, it produced weapons for the Americans, including 115 cannons for the Navy. Mortar shells produced here helped win the battle at Yorktown. The furnace also produced stoves, pots, kettles, doors, and other items. Today, the furnace, waterwheel, blast machinery, ironmaster's mansion, and other structures have been restored. Normal operations of the furnace and farm are re-created by staff in 19th-century costumes.

Lenape Trail leaves Hopewell Furnace on a gravel road between the visitor center and the restored area. Turn right onto Colliers Trail just before leaving Hopewell Furnace National Historic Site (2.9 mi.) [9]. Continue across Park Road (3.1 mi.) [10], then climb a steep hill over a series of switchbacks to the trailhead (3.6 mi.) [1].

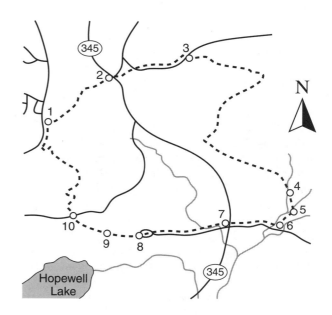

1. Trailhead
2. Route 345
3. Leave Mill Creek Trail
4. Raccoon Trail
5. Gravel road
6. Hopewell Road
7. Route 345
8. Hopewell Furnace
9. Colliers Trail
10. Park Road

14. Neshaminy State Park

- Watch oceangoing ships being pushed by tugboats.
- Walk the sandy shores of the only estuary in Pennsylvania.
- Swim in a large pool.
- See unusual birds and plants.

Area Information

Neshaminy State Park is the only state park in Pennsylvania where you can explore an estuary environment, watch the tide rise and fall, and stand at sea level. Both freshwater and saltwater animals and plants mingle in the brackish water. Estuaries and adjoining marshes are among the most fertile habitats in the world. Most of our valuable fishes along the Atlantic Coast depend on estuaries, as do numerous birds and mammals. During spring and fall migrations, you will see many unusual waterfowl. Several of the plants that grow here grow nowhere else in Pennsylvania.

But the 330-acre park protects only a tiny portion of the estuary. The river channel, once shallow and weedy with numerous small islands, has been dredged to allow passage of large ships. The removal of the soft, shallow bottom eliminated most mussels and aquatic plants and the animals that ate them. The water became dirtier because there are fewer plants to filter the water and because pollution increased. Water became so polluted that migratory fish such as shad, striped bass, and eels could not pass through. The degradation of estuaries has probably caused greater wildlife catastrophe than any other single type of habitat destruction in America.

The Delaware River estuary is far from clean, but it has improved. You can expect to see abundant wildlife in and around Neshaminy State Park. The best times to watch migratory waterfowl are during March and again during October–November. Several species that breed far to the north spend winters in the area. April is a splendid time for blossoming flowers along Neshaminy Creek.

Most of the park was a gift to the Commonwealth in 1956 by Robert R. Logan.

Directions: Neshaminy State Park is located on the northeast side of Philadelphia, on the banks of the Delaware River and Neshaminy Creek. Exit Interstate Route 95 at Pennsylvania Route 132, drive east, then turn left at the T to the park entrance.

Hours Open: The park is open year-round from 8:00 A.M. to sunset.

Facilities: Neshaminy is a day-use park with trails for hiking and biking, a swimming pool, play areas, and numerous picnic areas and pavilions. A portion of the park separated from the day-use area by Neshaminy Creek is a marina and boat launch with shore fishing areas.

Permits and Rules: All children age nine and under must be supervised by an adult at the swimming pool. Alcoholic beverages are prohibited. Boats must have either a state park launching permit, a state park mooring permit, or a current Pennsylvania Fish and Boat Commission registration. Outdoor recreational activities are restricted to locations where signs or physical improvements designate the appropriate use. Fires and the disposal of hot coals are restricted to provided facilities. Trash and litter must be placed in containers provided for this purpose, and disposal is limited to items accumulated during the use of the park. Pets must be leashed and controlled at all times, and they are not allowed at the swimming area. Do not swim in the Delaware River or Neshaminy Creek.

Further Information: Department of Conservation and Natural Resources, Neshaminy State Park, 3401 State Road, Bensalem, PA 19020-5930; phone 215-639-4538.

Other Areas of Interest

Visit the site where General George Washington's army crossed the Delaware River to attack the British at **Washington Crossing Historic Park,** P.O. Box 103, Washington Crossing, PA 18977; phone 215-493-4076.

For information about **Philadelphia,** write to Philadelphia Convention and Visitors Bureau, 1515 Market Street, Suite 2020, Philadelphia, PA 19102; phone 800-537-7676 or 215-636-1666.

Neshaminy State Park

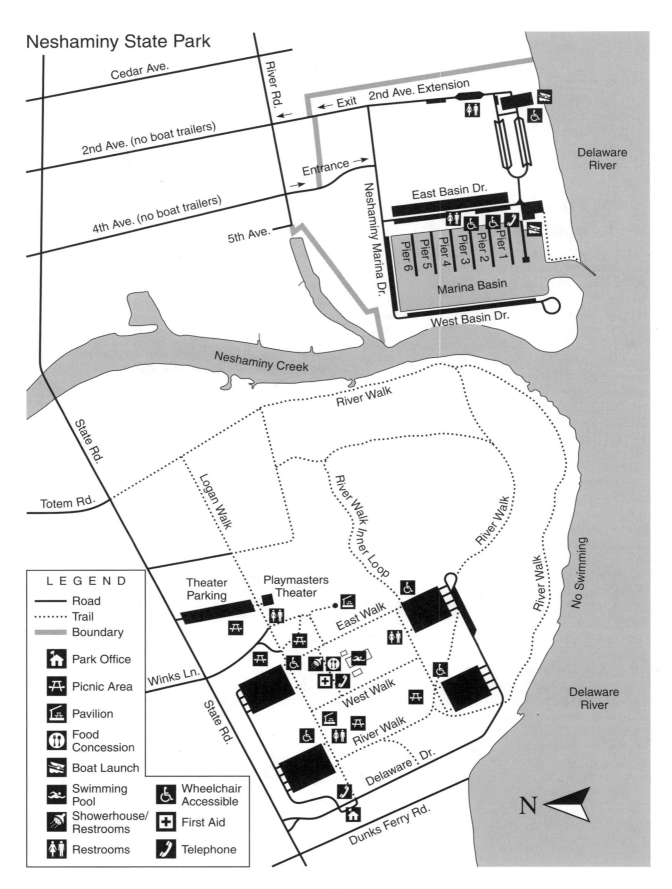

Cedar Ave.

River Rd.

2nd Ave. (no boat trailers)

Exit ← 2nd Ave. Extension

Entrance →

4th Ave. (no boat trailers)

5th Ave.

Delaware River

East Basin Dr.

Neshaminy Marina Dr.

Pier 6 Pier 5 Pier 4 Pier 3 Pier 2 Pier 1

Marina Basin

West Basin Dr.

Neshaminy Creek

River Walk

State Rd.

Logan Walk

River Walk Inner Loop

River Walk

River Walk

River Walk

No Swimming

Totem Rd.

LEGEND
—— Road
······ Trail
▬▬ Boundary

Theater Parking

Playmasters Theater

East Walk

Winks Ln.

Park Office

Picnic Area

West Walk

Pavilion

Food Concession

Boat Launch

River Walk

Swimming Pool

Showerhouse/ Restrooms

Restrooms

Wheelchair Accessible

First Aid

Telephone

State Rd.

Delaware Dr.

Delaware River

Dunks Ferry Rd.

N

River Walk 👢👢

Distance Round-Trip: 1.9 miles

Estimated Hiking Time: 1 hour

Caution: Watch for bicycles and park vehicles on the trail. Some portions of the trail might be wet.

Trail Directions: As you enter the park on Delaware Drive, turn left and park in the first of two large parking lots. The trailhead is at a kiosk marked "River Walk Trail" **[1]** at the end of this parking lot. As you face the kiosk from the parking lot, it is on the left side of the parking lot, not on the right as shown on the park map. The kiosk faces a paved trail. River Walk is a gravel trail to the left of the kiosk, perpendicular to the paved trail.

River Walk winds through a picnic area, past a play area on the left, to a fork (.07 mi.) **[2]**. Take the left fork. Just as you break out of the trees and the picnic area and the gravel trail curves left, turn right onto a grassy trail (.16 mi.) **[3]**, walk to a paved road, and turn left. This is Delaware Drive. To your right is the Delaware River estuary. You will probably see many pleasure boats and perhaps, if the tide is in, a tug pushing a huge barge upriver. Far to the right, facing downriver, you can see the Philadelphia skyline. Gulls bob up and down on the water and search for food from the air currents. During the spring or fall migration periods, you will see a variety of waterfowl. This is the heart of the Atlantic Flyway.

Leave the road as soon as it gets close to the river (.3 mi.) **[4]**. A sandy trail begins where the paved road curves away from the river. To the left is a parking area that is not used. You will have to contend with numerous unmapped spur trails. This is a heavily used park, and people wander all over. Use your navigational skills to stay on River Walk. This is not difficult because you know that it follows close to the Delaware River and Neshaminy Creek. About .76 mi. from the trailhead, the trail starts to follow the top of a raised levee **[5]**. The spoils area is to your left, an area that varies from dry sand to mucky marsh. Look for purple loosestrife and giant reed. Both are exotic plants that have crowded out native plants. These exotics are not very useful to wildlife.

As the trail curves left along Neshaminy Creek, look at the lush aquatic vegetation close to shore.

Identify wild rice and other plants. Some of the plants in this area are rare or endangered. Before the Delaware River was dredged, these plants were not confined to the shoreline.

There is a major trail fork about a mile from the trailhead **[6]**. Take the right fork. About 90 feet past this fork, you descend a set of wooden steps with an unusual rope handrail. This next stretch of the trail takes you close to Neshaminy Creek through a wooded area. Identify silver maple, alder, ash, and willow. You can see the state park marina across the creek. Turn left when you reach a gravel road (1.3 mi.) **[7]**. This road makes a hard left turn, but you go straight on another gravel road (1.4 mi.) **[8]**. After a long straight stretch, by a beautiful stand of birch, the trail curves right, into an open area. Turn left at a paved road (1.5 mi.) **[9]**, where you are facing a high tower. Keep straight on this paved road through the most developed section of the park, back to the trailhead (1.9 mi.) **[1]**.

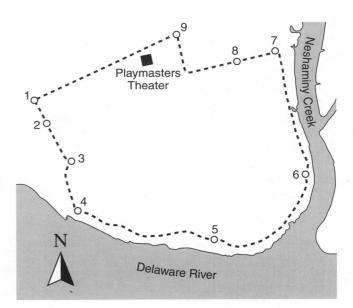

1. Trailhead	6. Major fork
2. Fork left	7. Gravel road
3. Fork right	8. Intersection
4. Leave road	9. Paved road
5. Levee	

River Walk Inner Loop 👢👢

Distance Round-Trip: 1.6 miles

Estimated Hiking Time: 1 hour

Caution: You can expect to get your feet wet. Watch for bicycles and park vehicles on parts of this trail. Signs warn that for this reason, hikers should not wear music headphones on the trails.

Trail Directions: From the park entrance off State Road, turn onto Delaware Drive, then turn left into the first of two large parking areas. The trailhead for River Walk Inner Loop is the same trailhead used for River Walk. It is located by a kiosk at the far end of the parking area facing a paved trail **[1]**.

Start your hike on the gravel trail, on the left side of the kiosk. Walk through the picnic area and past a playing field. At the first fork, take the left, or straight, fork (.07 mi.) **[2]** and continue out of the picnic area and scattered trees to an open area, where the trail forks again (.16 mi.) **[3]**. Take the left fork across a grassy road and between two unused parking areas. This is where the Inner Loop separates from River Walk. The Inner Loop does not take you to the estuary, but it provides a better look at the spoils area than the main River Walk.

You are now entering the spoils area, a mix of sand and soft, marshy pockets. How do you think this area formed? Can you visualize the Delaware River flooding this area, depositing sand and silt?

Look in a marshy area between the trail and the parking area to your right for unusual plants. Some of the plants growing here may be rare or endangered. Stay on the trail so you do not disturb the plants. Watch for killdeers scurrying over the sand or over the parking areas. These common birds make their nests right in the open on sand, on pebbles, or even on the parking areas. If you see one that appears to be dragging a broken wing, it is probably trying to lure you away from its nest.

Inner Loop crosses diagonally between the two unused parking areas and crosses the end of Delaware Drive (.46 mi.) **[4]**. The only motor vehicles using this part of Delaware Drive are official park vehicles. Continue into the heart of the spoils area. The nature of this area depends a lot on how wet it is. If the marshy pockets have standing water, you might see mallards, wood ducks, or wading birds. Beautiful wildflowers bloom from spring through late summer. Look for lesser celandine, blue toadflax, bladder campion, and purple loosestrife.

Your chances of seeing a wood duck improve after passing an intersection, where you take the left fork (.74 mi.) **[5]** and walk along the edge of a wet wooded area. As their name implies, wood ducks like to be around trees. They nest in hollow trees, though without artificial nesting cavities erected by groups such as Ducks Unlimited and the Pennsylvania Game Commission, wood ducks might be a disappearing species. Their population was threatened by the fashion industry, which used their brilliantly colored feathers, and by dwindling nesting habitat. But they have rebounded in the latter half of the 20th century, and now they are common in Pennsylvania.

Nearing the end of the wooded area, fork left (.97 mi.) **[6]**. Return across the edge of the spoils to the unused parking area (1.27 mi.) **[7]**. Follow the grassy road behind the parking area to complete the loop **[3]**, then turn right to the trailhead (1.6 mi.) **[1]**.

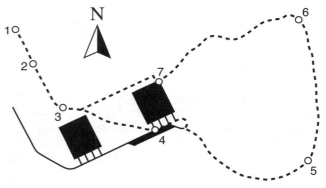

1. Trailhead
2. First fork
3. Second fork
4. Delaware Drive
5. Woodland fork
6. Leave woodland
7. Parking area

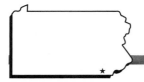

15. Susquehannock State Park

- View the Susquehanna River from atop high cliffs.
- See the world's first bald eagle sanctuary.
- Recall a vastly different time in this highly developed part of the state at historic sites.

Area Information

Most people come to Susquehannock State Park for its magnificent view of the Susquehanna River. From the top of a 380-foot cliff, you can see the Conowingo Pool, created by a dam in Maryland. One of the several islands below, Mt. Johnson Island, was the first designated bald eagle sanctuary. Also within view downriver is the Peach Bottom Atomic Energy Plant. In stark historic contrast is the stone foundation of the home of Thomas Neel, a Revolutionary War veteran. This park provides wonderful insight to the development of the lower Susquehanna River area.

Within the 224-acre park are a maze of trails through a surprisingly unspoiled forest. Birders can collect a good variety of sightings, ranging from eagles and other raptors to waterbirds to birds of the forest.

Directions: From Pennsylvania Route 272 about 14 miles south of Lancaster, take Pennsylvania Route 372 west to Susquehannock Drive. There, turn south to Park Drive, which is the only road into the park.

Hours Open: The park is open from 8:00 A.M. to sunset.

Facilities: Two ballfields, a playground, an organized group camping area (by reservation only), picnic tables, a picnic pavilion, water, and restrooms are near the park office. By the parking lot at the end of Park Road and near Hawk Point Overlook are picnic tables, a picnic pavilion, restrooms, and water. There is a special handicap parking area near Hawk Point Overlook.

Permits and Rules: Pets must be leashed and under control. Alcohol is not allowed.

Further Information: Department of Conservation and Natural Resources, Susquehannock State Park, c/o Gifford Pinchot State Park, 2200 Rosstown Road, Lewisberry, PA 17339-9787; phone 717-432-5011.

Park Trails

Pine Tree Trail 👢👢👢—.25 mile—This trail begins at the organized group tenting area and drops down a steep hillside to Rhododendron Trail.

Holly Trail 👢👢👢—.33 mile—This trail offers a look at mostly hilltop habitat between Fire Trail and Rhododendron Trail.

Susquehannock State Park

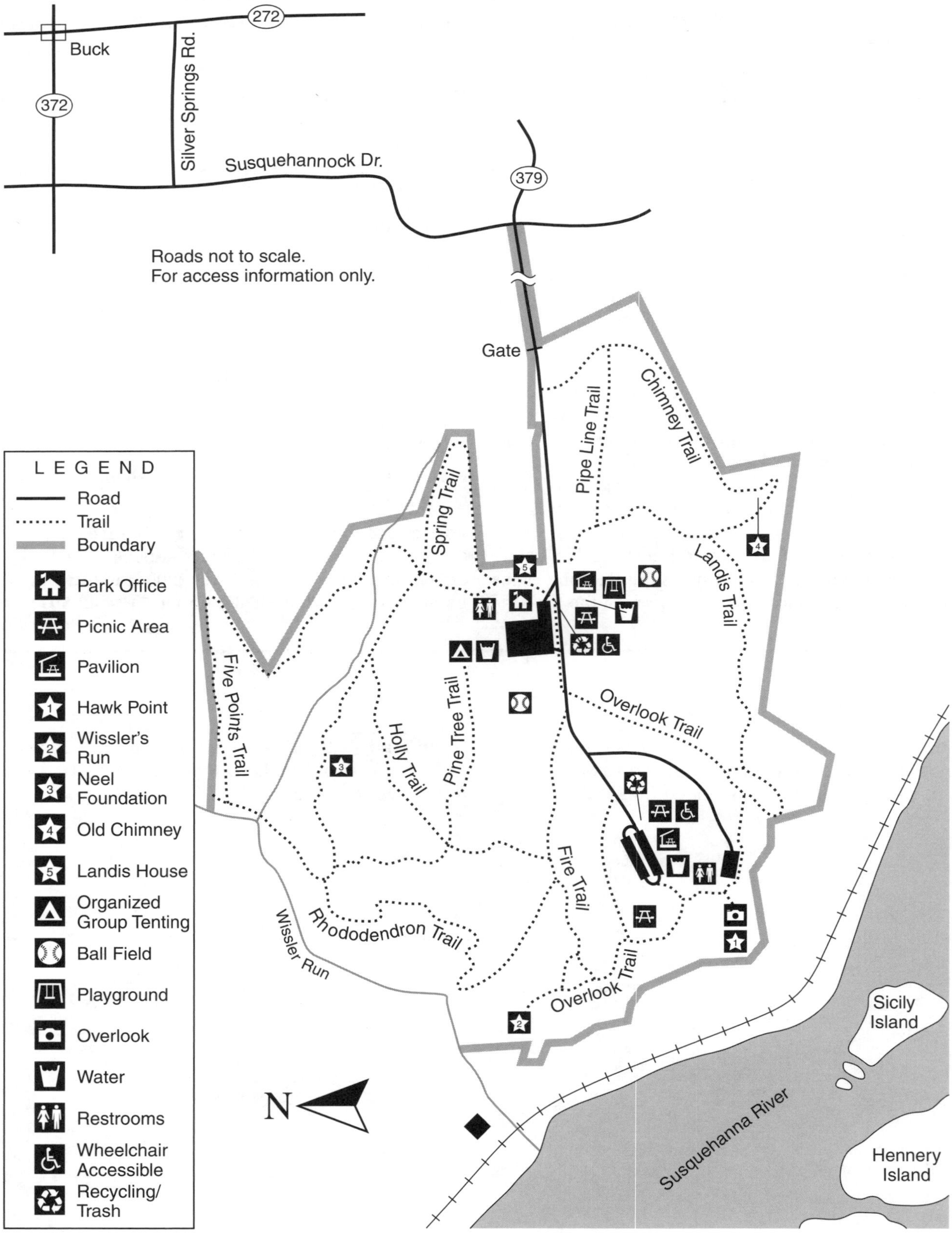

Buck

272

372

Silver Springs Rd.

Susquehannock Dr.

379

Roads not to scale.
For access information only.

Gate

Pipe Line Trail

Chimney Trail

Landis Trail

Spring Trail

Five Points Trail

LEGEND

——	Road
······	Trail
▬▬	Boundary
🏠	Park Office
⛱	Picnic Area
🏗	Pavilion
★	Hawk Point
★2	Wissler's Run
★3	Neel Foundation
★4	Old Chimney
★5	Landis House
▲	Organized Group Tenting
⚾	Ball Field
🎠	Playground
📷	Overlook
🚰	Water
🚻	Restrooms
♿	Wheelchair Accessible
♻	Recycling/ Trash

Holly Trail

Pine Tree Trail

Overlook Trail

Fire Trail

Rhododendron Trail

Wissler Run

Overlook Trail

N

Susquehanna River

Sicily Island

Hennery Island

Rhododendron Trails 👢👢👢👢👢

Distance Round-Trip: 2.18 miles

Estimated Hiking Time: 2 hours

Cautions: Parts of Rhododendron Trail are very steep, are very narrow, or pass over roots and boulder fields where footing is precarious. Overlook Trail passes along the edge of a 380-foot cliff. Stay on the trail and overlook areas, and watch children closely.

Trail Directions: Three trails are combined here because they form a convenient loop taking you through a magnificent forest that is becoming rare in southeast Pennsylvania, to the spectacular overlooks that make this park popular, and through history. Stop in the parking area adjacent to the Landis House. An information station **[1]** by this parking area has a wooden map showing park trails. Walk down a service road between the park office and the Landis House toward the restrooms to reach the head of Rhododendron Trail **[2]** after just .07 mi.

Rhododendron Trail immediately descends, getting progressively steeper. After .22 mi. you come to a three-way split in the trail **[3]**. The left fork is Rhododendron Trail. Another split occurs at .28 mi. **[4]**. Take the right fork, continuing downhill.

The Neel Foundation, once the home of a Revolutionary War veteran, rests under a huge, gnarly old beech tree **[5]**, .36 mi. along the trail. The trail becomes narrower here. Rhododendron, for which the trail was named, becomes an important part of the forest community as you continue down the trail.

Another fork at .53 mi. might be confusing **[6]**, though it is marked with signs. The map supplied by the park shows that these trails do not all meet at the same place, but they do. Pine Tree Trail splits uphill to the left, Five Points Trail to the right. Rhododendron Trail might be considered the straight fork, going downhill. Here you are almost to Wissler Run. Across and above the small creek is a two-lane hard road. Footing becomes more difficult as the trail crosses a boulder field, rock outcroppings, and fallen trees.

The trail makes an abrupt left turn away from the creek and begins climbing **[7]** at .72 mi. Switchbacks are necessary on the steep hillside. Footing is poor over odd-shaped rocks. Orange rectangular trail markers will help keep you from zigging when you should be zagging on a switchback.

Approaching the top of a knob, you might get glimpses of the Conowingo Pool through the leaves. Just as it seems you are getting to the top of this hill, the trail descends again to the bottom of a valley and another fork in the trail **[8]**, 1.08 mi. from the trailhead. The right fork is Phites Eddy Trail. Rhododendron Trail turns uphill to the left.

After a long, steep climb, Rhododendron Trail ends after 1.25 mi. when it meets Fire Trail **[9]**. Turn right. After a total distance of 1.34 mi., you come to Overlook Trail **[10]**. Turn right here toward the Wissler Run Overlook **[11]**. This is 1.41 mi. from your start. From here you can see far upriver to the Holtwood Dam. With binoculars you can usually observe several species of raptors, waterfowl, and waterbirds. Black vultures often soar close to the overlook.

Backtrack from here, continuing on Overlook Trail past the end of Fire Trail along the top of the 380-foot cliff to Hawk Point Overlook (1.69 mi.) **[12]**, which requires a short detour off the trail. Below and downriver you will see the first bald eagle sanctuary, Mt. Johnson Island, and across the river the Peach Bottom Atomic Energy Plant.

Return to Overlook Trail, and turn right to complete the loop. Landis Trail **[13]** intersects at 1.88 mi. Turn left to stay on Overlook Trail, past another meeting with Landis Trail (1.93 mi.) **[14]**, to the end of Overlook Trail (1.96 mi.) at the edge of the forest. Cross the open area back to the parking lot and information station **[1]** for a total distance of 2.18 mi.

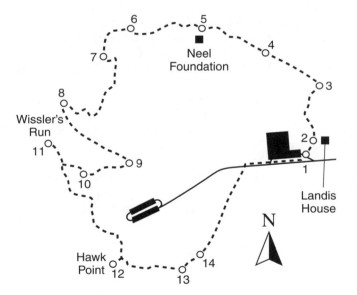

1. Information station
2. Rhododendron Trail trailhead
3. Three-way split
4. Holly Trail fork
5. Neel Foundation
6. Pine Tree and Five Points trails fork
7. Start climbing
8. Phites Eddy Trail fork
9. Fire Trail
10. Overlook Trail
11. Wissler Run Overlook
12. Hawk Point Overlook
13. Landis Trail fork
14. Landis Trail fork again

Chimney/Landis/ Pipeline Trails 🥾🥾🥾

Distance Round-Trip: .96 mile

Estimated Hiking Time: .5 hour

Caution: You could get your feet wet in a couple of places, and there are short, steep stretches that are slippery in wet weather, but generally this is a friendly trail. Stay on the trail, especially the downhill stretch, to avoid private land. You might encounter poison ivy along this trail.

Trail Directions: Chimney Trail leads to an old chimney, perhaps a remnant from the old charcoal industry. By combining with a short section of Landis Trail and most of Pipe Line Trail, it forms a complete loop. Watch for a variety of songbirds, squirrels, and white-tailed deer. Chimney Trail begins near a small parking area adjacent to the park entrance gate, on the left side as you enter. A sign **[1]** marks the trailhead. This is closer to the gate than the map indicates.

The trail is level for a few hundred feet, then starts to descend, only slightly at first. After .13 mi., it crosses Pipe Line Trail **[2]**. The state park map indicates that Pipe Line Trail approaches from the west and ends here, but actually it continues for some distance to the east. So instead of a T, this is a crossroads. Continuing straight on Chimney Trail, you will see posted private-property signs to your left, not far from the trail. Long, straight tulip trees form a high forest canopy. If you can identify any birds in the canopy, note how they are different from the birds that occupy the lower vegetation.

The trail becomes progressively steeper. At .33 mi., it forks **[3]**. The right fork, which crosses a spring seep, bypasses the old chimney. You might enjoy a short detour to this spring. Someone took the time to frame the spring with well-laid stones. Take the left fork to the remains of the chimney (.38 mi.) **[4]**. Unfortunately, a large tree fell on the chimney not

long before we hiked this trail, virtually leveling it. But it is still interesting. Parts of the base of the chimney remain almost intact.

Just below the chimney, a sign directs you across the spring, where you begin climbing back up the hill. Soon you pass the opposite end of the cutoff that you passed on the way down. After a brief steep stretch, you reach a sign **[5]** marking the end of Chimney Trail (.48 mi.). Turn right here onto Landis Trail. The steepest part of the trail is behind you. All that remains is a moderate climb to Pipe Line Trail **[6]** (.62 mi.), where you turn right to return to Chimney Trail **[2]**. Turn left to return to the trailhead **[1]** for a round-trip distance of .96 mi.

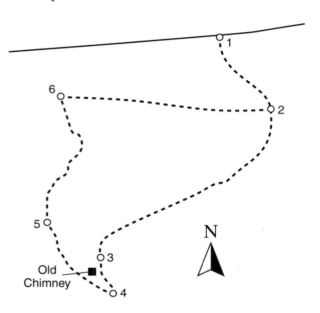

1. Chimney Trail trailhead
2. Cross Pipe Line Trail
3. Fork
4. Old chimney
5. Landis Trail
6. Pipe Line Trail

Central

With the fewest people, the most rugged terrain, and the majority of the public land, the central region is Pennsylvania's great outdoor playground. This region roughly extends from the Susquehanna River west to Laurel Ridge and the Allegheny National Forest, and from New York in the north to Maryland in the south.

Topography

Most of the highest land in Pennsylvania, above 2,000 feet elevation, is in the central region. From the New York border south roughly to Interstate Route 80 is a part of the Appalachian Plateau known as the Allegheny Highlands. This is some of the most rugged, heavily forested, lightly populated land in the state. It has the highest proportion of public land, including several state forests, state parks, and part of the Allegheny National Forest.

South of the Allegheny Highlands are the Appalachian Mountains, primarily the Ridge and Valley Province with rugged and forested ridges separated by broad, rolling valleys. Valleys hold most of the human population and agriculture. To the west are the Allegheny Mountains, including Mount Davis, peaking at 3,213 feet, which is the highest elevation in the state. It is located in southern Somerset County, near the Maryland border. The second-highest point, 3,146 feet, is Blue Knob, in Blue Knob State Park, located in northern Bedford County. East of the Ridge and Valley Province, separated by the Cumberland Valley, are the Blue Ridge Mountains.

Major Rivers and Lakes

The West Branch Susquehanna River drains the southern side of the Allegheny Highlands and the northern slopes of the Appalachian Mountains. The Juniata River, also a tributary of the Susquehanna River, flows through the Appalachian Mountains, draining much of the central part of the state. The Allegheny River, primarily a western Pennsylvania river, starts from a spring in Potter County.

There are no major natural lakes. Raystown Lake, 8,300 acres, is the largest human-made lake. It is located in Huntingdon County. Smaller lakes are located in many state parks.

Common Plant Life

Across the Allegheny Highlands and south along the Allegheny Mountain ridges into Maryland is one of the largest contiguous forests in the eastern United States. Termed Allegheny hardwood, it is also one of the most valuable forests, characterized by black cherry, red maple, sugar maple, yellow poplar, and white ash. Most of the black cherry in the world comes from central Pennsylvania. One of the most beautiful woods, it is used to make fine furniture and veneer. Beech, eastern hemlock, white pine, northern red oak, white oak, and chestnut oak are also common in some areas. Sycamore, silver maple, and willow are common in the major valleys.

Ferns dominate the lower vegetation in vast areas. This is due to browsing by deer, which eat most other plants. Mountain laurel, the state flower, is abundant throughout, mixing with rhododendron south of the northern-tier counties.

Agriculture dominates the broad, rolling valleys of the Appalachian Ridge and Valley Province. Dairy farms make up a large portion of this.

Common Birds and Animals

White-tailed deer are abundant throughout the central region. Black bears are most numerous in the Allegheny Highlands but are also seen throughout the region. Smaller mammals include gray squirrels, fox squirrels, red squirrels, cottontail rabbits, opossums, beavers, raccoons, striped skunks, and muskrats.

The Allegheny Highlands are also home to the only wild Pennsylvania elk herd. While elk were native to the state, they were eliminated by market hunting. The current herd descends from western elk. Coyotes have reestablished themselves. About twice the size of western coyotes, these might better be described as eastern brush wolves. Efforts are underway to reestablish river otters and fishers, which are also natives.

Ruffed grouse, the state bird, and wild turkeys thrive from north to south, especially along the edges of farms and in areas that have recently been timbered. The forests of this region are critical habitat for many songbirds and hawks that require unbroken forest.

Climate

North-central Pennsylvania has the coolest climate in the state, with an average growing season of about 120 days. Average midsummer temperatures range from about 80 degrees F in the north and 86 degrees F in the south to lows of 54 degrees F in the north and 62 degrees F in the south. Expect midwinter temperatures to range from 16 to 34 degrees F in the north and 22 to 40 degrees F in the south. Snow covers the ground during most of the winter in the north and at higher elevations in the south.

Best Features

- Susquehanna River
- West Branch Susquehanna River
- Juniata River
- Pine Creek Gorge
- Cumberland Valley
- Blue Knob
- Blue Ridge
- Allegheny Mountains
- Allegheny Highlands

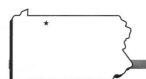

16. Allegheny National Forest— McKean County

- Fish for some of the largest walleyes and muskellunge in the northeast on the Allegheny Reservoir.
- Swim in cool water at Kiasutha.
- Walk through a virgin forest.

Area Information

The northeast corner of the Allegheny National Forest is in McKean County, an area of 135,396 acres of public land. Most of the land is rugged hills. Nearly all is covered by dense forest. It includes the highest elevations in the Allegheny National Forest, above 2,200 feet. Two large bays of the Allegheny Reservoir, Sugar and the Kinzua Creek Arm, extend into McKean County.

At the Tionesta Scenic Area, a 2,000-acre tract located about 8 miles south of Kane on Forest Route 133, and the adjoining Tionesta Research Natural Area, also about 2,000 acres, you get the rare opportunity to see 300- to 400-year-old beech, hemlock, and sugar maple trees. In 1985, one of the most violent tornadoes ever recorded tore through this area, leaving a wide path. This offers a stark contrast and a good study in forest succession. It has been designated a national natural landmark. Special rules for this area prohibit camping, fires, and motor vehicles or mountain bikes off open roads.

Along trails throughout the Allegheny National Forest you will see awesome rock outcrops high on the hillsides, and boulders the size of houses that have tumbled into narrow valleys. Wildlife is abundant, most notably white-tailed deer. You can expect to see several on a typical hike, if you walk quietly and keep a sharp lookout. This is also black bear and wild turkey country. Bird-watchers should be able to add a few species to their life lists.

Directions: The Allegheny National Forest covers most of the western third of McKean County. The major communities are Bradford, on U.S. Route 219 near the New York border, and Kane, on U.S. Route 6 in the southern part of the county.

Hours Open: The Allegheny National Forest is open year-round, around the clock.

Facilities: There are several campgrounds; picnic areas; and trails for hiking, biking, and cross-country skiing. A swimming beach is located on the Kinzua Creek Arm of the Allegheny Reservoir at Kiasutha Campground. Fishing for walleye, muskellunge, smallmouth bass, and northern pike is good in the Allegheny Reservoir. Uncounted miles of streams hold native brook trout, and many are stocked with brown, brook, and rainbow trout.

Permits and Rules: Motor vehicles are not allowed off designated roads and trails. Do not carve, chop, cut, or damage any live trees. Do not damage or remove any historical or archaeological items. Extensive rules limit camping outside designated campgrounds. Watch for posted restrictions on fires.

Further Information: Bradford Ranger District, Star Route, Box 88, Bradford, PA 16701; phone 814-362-4613.

Other Areas of Interest

Contact **Allegheny National Forest Vacation Bureau,** 10 East Warren Road, Drawer G, Custer City, PA 16725; phone 814-368-9370.

Park Trails

Johnnycake Trail 👢👢👢👢—2.3 miles—Hike from Tracy Ridge Campground to the shore of the Allegheny Reservoir through rock outcrops and hardwood forest. There is a magnificent stand of huge white pine on the North Country Trail near the intersection with Johnnycake Trail.

Tracy Ridge Trail 👢👢👢👢—2.7 miles—Hike from Tracy Ridge Campground to the North Country National Scenic Trail and connect with Johnnycake Trail to make a loop.

Rimrock Trail Loop 👢👢👢—8.3 miles—This hike from Route 59 to the edge of the Kinzua Arm of the Allegheny Reservoir is almost too long for a one-day hike.

Allegheny National Forest

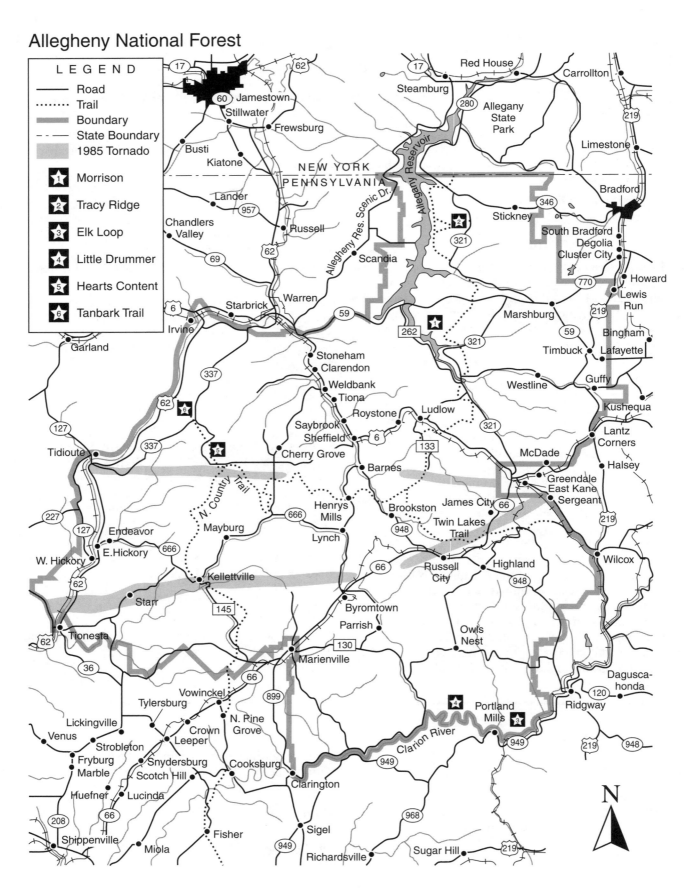

LEGEND

— Road
.... Trail
━━ Boundary
—·— State Boundary
░ 1985 Tornado

⭐1 Morrison
⭐2 Tracy Ridge
⭐3 Elk Loop
⭐4 Little Drummer
⭐5 Hearts Content
⭐6 Tanbark Trail

Interpretive Trail 👢👢

Distance Round-Trip: 3 miles

Estimated Hiking Time: 1.5 hours

Caution: A few places on this loop are moderately steep, but only for short distances. Roots and rocks are scattered along the trail. Wear bright-orange clothing during hunting season.

Trail Directions: This loop circles one of the highest points on the Allegheny National Forest, more than 2,240 feet in elevation, and passes through huge boulders.

From Route 59 between Route 219 and Route 6, turn north on Pennsylvania Route 321 about 11 mi. to the entrance to Tracy Ridge Camping Area at a large sign that also marks this as a trailhead. Turn left at the sign, passing an Interpretive Trail sign on the right, and continuing to a small parking area on the right side of the road, where there is another Interpretive Trail sign. This is your trailhead **[1]**.

The trail starts as a mowed path. Small circular fence enclosures are intended to protect young trees from deer. You will see two different trail blazes, gray diamonds and white diamonds. You will be following the gray diamonds through this entire loop; however, white diamonds seem to be scattered indiscriminately through the route, also. You will stay on course if you follow the gray diamonds, except at intersections, because other trails appear to use gray diamond blazes as well. The gray diamonds contain black arrows directing you through any confusing turns in the trail. The mowed area lasts only about 200 feet.

At the edge of a field, about 800 feet from the trailhead, angle left, across the field by the shortest route. You can see a gray diamond on the other side. This area is maintained as a field for wildlife habitat. Fields are important to animals such as wild turkeys, which come here to feed on grasshoppers. Observe the stages of forest succession as you move away from the field. Stone piles along the trail are fading evidence that this was once a farm. You will be able to pick blueberries here when they are ripe. These are a favorite food of black bears, which are common in this area. Vegetation becomes older as you get farther from the field, culminating in maturing hardwood forest composed mainly of maple and oak, with some hickory and cucumber tree.

Turn left, downhill, at a T (.4 mi.) **[2]**. The trail becomes rocky down this mild slope. The down slope is short, and soon you begin to climb through huge boulders. Ferns and striped maple are the predominate low vegetation. This is evidence of a high deer population, as these are not preferred foods for deer. Virtually anything a deer might eat is gone.

At the top of the ridge, after you pass between two large boulders, a spur trail cuts left. Ignore it and follow the gray diamonds to the right. Tracy Ridge Camping Area is now visible to the left, if any of the campsites are occupied. Continue along, or near, the top of the ridge to the intersection with Tracy Ridge Trail, which forks right, and Johnnycake Trail, which forks left (1.2 mi.) **[3]**. You are now at 2,245 feet elevation, one of the highest points in the Allegheny National Forest. Turn left at the sign marking this intersection, following Johnnycake Trail.

There is no sign where Interpretive Trail forks left, away from Johnnycake Trail (1.4 mi.) **[4]**. There is almost no low vegetation in this area. In fact, there is almost nothing green within reach of deer. This changes on a steeper slope just before you reach the gravel road that is the entrance road for the camping area. From here you can see your vehicle in the trailhead parking area to the left (3 mi.) **[1]**.

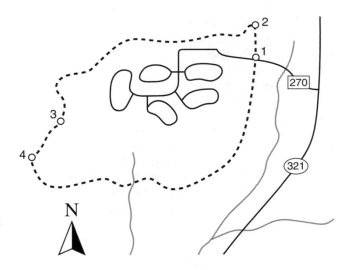

1. Trailhead
2. T
3. Tracy Ridge Johnnycake trails
4. Leave Johnnycake Trail

Morrison Trail 🥾🥾🥾

Distance Round-Trip: 5.3 miles

Estimated Hiking Time: 3 hours

Caution: Parts of this trail are steep. Spring seeps make the trail wet in many places. All stream crossings are over stepping stones. Roots and rocks interfere with footing more often than not.

Trail Directions: The trailhead parking area is marked by a sign along Pennsylvania Route 59 between the Morrison Bridge, over the Kinzua Creek Arm of the Allegheny Reservoir, and Marshburg. The trailhead is by a kiosk at the back center of the parking area **[1].** A map of the hiking trail is on the back of the kiosk, where you can see that there is a long loop, called the Morrison Trail Loop, and a longer loop, called the Rimrock Trail Loop.

White diamond trail blazes mark the Morrison Trail Loop. You are starting on top of a ridge, at an elevation of about 2,100 feet, through a forest of maple, oak, hickory, and black cherry, with some beech, birch, and hemlock. Hemlock becomes more common over the side of the hills, closer to creeks and springs. You can expect to see deer in this area, along with gray squirrels, wild turkeys, and bears. The black-color phase of gray squirrels are fairly common. Fox squirrels, which are unusual in this part of the state, can be seen at lower elevations. Bird-watchers should be able to identify many species, perhaps even the elusive northern goshawk.

The terrain is relatively level to a **T** (.5 mi.) **[2]** by a rock outcrop. This is where the trail completes a loop. Turn right and begin dropping in elevation. You will see a forest opening as you approach a small stream. Apple trees here will attract deer and bears when the apples start falling to the ground. The opening and apple trees are evidence that this was probably the site of a homestead many years ago. Many more boulders are exposed over the side of the hill. Cross the stream on stepping stones to a fork in the trail (.7 mi.) **[3].** Turn left. The right fork is the longer Rimrock Trail Loop.

Now you drop quickly through a steep, narrow valley, crossing the stream several times. The trail map does not accurately reflect the stream crossings. Many huge boulders protrude from the side of the hill, and many have rolled to the bottom of the valley. Numerous springs seep across the trail. Hemlocks dominate the forest along the creek. Pretty white pebbles cover the trail in places. Finally you arrive at an intersection close to the point where the stream

you have been following flows into Morrison Run (1.3 mi.) **[4].** This intersection is before Morrison Run. Turn left along the left side of the stream, not on the right as indicated on the trail map. You are now at an elevation of about 1,500 feet, roughly 600 feet below the trailhead. From here, you begin your climb back out.

The climb back toward the top of the plateau is more gentle than the descent. You will cross the stream a couple of times before passing through a notch in the hillside. This is evidence that you are following an old road grade. Just past the notch is one of the most beautiful sights along the trail, where Morrison Run drops over a small falls between two boulders into a deep pool. This is approximately the halfway point on the loop (2.7 mi.) **[5].** A boulder here just the shape and height to make a good seat appears to have been a gift to hikers. Find a bug and throw it into that pool, and a brook trout will almost certainly dart out from its lair and eat it.

After crossing to the right side of the stream again, you pass another forest opening and apple trees. The stream is getting very small when you cross back to the left, then climb the side of the hill and turn sharply left (3.7 mi.) **[6].** This begins the last and easiest leg of this triangular trail across the top of the plateau, through mountain laurel thickets, past abandoned oil wells and across a couple of unused roads to complete the loop by the rock outcrop (4.8 mi.) **[2].** Turn right to return to the trailhead (5.3 mi.) **[1].**

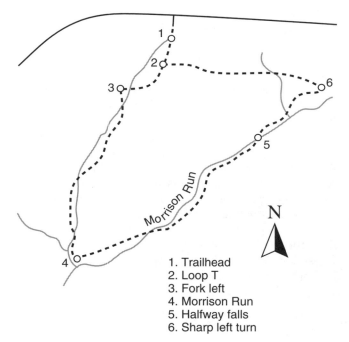

1. Trailhead
2. Loop T
3. Fork left
4. Morrison Run
5. Halfway falls
6. Sharp left turn

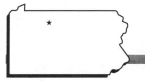

17. Kinzua Bridge State Park

- See a railroad bridge that was once considered one of the human-made wonders of the world.
- Get a lesson on the history of the forest industry.
- Hike through the Kinzua Creek valley and stop to fish for trout.
- Stand atop one of the best panoramas of the Allegheny Highlands.

Area Information

When Kinzua Bridge was built in 1882 as a branch of the Erie Railroad to haul coal northward, it was the highest and longest railroad bridge in the world. It took just 94 days for a 40-man crew to build the original bridge. It was 301.5 feet high and 2,053 feet long. Many people thought the original bridge was made of wood because the tubular wrought-iron columns looked like timbers. The bridge swayed in the wind. Sometimes hemlock bark was blown off the cars. Many people believed the bridge might collapse, but it survived a train wreck.

Surprisingly, this route saved just eight miles of track. Nevertheless, it served as an important link in the forest industry, transporting logs and hemlock bark, which was used to extract chemicals. During the next few years, larger and heavier railroad cars and locomotives appeared, which made it necessary to rebuild the bridge in 1900. By this time, it was the fourth-highest railroad bridge in the world. It was used until 1959. Four years later, Kinzua Bridge State Park was established. The bridge is on the National Register of Historic Civil Engineering Landmarks.

Today, it is hard to imagine that during the 19th century the forest had been completely stripped from this area. All you can see from the bridge is trees in every direction. This is one of the best places to see the flaming fall foliage, usually during early October. Kinzua Creek, which flows 300 feet below the bridge, is one of the finest trout streams in north-central Pennsylvania.

No trains crossed the bridge from 1959 until 1987, when the Knox and Kane Railroad began running excursion trains. The train makes scheduled runs from June to October.

Directions: Signs leading to Kinzua Bridge State Park start at Mt. Jewett, which is on U.S. Route 6 between Kane and Smethport. Drive north 4 miles on Pennsylvania Route 3011 to the park entrance. Turn north from Interstate Route 80 onto U.S. Route 219, then turn east on Route 6 to Mt. Jewett.

Hours Open: The park is open year-round 8:00 A.M. to sunset.

Facilities: This is a day-use park, except for a group camping area that is available only by reservation. There are picnic tables, a picnic pavilion, restrooms, and a concession store. Trout fishing is very good in Kinzua Creek, but from the park, you must make a long, steep climb to reach the creek. There are much easier places from which to access this creek.

Permits and Rules: Alcoholic beverages are prohibited. Outdoor recreational activities are restricted to locations where signs or physical improvements designate the appropriate use. Fires and the disposal of hot coals are restricted to provided facilities. Pets must be leashed and controlled at all times. There are no litter-disposal containers. All trash must be carried out. You must get off the bridge before a train crosses. Do not feed wild animals. Soliciting and posting signs are prohibited. Park only in designated areas.

Further Information: Department of Conservation and Natural Resources, Kinzua Bridge State Park, S Bendigo State Park, P.O. Box A, Johnsonburg, PA 15845; phone 814-965-2646.

Other Areas of Interest

The **Knox and Kane Railroad** runs excursion trains through the Allegheny National Forest and over the Kinzua Bridge. For a schedule and more information, write to Knox and Kane Railroad, P.O. Box 422, Marienville, PA 16239; phone 814-927-6621.

Aspen Trail 👢👢👢👢

Distance Round-Trip: 1.7 miles

Estimated Hiking Time: 1.5 hours

Caution: Portions of the trail are very steep and slippery. Do not walk onto the bridge if you are afraid of heights. Keep children strictly under control on the bridge.

Trail Directions: Drive into the main parking area, or walk to the main parking area from the overflow parking area. Start your hike on a blacktop path at the end of the parking area **[1]**. Ahead you can see a round metal kiosk. Two blacktop trails lead to the kiosk (.06 mi.) **[2]**. One winds down the gentle slope for wheelchair access. Stop at this kiosk to learn some of the history of Kinzua Bridge.

A sign by the kiosk directs you to the right on Aspen Trail toward an overlook on a blacktop path. Turn left onto the overlook for an excellent view of this imposing structure (.12 mi.) **[3]**. The upper level of the overlook is the farthest point on the trail accessible to wheelchairs. A lower level provides the best view.

Past the overlook, Aspen Trail turns right, uphill, on a wide path surfaced with wood chips. Trail blazes are orange. Turn left at the first major fork (.3 mi.) **[4]** onto a wide, grassy path. The right fork connects Aspen Trail to the group camping area. A sign marks this intersection. A wood chip trail forks right to the overflow parking area 250 feet farther along Aspen Trail. This intersection is not shown on the park map, but it is marked with a sign. Aspen Trail curves left past this intersection, beginning a steep descent to the bottom of the Kinzua Creek valley.

This section of the trail is dirt, which is very slippery when wet. Farther down this slope, it is apparent that you are walking on an old roadbed. Aspen Trail cuts away from this road close to the bridge. Watch for double orange trail blazes. There is no sign, and the road is not on the park map. From here, your trail is narrow and rocky. Watch out for pipes and cables crossing the trail.

At the bottom of the hill, you cross Kinzua Creek on a wooden footbridge (.8 mi.) **[5]**. Here you see quaking aspen trees, the first and only indication of how this trail got its name. Turn right once you are across the bridge, following a dirt road almost to Kinzua Bridge. The forest is open near the creek. Follow the orange trail blazes uphill to the right before you get to the bridge.

Aspen Trail is very narrow and rocky on the north slope of the valley. Several spur trails can confuse the route as it winds between large sandstone boulders and switches back and forth if you lose track of the trail blazes. But since you can see Kinzua Bridge and know that you are walking toward the end of it, without crossing under it, there is no way you can get lost. If you take the wrong trail to the right, you run into private-property signs.

After a rigorous climb, you reach the railroad tracks and turn left to cross Kinzua Bridge (1.2 mi.) **[6]**. Stay off the bridge if you see or hear a train approaching. The train approaches slowly and you will have enough time to get off the bridge. The dizzying view of the Kinzua Creek valley from the bridge is one of the most beautiful overlooks in the state. After crossing the bridge to complete the loop, backtrack to the parking area (1.7 mi.) **[1]**.

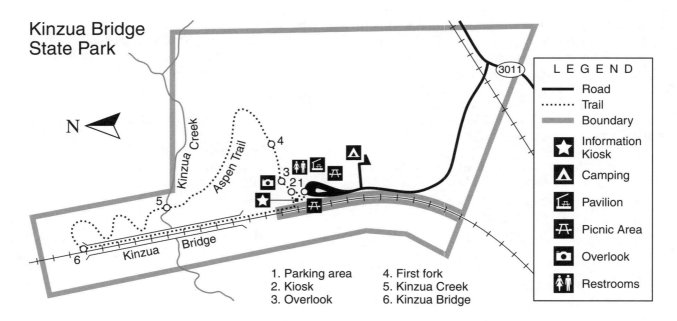

Kinzua Bridge State Park

1. Parking area
2. Kiosk
3. Overlook
4. First fork
5. Kinzua Creek
6. Kinzua Bridge

LEGEND
— Road
.... Trail
▬ Boundary
⭐ Information Kiosk
⛺ Camping
🏠 Pavilion
⛱ Picnic Area
◉ Overlook
🚻 Restrooms

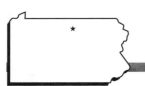

18. Leonard Harrison and Colton Point State Parks

- See the Grand Canyon of Pennsylvania.
- Tour the remote West Rim.
- Float through the canyon in a rubber raft.
- Fish for trout and smallmouth bass in Pine Creek.

Area Information

Leonard Harrison State Park and Colton Point State Park are contiguous; however, they are separated by the Pine Creek Gorge, which is better known as the "Grand Canyon of Pennsylvania." The only way to get directly to one from the other is a strenuous walk through the gorge, a task not to be taken lightly. The only practical way to travel between them is a drive of about 18 miles around the northern end of the gorge.

These two state parks both overlook the gorge, but they are quite different. Leonard Harrison State Park, on the east side, is highly developed, with a visitor center, a food concession, paved overlooks, and viewing scopes. This is the view of the gorge that most people see. Colton Point State Park, on the west side, might be nearly deserted at the same time that Leonard Harrison State Park is crowded. Its overlooks, which are just as spectacular, are less developed.

Pine Creek Gorge was formed when Ice Age glaciers blocked the northern flow of Pine Creek, forcing it to flow south, eroding what is now the most spectacular valley in the rugged Allegheny Highlands. Between Leonard Harrison State Park and Colton Point State Park, it is 800 feet deep. The area was designated a national natural landmark in 1968 by the National Park Service.

Directions: Leonard Harrison State Park is 10 miles west of Wellsboro on Pennsylvania Route 660, which ends in the park. Colton Point State Park is 5 miles south of U.S. Route 6, at Ansonia, on Colton Road.

Drive slowly and cautiously on this narrow, winding road.

Hours Open: The parks are open from 8:00 A.M. to sunset.

Facilities: Both Leonard Harrison State Park and Colton Point State Park offer campsites for tents or RVs with sanitary dump stations, picnic tables, picnic pavilions, restrooms, and drinking water. Leonard Harrison State Park has a food concession and an interpretive center that displays area history and wildlife.

Permits and Rules: Alcoholic beverages are prohibited. Outdoor recreational activities are restricted to locations where signs or physical improvements designate the appropriate use. Fires and the disposal of hot coals are restricted to provided facilities. Trash and litter must be placed in containers provided for this purpose, and disposal is limited to items accumulated during the use of the park. Pets must be leashed and controlled at all times, and they are not allowed at the overnight camping facilities.

Further Information: For both parks contact Department of Conservation and Natural Resources, Leonard Harrison State Park, RR 6, Box 199, Wellsboro, PA 16901-8970; phone 717-724-3061.

Other Areas of Interest

Tioga State Forest provides 159,466 acres of public land adjoining these state parks. Contact Tioga State Forest, Forest District 16, P.O. Box 94, Route 287 South, Wellsboro, PA 16901; phone 717-724-2868.

Canoeing and rafting on **Pine Creek,** horseback tours of the **Pine Creek Gorge,** and airplane rides over the gorge are available. Contact Tioga County Tourist Promotion Agency, 114 Main Street, Suite B, Wellsboro, PA 16901; phone 717-724-0635 or 800-332-6718.

Park Trails

Turkey Path Trail 🥾🥾🥾🥾—2 miles—Cross the bottom of Pine Creek Gorge in either direction between Colton Point State Park and Leonard Harrison State Park.

Rim Trail 🥾🥾🥾—1.5 miles—This trail loops through Colton Point State Park and includes Lookout Trail.

Leonard Harrison and Colton Point State Parks

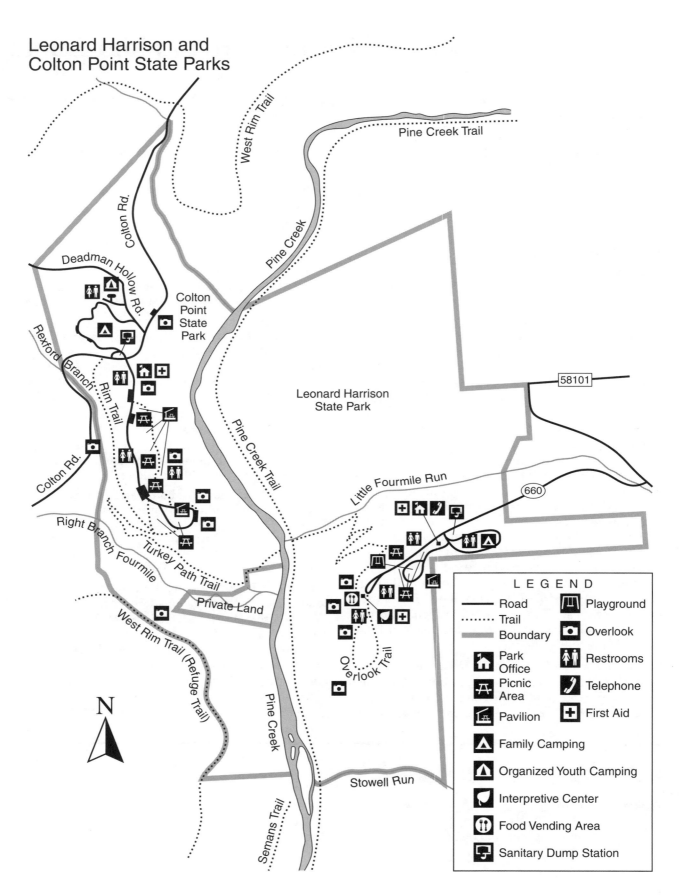

West Rim Trail

Pine Creek Trail

Pine Creek

Colton Rd.

Deadman Hollow Rd.

Colton Point State Park

Rexford Branch

Rim Trail

Colton Rd.

Leonard Harrison State Park

58101

Little Fourmile Run

660

Right Branch Fourmile

Turkey Path Trail

Private Land

West Rim Trail (Refuge Trail)

Pine Creek Trail

Overlook Trail

N

Pine Creek

Stowell Run

Semans Trail

L E G E N D

——	Road	🎠	Playground
····	Trail	📷	Overlook
▬▬	Boundary		
🏠	Park Office	🚻	Restrooms
🏕	Picnic Area	☎	Telephone
🏛	Pavilion	✚	First Aid

🔺 Family Camping

🔺 Organized Youth Camping

🍃 Interpretive Center

🍴 Food Vending Area

🚽 Sanitary Dump Station

68

Overlook Trail (Leonard Harrison State Park) 👢👢👢👢

Distance Round-Trip: .8 mile

Estimated Hiking Time: .5 hour

Caution: Parts of the trail are very close to sheer drops. Roots interfere with footing in some of the steepest places.

Trail Directions: Bring binoculars and a field guide to birds on this hike. When the birds are active, you might see numerous raptors soaring over the gorge and elusive forest songbirds.

The end of Pennsylvania Route 660 is a loop, with parking. At the apex of this loop **[1]** is a portal through a building, between a food concession and an interpretive center. Walk through this portal to an area paved with stones. You will pass the trailhead of Turkey Path Trail, then an overlook. Take a few minutes to study a display of trees here.

From this overlook, in addition to a spectacular view of the Grand Canyon of Pennsylvania, you get a view of the Allegheny Highlands beyond the gorge. Notice that all of the hilltops are about the same height. Though the terrain is hilly, this is actually a plateau. The valleys were formed by erosion. There is a wooden map of the area, including trails, in a pavilion that you pass on your left. Past the pavilion, follow a gravel path to the left around restrooms to a sign marking Overlook Trail.

The trail passes downhill behind the restrooms and splits .15 mi. from the end of Route 660 **[2]**. There is a bench at this split and an odd-looking stone structure. Can you figure out what it is? Take the right fork. You will be returning on the other fork.

You descend quickly to a bench at the edge of the gorge (.25 mi.) **[3]**. This bench is shaded on all sides by pine, oak, aspen, and birch trees and mountain laurel. Crude steps have been constructed to help you down the steepest part of the trail past the bench. But there are also many roots that could trip you. Stay on the trail and keep kids under control. You are walking along high ledges.

You arrive at Otter View, one of the best views of the gorge, at the lower extremity of the trail (.4 mi.) **[4]**. Far below you see Pine Creek flowing to the

south, and Pine Creek Trail, which follows an old railroad grade. On windy days especially, turkey vultures and various hawks soar on air currents, sometimes passing just a few feet from the overlook. You might even be treated to the sight of a bald eagle, though they are usually far below. Bald heads identify turkey vultures. Bald eagles are not bald but have brilliant white heads and tails. Identifying hawks is more difficult. During spring, you will probably see inflatable rafts and canoes on their journeys downstream. Raft and canoe rentals and guides are available at Ansonia, at the head of the gorge.

From Otter View, the trail turns left and begins climbing a steep course through a tributary valley. A bench about halfway up this climb (.6 mi.) **[5]** offers a well-deserved rest. Here you might try to identify some of the trees that were displayed on the overlook near the head of the trail. Timid forest songbirds here are quite a contrast to the raptors that soar over the gorge.

Ignore a trail that forks right at this bench and continue uphill. Ignore another fork to the right 335 feet up the trail. This fork leads to the park office, according to a sign. You return to the start of the Overlook Trail loop (.67 mi.) **[2]** after walking about 25 feet farther. Continue to Route 660 for a total distance of .8 mi.

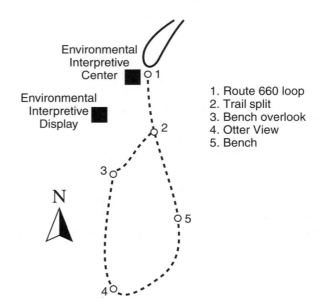

1. Route 660 loop
2. Trail split
3. Bench overlook
4. Otter View
5. Bench

Lookout Trail (Colton Point State Park) 👢👢

Distance Round-Trip: .93 mile

Estimated Hiking Time: .5 hour

Caution: The trail follows a very high, steep slope. Large roots protrude through the trail along the steepest stretch.

Trail Directions: The park map is inaccurate, but the developed area of Colton Point State Park is small, so you should be able to find your way around using these directions. Turn left from Colton Point Road at the well-marked park entrance onto a blacktop road, then park opposite the contact station, a small shack where campers register on the honor system. A wooden sign/map here provides a better picture of the area than the park map. A one-way gravel road that forks left just past the contact station is the head of Lookout Trail **[1]**, as indicated by a sign.

Walk about 250 feet along this one-way road to an overlook at the rim of the gorge (.05 mi.) **[2]**. You look primarily up the gorge. Distant cliffs are an unusual sight in the Allegheny Highlands. Even here in the canyon, most of the sides are forested. You might wonder how enough topsoil accumulated on these nearly vertical walls for trees to sprout. Relate this to other Pennsylvania trails where you get a close-up view of trees growing out of bare rock on a much smaller scale.

Turn right at this overlook, following the canyon rim. You will see dark-red paint blazes on trees. Lookout Trail follows these red blazes; however, these red blazes are for Rim Trail, a longer trail that shares the same course as Lookout Trail.

This is the quiet side of the canyon. You walk beneath a forest of maple, oak, pine, hemlock, and birch trees and mountain laurel on a dirt path. Some of the hemlocks and white pines are very large. There are no guardrails along most of the rim. The one-way road swings to the right away from the trail, by a small parking area, just before you arrive at Barbour

View (.27 mi.) **[3]**. Here again you can see primarily up the gorge, but you can also see the overlooks across the canyon to your right, on rocky cliffs, at Leonard Harrison State Park.

Up to this point, the trail could be traversed by wheelchair, but not beyond. You go by rest rooms just past Barbour View, then make a gentle descent to an unnamed overlook that is lined with pipes set in stone posts (.39 mi.) **[4]**. The canyon wall is so steep here that you seem to hang over Pine Creek.

Continue along a steeper descent to Harrison View (.47 mi.) **[5],** a long view down the gorge. Across the canyon, you are now close enough to see people walking along the overlooks at Leonard Harrison State Park, though you might not be able to recognize them as humans. The loop at the end of the blacktop park road and a parking area, lined with guardrails, is visible 175 feet to the right, or directly away from the gorge. Red trail blazes continue down along the rim, but this is Rim Trail only. You can either walk to the blacktop road and follow it to the right back to the trailhead, or better yet, return along Lookout Trail, for a total distance of .93 mi. **[1]**.

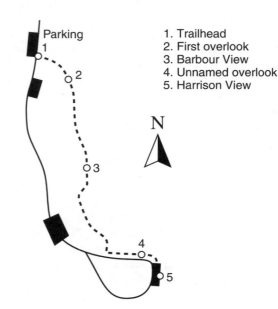

Parking
1

2

N

3

4

5

1. Trailhead
2. First overlook
3. Barbour View
4. Unnamed overlook
5. Harrison View

19. Sizerville State Park

- Hike one of the most challenging short trails in the state.
- Swim in a guarded pool.
- See an example of every large mammal species that exists in Pennsylvania.

Area Information

A small park, just 386 acres, with a small campground, Sizerville State Park does not get a lot of attention. It is tucked away in a deep, narrow valley on the border between Cameron County and Potter County, deep in the Allegheny Highlands. In 1917, this valley was chosen as the site for the reintroduction of beavers, which had become extinct in Pennsylvania. They were brought from Wisconsin and stocked along East Branch Cowley Run. You can still see their descendants in the valley.

Another native species that had also become extinct in the state, the elk, was also reintroduced into this area. Although elk are not common in the park, the best elk-viewing areas are nearby. White-tailed deer and black bears are abundant. You might even hear the haunting cries of eastern coyotes on cool, crisp nights, and rumors persist of mountain lion sightings in the area.

Sizerville is one of Pennsylvania's older state parks. It opened to public use in 1924. The first physical improvements were made three years later. The current character of the park is attributed to the CCC, which planted the pine trees you see in the park and bordering state forest lands.

Directions: The entrance to Sizerville State Park is on Pennsylvania Route 155, 7 miles north of Emporium. Turn left, as indicated by a sign, onto East Cowley Run Road.

Hours Open: The park is open year-round. Day-use areas are open from 8:00 A.M. to sunset.

Facilities: This small park provides a swimming pool, more than 200 picnic tables, picnic pavilions, 10 campsites with electricity for tents or RVs, five walk-in tent sites without electricity, trout fishing, and hiking trails.

Permits and Rules: Alcoholic beverages are prohibited. Outdoor recreational activities are restricted to locations where signs or physical improvements designate the appropriate use. Fires and the disposal of hot coals are restricted to provided facilities. Trash and litter must be placed in containers provided for this purpose, and disposal is limited to items accumulated during the use of the park. Pets must be leashed and controlled at all times, and they are not allowed at the swimming area or in overnight camping facilities. Posting signs and soliciting are prohibited. All children age 9 and under must be accompanied by a responsible adult at the swimming area. Camp only in designated camping areas, and minimize your impact.

Further Information: Department of Conservation and Environmental Resources, Sizerville State Park, RR 1, Box 238-A, Emporium, PA 15834-9608; phone 814-486-5605.

Other Areas of Interest

Visit the birthplace of famous western movie star Tom Mix and a monument dedicated to the **Bucktail Regiment** of Civil War fame. Write to Cameron County Tourist Promotion Agency, P.O. Box 118, Driftwood, PA 15832; phone 814-546-2665.

Sinnemahoning State Park is one of few places in Pennsylvania where you are likely to see both bald eagles and golden eagles. Write to Department of Conservation and Natural Resources, Sinnemahoning State Park, RR 1, Box 172, Austin, PA 16720.

See the **Pennsylvania elk herd.** Write to District Forester, P.O. Box 327, Emporium, PA 15834; phone 814-486-3353.

Park Trails

Campground Trail —.7 mile—This is an easy walk for the whole family.

North Slope Trail —.5 mile—Walk a loop on the lower slope of the valley.

Sizerville State Park

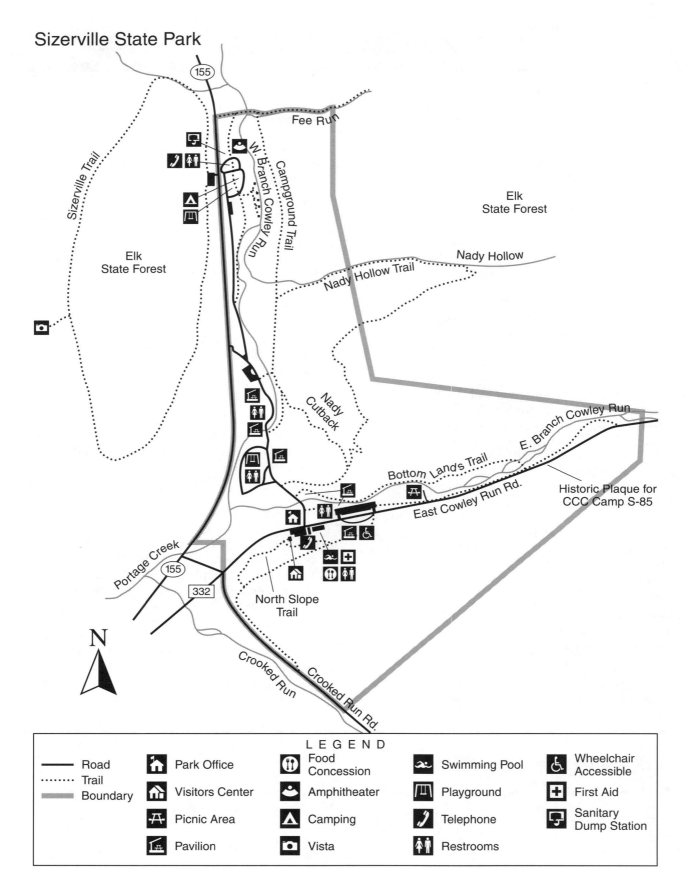

155

Fee Run

Elk
State Forest

W. Branch Cowley Run

Campground Trail

Sizerville Trail

Elk
State Forest

Nady Hollow

Nady Hollow Trail

Nady
Cutback

E. Branch Cowley Run

Bottom Lands Trail

East Cowley Run Rd.

Historic Plaque for
CCC Camp S-85

Portage Creek

155

332

North Slope
Trail

N

Crooked Run

Crooked Run Rd.

L E G E N D

—— Road	Park Office	Food Concession
···· Trail	Visitors Center	Amphitheater
Boundary	Picnic Area	Camping
	Pavilion	Vista

Swimming Pool	Wheelchair Accessible
Playground	First Aid
Telephone	Sanitary Dump Station
Restrooms	

Nady Hollow Trail 👢👢👢👢

Distance Round-Trip: 1.63 miles

Estimated Hiking Time: 2 hours

Caution: Do not attempt this trail unless you are in good physical condition. Parts of it are extremely steep with footing on slippery dirt and loose rock. You will climb about 600 feet in elevation.

Trail Directions: From the main park road, East Crowley Run Road, turn left, just before the swimming pool, toward the campground. The trailhead is on the right side of the road, but it is marked by a sign on the left side of the road **[1]**.

Begin walking up a set of wooden steps through a pine plantation. Follow both green and orange trail blazes. The pines soon give way to sugar maple, black cherry, and oak trees. The trail swings left about .13 mi. from the trailhead. At this point, light-blue trail blazes continue straight up the steep hill. If you feel adventurous, you can follow these blue blazes up the steepest part of the hill for a slightly longer loop of about 2 mi. This trail climbs about 100 feet higher in elevation than Nady Hollow Trail, but following it can be difficult. Do not attempt it without a map and compass. Even if you intend to stay on Nady Hollow Trail, take a short detour along the blue trail blazes to an unusual spring. It seeps from the hillside in a steady flow even under drought conditions, but then disappears within about 100 yards.

Continuing on Nady Hollow Trail, swing left, away from the blue blazes, with the orange and green blazes to a fork (.15 mi.) **[2]**. Take Cutback Trail, following the green trail blazes to the left if you are tired of climbing. It descends from here for a loop of about .6 mi. Take the right fork following orange trail blazes for the full loop of Nady Hollow Trail.

The full loop of Nady Hollow Trail continues up the steep hill, using switchbacks in the steepest area and eventually crossing the rounded ridge. Watch how the makeup of the forest changes as you climb in elevation. Wild grapevine and shagbark hickory become more common higher on the slope. The grapevine thins out at the top of the ridge, but hickory is a major forest component. Expect to see deer in this area. Deer like it here because it is relatively cool, and

they can see danger from a long distance through the mature timber. Walking is more pleasant on top of the ridge, but not for long. Soon you begin a steep descent into a small valley, where you strike an old woods road and see blue blazes to the right. This is the apex of the loop (.8 mi.) **[3]**. Turn sharply left, down the valley.

Shortly after the small valley drops to the level of the valley of West Branch Crowley Run, Nady Hollow Trail intersects with Campground Trail (1.25 mi.) **[4]**. This intersection is marked by a sign. Turn left, following both orange and white trail blazes. Do not cross the first wooden footbridge (1.35 mi.) **[5]**. Follow the white trail blazes across a smaller footbridge, keeping West Branch Cowley Run to your right. This section of the trail rises above the creek on a very steep slope, passing the lower end of Cutback Trail (1.44 mi.) **[6]**. The trail ends in a small picnic area. Continue straight ahead, between the paved road and the hillside, to return to the trailhead (1.63 mi.) **[1]**.

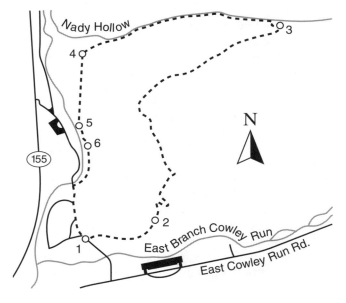

1. Trailhead
2. Cutback Trail
3. Apex of loop
4. Campground Trail
5. First footbridge
6. Cutback Trail

Bottom Lands Trail 👢👢

Distance Round-Trip: .9 mile

Estimated Hiking Time: .5 hour

Caution: This trail crosses several damp areas where you could get your feet wet. Expect biting insects during spring and early summer.

Trail Directions: This is an easy hike for the whole family. Bring field guides to identify trees and wildflowers.

Enter the park on East Cowley Run Road, then turn left toward the camping area by park headquarters. Pull into a parking area on the right immediately after crossing a bridge. The trailhead is at this parking area, but it is marked by a sign on the opposite side of the road **[1]**. Follow pink trail blazes up the valley, with East Branch Cowley Run on your right. Bottom Lands Trail swings along the hillside, around a picnic pavilion, and then drops to the edge of the stream. You should see numerous wildflowers. Watch for orange touch-me-nots in the damper soils. If you pinch these flowers lightly when they bloom during early summer, they pop.

Pine and hemlock shade most of the trail. The pine was planted by the CCC during the 1930s, after the timber had been cut from this area and from most of Pennsylvania. The trail swings away from the stream just as you are passing the remains of an old dam (.3 mi.) **[2]**.

You can see most of the major trees in this part of the Allegheny Highlands on the flat bottomland, or on the side of the hill to your left. See if you can identify eastern hemlock, white pine, sugar maple, beech, black cherry, northern red oak, shagbark hickory, and sweet birch.

The trail turns right, crossing East Branch Cowley Run on a wooden footbridge (.4 mi.) **[3]**. Look upstream at a small log dam. This creates a pool that is good trout habitat and a waterfall that aerates the water. Between the dam and the bridge, a log and rock fill has been placed by the roots of a pine tree to prevent the stream from eroding under the roots. This also narrows the stream channel, which improves trout habitat. Streams warm too quickly when they are wide and shallow.

Follow the trail across a second, smaller wooden footbridge to an intersection with a mowed grass path (.5 mi.) **[4]**. This is the apex of the loop. Turn right, following East Branch Cowley Run downstream, parallel to a paved road on your left. Watch for a sign that marks the border between Cameron County and Potter County on the side of the road (.7 mi.) **[5]**, where the mowed grass path blends into the day-use area. Continue straight, through a picnic area and a parking area. You can see pink trail blazes again at the lower end of the parking area behind a small stone building. This was a restroom facility, but it is no longer in use. Continue straight, by a split-rail fence, to another paved road. From here, you can see the small parking area at the trailhead to your right. The complete loop is .9 mi. **[1]**.

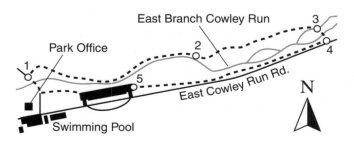

1. Trailhead
2. Dam remains
3. Footbridge
4. Mowed grass path
5. County line

20. Ole Bull State Park

- Relax in some of the wildest, most remote country in Pennsylvania.
- Visit the site of Ole Bull's castle.
- Swim in the cool water of Kettle Creek.

Area Information

From belted kingfishers plunging into Kettle Creek to pileated woodpeckers hammering trees on the steep hillsides, Ole Bull State Park is a bird-watcher's paradise. This is the Black Forest of Pennsylvania, some of the wildest country in the state, so named because the earliest white settlers thought it resembled the Black Forest of Germany. The forest those early settlers saw, much of it towering white pine and eastern hemlock, was cut during the 19th and early 20th centuries. Some of it was used as masts for the great sailing ships. Today the forest is different, mostly northern hardwoods, but it is dense and beautiful, one of the greenest places on Earth.

The park is named for Ole Bornemann Bull, a famous Norwegian violinist. While touring the United States during the 1850s, Bull decided to settle in Potter County with a group of fellow Norwegians. But life was hard here. The group disbanded within a year and moved west into Michigan and Wisconsin.

Soon after Ole Bull's colony left, the logging industry moved into the area. Two rail lines were built to haul logs to the sawmills. The grades are still visible in some places. Following several phases of logging and forest fires, when the land was of no further use to the logging companies, it was purchased by the Commonwealth of Pennsylvania. A small picnic site was established in 1925 at the current site of Ole Bull State Park. The CCC made further developments during the 1930s, enlarging the park to 125 acres.

Directions: Getting here is half the fun. Ole Bull State Park is located on Pennsylvania Route 144, 18 miles south of Galeton, on U.S. Route 6, and 26 miles north of Renovo, on Pennsylvania Route 120. An alternate route from the north follows Pennsylvania Route 44 south from Route 6 at Sweden Valley to Route 144. Both Route 44 and Route 144 are narrow, winding roads through some of the most beautiful forested hills on the planet. There are several fabulous scenic overlooks at roadside pull-offs.

Hours Open: The park is open year-round. Day-use areas are open from 8:00 A.M. to sunset.

Facilities: The park has two camping areas along Kettle Creek with 81 campsites for tents or RVs, a guarded swimming area at a small dam on Kettle Creek, excellent trout fishing in Kettle Creek, picnic tables and pavilions, and a play area. A mountain bike trail connects to trails in the Susquehannock State Forest.

Permits and Rules: Alcoholic beverages are prohibited. Outdoor recreational activities are restricted to locations where signs or physical improvements designate the appropriate use. Fires and the disposal of hot coals are restricted to provided facilities. Trash and litter must be placed in containers provided for this purpose, and disposal is limited to items accumulated during the use of the park. Pets must be leashed and controlled at all times, and they are not allowed at the swimming area or in overnight camping facilities. Soliciting and posting signs are prohibited. All children age 9 and under must be supervised by a responsible adult at the swimming area. Fishing is prohibited between the wires at the dam basin and in the swimming area.

Further Information: Department of Conservation and Natural Resources, Ole Bull State Park, HCR 62, Box 9, Cross Fork, PA 17729-9701; phone 814-435-5000.

Other Areas of Interest

The **Susquehannock State Forest** provides 264,000 acres of public land with numerous trails for hiking and biking. Write to Susquehannock State Forest, Forest District 15, P.O. Box 673, Coudersport, PA 16915; phone 814-274-8474.

Potter County is an outdoor recreation paradise. For information phone the Potter County Visitors Association, 1-888-POTTER-2.

Park Trails

Daugherty Loop Trail —1.2 miles—Hike up Ole Bull Run, on part of the Susquehannock Trail, then complete a loop following an old railroad grade.

Ole Bull State Park

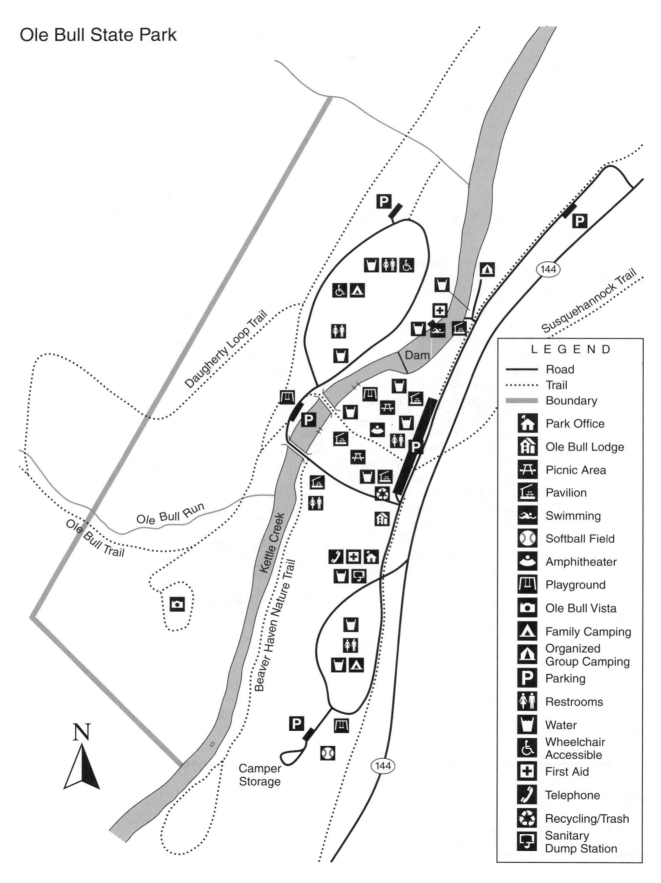

LEGEND

——	Road
····	Trail
▬	Boundary
🏠	Park Office
🏛	Ole Bull Lodge
⛏	Picnic Area
⛺	Pavilion
🏊	Swimming
⚾	Softball Field
🎭	Amphitheater
🎠	Playground
📷	Ole Bull Vista
▲	Family Camping
▲	Organized Group Camping
P	Parking
🚻	Restrooms
🚰	Water
♿	Wheelchair Accessible
✚	First Aid
☎	Telephone
♻	Recycling/Trash
🚽	Sanitary Dump Station

Daugherty Loop Trail

Susquehannock Trail

144

Dam

Ole Bull Run

Ole Bull Trail

Kettle Creek

Beaver Haven Nature Trail

Camper Storage

144

N

Castle Vista Trail 👢👢👢

Distance Round-Trip: .5 mile

Estimated Hiking Time: .5 hour

Caution: This trail is very steep. Do not cross the split-rail fence at Castle Vista. The ground is slippery with loose rocks at the edge of a high cliff. Children should be closely supervised.

Trail Directions: Castle Vista Trail is short and steep, with a great view and an interesting bit of history. Bring your camera.

Turn off the main park road toward Camping Area #1. The trailhead is a dirt road that forks left after crossing a bridge over Kettle Creek, by a flagpole and a kiosk **[1]**. There is a small parking area about 150 feet from the trailhead, by a play area.

Follow orange trail blazes along the dirt road past a trail sign and a bench where Daugherty Loop Trail forks acutely right, only 225 feet from the trailhead, straight to another trail sign and bench where Castle Vista Trail forks right, toward Castle Vista (.07 mi.) **[2]**. This sign warns that you will encounter steep cliff conditions that are slippery when wet, and that you should wear proper footgear. Follow red trail blazes from this point.

You begin a steep climb on a wide dirt and gravel path from the trail sign. Susquehannock Trail forks right partway up the hill (.1 mi.) **[3]**. This is marked by a sign. On the park map, this is named Ole Bull Trail, which is part of the Daugherty Loop Trail.

Continue uphill past another bench. Look at Ole Bull Creek, below to your right, where you will see several stream-improvement structures intended to improve trout habitat. A fourth bench has been placed at the top of the steep climb, where the trail curves left and splits (.2 mi.) **[4]**. This begins the loop portion of Castle Vista Trail. Ahead, through the inside of the loop, you can see the back of a large sign. Take the right fork to Castle Vista (.26 mi.) **[5]**.

Castle Vista is atop a large sheer rock outcrop. As you sit on either of two benches, you look over a split-rail fence across the steep valley of Kettle Creek. All you can see in any direction is forest. If you carefully look over the cliff, you can see small pieces of Kettle Creek sparkling in the sunlight. This is one of the finest freestone trout streams in Pennsylvania.

Behind you is a depression in the bedrock. This is all that remains of the "castle" of Ole Bornemann Bull. Actually, it was a log cabin, and it never was completed. Winters are long and harsh in the Allegheny Highlands, and the ground is steep and rocky. Beautiful as it was, it was not a good place for a colony.

Complete this short loop around Castle Vista (.3 mi.) **[4]**, then backtrack to the trailhead (.5 mi.) **[1]**.

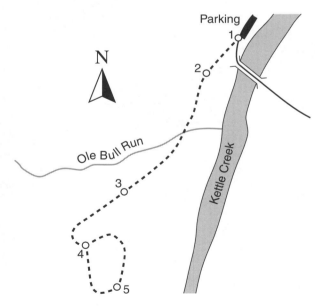

1. Trailhead
2. Castle Vista sign
3. Susquehannock Trail
4. Trail splits
5. Castle Vista

Beaver Haven Nature Trail 🥾

Distance Round-Trip: 1.1 mile

Estimated Hiking Time: .5 hour

Caution: Biting insects can be a problem. Bring insect repellent. This is a narrow trail with a few roots across it.

Trail Directions: From the main park road, turn toward Camping Area #1. The trailhead is on the left side of the road before you cross Kettle Creek, behind a picnic pavilion **[1]**. A wooden sign does not name the trail, but it does have a trail map and other information.

This narrow, wood chip-covered trail follows Kettle Creek downstream. It reveals a strikingly different ecosystem than the surrounding highlands. Lush vegetation covers the ground. Look for skunk cabbage on the wetter ground. Wildflowers are abundant. One of the most beautiful, and most unusual in this area, is the Turks cap lily. Sycamores dominate the forest canopy, except where pines and other conifers have been planted by the CCC.

Small ponds near the trail wiggle with life. The dark, stagnant water of isolated pools is an incubator for frogs and insects. Pools that are connected to the creek are nurseries for small fish. This is also wood duck habitat. These pools were created when Kettle Creek flooded or when the meandering creek changed channels. The floodplain is relatively wide here. In some other areas, the steep hills slope right to the edge of the creek.

A few unmapped trails connect Beaver Haven Nature Trail to the campground that you can see to your left. Soon after entering a pine plantation, your trail splits immediately after crossing a wooden footbridge (.4 mi.) **[2]**. This starts the loop portion of the trail. Notice a crabapple tree at the end of the bridge. The fruit of this small, thorny tree is an important food for several species of wildlife. Take the right fork, beneath the overhanging limbs of several spruce trees, then between tightly packed rows of pines. These conifers were planted by the CCC during the 1930s, when few trees were left standing in the area.

At the apex of the loop (.5 mi.) **[3]**, another trail that is blazed with yellow circles continues straight ahead. This is too new to be on the park map. It leads through Susquehannock State Forest land to a fly-fishing area downstream on Kettle Creek. You can see a few larch trees in this area, also planted by the CCC. Curve left here, staying on the wood chip path. You will have to look carefully, though, because Beaver Haven Nature Trail becomes less distinct.

Two benches are placed at the edge of a field, close to the beaver dam. You might have to get off the trail to see the beaver dam. Look for birds here that you will not see in the forest. From here, you can see the footbridge where you complete the loop (.7 mi.) **[2]**. Follow the trail upstream to return to the trailhead (1.1 mi.) **[1]**.

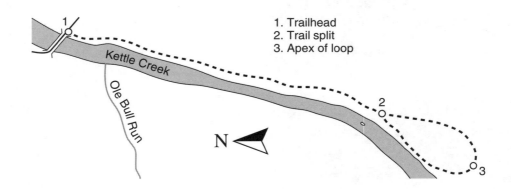

1. Trailhead
2. Trail split
3. Apex of loop

21. Allegheny National Forest— Elk County

- Float the Clarion River.
- Fish in many miles of trout streams.
- Enjoy year-round outdoor activities.

Area Information

With more than 111,500 acres of the Allegheny National Forest inside its borders, Elk County can boast one of the finest outdoor playgrounds in the East. In contrast to the eastern part of the county, the Allegheny National Forest in the western part of the county is some of the most gentle terrain in the Allegheny Highlands between the Tionesta Creek and Clarion River drainages. Many miles of trails for hiking, biking, cross-country skiing, and ATV riding will take you into beautiful hardwood and coniferous forests, to hidden streams teeming with wild brook trout, and into areas managed for grouse, turkeys, and other wildlife.

The Clarion River, along the southern border of the Allegheny National Forest, has been designated a National Wild and Scenic River. It is popular with canoeists during spring downriver from Ridgeway. Fishing for trout and smallmouth bass is good and improving from a period when acid mine drainage and other pollution nearly made it dead water.

Directions: The Allegheny National Forest is in the northwestern portion of Elk County. The Ridgeway Ranger Station is located off Pennsylvania Route 948 about 2 miles north of the center of Ridgeway.

Hours Open: The national forest is open year-round. Day-use areas are open from 6:00 A.M. to 10:00 P.M.

Facilities: Allegheny National Forest facilities in Elk County include camping areas for tents and RVs; a canoe launch on the Clarion River; picnic areas; trails for hiking, biking, cross-country skiing, and ATVs; many miles of trout streams; and swimming at Twin Lakes Recreation Area.

Permits and Rules: ATVs are allowed only on designated ATV trails. Horses and pack animals are not allowed on hiking trails. Do not carve, chop, cut, or damage any live trees. Do not damage or remove any historical or archaeological items. Extensive rules limit camping outside designated campgrounds. Watch for posted restrictions on fires.

Further Information: Marienville Ranger District, HC 2, Box 130, Marienville, PA 16239, phone 814-927-6628; Allegheny National Forest, P.O. Box 847, Warren, PA 16365, phone 814-723-5150.

Other Areas of Interest

East Branch Lake, in the northeast corner of Elk County, offers boating and fishing for both cold-water and warm-water species. Write to Resource Manager, East Branch Lake, U.S. Army Corps of Engineers, RD #1, Wilcox, PA 15870; phone 814-965-2065. For 24-hour lake information, phone 814-965-4762.

Elk County is part of the home range of the only **wild Pennsylvania elk herd.** For information about services and other Elk County attractions, write to Elk County Visitors Bureau, P.O. Box 838, St. Marys, PA 15857; phone 814-834-3723.

Park Trails

Twin Lakes Trail 👢👢👢—14.7 miles—Hike from the North Country National Scenic Trail along South Branch Tionesta Creek to Twin Lakes Recreation Area.

Loleta Trail 👢👢👢—3.2 miles—Loop through hardwood forest from the site of a ghost town.

Mill Creek Trail 👢👢👢—9 miles—This trail connects the Brush Creek trailhead with the Twin Lakes Trail along the Mill Creek Valley. Mill Creek is an excellent trout fishing stream.

Allegheny National Forest

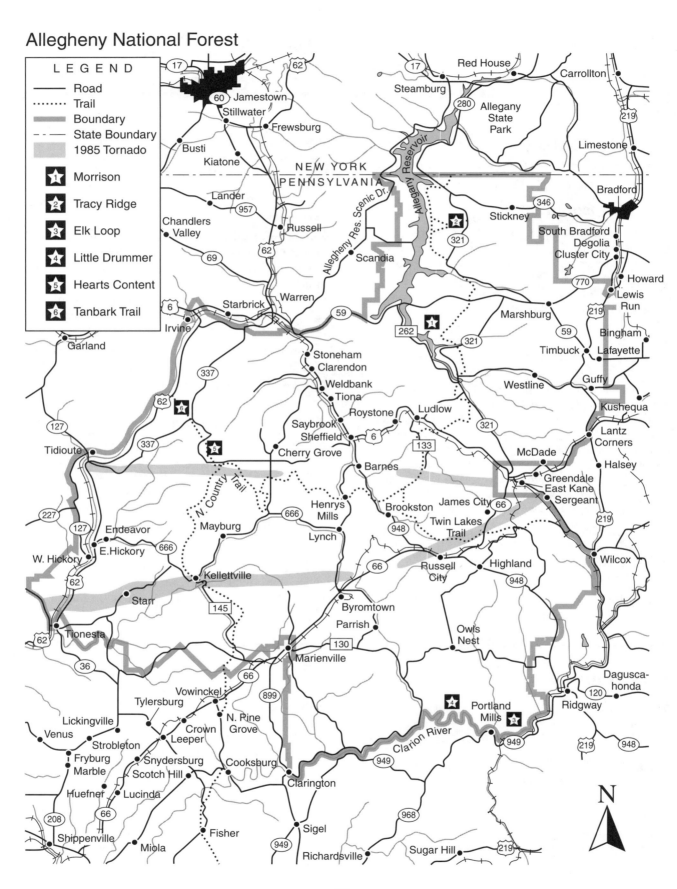

LEGEND
—— Road
······ Trail
━━ Boundary
—·— State Boundary
░ 1985 Tornado

⭐1 Morrison
⭐2 Tracy Ridge
⭐3 Elk Loop
⭐4 Little Drummer
⭐5 Hearts Content
⭐6 Tanbark Trail

Little Drummer Historical Pathway 👢👢

Distance Round-Trip: 3.4 miles

Estimated Hiking Time: 2 hours

Caution: Wear bright orange clothing if you hike during spring or fall hunting seasons. This area, like many of the best wildlife habitats, has been developed and protected by hunting license funds and private hunters' organizations. Waterproof hiking boots will be necessary to keep your feet dry on the long loop.

Trail Directions: Pick up the Little Drummer Historical Pathway interpretive booklet at the Ridgeway Ranger Station about 2 miles north of Ridgeway on Route 948, or at the Marienville District Ranger Station 2.5 miles north of Marienville on Pennsylvania Route 66. Hiking this trail with the booklet provides an outstanding education in wildlife management. Numbered wooden posts along the trail correspond with numbers in the booklet.

At Ridgeway, turn off Pennsylvania Route 948 onto Laurel Mill Road at the west side of town. Drive about 8 miles to a sign on the right side of the road that marks Little Drummer Historical Pathway, and turn right into a small gravel parking area. The trailhead is a kiosk by a gate at the end of the parking area **[1]**.

Begin the hike following a service road past the gate. The trail is blazed with off-white diamonds and hiker decals on brown plastic posts. Turn left where the trail splits at interpretive station 2 (.08 mi.) **[2]**. This starts the loop portion of the trail on a wide grassy road. Plastic tubes alongside the road protect

fruit-bearing bushes until they grow tall enough to survive browsing deer.

Cross over a gas line right-of-way at interpretive station 7 (.6 mi.) **[3]**. At a fork by interpretive station 9 (.7 mi.) **[4]** you must decide whether to hike the short loop or to continue on the complete loop. If you want to hike the short loop, continue straight toward Cole Run Pond, then take a right fork at interpretive station 10 and skip ahead to trail highlight **[7]** for a total hiking distance of 1.4 mi.

Continuing on the long loop, take the left fork by interpretive station 9 onto a narrower dirt path. You are now circling Cole Run Pond and the adjacent wetland on first a log skidding trail, then, past interpretive station 19, on a railroad bed. Expect wet feet on this stretch of the trail if your footgear is not waterproof.

Turn right along an abandoned gas line by interpretive station 27 (1.3 mi.) **[5]**. Except for a detour around a wet area, you follow the gas line to a right turn at interpretive station 29 (1.8 mi.) **[6]**. Savannahs like this, grassy areas with just a few scattered trees, are unusual in the densely forested Allegheny Highlands, except near wetlands. After passing a larch plantation, stop at a bench near several high anthills for a pleasant view of Cole Run Pond.

Turn left at interpretive station 10 after crossing the earthen dam that creates Cole Run Pond (2.6 mi.) **[7]**. About 200 feet past this turn, you are again following an old railroad bed. Two long boardwalks keep your feet dry over a wet area.

Do not be confused by a mowed grass pipeline near interpretive station 14. Cross it at a left angle, watching ahead for a post decal (3 mi.) **[8]**. The loop is complete at interpretive station 2. Turn left to return to the trailhead kiosk (3.4 mi.) **[1]**.

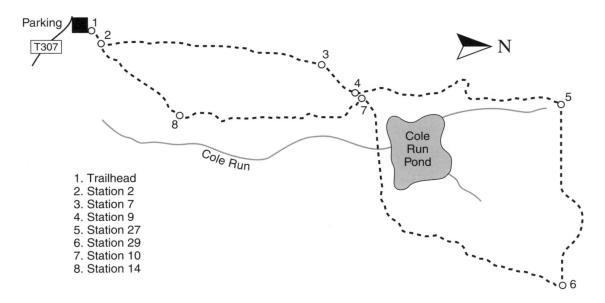

1. Trailhead
2. Station 2
3. Station 7
4. Station 9
5. Station 27
6. Station 29
7. Station 10
8. Station 14

Elk Loop 👢👢

Distance Round-Trip: 1 mile

Estimated Hiking Time: .5 hour

Caution: Wear bright orange clothing during spring and fall hunting seasons.

Trail Directions: Drive about 3 miles west from Ridgeway on Laurel Mill Road, Township Road 307, then turn right into a gravel parking area that is separated from the road by a split-rail fence. This is the Laurel Mill Cross-Country Skiing/Hiking Area. The trailhead is at a kiosk near the end of the parking area **[1]**. This is one of the most pleasant trailheads you will ever find. A pavilion contains a couple of picnic tables and a woodstove. During winter the pavilion can be completely enclosed into a warming hut. Several railroad spikes have been driven into a timber above the stove for hanging wet clothes.

Study the trail map at the kiosk. Laurel Mill Cross-Country Skiing/Hiking area consists of six loop trails. Three are north of Laurel Mill Road, three are south of the road. Several benches and cooking grills are scattered along the loops. Try the shortest loop, Elk Loop, as a sample. This is one of the easiest trails in the Allegheny Highlands, yet you get a good look at a hardwood forest with a good chance of seeing wildlife if you hike early or late in the day. You will probably be tempted to return next winter for cross-country skiing.

As you face the kiosk, walk to your left past the pavilion and a brown shed. A wide dirt and grass trail gently descends through a hardwood forest of black cherry, red oak, sugar maple, and basswood.

Trail blazes are blue diamonds. Watch for sharp turns at double diamonds.

Deer and wild turkeys are abundant in this area. You can also expect to see a fair variety of songbirds if you carry binoculars. Some species inhabit the forest canopy. Others are ground feeders. The lack of intermediate vegetation eliminates some species. For a contrast to these conditions, hike the Little Drummer Historical Pathway, about 5 miles west, where you hike through a greater variety of habitats. Would you expect to see more or fewer species there?

Turn left at an intersection that is marked by a metallic trail map on a wooden post (.5 mi.) **[2]**. This is the apex of the loop. A mild climb takes you back to the trailhead, passing between a restroom and the pavilion (1 mi.) **[1]**.

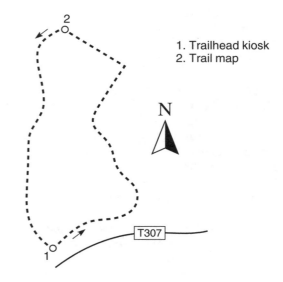

1. Trailhead kiosk
2. Trail map

22. Little Pine State Park

- Climb some of the highest and steepest hills in the state to awesome vistas.
- Fish in Little Pine Lake and Little Pine Creek.
- Visit during winter for sledding, cross-country skiing, ice fishing, snowmobiling, and ice skating.

Area Information

Little Pine State Park is toward the southern end of the Allegheny Highlands where the valleys are very deep. This is some of the wildest, most rugged, and beautiful terrain in the state. Elevation changes about 1,000 feet from Little Pine Creek to the surrounding ridges. Other than the developed day-use area near Little Pine Lake, the land is covered in dense forest. You can observe changes in this forest, from sycamore groves and pine plantations on the valley floor to mixed hardwoods on the hillsides and scrubby pines and oaks at the highest elevations.

Iroquois and Algonquins hunted here before the coming of white settlers. The forest began to lose its primitive character in 1809, when two sawmills were built by Little Pine Creek. A logging village, English Mills, was at the location of the park campground. You can see the small community cemetery here. Logs were floated down Little Pine Creek to Williamsport, known then as the logging capital of the world, by splash dams that were broken to create a rush of water down the otherwise small stream.

The CCC built a camp here in 1933. The pine plantations you see in the area were part of its accomplishments. When the CCC left in 1937, the land was turned over to the Bureau of State Parks. The dam that backs up Little Pine Lake was built in 1950 for flood control and recreation. The park was used as a picnic area until a campground was constructed in 1958. The newer facilities were built after Hurricane Agnes caused a huge flood in 1972.

Directions: The park is located on Pennsylvania Route 4001, 4 miles north of Pennsylvania Route 44 at Waterville and 8 miles south of Pennsylvania Route 287 at Center English.

Hours Open: The park is open year-round. Day-use areas are open from 8:00 A.M. to sunset.

Facilities: The campground has 104 campsites, of which 98 can accommodate RVs up to 30 feet in length. Some sites have electricity. The park also has swimming, fishing, and boating on Little Pine Lake; boat rentals; fishing in Little Pine Creek; several trails that connect to Tiadaghton State Forest; 300 picnic tables; and four picnic pavilions.

Permits and Rules: Alcoholic beverages are prohibited. Boats must have either a state park launching permit, a state park mooring permit, or a current Pennsylvania Fish and Boat Commission registration. Only nonpowered and electric-powered boats are allowed. Outdoor recreational activities are restricted to locations where signs or physical improvements designate the appropriate use. Fires and the disposal of hot coals are restricted to provided facilities. Trash and litter must be placed in containers provided for this purpose, and disposal is limited to items accumulated during the use of the park. Pets must be leashed and controlled at all times, and they are not allowed at the swimming area or in overnight camping facilities. Posting signs and soliciting are prohibited. All children age 9 and under must be accompanied by a responsible adult at the swimming area.

Further Information: Department of Conservation and Natural Resources, Little Pine State Park, 4205 Little Pine Creek Road, Waterville, PA 17776; phone 570-753-6000.

Other Areas of Interest

For more information about outdoor recreation and events in the area, write to **Lycoming County Tourist Promotion Agency,** 454 Pine Street, Williamsport, PA 17701; phone 800-358-9900 or 570-327-7700.

Park Trails

Spike Buck Hollow Trail 👢👢👢👢—2 miles—See high overlooks and rock outcrops on this difficult trail.

Lake Shore Trail 👢👢👢—5 miles—You can expect to see several wildlife species on this trail, which follows the undeveloped side of Little Pine Lake.

Button Ball Trail 👢👢—.5 mile—This trail is used primarily by anglers who fish Little Pine Creek below the dam.

Little Pine State Park

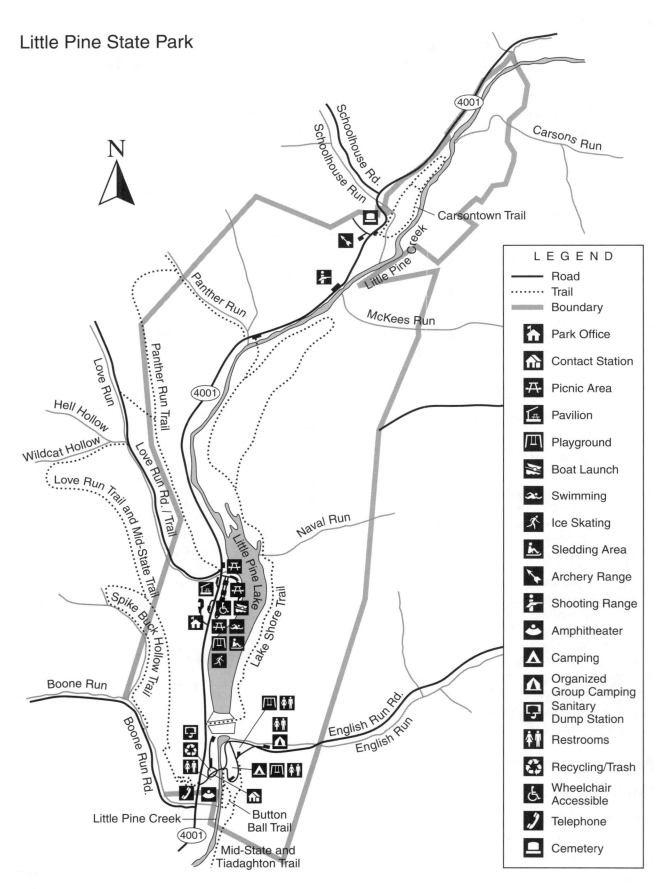

Panther Run/Love Run Trails/ Love Run Road 🥾🥾🥾🥾🥾

Distance Round-Trip: 2.8 miles

Estimated Hiking Time: 2 hours

Caution: Do not attempt this trail unless you are in good physical condition. Wear proper hiking boots. This trail is very steep, and it climbs about 1,000 feet in elevation. Some areas cross jagged rocks.

Trail Directions: Your trailhead is on the north side of the day-use area, on Route 4001. If you are driving north, it is on the left side of the road, marked by a trail sign where a dirt road meets Route 4001 **[1]**. There is a parking area on the right side of Route 4001 by a small picnic area.

About 50 feet past the trail sign is a kiosk with a wooden map of the park trails. Begin your hike on a very steep path behind the kiosk. This is not a well-worn path, so you will have to watch the dark-green blazes, which blend into the background. The forest is maple, oak, birch, and pine. Wild grapevine hangs from many of the trees. Patches of mountain laurel bring color to the forest when they bloom in late June.

White pine saplings are abundant about halfway up the hill. Small rock outcrops appear in the same area. The slope becomes less severe where the trail crosses the first larger rock outcrop (.3 mi.) **[2]**. This is a good place to rest and study the changing habitat. Underbrush is thinner, giving you a better view through the trees. Oak makes up a greater share of the trees at this elevation. Past here, you walk on top of a rocky hogback ridge. Walking is very pleasant along a gentle downhill slope through small white pines, especially during summer when it is noticeably cooler, breezier, and less humid than in the valley. The ridge is so narrow and steep that you can see far down both sides at the same time. Only dark shadows under the dense forest canopy limit your vision. Long, jagged rock outcrops crown the ridge in many places. Thick moss covering the rocks on the trail makes it feel as if you are walking on a padded carpet.

But you have not finished climbing. Look at the high ridge to your left. That is about how high you will climb. It is well worth the effort, though, because the rock outcrops and the scenery become increasingly impressive to an old flagstone quarry at the top (1 mi.) **[3]**. Examine the changes the forest has made. The small quarry is surrounded by quaking aspen and table mountain pine. Table mountain pine is very unusual this far north.

Scale the cliff at the far end of the quarry and look back at the view. Pause here for a lunch break. Past the quarry, the trail follows an old road to an intersection marked by a trail sign (1.1 mi.) **[4]**. The sign indicates Mid State Trail and Panther Run Trail straight ahead, and Love Run Trail behind you. Turn left here, down an old road. You are now following both orange and green trail blazes. The road is wide, level, and grassy but so steep it is a toe cruncher.

Turn left where this road meets another dirt road at the bottom of the valley (1.4 mi.) **[5]**. This is Love Run Road, which is closed to vehicles. Another sign marks this intersection. This road drops at a more pleasant angle, passing a camp (1.9 mi.) **[6]** before reaching the trailhead at Route 4001 (2.8 mi.) **[1]**.

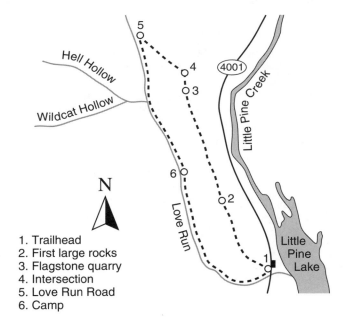

N

1. Trailhead
2. First large rocks
3. Flagstone quarry
4. Intersection
5. Love Run Road
6. Camp

Carsontown Trail 👢👢

Distance Round-Trip: 1.1 miles

Estimated Hiking Time: .5 hour

Caution: Biting insects can be a problem along this trail. Staying on the trail can be challenging along Little Pine Creek because it is not blazed.

Trail Directions: This trail is often used by anglers to reach a special-regulations section of Little Pine Creek where only artificial lures may be used. Bring field guides for birds and wildflowers. It is a good family hike where you see a forest that is much different than the forest on the steep hillsides as well as many wildflowers. You can also expect to see birds that only live near water.

The trailhead is toward the northern end of the park, near the archery range. It is on the right side of the road if you are driving north, by a small parking area. A sign marks the trailhead **[1]**. It begins as a wide, mowed grass path through a small forest opening. The trail splits into the loop portion after about 100 feet, still in the opening. Take the right fork straight toward Little Pine Creek. After passing between a few white pines and crossing a rocky flood channel, which is dry in normal summer conditions, you enter a large sycamore stand on the level flood-plain. The trail is much narrower here, almost hidden by tall grass. Watch to your right for wood ducks in a small pool.

Sneak up to the edge of the creek (.1 mi.) **[2]**. Several bird species will probably be fishing. Watch for belted kingfishers perched on limbs that overhang the water, for great blue herons wading in the water, and for common mergansers swimming and diving. Early in the morning and late in the evening, you might also see raccoons or mink hunting along the shoreline. Watch for deer anywhere along the trail. Look into the water for small piles of pebbles. These

are beds where smallmouth bass laid their eggs during late May or early June.

The land is also flat across the creek; however, pine and spruce are mixed with the sycamore trees. These were planted by the CCC. Can you guess why this land is so flat? Look at the rock and gravel bar between the trees and the creek before the first bend in the creek. Can you guess how it was created? It was by the same forces that made the valley floor flat.

By now, if you are an angler who did not bring a fishing rod, you are wishing you had. This is a fine trout stream. Aquatic insect hatches are very good during May and June. Use terrestrial flies during summer.

The trail turns sharply left before the second left turn in the creek (.6 mi.) **[3]**. You follow an old railroad grade, crossing a footbridge (1 mi.) **[4]** before returning to the trailhead (1.1 mi.) **[1]**.

1. Trailhead
2. Little Pine Creek
3. Leave creek
4. Footbridge

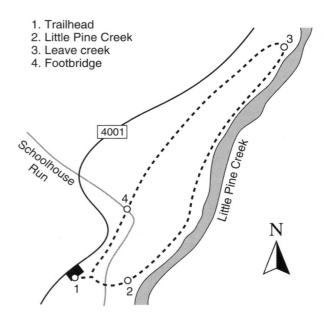

23. Parker Dam State Park

- Witness the results of the largest tornado ever recorded in Pennsylvania.
- Examine relics of 19th-century logging.
- Share a quiet valley with beavers.
- Fish for a variety of warm-water and cold-water species.

Area Information

Like many of Pennsylvania's older state parks, Parker Dam State Park has its roots in the CCC. The CCC built a dam here in 1934, but it was destroyed by the great flood of 1936. Two years later it was replaced by the present dam. The CCC built stone picnic shelters, the visitor center, the interpretive center, and the family cabins. All of the original forest had been cleared by loggers during the previous century, so the CCC also did considerable planting of trees.

The 20-acre lake is stocked with trout by the Pennsylvania Fish and Boat Commission during spring, and again for the ice fishing season. Anglers also catch largemouth bass, crappies, bluegills, and catfish. Nonpowered boats and electric-powered boats are allowed on the lake. A large, sandy swimming beach attracts summer crowds.

Directions: The entrance to Parker Dam State Park is off Pennsylvania Route 253 between Interstate Route 80 and the village of Penfield. The turnoff from Route 253 onto Mud Run Road is well marked. The park is about 2 miles down this road.

Hours Open: The park is open from 8:00 A.M. to sunset year-round.

Facilities: The park is open to nonpowered and electric-powered boating, and there is a sandy swimming beach. Rowboats and paddleboats are available to rent in season. There are 110 campsites for tents or RVs, with showers and sanitary dumping facilities, and 16 family cabins, all of which can be reserved. A food concession is located near the swimming beach. Picnic tables and pavilions, some with electricity, are dispersed around the park. An environmental interpretive program is conducted during summer. There are also ballfields, playgrounds, and volleyball areas.

Permits and Rules: Alcoholic beverages are prohibited. Boats must have either a state park launching permit, a state park mooring permit, or a current Pennsylvania Fish and Boat Commission registration. Outdoor recreational activities are restricted to locations where signs or physical improvements designate the appropriate use. Fires and the disposal of hot coals are restricted to provided facilities. Trash and litter must be placed in containers provided for this purpose, and disposal is limited to items accumulated during the use of the park. Pets must be leashed and controlled at all times, and they are not allowed at the swimming area or in overnight camping facilities. Do not feed waterfowl.

Further Information: Parker Dam State Park, RD 1, Box 165, Penfield, PA 15849-9799; phone 814-765-0630.

Other Areas of Interest

Moshannon State Forest, Forest District 9, P.O. Box 952, Clearfield, PA 16830; phone 814-965-3741.

Park Trails

Trail of New Giants 👢👢👢—1 mile—This trail was cut through the path of a 1985 tornado that was the worst ever recorded in the state. This area has been set aside as the Windstorm Natural Area.

Skunk Trail 👢👢👢—1.4 miles—This trail connects Souder's Trail with Mud Run Road. Hikers see a second-growth hardwood forest.

Logslide/Stumpfield Trails 👢👢👢—1.2 miles— A pipeline connects these trails, forming a loop that passes a re-creation of a log slide and a succession forest.

Parker Dam State Park

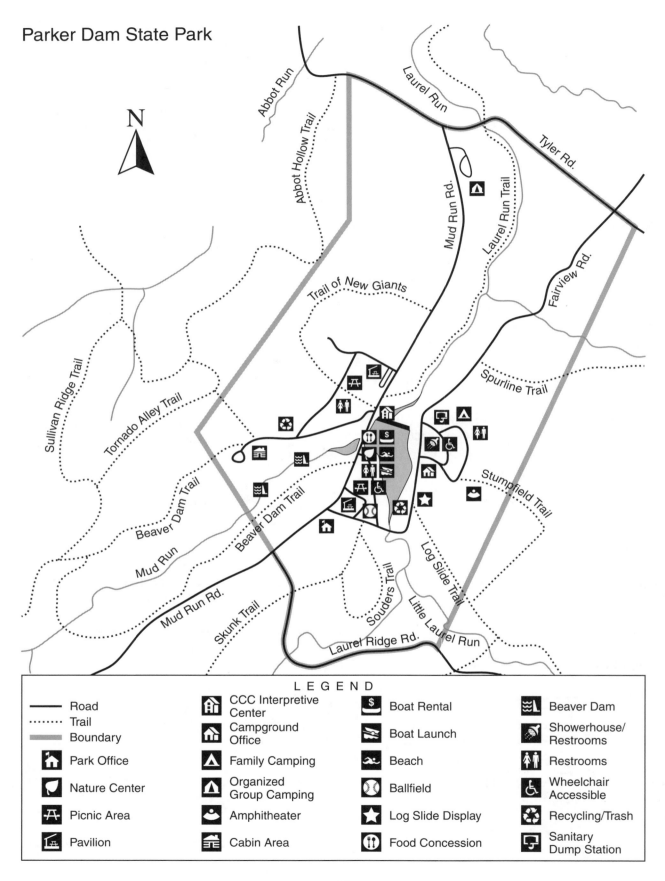

N

LEGEND

—— Road	CCC Interpretive Center	$ Boat Rental	Beaver Dam
···· Trail	Campground Office	Boat Launch	Showerhouse/Restrooms
▬▬ Boundary	Family Camping	Beach	Restrooms
Park Office	Organized Group Camping	Ballfield	Wheelchair Accessible
Nature Center	Amphitheater	Log Slide Display	Recycling/Trash
Picnic Area	Cabin Area	Food Concession	Sanitary Dump Station
Pavilion			

Beaver Dam Trail 🥾🥾

Distance Round-Trip: 2.8 miles

Estimated Hiking Time: 1.25 hours

Caution: Numerous roots stick up through the trail in some areas. Wear a piece of bright orange clothing if you hike here during hunting season. Do not take pets on this hike since they are not allowed in the cabin area through which you will pass.

Trail Directions: The trailhead **[1]** is off Mud Run Road between park headquarters and the lake, going from park headquarters on the left by the restrooms. There is a large parking area here. This trail loops through a shallow valley that has been set aside for the propagation of beavers. Hike it early in the morning or in the evening for the best chances of seeing beavers, white-tailed deer, gray squirrels, and other wildlife.

As you face the restrooms from the road, the trail goes to the right of the restrooms and swings left into the woods. After the second small footbridge, you enter a dense hemlock stand, emerge into a small opening after about 500 feet, then go back into mixed forest that includes cherry, maple, hemlock, and oak. You are very close to Mud Run Road when you begin following a straight, wide grade (.6 mi.) **[2]**. Clues to the history of this grade are shallow depressions that run across the grade. This is where railroad ties have rotted away. This railroad was used to haul timber.

Along this old railroad grade, you pass through a red pine plantation. Virtually all of the trees in this area were cut during the 19th century. The CCC planted numerous pines during the 1930s. The trail swings away from the road at about the end of the pine plantation 1.1 mi. from the trailhead **[3]**, going gently down to Mud Run, where you cross a long boardwalk. This is the upper end of your loop. The creek is slow moving and meandering. Downstream to your right is a beaver pond.

Turn right after crossing the footbridge to a bench that you can already see (1.3 mi.) **[4]**. Stop here and study the beaver dam and pond. Is this an old pond or a new pond? The amount of sediment in the pond gives you the answer. There is so much sediment that small grassy islands have formed. Slightly to your left is the beaver lodge, a large, rounded pile of sticks. Entrances to it are underwater, which provides protection from predators and gives beavers access under the ice, where they store food, during winter. Farther to the left is the dam. You have heard the

phrase "busy as a beaver." Think how busy beavers were constructing that dam one stick at a time. In front of you is a wooden box on a pole. This is a human-made wood duck nesting box, meant to replicate a hollow tree.

You might also see wildlife that you do not normally see in a forest. Red-winged blackbirds nest along the edges of the pond. Cedar waxwings and other birds catch insects in flight. If you see an animal swimming that is too small to be a beaver, it might be a muskat. Raccoons and mink hunt along the shoreline. This large forest opening created by beavers provides the forest with habitat diversity.

Past the bench, the trail swings uphill to the left, out of the open area and, by a large white oak, into mixed forest. You reach an intersection with Snow Trail (1.6 mi.) **[5]** after a moderate climb. Turn right at this T, going into a gentle decline. Gray squirrels are abundant in this mixed forest of maple, oak, hemlock, beech, and hickory. A bench on this slope is a good place to sit quietly and watch for squirrels, turkeys, and deer.

The end of the trail is at the access road in the cabin area (2.2 mi.) **[6]**. Turn left and follow this road to Mud Run Road. You can take a shortcut through a picnic area and past a pavilion to Mud Run Road (2.8 mi.) **[7]**. Turn right, crossing a causeway over the lake, back to the trailhead where you began **[1]**. You pass a food concession along the way. The total distance of the loop is 2.8 mi.

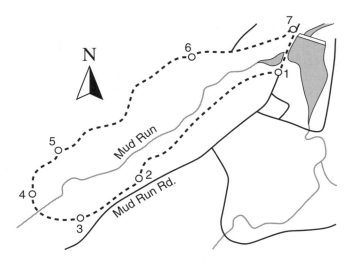

1. Trailhead
2. Railroad grade
3. Leave railroad
4. Beaver pond bench
5. Snow Trail
6. Cabin area
7. Mud Run Road

Souders Trail 🥾🥾

Distance Round-Trip: 1 mile

Estimated Hiking Time: .5 hour

Caution: Watch for black bears when blueberries are in season. Wear bright orange clothing during hunting season.

Trail Directions: Turn off Mud Run Road at the park office. Park in the large picnic area to the left. Walk down the road about 350 feet to the trailhead on your right, which is marked by a sign **[1]**. This sign notes that the trail was built by the Neighborhood Youth Corps. Walk past the sign into a secondary-growth forest of red maple, black cherry, hemlock, and oak. The forest floor is dominated by ferns, indicating a high deer population. Do you know why?

You will pass the rotting remains of several numbered posts along the trail. This was an interpretive trail with a brochure to explain each post, but this program was discontinued. You will have to interpret on your own. A field guide to trees will be helpful.

Look at the rotting tree stumps. These are reminders of a logging boom more than a century ago. Examine a pine tree on your left. It is just clinging to life. Part of its split trunk is dead. Woodpeckers have made numerous holes in it. Some might lead to dens in the hollow trunk, perhaps used by birds or flying squirrels. One of the biggest threats to several wildlife species is the lack of den trees. The trail splits after about 300 feet. Take the left fork. You will be returning on the other fork.

After passing a small forest opening, watch for a birch tree growing out of a stump. You will pass a bench just as the trail starts climbing up a hillside. Look at the trees to your left, on the downhill side of the trail, then at the trees uphill to your right. How are they different, and why? Examine the sandstone boulders scattered on the forest floor. Why would there be sandstone here?

Past the bench, the trail drops again, with the help of steps, close to Laurel Run. Here you will see a sign that explains the stone wall in front of you (.3 mi.) **[2]**. This stone wall was built during the 19th century to maintain water depth and channel logs that were floated down to Parker Dam. A small spur trail forks left to the creek here. It is hard to imagine logs floating on this small creek. Splash dams were built across the creek, then broken to create a torrent deep enough to float huge pine logs.

Continue by walking along the stone wall. The trail swings away from the creek, where you pass an unusually large white pine between the trail and the creek. It might have escaped the loggers' axes because its trunk divides, making it useless for lumber.

Soon you come into an open area that is covered with blueberry bushes. Blueberries are a favorite food of black bears and make great pies. Small pine trees are beginning to invade the edge of this opening. The trail swings right out of the opening, across a footbridge (.55 mi.) **[3]**, and starts winding uphill. This is the apex of the loop.

The climb is gentle at first. Steps ease the steepest part of the climb near the top of the hill. There is a split-log bench here, just before you reach a T at the intersection with Skunk Trail (.7 mi.) **[4]**. You can see a long way through the forest here because there is little low vegetation. Notice how the forest is different here than it was at the valley floor. The melodies of songbirds may be broken by the cawing of crows. And you might be treated to the sight of a pileated woodpecker, a crow-size bird that makes the large holes you have seen in dead tree trunks.

You begin dropping gently after the intersection with Skunk Trail. The trail is wider. Turn left where the loop completes, back to the edge of the road (1 mi.) **[1]**. Turn left to return to the parking area.

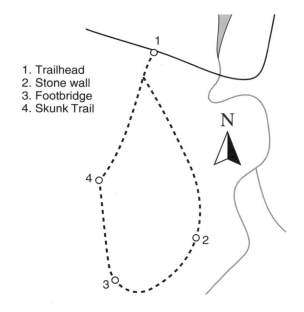

1. Trailhead
2. Stone wall
3. Footbridge
4. Skunk Trail

24. Black Moshannon State Park

- Explore the finest human-made bog in Pennsylvania, and see plants that are usually not found in this state.
- Beat summer heat at high elevations, and swim in the cool lake.
- Fish for bass, chain pickerel, and panfish in Black Moshannon Lake and for trout below the dam in Black Moshannon Creek and other nearby streams.

Area Information

Black Moshannon State Park, its name derived from a Native American word meaning "moose stream" and for its dark, tannin-stained water, is situated on the Allegheny Front, the line where the Allegheny Plateau meets the Appalachian Mountains. This is a large park, 3,394 acres, which contains 250-acre Black Moshannon Lake. The dam that creates this lake was constructed by lumbermen who built it on the site of a beaver dam. Some of the finest timber in the state was cut here, including white pines that were six feet in diameter. The bog around the lake formed when all of the trees were removed because the underlying sandstone is so close to the surface that drainage is poor.

The park was developed by the CCC and the WPA during the 1930s. Today the area around the bog is again forested, though the original white pine/hemlock forest is replaced by a secondary growth of hardwoods mixed with hemlock and red pine plantations.

Directions: The park can be reached by Pennsylvania Route 504 between Philipsburg and U.S. Route 220 at Unionville.

Hours Open: The park is open from 8:00 A.M. to sunset year-round.

Facilities: The 80-site family camping area for tents or trailers has washhouses with showers, a sanitary dump station, and flush toilets. Rustic and modern cabins can be rented weekly during summer and daily at other times. Nonpowered and electric-powered boating, fishing, and swimming are permitted in the lake. Two miles of bike trails are connected to other trails in Moshannon State Forest.

Permits and Rules: Alcoholic beverages are prohibited. Boats must have either a state park launching permit, a state park mooring permit, or a current Pennsylvania Fish and Boat Commission registration. Outdoor recreational activities are restricted to locations where signs or physical improvements designate the appropriate use. Fires and the disposal of hot coals are restricted to provided facilities. Trash and litter must be placed in containers provided for this purpose, and disposal is limited to items accumulated during the use of the park. Pets must be leashed and controlled at all times, and they are not allowed at the swimming area or in overnight camping facilities.

Further Information: Department of Conservation and Natural Resources, Black Moshannon State Park, RR 1, Box 183, Philipsburg, PA 16866-9519; phone 814-342-5960.

Other Areas of Interest

Moshannon State Forest surrounds Black Moshannon State Park. It contains the Quehanna Wild Area, the Marion Brooks Natural Area, and an extensive trail system. Write to District Forester, Bureau of Forestry, P.O. Box 341, Clearfield, PA 16830; phone 814-765-3741.

Park Trails

Moss-Hanne Trail —7.4 miles—Explore the Moshannon Bog Natural Area on this winding path. Boardwalks traverse otherwise inaccessible areas, yet it is still advisable to wear waterproof footwear. The full loop is 10.7 miles.

Indian Trail —1 mile—See a variety of habitats, including hawthorns and barberry bushes. Combine it with Seneca Trail and Hay Road Trail to form a loop.

Sleepy Hollow Trail —.6 mile—Examine a selective cut area, where specific trees were selected to be harvested.

Tent Hill Trail —.5 mile—This trail connects the camping area to park headquarters and the swimming beach.

Aspen Trail —.9 mile—An alternative route for a portion of Moss-Hanne Trail, this trail offers a glimpse of giant pine stumps and an aspen stand.

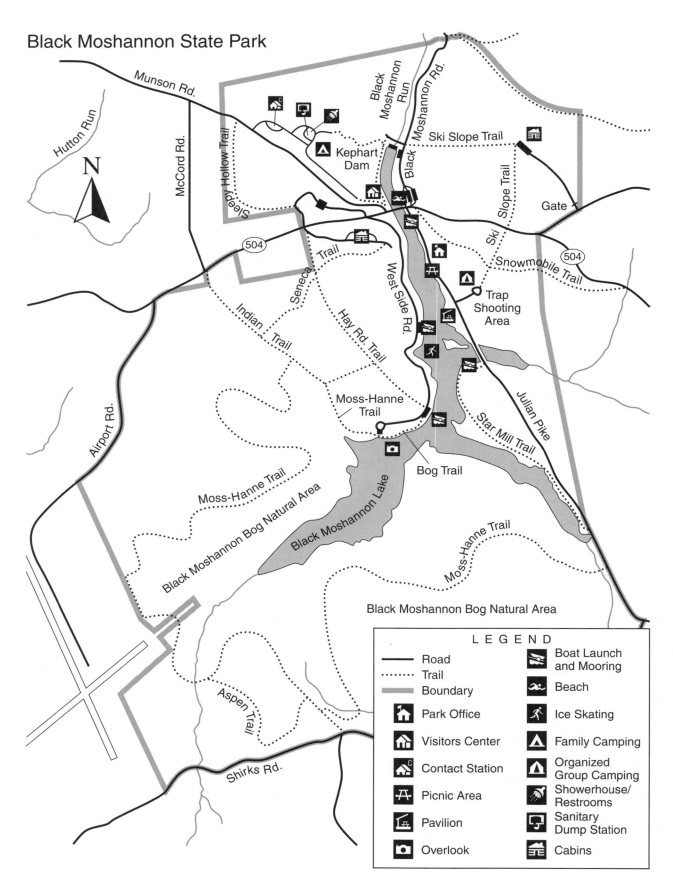

Black Moshannon State Park

Munson Rd.

Hutton Run

McCord Rd.

Sleepy Hollow Trail

Black Moshannon Run

Black Moshannon Rd.

Ski Slope Trail

Kephart Dam

Gate

504

Seneca Trail

Indian Trail

Hay Rd. Trail

West Side Rd.

Ski Slope Trail

Snowmobile Trail

504

Trap Shooting Area

Airport Rd.

Moss-Hanne Trail

Moss-Hanne Trail

Black Moshannon Bog Natural Area

Black Moshannon Lake

Bog Trail

Star Mill Trail

Julian Pike

Moss-Hanne Trail

Aspen Trail

Shirks Rd.

Black Moshannon Bog Natural Area

LEGEND

—	Road		Boat Launch and Mooring
····	Trail		Beach
▬	Boundary		Ice Skating
🏠	Park Office		Family Camping
🏠	Visitors Center		Organized Group Camping
🏠	Contact Station		Showerhouse/ Restrooms
⛱	Picnic Area		Sanitary Dump Station
🏛	Pavilion		Cabins
📷	Overlook		

Star Mill Trail 🥾🥾

Distance Round-Trip: 1.95 miles (includes return by Julian Pike)

Estimated Hiking Time: 1 hour

Caution: Expect biting insects during spring and early summer. Some places are soggy. Be cautious of vehicles during the return along Julian Pike.

Trail Directions: From Route 504, turn onto Julian Pike, past park headquarters to Boat Mooring Area No. 4. The trailhead **[1]** is at the end of the parking area, near the boat launch ramp, and is marked with a sign. From here, the trail follows the edge of the lake, providing close-up views of both aquatic and forest habitats. You will be following yellow trail blazes.

Walk beneath overhanging hemlock limbs to start the trail. Enjoy the yellow flowers of pickerelweed and the white flowers of lilies on the water while you walk through a forest that is a mix of hemlock, pine, oak, maple, birch, cherry, rhododendron, blueberry, and many other plants and shrubs. This edge between forest and aquatic habitats provides a rich environment for diverse wildlife.

Your chances of observing wildlife improve if you move quietly. This is one of the better places around the lake to see waterfowl. During summer, Canada geese are plentiful. You may also see mallards and wood ducks. Soon after the ice melts during late winter, and again when the cold north winds blow during late fall, black ducks, common mergansers, hooded mergansers, teal, ring-necked ducks, and other waterfowl from the north are common visitors. Wetlands such as this are valuable stopovers for migrating waterfowl where they can rest and feed. Watch for green herons during the morning or evening. Red-winged blackbirds nest and feed along the edges of the lake. You might even see crows feeding as they walk over floating vegetation. Deer browse in the forest. Mink and raccoons search along the shoreline for food. Songbirds fill the trees.

Watch for the yellow blazes and ignore several short trails between cabins on your left and the lake on your right. You pass through a red pine plantation about .2 mi. from the trailhead. These were planted to replace the white pine/hemlock forest that once stood here. Rotting stumps are a reminder of that old-growth forest. Hemlock and red maple have invaded this pine plantation in places. Observe how the composition of the forest changes, in some places dominated by hemlocks, in others by hardwoods. Can you guess why?

The strip of land between the lake and Julian Pike narrows before you reach a bench (.9 mi.) **[2]**. Pause here for a last chance to study the flora and fauna. There is a wood duck box, a human-made box on a pole intended for use as a wood duck nest, just past the bench. Note that there is nothing to prevent predators from entering the nest, so the chances of a successful nest are not good. The end of the trail is just ahead at Julian Pike (1 mi.) **[3]**. Watch for traffic if you return to the trailhead by way of Julian Pike.

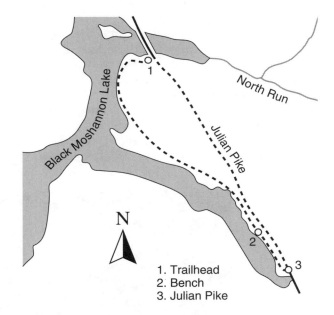

1. Trailhead
2. Bench
3. Julian Pike

Bog Trail 🥾

Distance Round-Trip: .47 mile (including return by West Side Road)

Estimated Hiking Time: 20 minutes

Caution: Carry insect repellent for mosquitoes and other biting insects.

Trail Directions: From Route 504, turn onto West Side Road. The trailhead **[1]** is at the far end of Boating Area No. 2, as indicated by a wooden post sign. This trail, which is accessible to wheelchairs, is short but sweet. Bring binoculars to watch birds and field guides for identifying birds and aquatic plants. The best variety of waterfowl can be seen during spring and fall migrations.

The trail begins on a smooth raised path through thick hemlocks for 180 feet, then continues along a boardwalk across the boggy edge of Black Moshannon Lake. You will see rotting stumps surrounded by pickerelweed and white lilies in the shallow water to the left, reminders of the forest that once stood here. When blueberries are ripe, you can pick them from the trail. A short distance to the right is the edge of the forest, primarily hemlock and rhododendron that conceal hardwoods farther from the water.

Turn left onto an observation deck at .2 mi. **[2]**. Signs on this viewing area explain the bog habitat. Some of the birds you might see here are great blue herons, common yellowthroats, swamp sparrows, Canada geese, song sparrows, mallards, wood ducks, and green herons. During spring or fall migrations

you might also see blue-winged teal, horned grebes, black ducks, mergansers, scaup, canvasbacks, and tundra swans. This is on the Atlantic Flyway, a major migration route for waterfowl that breed in the Arctic and sub-Arctic tundra.

Return to the main trail and turn left, where the trail turns back into the forest and the boardwalk ends. You pass an intersection with Moss-Hanne Trail, which forks left, then reach the end of Bog Trail at West Side Road (.3 mi.) **[3]**. A sign here notes that the Black Moshannon Bog Natural Area is the finest reconstituted bog area in the state. It contains numerous rare plants. You can either backtrack or return to the trailhead parking area along West Side Road (.47 mi.) **[1]**. Stop to examine an huge rotting tree trunk beside the road on this return trip.

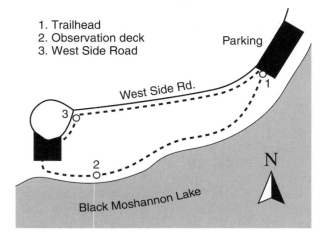

1. Trailhead
2. Observation deck
3. West Side Road

25. Reeds Gap State Park

- Relax in a quiet getaway that's just a short drive from the busy southeastern corner of the state.
- Swim in a guarded and uncrowded pool.
- Learn about forest ecology along one of the better interpretive trails in the Pennsylvania state park system.

Area Information

Reeds Gap State Park, a natural water gap in Thick Mountain, is close enough to the Harrisburg area for a one-day visit, but it is out-of-the-way enough to be serene. The back roads that visitors must travel to get here and the small camping area keep down crowds. As long ago as the 18th century, people recognized the area's beauty and came here for social gatherings.

Edward and Nancy Reed, for whom the area is named, built a dam and a water-powered sawmill in the mid-19th century. Their home still stands just outside the park. Remains of the dam can be seen from Honey Creek Trail. A steam-powered sawmill was built near the present park maintenance building around 1900.

The state bought the land in 1904, after the original forest was eliminated. The park was built by the CCC and dedicated in 1938. Swimming pools to replace an old dam that was constructed by the CCC were built in 1965, along with other facilities in later years.

Directions: Finding Reeds Gap State Park is a little more difficult compared to other state parks. Watch carefully for signs along narrow, winding roads. Some signs are small. Turn off U.S. Route 322 at Milroy and follow the signs for 7 miles. New Lancaster Valley Road passes through the park.

Hours Open: The park is open from 8:00 A.M. to sunset.

Facilities: There are 14 tent-only campsites, two guarded swimming pools, picnic tables, picnic pavilions, and a food concession adjacent to the swimming area.

Permits and Rules: Alcoholic beverages are prohibited. Boats must have either a state park launching permit, a state park mooring permit, or a current Pennsylvania Fish and Boat Commission registration. Outdoor recreational activities are restricted to locations where signs or physical improvements designate the appropriate use. Fires and the disposal of hot coals are restricted to provided facilities. Trash and litter must be placed in containers provided for this purpose, and disposal is limited to items accumulated during the use of the park. Pets must be leashed and controlled at all times, and they are not allowed at the swimming area or in overnight camping facilities.

Further Information: Department of Conservation and Natural Resources, Reeds Gap State Park, 1405 New Lancaster Valley Road, Milroy, PA 17063-9735; phone 717-667-3622.

Other Areas of Interest

Bald Eagle State Forest borders the park. See virgin timber at Snyder-Middleswarth State Forest Picnic Area and spectacular views along Locust Ridge Road and Siglerville-Millheim Pike. Write to Bald Eagle State Forest, P.O. Box 147, Laurelton, PA 17835; phone 717-922-3344.

Park Trails

Flicker Path —.5 mile—Hike through forested hillside from a picnic area near the west end of the park to an intersection with Blue Jay Trail near the northernmost point of the park by Reeds Gap Run. This can be used as an alternate route for a section of Blue Jay Trail.

Honey Creek Trail —1.8 miles—Loop through the southern third of the park and through Bald Eagle State Forest.

Reeds Gap State Park

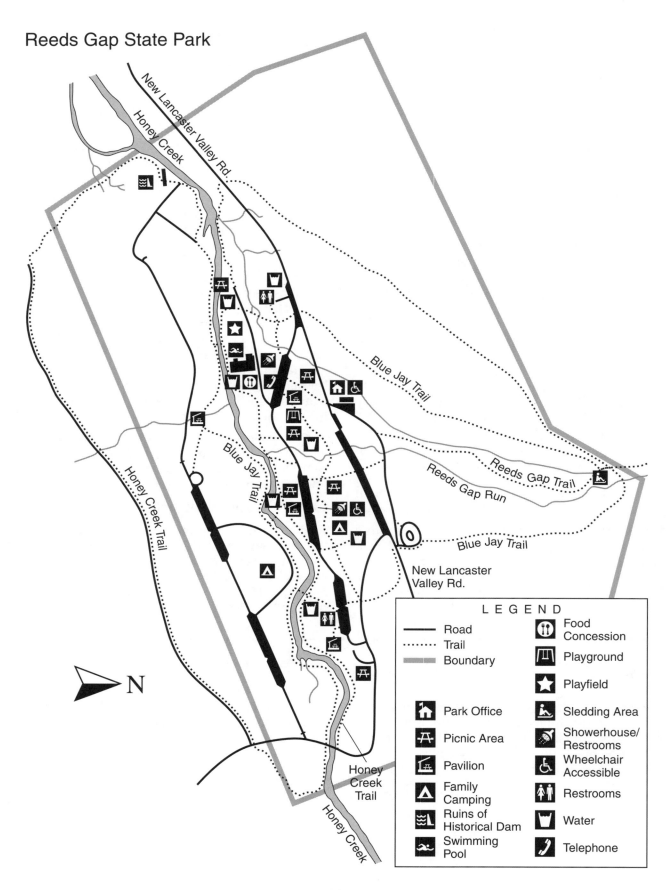

New Lancaster Valley Rd

Honey Creek

Blue Jay Trail

Blue Jay Trail

Reeds Gap Trail

Reeds Gap Run

Blue Jay Trail

Honey Creek Trail

New Lancaster Valley Rd.

Honey Creek Trail

Honey Creek

N

L E G E N D

—— Road	Food Concession
···· Trail	Playground
▓▓ Boundary	Playfield
Park Office	Sledding Area
Picnic Area	Showerhouse/ Restrooms
Pavilion	Wheelchair Accessible
Family Camping	Restrooms
Ruins of Historical Dam	Water
Swimming Pool	Telephone

Blue Jay Trail 👢👢👢

Distance Round-Trip: 1.45 miles

Estimated Hiking Time: 1 hour

Caution: Part of the trail is the border to the area of the park that is open to hunting. Wear bright orange clothing during hunting season. Watch blue trail blazes because ground traces of the trail disappear in places.

Trail Directions: From New Lancaster Valley Road, which runs through the park east to west, turn onto State Park Road, a one-way road that accesses all of the park day-use facilities. Go to Lot C, the last of three large parking areas along State Park Road. Blue Jay Trail is a loop, so there are several convenient places to begin a hike. Use Lot C because it is farthest from most park activity. Blue Jay Trail passes through the middle of this parking area by the restrooms. Use a walkway that crosses a ditch as the trailhead **[1].** Begin walking uphill through a pine plantation. After just a few steps you cross Reeds Valley Road. The trail is not visible, but you will see blue paint blazes ahead. Then at .07 mi. you cross New Lancaster Valley Road **[2].** Watch for traffic before crossing both roads.

Cross the road, angling left to a dirt track road that forks left three times. Keep going straight uphill past the forks, following the blue blazes into a dense second-growth forest. From here, the trail is clearly visible until you loop back down to New Lancaster Valley Road. Try to identify the mix of hemlock, maple, and oak trees. Principal species are red maple, red oak, and chestnut oak. You will also pass hickory trees. Farther uphill are numerous young white pine, and the ground becomes rockier.

You will see a very steep slope to your right where the trail reaches its maximum elevation and turns left. Immediately you drop to Reeds Gap Run and cross a footbridge (.4 mi.) **[3].** Feel the cool air near the stream. Watch for warblers in the low bushes. About 75 feet past the footbridge you reach an intersection with Reeds Gap Trail and Flicker Trail. Turn left onto a service road past a trail registry and a bench. This registry is for hikers who use Reeds Gap Trail to access Mid-State Trail. Blue Jay Trail cuts right off the service road after a few steps. Look for the blue blazes.

You now begin a comfortable descent that angles along the side of a steep slope. Watch for signs of wildlife. Wild turkeys, white-tailed deer, black bears, gray squirrels, and many smaller animals inhabit the area. Except for a small forest opening above the park dump area, it is all second-growth forest down to the

highway. The trail might be hard to distinguish across the opening, but you should see blue blazes on the opposite side.

Listen to children playing at the swimming pool as you get close to the bottom of the hill. After carefully crossing New Lancaster Valley Road (.87 mi.) **[4],** you will have to watch the trail blazes carefully. Walk straight across the road at the intersection with State Park Road, passing restrooms on your right and a horseshoe pit to your left, through a picnic area, past a marked intersection with Flicker Trail (.97 mi.) **[5],** to the edge of Honey Creek. You might stop for a cool drink at a water fountain between Flicker Trail and the creek. Turn left at the edge of the creek, going upstream to a footbridge.

Cross the footbridge and turn left at an intersection with Honey Creek Trail (1.04 mi.) **[6],** which goes right. A sign marks this intersection. Watch for trout rising to the water surface to feed on insects. Human-made stream improvements have been built in the stream to enhance trout habitat. Hemlock dominates the forest here on the valley floor, shading the creek, which helps keep it cool. This lower section of Blue Jay Trail follows the creek upstream past a second footbridge (1.3 mi.) **[7],** then cross a third footbridge (1.39 mi.) **[8].** You pass the camping area between the second and third footbridges.

Once across the bridge, walk straight uphill to the restrooms that you can see ahead, into the parking lot and back to the trailhead (1.45 mi.) **[1].**

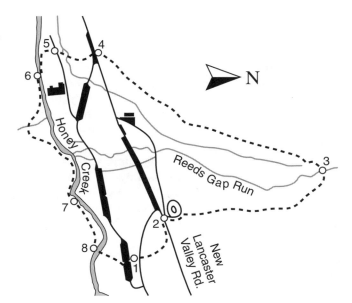

1. Trailhead
2. New Lancaster Valley Road
3. Reeds Gap Run
4. New Lancaster Valley Road
5. Flicker Trail
6. Honey Creek Trail
7. Second footbridge
8. Third footbridge

Interpretive Trail 🥾🥾

Distance Round-Trip: 1 mile

Estimated Hiking Time: .75 hour

Caution: Informational signs indicate that this trail is marked with green blazes, but it is not. Be prepared for biting insects during spring and early summer.

Trail Directions: Turn onto State Park Road, a one-way road, from New Lancaster Valley Road. The trailhead for Interpretive Trail is at a kiosk just below the steps at the lower end of Lot A, behind the food concession **[1]**. This trail circles a section of Honey Creek. It has several information stations that explain important aspects of the forest community. Through the entire length, Interpretive Trail follows the same route as parts of Honey Creek Trail or Blue Jay Trail.

Walk downstream along a dike between the swimming pool and Honey Creek to a footbridge. Turn left across the footbridge, then turn left again upstream to the first information station (.4 mi.) **[2]**, a plaque on a post that explains stream improvements in Honey Creek. Structures made of rock and wood improve trout habitat by creating an equal mix of pools and riffles. Stand very still and you might see trout moving about in the stream, occasionally attacking insects on the water surface.

As you continue upstream, the next information station is by a bench (.5 mi.) **[3]**. It explains how organic material decomposes on the forest floor. This is the process that contributes to the rich layer of topsoil.

The third information station is just past a second footbridge that you do not cross (.6 mi.) **[4]**. You are now at the edge of the tent camping area. This station explains how the forest changes with the seasons. Look around and try to imagine how this scene would be different during other seasons, and why.

Cross the third footbridge over Honey Creek to an information station that explains how the stream and forest are interrelated (.7 mi.) **[5]**. Can you understand why the plant community is different near a stream than it is up the hillside, and why animal life is more diverse close to a stream?

Turn left at this information station and begin moving downstream to an information station about forest layers (.8 mi.) **[6]**. You are now just below the upper end of Lot B, the middle of three large parking areas. Identify the layers of the forest, from the vegetation closest to the ground up to the forest crown, the top branches of the trees. If you study the forest, you will observe that some animals, red squirrels, for example, use the forest from top to bottom, while others primarily use just one layer. Name a few species that are generally seen in just one forest layer. Now, do you understand the relationship between forest layers and biodiversity?

Walk past the middle footbridge over Honey Creek, over a footbridge that crosses a small tributary stream, to an information post about a changing forest (.9 mi.) **[7]**. This station is beside a picnic area, and the trail joins a single-track dirt road. Can you see how human activity has changed the forest here? Imagine how drastically the wildlife community changed when the original hemlock and white pine forest that existed in this area was completely removed by loggers more than a century ago, and how it has regrown since then into a different type of forest.

Walk along the road to the kiosk at the trailhead **[1]**, completing a loop of nearly 1 mi. Apply what you have learned here to other trails.

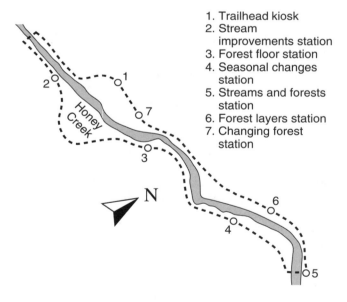

1. Trailhead kiosk
2. Stream improvements station
3. Forest floor station
4. Seasonal changes station
5. Streams and forests station
6. Forest layers station
7. Changing forest station

26. Greenwood Furnace State Park

- Visit the remains of a community that flourished a century ago because of the iron industry.
- Swim in the cool water of Greenwood Lake.
- Walk through a thriving forest that was laid to waste a century ago.

Area Information

The community of Greenwood Furnace was a busy place during the 19th century. Iron furnaces belched orange flames and ugly clouds of smoke into the air, creating a hellish scene. This is the only documented place in the state where two cold-blast furnace remains stand side by side. Cold blasts of air were pumped into the charcoal-fired furnaces by means of a steam engine or water-powered bellows. This was a vital operation in the growth of America. Iron produced here was used primarily to make railroad rails.

About an acre of forest had to be cut each day to make the charcoal to fuel each furnace. The forest around the community quickly disappeared. At one time, 127 buildings stood at Greenwood Furnace, and about 300 workers lived here with their families. Today only a few of those structures remain, but the forest has returned. In the place of the sooty town and the sounds of busy workers is a peaceful park and the sounds of children playing.

A park was established here in 1925, taking advantage of the dam and lake left by the industrial complex. Facilities in the park and surrounding state forest were improved by the CCC during the 1930s. The National Park Service recognized the Greenwood Furnace National Historic District in 1989.

Directions: Pennsylvania Route 305 passes through the park between Ennisville and Belleville, about 40 minutes southeast of State College.

Hours Open: The park is open from 8:00 A.M. to sunset.

Facilities: In addition to the historic remains of the community of Greenwood Furnace, the park offers an interpretive center, tent and trailer campsites, a sanitary dump station, swimming, numerous picnic tables, pavilions, and a food concession.

Permits and Rules: Alcoholic beverages are prohibited. Outdoor recreational activities are restricted to locations where signs or physical improvements designate the appropriate use. Fires and the disposal of hot coals are restricted to provided facilities. Trash and litter must be placed in containers provided for this purpose, and disposal is limited to items accumulated during the use of the park. Pets must be leashed and controlled at all times, and they are not allowed at the swimming area or in overnight camping facilities.

Further Information: Department of Conservation and Natural Resources, Greenwood Furnace State Park, RR 2, Box 118, Huntingdon, PA 16652-9006; phone 814-667-1800.

Other Areas of Interest

Whipple Dam State Park is a day-use facility for swimming, boating, and fishing. **Penn Roosevelt State Park** has primitive camping and picnic facilities by a small lake. For information about either, contact Greenwood Furnace State Park.

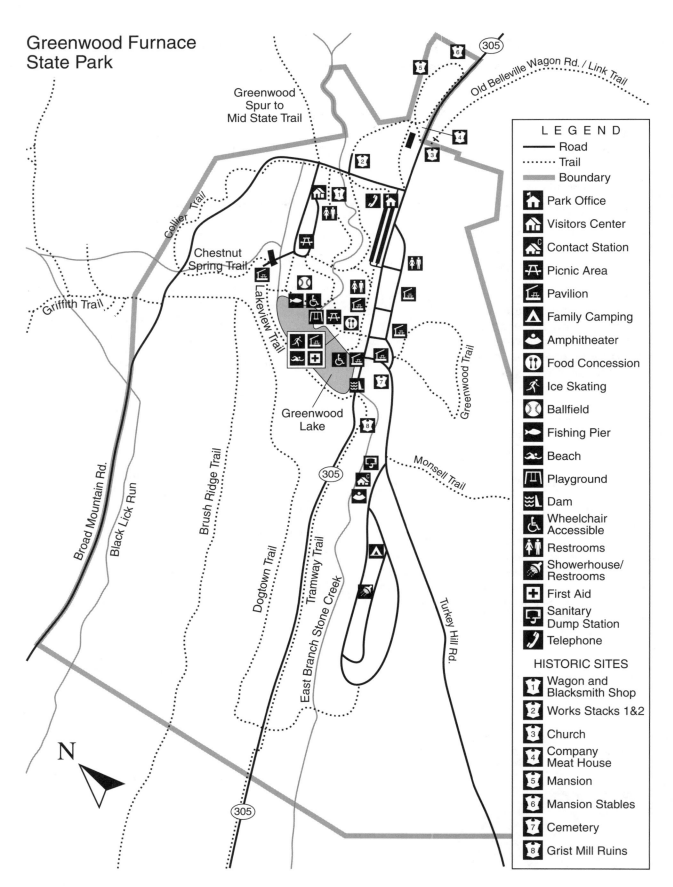

Greenwood Furnace State Park

Greenwood Spur to Mid State Trail

Old Belleville Wagon Rd. / Link Trail

Collier Trail

Chestnut Spring Trail

Griffith Trail

Lakeview Trail

Greenwood Lake

Greenwood Trail

Monsell Trail

Broad Mountain Rd.

Black Lick Run

Brush Ridge Trail

Dogtown Trail

Tramway Trail

East Branch Stone Creek

Turkey Hill Rd.

305

N

LEGEND
- —— Road
- ⋯⋯ Trail
- ▬ Boundary
- Park Office
- Visitors Center
- Contact Station
- Picnic Area
- Pavilion
- Family Camping
- Amphitheater
- Food Concession
- Ice Skating
- Ballfield
- Fishing Pier
- Beach
- Playground
- Dam
- Wheelchair Accessible
- Restrooms
- Showerhouse/ Restrooms
- First Aid
- Sanitary Dump Station
- Telephone

HISTORIC SITES
1. Wagon and Blacksmith Shop
2. Works Stacks 1&2
3. Church
4. Company Meat House
5. Mansion
6. Mansion Stables
7. Cemetery
8. Grist Mill Ruins

Greenwood Trail 👢👢👢

Distance Round-Trip: .6 mile

Estimated Hiking Time: 20 minutes

Caution: Some trail blazes are worn to show silver only.

Trail Directions: The trailhead for Greenwood Trail is in a parking area across Route 305 from the swimming beach. Walk between pavilions #6 and #7 on the gravel road that passes behind pavilion #6 and leads to the family camping area. A worn sign that marks the trailhead is visible on the hillside across the gravel road from pavilion #6 **[1]**.

Watch for round red metal trail blazes on trees. Silver arrows inside silver circles in the middle of these blazes point in the direction of the trail. Begin walking uphill to the left of the trailhead sign into a second-growth forest of oak, maple, hemlock, and pine. This hillside was bare soon after the iron furnaces started operating in 1834, if not before. Nature begins repairing itself immediately, but it took more than 150 years for the present forest to develop.

At first the trail is covered with wood chips, but they soon give way to bare ground as the climb gets steeper. Examine the signs of water erosion on the trail and compare that with the relative lack of erosion where vegetation covers the ground. This should give you some idea of the effects that erosion had after all of the trees were cut from these hills.

The trail takes a hard right turn at the top of the hill (.18 mi.) **[2]**. The next leg of the trail is relatively level, narrow, and rocky. At about .3 mi. you will see two signs that identify trees **[3]**. One is red maple, one of the most common trees in the state; the other is Juneberry. A few steps farther you pass another sign that identifies witch hazel.

The trail makes a hard right again, starting the last and downhill leg (.38 mi.) **[4]**. A sign here identifies rhododendron. Many people do not distinguish between rhododendron and Pennsylvania's state flower, the mountain laurel. But through much of the state, rhododendron is more abundant. It can be identified by its longer leaves.

Switchbacks ease the angle of the trail as the hill gets steeper. In places, the outside of the trail is lined with natural stones. You will pass several interpretive posts. You will see numbers on top of some, but most numbers have weathered away. As in many other state parks, interpretive brochures are no longer available, saving both money and litter. With the bottom of the trail in sight, you will see a sign that identifies black birch (.55 mi.) **[5]**. The trail completes its loop after a distance of .6 mi. **[1]**. You might want to visit a water fountain by pavilion #6. Let the water run for a few seconds. It will get cool.

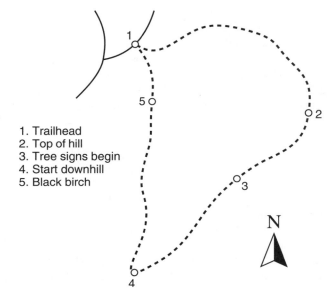

1. Trailhead
2. Top of hill
3. Tree signs begin
4. Start downhill
5. Black birch

A Walk Through Historic Greenwood Furnace 🥾🥾

Distance Round-Trip: 1.8 miles

Estimated Hiking Time: 1 hour

Caution: You will be crossing roads and streets, so watch for traffic. The parts of this route that follow Collier Trail and Chestnut Spring Trail are considerably rougher and steeper than the portion of the trail in the old Greenwood Furnace village. You might wish to eliminate that and make this a much easier trail. Since the reason for this hike is to examine the historic remains of Greenwood Furnace, you will frequently get off the path to investigate specific sites. The distance of this hike is only approximate and does not include side excursions.

Trail Directions: There are numerous places to start this trail. For this description, park by the park headquarters, in a large parking area, and use the intersection of Route 305 and Black Lick Road at park headquarters as the trailhead **[1].** Pick up a brochure entitled "A Walk Through Historic Greenwood Furnace" at park headquarters. It will explain what you will see on this hike. This will be a valuable and unique lesson in American history. Forget about the estimated hiking time. You should spend the better part of a day here.

Walk east on Route 305, passing the old Greenwood Furnace Church on your right and the old company meat house on your left. The church was built about 1865 and is still in use. Turn left by the mansion stables (.2 mi.) **[2],** off Route 305 onto an old road that passes the old mansion, which was home to the furnace manager, his family, and guests. As you continue and pass behind the company meat house, turn right at an intersection, following a road between the furnace stacks. A kiosk gives insight into the heart of the old industrial complex. Try to imagine roaring flames, thick gray smoke, constant noise, and sweaty men constantly working to produce molten iron. This was the heart of the community, its whole reason for existence.

At the furnace stacks, turn right onto Black Lick Road (.5 mi.) **[3].** Follow this road out of the village to the head of Collier Trail (.6 mi.) **[4],** past the bookkeeper's house, which was built in 1863 and is now a private residence. Turn right on Collier Trail and walk through the second-growth forest that has replaced the forest cut to fuel the iron furnaces. You can eliminate this more difficult section of the historic walk by following Black Lick Road to Chestnut Spring Trail and turning left. If you use Collier

Trail, cross Black Lick Road (.9 mi.) **[5]** and continue down Chestnut Spring Trail to a pavilion, then turn right onto Lakeview Trail (1 mi.) **[6].** This small lake was constructed to provide water power for a gristmill constructed in 1842 and to provide water for steam engines and other purposes of the ironworks.

Turn right when you come to Route 305 (1.3 mi.) **[7].** Be careful when you cross the road to the remains of the gristmill and onto Tramway Trail (1.36 mi.) **[8].** Turn left on Tramway Trail, passing the gristmill, looping back to Route 305, across the road from the end of Lakeview Trail (1.4 mi.) **[9].** It does not matter how you make this loop. Its only purpose is to let you see the crumbling foundation of the gristmill that once produced cornmeal and flour for the community. Transportation was a much slower affair a century ago. Communities had to be as self-sufficient as possible.

Follow Route 305 to the first right turn, which is a road to the family camping area. Follow this road to the old cemetery (1.48 mi.) **[10].** Just beyond is the site of the Monsell House, an old boardinghouse that was occupied until the 1960s.

Reverse direction from the cemetery and turn right at the first fork in the gravel road, passing a picnic area and three pavilions on your way back to Route 305 near park headquarters (1.8 mi.) **[1].** All of this is visible from the fork. Instead of going directly back to the trailhead, you might prefer to cross Route 305 to the food concession by the swimming beach.

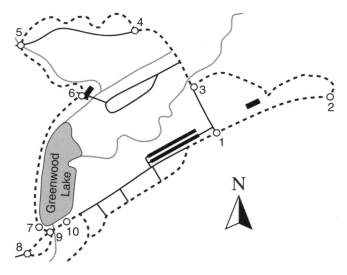

1. Trailhead (at park headquarters)
2. Left by stables
3. Black Lick Road
4. Collier Trail
5. Cross road
6. Lakeview Trail
7. Route 305
8. Tramway Trail
9. Route 305
10. Cemetery

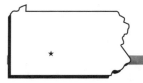

27. Canoe Creek State Park

- Fish for trophy bass and walleyes in Canoe Lake.
- Visit the remains of early-20th-century lime kilns.
- Swim at a guarded beach.

Area Information

Canoe Creek State Park is a day-use facility wrapped around a 155-acre lake. While it provides excellent outdoor recreation, the features that make it unusual are historical. Early in the 20th century, rich lime deposits were extracted for the iron and steel industries as well as for other purposes. Several old lime quarries are in the park. Two lime kilns operated here during the early 1900s. The remains of the Blair Limestone Company Kiln can be seen along Limestone Trail.

This 958-acre park was dedicated in 1979. Areas that have not been developed for recreation are managed to provide a variety of habitats for wildlife, including forest, field, and the marshy edges of the lake. Bird-watchers should be able to identify a wide variety of species, especially during migration periods. Human-made lakes such as Canoe Lake are providing valuable stopovers for waterfowl.

Directions: The park is located about 7 miles east of Hollidaysburg on U.S. Route 22. Turn north on Turkey Valley Road at the village of Canoe Creek and travel about .5 mile to the main park entrance.

Hours Open: The park is open from 8:00 A.M. to sunset.

Facilities: Day-use facilities include boating on Canoe Lake, with boat ramps on the east and west sides of the lake, swimming, picnic pavilions, numerous picnic tables, and trails for hiking and horseback riding.

Permits and Rules: Alcoholic beverages are prohibited. Boats must have either a state park launching permit, a state park mooring permit, or a current Pennsylvania Fish and Boat Commission registration. Only nonpowered and electric-powered boats are allowed. Outdoor recreational activities are restricted to locations where signs or physical improvements designate the appropriate use. Fires and the disposal of hot coals are restricted to provided facilities. Trash and litter must be placed in containers provided for this purpose, and disposal is limited to items accumulated during the use of the park. Pets must be leashed and controlled at all times, and they are not allowed at the swimming area.

Further Information: Department of Conservation and Natural Resources, Canoe Creek State Park, RR 2, Box 560, Hollidaysburg, PA 16648-9752; phone 814-695-6807.

Other Areas of Interest

Contact the **Allegheny Mountains Convention and Visitors Bureau,** Logan Valley Mall, Route 220 and Goods Lane, Altoona, PA 16602; phone 814-943-4183 or 800-84-ALTOONA.

Park Trails

Fisherman's Path 👢👢—1 mile—This trail provides access to the east side of the lake between the dam and a boat launch.

Beaver Pond Trail 👢👢—.7 mile—Follow the lakeshore and Canoe Creek toward the north end of the park.

Moore's Hill Trail 👢👢👢—2.7 miles—Moore's Hill Trail loops around the northern, less developed half of the park from Limestone Trail.

Canoe Creek State Park

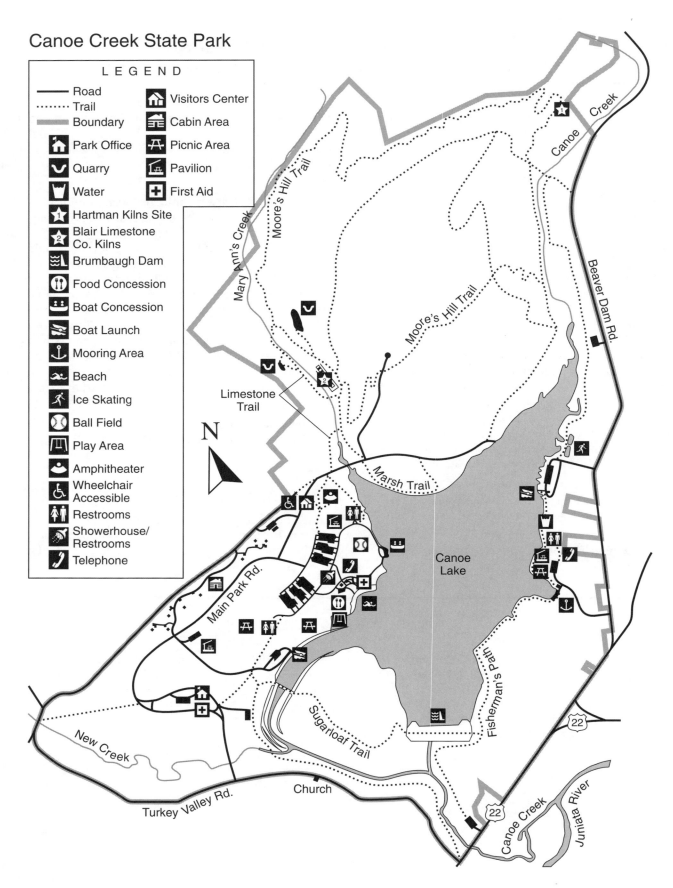

LEGEND

—— Road	🏠 Visitors Center
···· Trail	🏚 Cabin Area
▬▬ Boundary	🪑 Picnic Area
🏠 Park Office	🏛 Pavilion
⩗ Quarry	✚ First Aid
🪣 Water	
★ Hartman Kilns Site	
★2 Blair Limestone Co. Kilns	
〰 Brumbaugh Dam	
🍴 Food Concession	
👥 Boat Concession	
🏊 Boat Launch	
⚓ Mooring Area	
🏖 Beach	
⛸ Ice Skating	
⚾ Ball Field	
🎠 Play Area	
🎭 Amphitheater	
♿ Wheelchair Accessible	
🚻 Restrooms	
🚿 Showerhouse/ Restrooms	
☎ Telephone	

N

Moore's Hill Trail

Mary Ann's Creek

Canoe Creek

Beaver Dam Rd.

Limestone Trail

Marsh Trail

Canoe Lake

Main Park Rd.

Sugarloaf Trail

Fisherman's Path

New Creek

Turkey Valley Rd.

Church

22

22

Canoe Creek

Juniata River

Limestone Trail 👢👢👢

Distance Round-Trip: 1.21 miles

Estimated Hiking Time: 1 hour

Caution: This trail has sections that are steep, though short, with loose rocks in a few places.

Trail Directions: Drive on Main Park Road, following the signs to the Visitor Center Parking Area. A sign also directs you to Limestone Trail at the last turn. The trailhead is across a footbridge at the upper end of the parking area, marked with a sign [1]. This will take you to the small amphitheater on a gravel path, and beyond on mowed grass to a split in the trail.

Take the left fork to a paved road (.13 mi.) [2], turn right and walk 55 feet, then turn left by the first interpretive sign on Limestone Trail. This sign explains that you will take a walk to 1900 when this was the center of a booming limestone industry. The trail leads to a lime kiln and a few old quarries. You will also see the first sign marking this trail, a sign with a silhouette of a lime kiln.

After crossing Mary Ann's Creek you come to a gravel road (.24 mi.) [3]. Turn left and proceed to a fork near the kiln area (.33 mi.) [4]. Turn left across a bridge. You will have the opportunity to examine the kilns on the return leg of this loop. Here the trail is covered with wood chips as it climbs a mild slope through pole timber–size maple to a small footbridge, where the trail surface changes from wood chips to gravel.

Turn left at the next fork to examine a limestone quarry (.45 mi.) [5]. This fork is a narrow, steep gravel path. The quarry is a narrow notch cut out of the hillside, exposing solid limestone. In terms of modern quarries, it is small, maybe 30 feet deep. But remember that equipment was crude 100 years ago. Since operations were abandoned, trees have started to grow out of fallen rocks and on the hillside. Nature eventually reclaims everything. This spur trail continues past the quarry and down a set of steps to the main trail (.5 mi.) [6].

Curve right, crossing a footbridge over Mary Ann's Creek and another, smaller footbridge over a marshy area, then curve sharply to the right again and up a steep slope to an intersection with Moore's Hill Trail (.61 mi.) [7]. Take the right fork to stay on Limestone Trail. This portion of the trail is rocky and moderately steep. Pass by a left fork, which leads to another limestone quarry (.76 mi.) [8]. If you choose to examine this quarry, the spur trail is a round-trip of about .2 mi.

Soon after this spur, you get a view of the lime kilns from above, and you begin descending on a mowed grass path until you reach the Blair Limestone Company Kilns Historic Site. A horse trail forks left adjacent to the kilns (.83 mi.) [9]. Take time to explore the kilns. You can walk in and around them. This was a vital component of the iron and steel industry during the period of America's emergence as a world power before World War I. The United States could not have become the superpower it is today without these kilns. Think about that before you move on.

Moore's Hill Trail also intersects from the left in the kiln area (.86 mi.) [10]. To return to your trailhead, continue down the gravel road and complete the loop at the first footbridge (.87 mi.), then follow your backtrack to the footbridge by your parking area (1.21 mi.) [1].

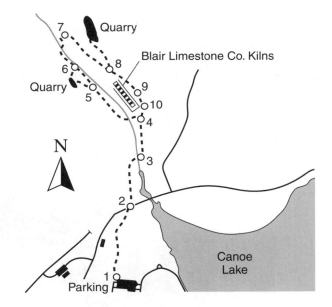

1. Trailhead	6. Main trail
2. Paved road	7. Moore's Hill Trail
3. Gravel road	8. Spur to second quarry
4. Bridge by kilns	9. Horse trail
5. Quarry fork	10. Moore's Hill Trail

Marsh Trail 👢👢

Distance Round-Trip: .9 mile

Estimated Hiking Time: .5 hour

Caution: Watch out for swamp sumac, also known as poison sumac, along this trail. Be prepared to deal with biting insects during spring and early summer. Watch for horses along the road portion of this loop.

Trail Directions: Drive on Main Park Road, following the signs to the Visitor Center Parking Area. A sign also directs you to Limestone Trail at the last turn. The trailhead is across a footbridge at the upper end of the parking area, marked with a sign **[1]**.

Limestone Trail is gravel to a small amphitheater, and grass beyond to a fork. Take the left fork to a paved road (.1 mi.) **[2]**. Turn right on this road. Eighty feet past a bridge, a sign directs you to the right on Marsh Trail (.2 mi.) **[3]**. This is a wide, grassy trail. Watch along both sides for poison sumac. This is a shrub that can grow to a height of 20 feet, though it is not this tall here. It produces a white fruit about the size and texture of blueberries. Its sap can cause painful skin irritation.

Peer through the thick vegetation to your right at a small bay. This is a beautiful scene framed by a mountain ridge in the background. Canada geese and mallards can often be seen here, as well as turtles sunning themselves on logs. During the spring and fall migrations, you might see a larger variety of waterfowl. The marshy lake edge is a rich habitat. Watch for wildlife such as red-winged blackbirds, which nest here, and herons. Raccoons and muskrats might be observed early in the morning or in the evening. The elusive mink is also here, but seldom seen.

Notches have been cut in the thick vegetation to get you closer to the lake. A thick band of cattails line the shore. Is this broad-leaved cattail or narrow-leaved cattail? While you cross a small footbridge, identify duck potato and water lily. How can you distinguish duck potato from pickerelweed or arrow arum?

Marsh Trail turns left toward a T at a road (.5 mi.) **[4]**. This is a paved road, but it has deteriorated to the point that it looks more like a gravel road. Turn left to complete the loop (.7 mi.) **[3]** and retrace your steps to the Limestone Trail head at the Visitor Center Parking Area (.9 mi.) **[1]**. Count all of the rabbits on this return leg.

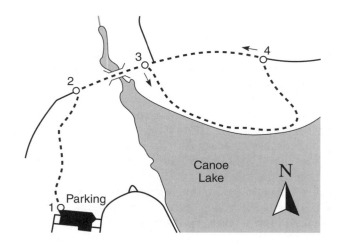

1. Trailhead
2. Paved road
3. Marsh Trail
4. Road T

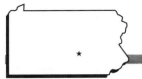

28. Little Buffalo State Park

- Watch a gristmill in operation.
- Visit a car that operated here on a narrow-gauge railroad.
- Hike to secluded fishing spots.
- Swim in a half-acre pool.

Area Information

Little Buffalo State Park covers 380 rolling acres of reverting farmland. Its major feature is 88-acre Holman Lake, an impoundment of Little Buffalo Creek. Trout are stocked various times each year into this lake and into the creek both above and below the lake. Anglers might also catch bass, pickerel, and panfish. Special big bass regulations encourage the growth of trophy bass. Rowboats and canoes can be rented at the boat concession.

Several park features will appeal to history enthusiasts. Shoaff's Mill is a fully restored 18th-century grinding mill that still operates from May through October. A restored railroad car is displayed on the old Sherman's Valley Railroad right-of-way. There are also a restored tavern that began operation in the 1790s, a cemetery that dates to the mid-1700s, and a covered bridge that was repaired after heavy snow crushed part of the roof in 1993.

Directions: Turn west off Pennsylvania Route 34 between New Bloomfield and Newport.

Hours Open: Day-use areas are open from 8:00 A.M. to sunset. The park is open year-round. The swimming pool is open between 11:00 A.M. and 7:00 P.M. from Memorial Day weekend through Labor Day, unless otherwise posted.

Facilities: Lakeside facilities include two boat launches, a boat rental, and a handicapped-accessible fishing pier. There are also a swimming pool, a playground, picnic areas, a food concession, restrooms, and a shower house.

Permits and Rules: Only nonpowered and electric-powered boats are allowed. Boats must display either a state park launch permit or a current Pennsylvania boat registration. Outdoor recreational activities are restricted to locations where physical improvements or signs designate the appropriate use. Fires and disposal of coals are limited to facilities provided. Place trash in designated recycling facilities.

Further Information: Department of Conservation and Natural Resources, Little Buffalo State Park, RR 2, Box 256A, Newport, PA 17074-9428; phone 717-567-9255.

Other Points of Interest

Hoverter & Sholl Box Huckleberry Natural Area, located about a mile south of New Bloomfield, is a 10-acre area that contains a rare colony of box huckleberry. This is a single plant estimated to be 1,300 years old. Contact District Forester, Box 67, Blain, PA 17006; phone 717-536-3191.

For information about local private attractions, contact **Perry County Tourist and Recreation Bureau,** Box 447, New Bloomfield, PA 17068; phone 717-834-4912.

Park Trails

Exercise Trail 👢👢👢—1.2 miles—Various exercises are suggested at numbered stations.

North Side Trail 👢👢👢👢—2.5 miles—Watch for poison ivy along the most difficult trail in the park. It can be combined with other trails to form a loop around the park.

Creek Side Trail 👢👢—1 mile—Watch for wildlife along Little Buffalo Creek, or try your luck at fishing.

Little Buffalo State Park

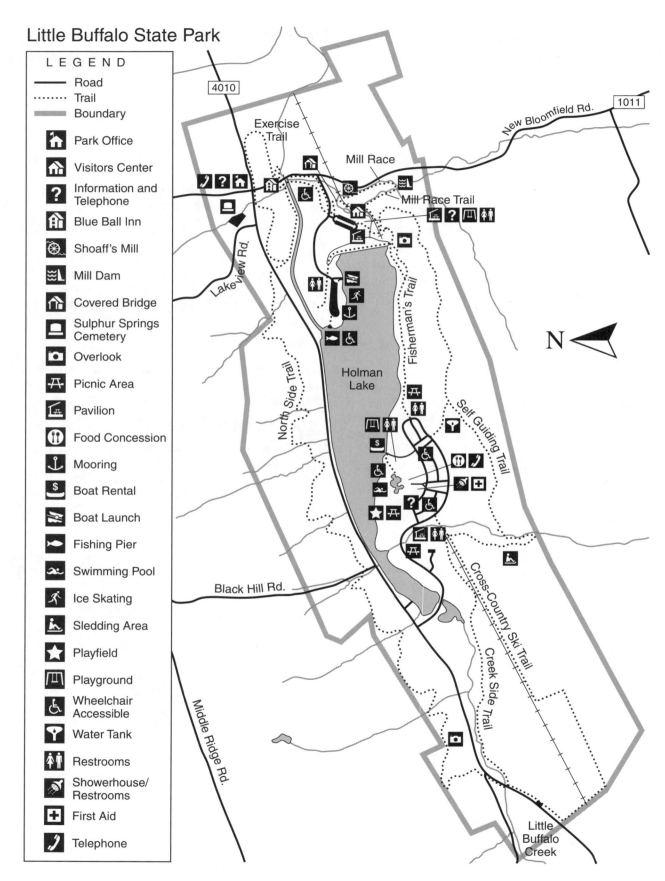

Mill Race Trail 🥾🥾

Distance Round-Trip: .6 mile

Estimated Hiking Time: Less than .5 hour

Caution: You could get your feet wet along this trail. Watch for slippery rocks and poison ivy.

Trail Directions: From State Route 4010 near park headquarters, take New Bloomfield Road, State Route 1011, south about 1,000 feet to the access road to a parking lot below the Holman Lake Dam and the boat mooring area. Begin this hike at the entrance to the parking lot, by a gate and a sign that points to the mill **[1]**. A pleasant little trail, Mill Race Trail takes you on an historical tour. You will learn how an old grist, or grinding, mill works.

Begin walking along an access road. After just .05 mi., you cross Clay's Bridge **[2]**, a covered wooden span over the original Little Buffalo Creek bed. Just after the bridge, go straight up a set of stairs onto an abandoned railroad grade. This is the old Newport and Sherman's Valley Railroad right-of-way. Notice how much narrower it is than a modern railroad. It was built in 1880 to haul lumber, tanbark (bark used to tan leather), freight, and passengers. You can see Shoaff's Mill to your left. Turn right. You will get a closer look at the mill as you complete this short loop.

Walking is easy on the level railroad grade. After crossing a small creek at .13 mi., you should see a sign indicating a left turn for Mill Race Trail **[3]**. White arrows on trees mark the trail, which follows up the creek. Stones, roots, and a gentle incline make footing a bit more difficult. As a small footbridge comes into sight you will cross a wet area, climb a short set of steps, then turn left onto the footbridge **[4]** (.3 mi.). Look to your right at the small dam. A gate in this dam, when closed, directs water into the mill race. This water powers the wheel that turns the grinding stones at Shoaff's Mill.

As you walk along the dike on the lower side of the millrace, notice how it was constructed by digging a long trench and piling the dirt on the downhill side to form the dike. The size of some of the trees growing on the dike indicates how long ago it was constructed. Shortly before reaching the mill you will see the scoop that was used to dig the millrace after the ground had been loosened by a plow.

Shoaff's Mill **[5]** is a distance of .52 mi. from the beginning of this hike. It was constructed in the 1830s to grind wheat and buckwheat flour, cornmeal, and livestock feed. Operations ceased in the 1940s. After restoration, it is now operated for demonstration. Several grindstones are on display in front of the mill. From here you can see to your left the covered bridge you crossed as you were starting the hike. Return the way you came.

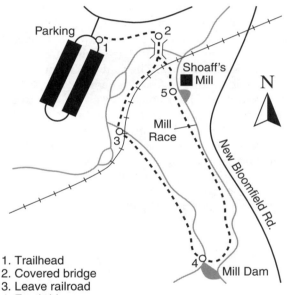

1. Trailhead
2. Covered bridge
3. Leave railroad
4. Footbridge
5. Shoaff's Mill

Fisherman's Trail 🥾🥾🥾

Distance Round-Trip: 2.52 miles

Estimated Hiking Time: 1.5 hours

Caution: While most of this trail is level, in some places rocks interfere with footing.

Trail Directions: A peaceful forest trail with excellent views of Holman Lake, Fisherman's Trail starts by the restrooms at the end of the parking lot by the Holman Lake Dam **[1]**. You reach this by taking New Bloomfield Road, State Route 1011, south for about 1,000 feet from park headquarters. A wood sign here shows park trails. Walk between the sign and the restrooms and continue between pavilion #3 and the Moore Pavilion. Cross the small creek, which is an outflow from the dam. Just past the creek is an old railroad car that was used on the Newport and Sherman's Valley Railroad. Take time to look at this car to see how people traveled a century ago. If we can overlook how much slower transportation was then, it seems like a very pleasant way to travel.

After a sharp left then a sharp right, you come to a set of steps **[2]** (.09 mi.). The trail forks just above the steps. A sign indicates that Fisherman's Trail is the right fork. Switchbacks make the climb less grueling here. Hemlock trees dominate the forest, providing cool shade. Yellow dots and white arrows on trees mark the trail. Soon the lake becomes visible to the right. The best view is at a scenic overlook **[3]**, .18 mi. from starting the trail. You will want to pause here, lean against the wood fence or sit on the bench to catch your breath from the climb, and take in the peaceful setting. Notice that hardwoods dominate the forest on the opposite side of the lake.

The trail begins to drop gently after the overlook. More boulders protrude from the ground in this area, possibly making it difficult to follow the trail. But you should have no difficulty if you watch for the yellow dots and white arrows.

At .33 mi. **[4]**, another trail intersects from the right on an acute angle. Fisherman's Trail becomes wider and more level with better footing at this point. Anglers may be tempted to stop to wet a line. Restrooms and a picnic area **[5]** are conveniently located at .61 mi., nearing the end of the trail at the parking lot **[6]** (.71 mi.). Squirrels are numerous in this area, thanks to a variety of oaks that grow here.

If you wish to hike back to the starting point without backtracking, walk through the parking lot along the blacktop drive uphill to your far left. At 1 mi. you will see a maintenance building and an access road to your left. Walk down this access road to the head of the Story of the Forest Self-Guiding Nature Trail and Creek Side Trail **[7]** (1.02 mi.). The Self-Guiding Nature Trail is the left fork. Pick up a paper that describes the 25 stations of this trail here. At these stations, you will learn about various stages of forest regeneration. This area had previously been logged, then farmed. Now forest is reclaiming the land. You will also see the remains of a charcoal hearth and walk along the path where charcoal was hauled.

After 2.43 mi. you return to Fisherman's Trail near the head of the steps **[2]** above the old railroad car. Total distance back to the parking lot where you began this hike **[1]** is 2.52 miles.

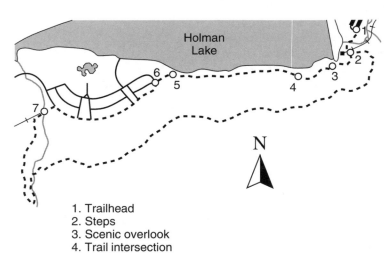

1. Trailhead
2. Steps
3. Scenic overlook
4. Trail intersection
5. Restrooms and picnic area
6. Parking lot
7. Head of self-guiding nature trail

29. Trough Creek State Park

- Walk down a few steps into the ice mine, where cold air escapes from inside the mountain.
- See a boulder balanced precariously on a high cliff.
- Hike over sheer mountain ledges and through scenic boulder fields.

Area Information

According to local legend, Edgar Allen Poe visited Great Trough Creek in 1870 and wrote his poem "The Raven" after seeing the numerous ravens that nested on the cliffs above the creek. Today, it is easy to understand how the natural beauty of Trough Creek State Park could attract and inspire someone as notable as Poe. But while the terror Poe created existed only on paper, humankind brought a century-long real-life nightmare to Great Trough Creek.

Water power attracted the first industry in 1780, a gristmill. In 1790, a bloomery was built to make iron. That was followed by an iron furnace in 1832. The iron industry left following the Civil War, but in 1913 a railroad was built through the valley to extract the timber. In five years the timber was gone, leaving the land prone to fires and floods.

The arrival of the CCC in 1933 marked the rebirth of the Great Trough Creek valley as a place of natural splendor. The CCC planted trees and built park facilities. Three years later, the park opened.

Most people who camp at Trough Creek State Park are actually here to boat and fish at Raystown Lake, which touches the north end of the park. But this 554-acre park is a lot more than a quiet relief from the busy lake. Its narrow gorge is one of the most picturesque places in central Pennsylvania.

Directions: Trough Creek State Park is on the east side of Raystown Lake. From Huntingdon, drive south on Pennsylvania Route 26 about 16 miles, then turn east on Pennsylvania Route 994, near Entriken, about 5 miles to the park entrance road.

Hours Open: The park is open year-round. Day-use facilities are open from 8:00 A.M. to sunset.

Facilities: Trough Creek State Park has 32 campsites for tents or RVs; a sanitary dump station; five picnic areas; fishing for trout, bass, and panfish in Great Trough Creek; and several hiking trails.

Permits and Rules: Alcoholic beverages are prohibited. Outdoor recreational activities are restricted to locations where signs or physical improvements designate the appropriate use. Fires and the disposal of hot coals are restricted to provided facilities. Trash and litter must be placed in containers provided for this purpose, and disposal is limited to items accumulated during the use of the park.

Further Information: Department of Conservation and Natural Resources, Trough Creek State Park, RR 1, Box 211, James Creek, PA 16657-9302; phone 814-658-3847.

Other Areas of Interest

Raystown Lake, an 8,300-acre human-made impoundment, is one of the most popular lakes in Pennsylvania for boating and fishing. It is widely known for bass and striper fishing. For information contact Manager, Raystown Lake, U.S. Army Corps of Engineers, RR 1, Hesston, PA 16647; phone 814-658-3405.

Park Trails

Raven Rock Trail 👢👢👢—.2 mile—Walk from Balanced Rock to a dead end at Great Trough Creek and see rock outcrops.

Laurel Run Trail 👢👢👢—1.3 miles—Follow the course of Laurel Run, then cross a low mountain to Ice Mine Trail.

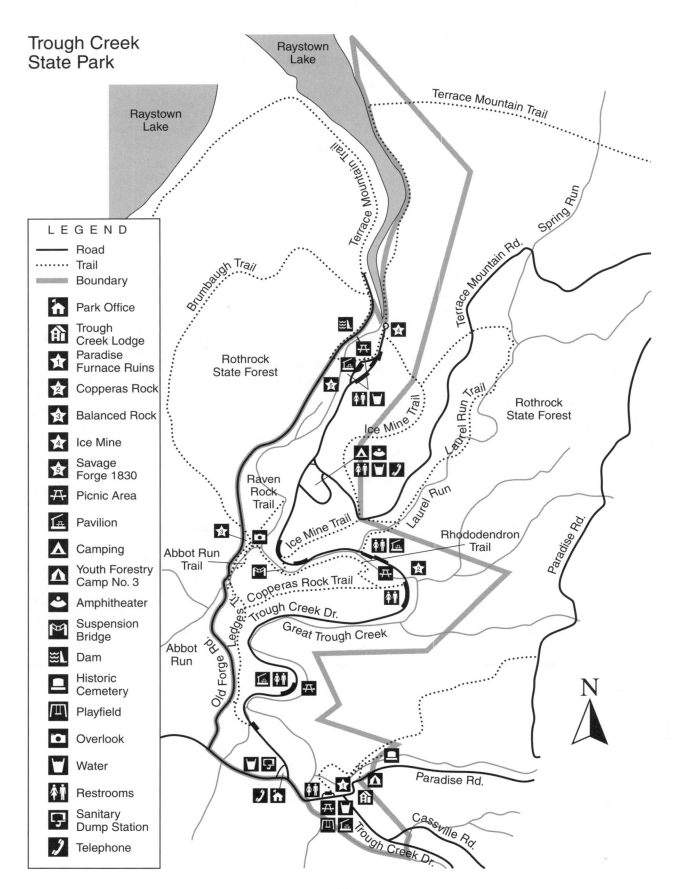

Trough Creek State Park

LEGEND

— Road
···· Trail
▬ Boundary

🏠	Park Office
🏛	Trough Creek Lodge
★	Paradise Furnace Ruins
★2	Copperas Rock
★3	Balanced Rock
★4	Ice Mine
★5	Savage Forge 1830
🪑	Picnic Area
🏕	Pavilion
⛺	Camping
⛺	Youth Forestry Camp No. 3
👥	Amphitheater
🌉	Suspension Bridge
〰	Dam
⬛	Historic Cemetery
🛝	Playfield
📷	Overlook
🪣	Water
🚻	Restrooms
♿	Sanitary Dump Station
📞	Telephone

Raystown Lake

Terrace Mountain Trail

Spring Run

Terrace Mountain Trail

Terrace Mountain Rd.

Brumbaugh Trail

Rothrock State Forest

Rothrock State Forest

Ice Mine Trail

Laurel Run Trail

Laurel Run

Raven Rock Trail

Ice Mine Trail

Rhododendron Trail

Paradise Rd.

Abbot Run Trail

Ledges Trail

Abbot Run

Copperas Rock Trail

Trough Creek Dr.

Great Trough Creek

Old Forge Rd.

Paradise Rd.

Cassville Rd.

Trough Creek Dr.

N

Rhododendron/Abbot Run/ Ledges/Copperas Trails

👢👢👢👢

Distance Round-Trip: 1.6 miles

Estimated Hiking Time: 1 hour

Caution: A sign at the trailhead warns, "Caution. Sections of this trail are narrow and steep with vertical cliffs. Proper footwear and adult supervision are required. Please stay on trail." Rocks and roots cover much of this hike.

Trail Directions: Plan this hike with plenty of time to linger at Rainbow Falls and Balanced Rock.

Drive down Trough Creek Drive about 1.5 miles past park headquarters, then turn into a parking area on the left side of the road just before crossing a bridge over Great Trough Creek. The trailhead is near the creek, marked by a sign that has colored arrows pointing to various trails and destinations **[1]**. The arrow colors correspond to the trail blazes: blue for Ledges Trail, yellow for Balanced Rock, green for Rhododendron Trail, and red for Copperas Rock Trail.

Begin climbing a moderately steep grade from the trailhead. The trail splits after 225 feet. Turn right, following the sign and green blazes on Rhododendron Trail toward Balanced Rock and Rainbow Falls. The forest is a mix of hardwoods and hemlock. When you get into thick rhododendron and to the first ledge, the trail turns left and uphill around the ledge, then descends the steep hillside past the ledge using switchbacks. These switchbacks will take you down alongside the ledge (.2 mi.) **[2]**. Observe how this ledge is cracking and will eventually tumble into the creek. This is the work of water that seeps into the cracks and then expands as it freezes.

Rhododendron Trail continues descending to the valley floor, which it follows for about 1,000 feet. Watch for trout feeding in the creek. After climbing over rocky ledges, the trail descends again to a suspension bridge (.5 mi.) **[3]**. A sign here indicates that you are now on Abbot Run Trail going toward Balanced Rock and Rainbow Falls. Follow yellow trail blazes from this point. Though rocks and roots still interfere with footing, Abbot Run Trail is much wider and smoother than Rhododendron Trail. A favorite hike in this park starts at the suspension

bridge and ends at Balanced Rock. This is a gorgeous trail, climbing gently along a rock ledge to a footbridge at the base of Rainbow Falls (.6 mi.) **[4]**. This is most impressive during spring. Not much water flows over the waterfall during summer, yet even then you will feel refreshed by the cool air.

Begin climbing rock steps immediately after crossing the footbridge. After 73 steps, depending on how you count them, the trail splits. Take the right fork to Balanced Rock (.7 mi.) **[5]**. You will wonder what is holding this precarious boulder in place. Almost straight below it you will see Great Trough Creek. An interpretive sign explains how Balanced Rock moved to its present position and how it will eventually fall into the creek.

Facing the interpretive sign, you are at a four-way intersection. Balanced Rock is to the right. The trail you just climbed is behind you. Raven Trail is straight ahead. Turn left and walk toward a green trail blaze. You will actually be following yellow trail blazes along Abbot Run to a footbridge (.86 mi.) **[6]**. A sign across the footbridge points you uphill on Ledges Trail, following blue trail blazes.

Ledges Trail starts with a steep climb to an overlook (.9 mi.) **[7]**. Be careful here. The trail bends right past the overlook, up an even steeper climb. Mercifully, the trail levels along the top of the ridge before reaching Copperas Trail (1.1 mi.) **[8]**. Did you notice that mountain laurel replaced rhododendron on top of the ridge?

Follow Copperas Trail downhill to complete the loop, then turn right to the trailhead (1.6 mi.) **[1]**.

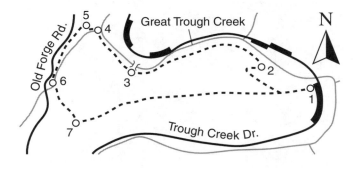

1. Trailhead
2. Side of ledge
3. Suspension bridge
4. Rainbow Falls
5. Balanced Rock
6. Abbot Run bridge
7. Overlook
8. Copperas Trail

Ice Mine Trail 👢👢👢

Distance Round-Trip: 1.2 miles

Estimated Hiking Time: 1 hour

Caution: A sign at the trailhead warns, "Caution. Sections of this trail are narrow and steep with vertical cliffs. Proper footwear and adult supervision are required. Please stay on trail." Your hiking boots should have good ankle support. You will cross spectacular boulder fields where it is easy to twist an ankle.

Trail Directions: Drive to the end of Trough Creek Drive and park by the ice mine. This interesting little hole in the ground was probably made by miners searching for iron ore. Cool air flows from the mountain into the ice mine. Walk down the steps and feel the air cool to near freezing. However, this phenomenon decreases in late summer.

The trailhead is adjacent to the ice mine, marked by a sign **[1]**. The trail begins with a moderately steep climb through a boulder field. During this hike you will be passing through a mixed forest of hemlock,

pine, red oak, and mountain laurel. You are following red trail blazes. Toward the top of the ridge, the incline is less steep, and you pass out of the boulder field. Signposts mark the intersection with Laurel Run Trail (.2 mi.) **[2]**, which comes from the left. Continue straight. Ice Mine Trail becomes much narrower, but less rocky. Only about 100 yards farther you come to another intersection with Laurel Run Trail. This is also marked by a sign. Follow Ice Mine Trail to the right.

Soon you start descending, and the trail winds through another boulder field. Watch for cars when you cross a dirt road (.8 mi.) **[3]**. Ice Mine Trail is marked by a sign on each side of the road. Another points uphill toward Laurel Run Trail. Continue straight across the road and by some very large boulders. Five steps fashioned with natural stone climb into a boulder field about 100 feet past the dirt road. Here you walk along a steep, rocky ledge. Stay on the trail.

Continuing through the boulder field you will see a sign that says, "Trail three way split." Three arrows in different colors are also on this sign. Follow the trail to the right and red trail blazes over more steps through the boulder field. The trail winds and is very steep in places, until you leave the boulder field, where the trail becomes wider.

You can hear Great Trough Creek as you approach the end of Ice Mine Trail at the edge of Trough Creek Drive, in a small parking area (1.2 mi.) **[4]**.

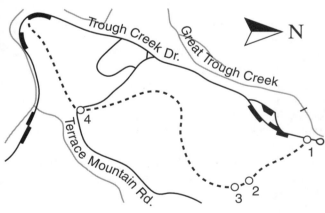

1. Trailhead
2. Laurel Run Trail
3. Dirt road
4. Trough Creek Drive

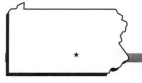

30. Colonel Denning State Park

- Camp and hike on Blue Mountain.
- Swim or fish for trout in Doubling Gap Lake.
- Watch, very cautiously, for rattlesnakes on the rocky hillsides.

Area Information

Colonel Denning State Park is just far enough from Harrisburg, just hard enough to reach, and just unspectacular enough to keep down the crowds. But if you enjoy mountain scenery and climbing through rocky forest, you will enjoy this park. It opened as a recreation area about 1930, but as with so many of our older state parks, major improvements were not made until the CCC came a few years later.

The 273-acre park is nestled in Doubling Gap, an S-turn in Blue Mountain. It is named for William Denning, who was actually not a colonel but a sergeant during the American Revolution. Denning built an unusual type of cannon that consisted of strips of iron, resulting in a lighter weapon.

Directions: The park is on Pennsylvania Route 233 about halfway between Newville and Landisburg in northern Cumberland County.

Hours Open: The park is open year-round. Day-use areas are open from 8:00 A.M. to sunset.

Facilities: The campground has 52 sites for tents or RVs. Fish in the lake or swim at a guarded beach from Memorial Day weekend through Labor Day between 11:00 A.M. and 7:00 P.M. There is a food concession near the swimming beach. Two pavilions and more than 200 picnic tables are placed at convenient locations.

Permits and Rules: Alcoholic beverages are prohibited. Boats must have either a state park launching permit, a state park mooring permit, or a current Pennsylvania Fish and Boat Commission registration. Only nonpowered and electric-powered boats are allowed. Outdoor recreational activities are restricted to locations where signs or physical improvements designate the appropriate use. Fires and the disposal of hot coals are restricted to provided facilities. Trash and litter must be placed in containers provided for this purpose, and disposal is limited to items accumulated during the use of the park. Pets must be leashed and controlled at all times, and they are not allowed at the swimming area or in overnight camping facilities.

Further Information: Department of Conservation and Natural Resources, Colonel Denning State Park, 1599 Doubling Gap Road, Newville, PA 17241-9756; phone 717-776-5272.

Other Areas of Interest

See a stand of virgin hemlock at **Hemlocks Natural Area.** Write to Tuscarora State Forest, Forest District 3, RD 1, Box 42-A, Blain, PA 17006; phone 717-563-3191.

Park Trails

Flat Rock Trail 👢👢👢👢—2.5 miles—Walk to a rock outcrop in the Tuscarora State Forest where on a clear day you can see to the Potomac River.

Old Doubling Gap Road Trail 👢👢—2.6 miles—Leave the north end of the park on an old gravel road. Walking is easy.

Colonel Denning
State Park

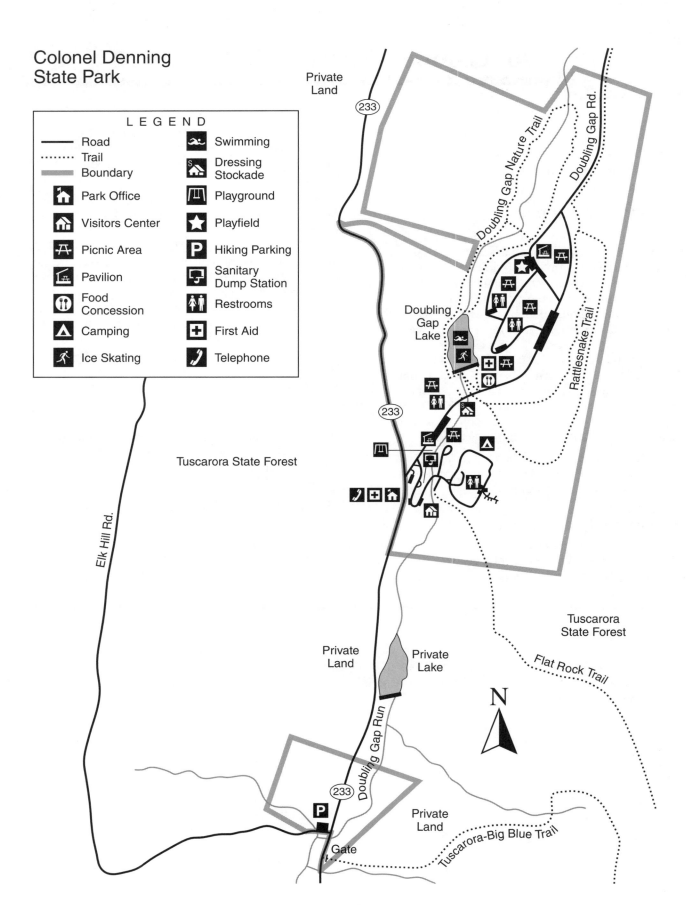

LEGEND

—— Road	🏊 Swimming
···· Trail	🏠 Dressing Stockade
▬▬ Boundary	🎢 Playground
🏠 Park Office	⭐ Playfield
🏠 Visitors Center	P Hiking Parking
🎪 Picnic Area	🚮 Sanitary Dump Station
🏕 Pavilion	🚻 Restrooms
🍴 Food Concession	✚ First Aid
⛺ Camping	☎ Telephone
⛸ Ice Skating	

Private Land

Tuscarora State Forest

Elk Hill Rd.

Doubling Gap Nature Trail

Doubling Gap Rd.

(233)

Rattlesnake Trail

Doubling Gap Lake

(233)

Tuscarora State Forest

Private Land

Private Lake

Flat Rock Trail

Doubling Gap Run

N

(233)

Private Land

Tuscarora-Big Blue Trail

P

Gate

Rattlesnake Trail 👢👢👢

Distance Round-Trip: 1.9 miles

Estimated Hiking Time: 1 hour

Caution: Most of this trail is rocky. It is well named, so watch out for rattlesnakes. Rattlesnakes are very timid. Your odds of seeing one are slim. But if you want to see one, walk quietly and watch the ground around you. Their venom can be fatal, so if you find one, do not approach it too closely. And do not assume you are safe by keeping your distance—there might be more than one. Snake-proof leggings and a snakebite kit are wise precautions. Look first before stepping over rocks and logs. Do not harm the rattlesnakes. They are becoming uncommon and are protected by law.

Trail Directions: Drive in the main park road past the ranger station to the large parking area below Doubling Gap Lake. A sign marks this as Parking #1 and the trail center. A sidewalk at the upper end of this parking area passes through a dressing stockade for the swimming area. Use the start of this sidewalk as your trailhead **[1]**.

Walk through the dressing stockade and turn right at the paved road. Cross a bridge to a "Rattlesnake Trail" sign on the right. Cross a ditch, then follow yellow trail blazes up a steep hill to a fork (.07 mi.) **[2]**. Turn right. Thick hemlocks form a dense canopy over the trail and the lower ground to your right. To your left, the forest is mostly hardwoods with a few scattered pines. As you rise in elevation, you leave the hemlocks behind.

Rattlesnake Trail is not a well-worn path. Perhaps the name prevents it from getting more traffic. Indeed, it is fittingly named. This is serious rattlesnake country, the heart of timber rattlesnake range. The rattlesnake is a large snake, rarely reaching 6 feet in length but more commonly 3 to 4 feet. It has two color phases, light and dark, both of which can be found in this area.

Keep the yellow trail blazes in sight as much as possible. Watch for turns when you see double yellow slashes. If the trail completely disappears, you might have to scout for the next trail blaze. An

intersection .26 mi. into the trail can be confusing **[3]**; it does not appear on the park map. If you go straight on the more distinct trail, you will go to the campground. Turn left, uphill, to remain on Rattlesnake Trail.

After a long climb, the trail swings left, through a small cut, and becomes very rocky (.5 mi.) **[4]**. You are entering the area where you are most likely to see rattlesnakes. Stay on the trail and look around on the ground very carefully. When you find a comfortable seat, pause to listen to and watch the songbirds in this mature hardwood forest. But examine the area very cautiously before sitting.

A sharp left turn by a triple yellow trail blaze puts you on a barely visible old road (1.2 mi.) **[5]**. Follow this downhill to a dirt road, where you turn left again (1.3 mi.) **[6]**. This is Doubling Gap Road, which you will follow back to the trailhead. Watch out for motor vehicles. Turn left at the first fork (1.38 mi.) **[7]**. This is the only intersection that might be confusing. Ignore two more roads that cut to the right. Doubling Gap Road is paved past the second of these. Follow the pavement around a sweeping right turn to your trailhead (1.9 mi.) **[1]**.

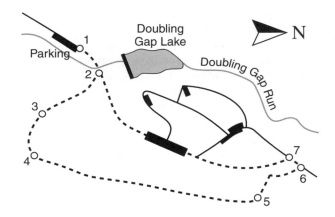

1. Trailhead
2. Fork
3. Unmapped fork
4. Very rocky area
5. Old road
6. Doubling Gap Road
7. First fork

Doubling Gap Nature Trail

👢👢👢

Distance Round-Trip: 1.4 miles

Estimated Hiking Time: 1 hour

Caution: Watch for wet, slippery, and unstable footing. This trail is very steep in a few places. There are no trail blazes, and several spur trails are not marked by signs.

Trail Directions: This is one of the better interpretive trails in the state. Stop to read each of the excellent interpretive signs, then study the forest around you to understand the meanings.

Drive in the main park road to the parking area near the beach and the outlet of Doubling Gap Lake. Use the sidewalk that starts at the end of the parking lot closest to the lake as your trailhead **[1]**. Walk through the dressing stockade and across the paved road toward the outlet, where you will see a kiosk. Walk up the breast of the dam on a set of stone steps. Turn left and cross the dam, then turn right on a walkway that is accessible to wheelchairs (.06 mi.) **[2]**. A small picnic area and parking area to your left could also be used as a trailhead.

A trail sign confirms that you are on Nature Trail when you leave the sidewalk and begin a sloping dirt trail. Phoebes and other songbirds serenade you in the lakeside forest of tulip tree, oak, and pine. Crows squawk in the distance. This side of the small lake is popular with anglers. You can see the beach on the opposite side.

At the head of the lake you cross a small wooden footbridge over a tributary to Doubling Gap Run and see some large hemlock trees. Several spur trails could make this area confusing if you do not watch the signs. Ignore a spur that forks to the right just past the footbridge. A Nature Trail sign directs you to the left at the next intersection (.24 mi.) **[3]**. You can see a wooden footbridge crossing Doubling Gap Creek on the right fork. This is where Nature Trail splits to form a loop. You will be returning over that footbridge.

The first interpretive sign on the trail is about 425 feet past this intersection. It describes how each member of the forest community contributes to the ecology. Look for examples around you. Your trail rises from the interpretive sign, moving away from Doubling Gap Run and through mature pine trees to the end of a ridge, then turns sharply right, downhill to a small wooden footbridge and an intersection (.5 mi.) **[4]**. To the right is the cutoff that forms the short loop of Nature Trail.

Continue straight ahead, uphill, on the long loop to an interpretive sign that describes seasonal changes in the forest. The trail becomes narrower, and the forest changes to primarily beech as you walk to another interpretive sign about changes brought to the forest by humans. After the trail winds closer to Doubling Gap Run, read the interpretive sign about the connection of the creek with the forest community. You cross Doubling Gap Run on a larger footbridge at the apex of your loop (.8 mi.) **[5]**, then swing right.

Interpretive signs on this stretch of the trail describe forest layers and the forest floor. Between these signs, you pass the cutoff trail for the short loop, where you see a footbridge to the right (.9 mi.) **[6]**. Do not cross Doubling Gap Run until the next footbridge (1.2 mi.) **[7]**. You have completed the loop about 70 feet past the bridge. Turn left and backtrack to the trailhead (1.4 mi.) **[1]**.

1. Trailhead
2. End of dam
3. Trail loop split
4. Cutoff trail
5. Cross creek
6. Cutoff trail again
7. Lower bridge

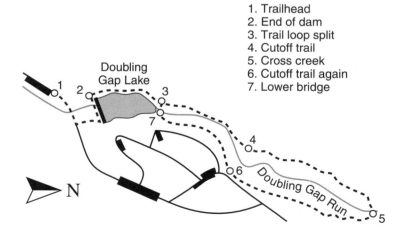

31. Blue Knob State Park

- Stand atop the second-highest point in Pennsylvania.
- Feel the temperature drop as you rise in elevation from the bottom of the mountain.
- Ski down the highest vertical drop of any ski slope in the state.

Area Information

One of the largest and most spectacular of Pennsylvania's state parks, Blue Knob is a hiker's paradise. About 17 miles of hiking trails course through 5,614 park acres. In addition, trails for biking, snowmobiling, horseback riding, and cross-country skiing guide you through secluded hollows, past abandoned homesteads, and through a succession of forest types. Trails can be combined for a variety of experiences and degrees of difficulty.

The crest of Blue Knob is at a ski resort that is leased from the park. It has the greatest vertical drop in the state—1,050 feet. Annual snowfall is about 12 feet. Temperatures are several degrees cooler than at surrounding cities and towns. Riding with your elbow out the car window, you can feel the temperature change as you drive up or down the mountain.

Views are far more spectacular than at the highest point in the state, Mt. Davis, because the highest point on Blue Knob is a peak, whereas Mt. Davis has a flat top. Blue Knob reaches an elevation of 3,146 feet. Mt. Davis is only 67 feet higher. From the peak of Blue Knob, and from overlooks on the trails, you can see as far as 42 miles in clear weather. The best views generally occur after cold fronts during fall, but summer is just as good a time to visit because of the cooler, less humid air on top of the mountain.

Directions: From the Pennsylvania Turnpike, turn north on Interstate Route 99 at Exit 11, then exit I-99 onto Pennsylvania Route 869, which enters the park at the village of Pavia.

Hours Open: The park is open year-round. Day-use areas are open from 8:00 A.M. to sunset.

Facilities: In addition to trails and the ski resort, Blue Knob State Park offers swimming in a pool from Memorial Day weekend to Labor Day; 42 campsites for tents or RVs, 25 with electric hookups; pavilions; and about 200 picnic tables. Anglers can catch stocked and native trout in Bob's Creek and its tributaries.

Permits and Rules: Alcoholic beverages are prohibited. Outdoor recreational activities are restricted to locations where signs or physical improvements designate the appropriate use. Fires and the disposal of hot coals are restricted to provided facilities. Trash and litter must be placed in containers provided for this purpose, and disposal is limited to items accumulated during the use of the park. Pets must be leashed and controlled at all times, and they are not allowed at the swimming area or in overnight camping facilities.

Further Information: Department of Conservation and Natural Resources, Blue Knob State Park, 124 Park Road, Imler, PA 16655-9207; phone 814-276-3576.

Park Trails

Rock 'n' Ridge Trail 👢👢👢—2.8 miles—Loop up the mountain from the swimming pool area.

Homestead Trail 👢👢—1.8 miles—You can enjoy excellent bird watching in the fields and woods around old homestead sites.

Saw Mill Trail 👢👢👢—3.5 miles—This trail follows service roads and other openings to connect the Willow Springs Picnic Area with Knob Road.

Chappell's Field Trail 👢👢—2.5 miles—Start at the Chappell's Field unloading area and loop through a relatively gentle section of Blue Knob.

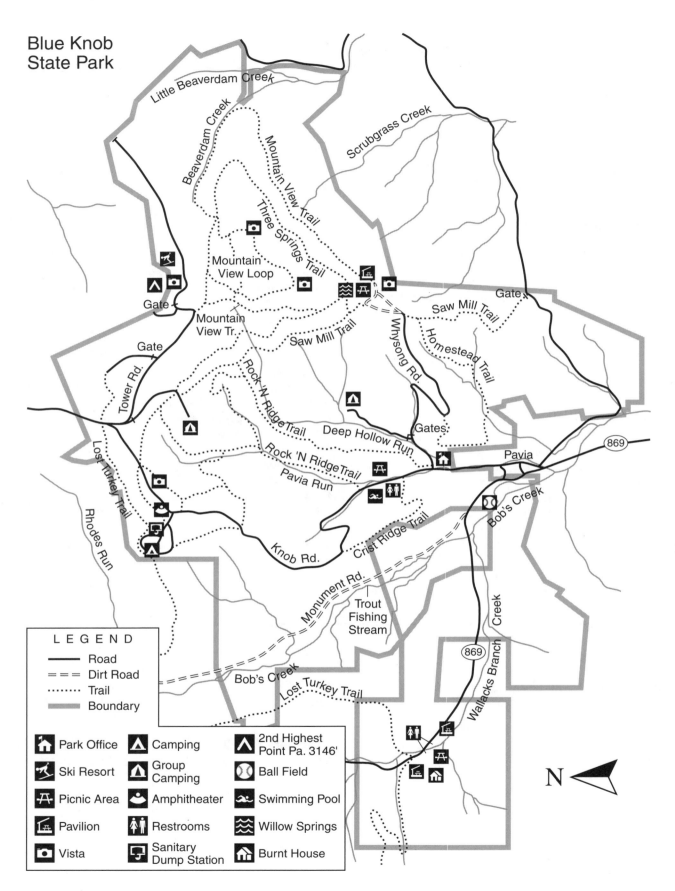

Blue Knob
State Park

LEGEND

— Road
= = = Dirt Road
.... Trail
▬▬ Boundary

Park Office
Ski Resort
Picnic Area
Pavilion
Vista

Camping
Group Camping
Amphitheater
Restrooms
Sanitary Dump Station

2nd Highest Point Pa. 3146'
Ball Field
Swimming Pool
Willow Springs
Burnt House

Mountain View Loop 🥾🥾🥾

Distance Round-Trip: 2 miles

Estimated Hiking Time: 1.25 hours

Caution: One section of this loop is very steep. In some places the trail is rocky and hard to follow, or very narrow and crowded by brush.

Trail Directions: Entering the park from the south, take Knob Road to Tower Road and turn right. Entering from the north, you are on Tower Road. The trailhead is on the southern side of the mountain at a sharp left turn by an electric substation, a fenced area containing several electric poles and marked "Danger High Voltage." The trailhead is marked by a white post with black letters **[1]**.

Mountain View Loop begins on a gravel road that is blocked to motor vehicles by a red and black gate. Trail blazes are two red slashes. Descend a mild slope, then start climbing at the intersection of Deep Hollow Trail (.1 mi.) **[2]**, which forks to the right. Continue on the gravel road until Mountain View Trail forks right at a sign .2 mi. from the trailhead **[3]**. This dirt trail immediately begins descending, still following double red slashes. Stay on Mountain View Loop past the intersection with Connecting Trail (.4 mi.) **[4]**. This intersection is also marked by a sign. Connecting Trail can be used to shorten this loop; however, it is not marked by a sign at the opposite end where it meets Mountain View Loop again.

Past the Connecting Trail intersection, Mountain View Loop becomes narrower before swinging left along the edge of a steep slope. Enjoy the blueberries here if they are in season.

Pavia Outlook (.8 mi.) **[5]** is the first and best of two overlooks on this trail. From a level platform lined by a circle of blocks, you see a stunning view of the Appalachian Ridge and Valley Province. While you relax in this pleasant setting, notice how the forest is different at this high elevation than it is at the bottom of the park, starting with the scrub oak around the platform.

These are very old and eroded mountains when compared with the Rocky Mountains of the American West. Long ago, they were much higher. Look for boulder fields on distant ridges. These were formed as the boulders tumbled after erosion cut beneath them.

This trail wraps around a ridge that juts from the side of Blue Knob. Past Pavia Outlook, the trail curves left to Queen Outlook (1 mi.) **[6]**. This undeveloped overlook has been mostly blocked by tree growth.

Following the trail past this point would be difficult if not for the double red slashes. It is no wider than a game trail and very rocky. An unmarked intersection is the end of Connecting Trail (1.3 mi.) **[7]**. Turn right, following Mountain View Loop and the double red slashes over stone steps. Turn left at a gravel road (1.4 mi.) **[8]**. There are two signs at this intersection. One points straight across the road to Beaverdam Creek. The other points to the overlooks you have visited. No signs point to your trailhead, and you are now leaving the double red slashes.

Your left turn on the gravel road will lead up a very steep hill and directly back to the trailhead. You can see an opening as you get past the worst of the climb, then a road in that opening comes into sight. You are near the crest of Blue Knob, when the ski resort comes into view. All that remains is a mild descent along the gravel road to complete the loop (1.7 mi.) **[3]** and return to the trailhead (2 mi.) **[1]**.

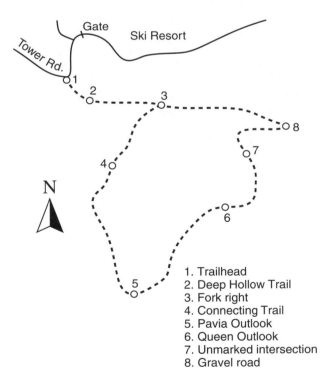

1. Trailhead
2. Deep Hollow Trail
3. Fork right
4. Connecting Trail
5. Pavia Outlook
6. Queen Outlook
7. Unmarked intersection
8. Gravel road

Crist Ridge Trail 👢👢👢

Distance One-Way: .9 mile

Estimated Hiking Time: .5 hour

Caution: Watch for thorns along the trail. If you bring children on this hike, keep them away from any mounds. The ants in these mounds bite. A steeper section toward the end of the trail has poor footing on roots, rocks, and gravel.

Trail Directions: This is an easy downhill hike through mature forest. Wildlife is abundant. Follow Knob Road about 1.2 miles north from park headquarters to the trailhead, which is marked with a white signpost with black letters **[1]**. You will be following orange trail blazes, but you will also see some white trail blazes.

Crist Ridge Trail starts down a gradual slope and soon narrows. The forest is a mix of oak, hickory, maple, cherry, and hemlock. Look for three massive oaks along the first few hundred yards. Wild grapevine hangs from some trees. You can pick blackberries in season. The view is limited by the dense forest. You can see just far enough to realize that you are walking along the spine of a narrow ridge. During early spring or winter, when there are no leaves on the trees, the view is much more impressive.

If you want to pause and watch for deer, squirrels, or birds, walk far enough off the trail to see over the side of the mountain so you can see farther.

Proceed straight across a small field (.5 mi.) **[2]**. The trail is overgrown with grass. Watch for an orange trail blaze at the far end of the field. Large ant mounds dot this field. Do not let these ants get on

you; they can inflict nasty bites. Bears consider these ants a delicacy. You might see mounds that have been torn apart by hungry bears. Your chances of seeing a bear here are better than in many other areas, but it is still unlikely. Even where bears are abundant, they are rare when compared to deer, and bears are very elusive.

A horseshoe curve to the left (.6 mi.) **[3]** leads into a steeper downhill slope where you leave the top of the ridge. Watch your footing on the rocks, roots, and gravel. You reach Knob Road at a white trail sign, near the swimming pool, after walking .9 mi. **[4]**.

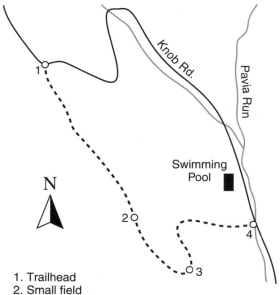

1. Trailhead
2. Small field
3. Horseshoe curve
4. Knob Road

32. Warriors Path State Park

- Follow the path taken by Iroquois warriors when they raided Cherokees and other Native American tribes.
- Launch your boat and fish in the Raystown Branch of the Juniata River.
- Relax in a lightly used park.
- Observe stark habitat changes from river bottom to ridge top.

Area Information

Warriors Path is a small state park, just 334 acres, nestled inside a meander of the Raystown Branch of the Juniata River. While the scenery is unspectacular, it is still lovely and relaxing. The undeveloped parts of the park are mostly mature hardwood forest. A thin strip of swamp follows the bottom of the valley along the river, where you can also find vegetation that is unusual in this part of the state. Shale cliffs can be seen across the river.

With nothing of the sort that tends to attract crowds and no camping, it provides a pleasantly quiet experience. Yet to those with a sense of history, especially those who try to feel history, this park offers an unusual opportunity. You can walk along the trail taken by warriors of the mighty Iroquois League as they made war on neighboring tribes.

The river has good fishing for smallmouth bass and rock bass, with fair fishing for walleyes and muskellunge. During summer, when the river is generally too low for boating, this is a fine place to wade in sneakers and shorts. Floating the river is popular during spring, when there is more flow.

Directions: Follow signs about 2 miles south from Saxton, a community located immediately south of Raystown Lake along Pennsylvania Route 913, just east of Pennsylvania Route 26.

Hours Open: This park is open from 8:00 A.M. to sunset from mid-April through the end of October. At other times, while the entrance road is gated, you may enter the park on foot.

Facilities: Warriors Path is a day-use park with picnic tables, pavilions, restrooms, a boat launch ramp on the Raystown Branch of the Juniata River, trails for hiking and cross-country skiing, and play areas.

Permits and Rules: Park in designated areas only. Alcoholic beverages are prohibited. Boats must have either a state park launching permit, a state park mooring permit, or a current Pennsylvania Fish and Boat Commission registration. Outdoor recreational activities are restricted to locations where signs or physical improvements designate the appropriate use. Fires and the disposal of hot coals are restricted to provided facilities. Trash and litter must be placed in containers provided for this purpose, and disposal is limited to items accumulated during the use of the park. Pets must be leashed and under control at all times. Soliciting and posting signs are prohibited.

Further Information: Department of Conservation and Natural Resources, Warriors Path State Park, c/o Trough Creek State Park, RR 1, Box 211, James Creek, PA 16657-9302; phone 814-658-3847.

Other Areas of Interest

For information about the **Raystown Lake** area, contact Raystown Country Visitors Bureau, Seven Points Road, RR 1, Box 222A, Hesston, PA 16647.

Park Trails

Reichenbaugh Trail —.2 mile—This trail connects Warriors Trail and Deer Trail. It can be used to make a shortened loop with Warriors and Deer trails.

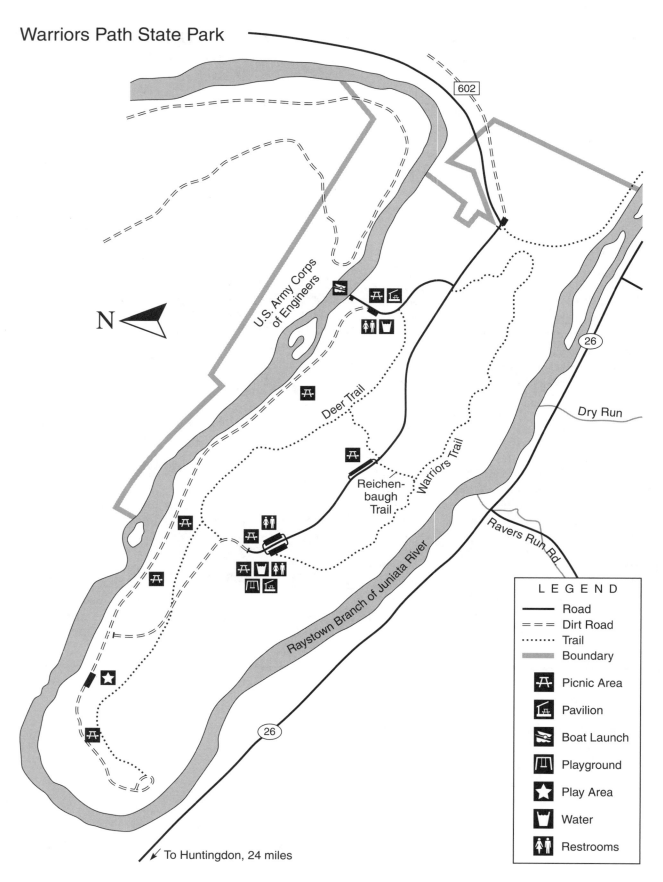

Warriors Path State Park

N

602

26

Dry Run

Ravers Run Rd

U.S. Army Corps of Engineers

Deer Trail

Reichen-baugh Trail

Warriors Trail

Raystown Branch of Juniata River

26

To Huntingdon, 24 miles

LEGEND
——— Road
= = = Dirt Road
.... Trail
▬▬ Boundary
⛏ Picnic Area
🏠 Pavilion
🚣 Boat Launch
🛝 Playground
★ Play Area
🪣 Water
🚻 Restrooms

Warriors Trail 👢👢

Distance Round-Trip: 1.5 miles

Estimated Hiking Time: .5 hour

Caution: This trail is groomed; however, there are still roots and rocks. It becomes very steep near the end, and this area can be slippery in wet weather.

Trail Directions: Drive to the parking lot by park headquarters at the end of the main park road. The trailhead for Warriors Trail is marked by a sign to the left of the restrooms **[1]**.

It is easy to see why Iroquois warriors chose this route. After a gentle climb, it follows the relatively level top of a low ridge. The forest is second-growth hardwoods, a mix of oaks, maple, hickory, and cherry. The largest trees are oaks, which probably sprouted after a forest fire. Though far different from the forest the Iroquois saw, it is still a pleasant forest and a lot less deadly. Reichenbaugh Trail forks left unnoticed at a sign that points ahead to Warriors Loop and behind to Warriors Trail (.4 mi.) **[2]**.

Reichenbaugh Trail crosses the main park road and continues to Deer Trail. Though it is hard to see, the road is less than 500 feet directly downhill. Continue on Warriors Loop. Try to identify several large tulip trees past the sign.

Stop along the trail at a convenient seat and try to get the feeling of a warriors' path. Close your eyes and imagine yourself being here 500 years ago and not being an Iroquois. The Iroquois were the most powerful group in what is now the Northeast. They were a league of six tribes—the Seneca, Huron, Mohawk, Tuscarora, Oneida, and Onondaga, and later a sev-enth, the Cherokee. Most likely it was the Senecas who used this trail. They were the most fearsome of all this powerful confederation. Woe to the unfortunate foes they captured. Try to imagine the terror of being pursued by them.

The Iroquois also had a highly developed civilization. Our current form of government borrows heavily from their near-Utopian society. Near-Utopian, that is, if you belonged to the Iroquois League.

Your trail continues along the ridge top to a sharp left turn (.7 mi.) **[3]**. If you intend to return to the trailhead, this is a good place to turn around. All that remains is a descent of a steep slope to the main park road (.9 mi.) **[4]**. Here you can turn left on this paved road to complete a loop to the trailhead (1.5 mi.) **[1]**.

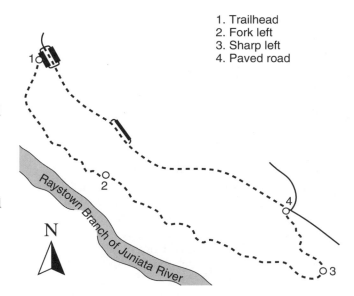

1. Trailhead
2. Fork left
3. Sharp left
4. Paved road

N

Deer Trail 👢👢

Distance One-Way: .7 mile

Estimated Hiking Time: .5 hour

Caution: Take insect repellent on this trail during spring or early summer.

Trail Directions: Use Deer Trail as a study in river-bottom habitat. It should help you understand why riparian areas are so critical to wildlife. Notice how trees and plants are different than those on higher ground and that there is more low vegetation.

After entering the park, drive less than .2 mile and turn right toward the boat launch, which is marked by a sign. The trailhead for Deer Trail is about 700 feet down this road, marked by a sign on the left, about 200 feet before the restrooms **[1]**. There is an alternate trailhead between the restrooms and a parking area.

This trail starts as a wide, mowed path. You might be able to pick blackberries here when they are ripe. Also note wild grapevine in the trees. These provide a favorite food for many animals, including wood ducks and ruffed grouse. Wildflowers—black-eyed Susans, morning glories, and several others—are abundant. Forest is only beginning to reclaim this area. For the first few hundred yards most trees are young, then you enter more mature growth. Look for oaks, hickories, maples, and tulip trees. The path is still wide but no longer grassy. Do you know why? Look above at the forest canopy that shades the forest floor. To the right, separated from the forest by a band of rhododendron, is a thick marshy area. Look for skunk cabbage along the edge. Which animals might live here that do not live in the forest away from the marsh and river?

After you start up a slight incline, a trail forks acutely left (.2 mi.) **[2]**. This is Reichenbaugh Trail, which crosses the main park road and connects with Warriors Trail. Continue straight. The marsh disappears as Deer Trail becomes steeper, then you enter a field, some of which is mowed. Stay out of the tall grass. Proceed to the left through this open area, along the tree line, to a service road (.7 mi.) **[3]**. Here you will see a sign designating this as the end of Reichenbaugh Trail, though it is not marked this way on the park map. Turn left on the service road to a parking area by the park office. You can complete this as a loop along the paved park road from the park office or combine it with Warriors Trail, which starts in this parking area and ends at the entrance to the boat launch area.

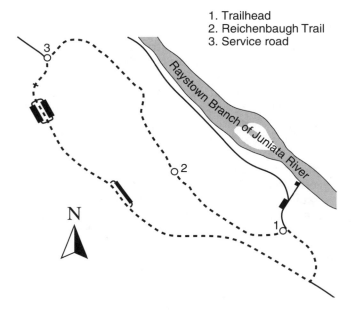

1. Trailhead
2. Reichenbaugh Trail
3. Service road

33. Kings Gap Environmental Education and Training Center

- Learn how to grow herbs.
- Visit a 32-room mansion built with local Antietam quartzite.
- Watch the Allegheny mound-building ants.

Area Information

Kings Gap, a 1,454-acre environmental education and training center, is situated on top of South Mountain. This is the northern terminus of the Blue Ridge Mountains, which extend south to Tennessee. Looking north and west from the mansion that serves as park headquarters, you see a panorama of the Cumberland Valley and beyond to Blue Mountain, which is part of the Appalachian Mountains and is not to be confused with the Blue Ridge Mountains.

Beginning in the 18th century, the forest in this area was cut at 20- to 25-year intervals and converted to charcoal, which was used as fuel in iron furnaces. Remnants from charcoal hearths can still be seen at Kings Gap. Wood smoldered in these hearths as long as two weeks during the charcoal-making process.

James McCormick Cameron bought land here in 1906 and built the mansion. The mansion is 200 feet long and has 32 rooms. It is constructed with Antietam quartzite that was quarried nearby. After it changed hands, the Commonwealth of Pennsylvania acquired the mansion and land in 1973.

While you are in the mansion day-use area, be sure to visit the mansion garden. The original garden provided food for the owners. Today, it is a demonstration area consisting of three sections. The herb garden contains more than 100 herbs that are used for food, medicine, dyes, and fragrances. At the native habitat garden you can learn how to attract wildlife to your own backyard. The compost demonstration area shows how to convert organic waste into compost.

Kings Gap is set up primarily for education. Information stations that explain forest ecology, some written in Braille, are located along some trails.

Directions: Take Exit 11 from Interstate Route 81, then drive south about 2.5 miles on Pennsylvania Route 233, turn left onto Pine Road, and drive about 2.5 miles to the well-marked entrance to Kings Gap Environmental Education and Training Center, where you turn right.

Hours Open: The grounds are open year-round from 8:00 A.M. to sunset. The office is open weekdays from 8:00 A.M. to 4:00 P.M.

Facilities: This is an environmental education center. There are no recreational facilities, except for several hiking trails and a few picnic tables.

Permits and Rules: There are no trash containers. All garbage must be taken home. Collecting plants or animals is prohibited.

Further Information: Department of Conservation and Natural Resources, Kings Gap Environmental Education and Training Center, 500 Kings Gap Road, Carlisle, PA 17013; phone 717-486-5031.

Other Areas of Interest

For information about this area, write to **Harrisburg-Hershey-Carlisle Tourism and Convention Bureau,** 25 North Front Street, Harrisburg, PA 17101; phone 717-231-7788 or 800-995-0969.

Park Trails

Boundary Trail 🥾🥾🥾—1.5 miles—Travel through an oak and pitch pine forest along the western boundary of the park.

Forest Heritage Trail 🥾🥾🥾—1.6 miles—See several charcoal hearths.

Kings Gap Hollow Trail 🥾🥾🥾—1.7 miles—Watch the habitat change with the elevation.

Rock Scree Trail 🥾🥾🥾—1.9 miles—Visit the site where the stone used to build the mansion was quarried.

Scenic Vista Trail 🥾🥾🥾—2.5 miles—Benches are strategically placed to provide panoramic vistas.

Whispering Pines Trail 🥾—.3 mile—Learn about a coniferous forest on this paved trail. Interpretive signs are in both script and Braille.

White Oaks Trail 🥾—.3 mile—Learn about deciduous forest ecology on a paved trail. Interpretive signs are in both script and Braille.

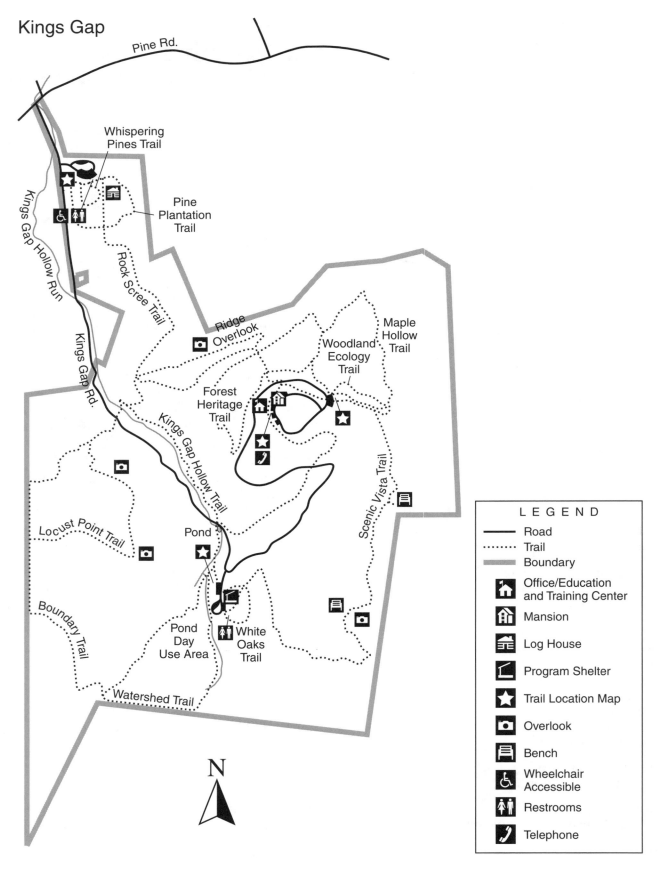

Kings Gap

Pine Rd.

Whispering Pines Trail

Pine Plantation Trail

Kings Gap Hollow Run

Rock Scree Trail

Ridge Overlook

Woodland Ecology Trail

Maple Hollow Trail

Kings Gap Rd.

Forest Heritage Trail

Kings Gap Hollow Trail

Scenic Vista Trail

Locust Point Trail

Pond

Boundary Trail

Pond Day Use Area

White Oaks Trail

Watershed Trail

N

L E G E N D

Road
Trail
Boundary
Office/Education and Training Center
Mansion
Log House
Program Shelter
Trail Location Map
Overlook
Bench
Wheelchair Accessible
Restrooms
Telephone

Watershed Trail 🥾

Distance Round-Trip: 1.7 miles

Estimated Hiking Time: 1 hour

Caution: Copperhead snakes, which are poisonous, are quite abundant in this area. Rocks and roots protrude through the trail in many places.

Trail Directions: Look for the structures built by Allegheny mound-building ants on this pleasant loop.

Drive to the Pond Day-Use Area, which is well marked on Kings Gap Road. A kiosk at the head of the parking area is your trailhead **[1]**. A sign here directs you to Watershed Trail and Boundary Trail on a gravel path that drops away from the trailhead through maple, oak, and pine to a T (.01 mi.) **[2]**. Turn left, as indicated by a signpost. Walk slightly less than 200 feet, then turn right across a small wooden footbridge, as directed by a trail sign. You will be following purple trail blazes. This is also the route to Boundary Trail, so do not be confused by signs.

If you have hiked several Pennsylvania trails, you should notice a striking difference in vegetation. Because of the low deer population, low vegetation such as blueberries and hardwood seedlings covers the forest floor. This provides better habitat for other mammals and songbirds. Try to identify birds by their songs.

This first leg of Watershed Trail gradually climbs a shallow valley. A large sign (.4 mi.) **[3]** explains the most interesting aspect of this trail, Allegheny mound-building ants. These red and black ants built tall mounds with material extracted from beneath the mounds. The mounds are incubation areas for their eggs. Bears will tear these mounds apart. Ants and eggs are delicacies to them.

Boundary Trail begins at a T, going to the right with green trail blazes. Turn left, following the purple blazes (.9 mi.) **[4]**. Watershed Trail continues to climb, becoming moderately steep by a rock outcrop (1 mi.)

[5]. You might see small round metal state park boundary signs in this area. Watch out for northern copperheads near the rocks. Northern copperheads possess poisonous venom. Though they generally flee from trouble, they will strike if you get too close.

Past the rock outcrop, you drop into a small valley and turn left at a signpost (1.1 mi.) **[6]**. Another trail, which is not on the park map, goes straight across the valley, blazed with white. Your left turn takes you down the valley. Observe that ferns are the predominant low vegetation in the damp soil close to the stream. Look in the small stream. Can you guess the origin of the white pebbles on the streambed?

Turn right when you reach a well-worn but unmarked and unmapped intersection (1.6 mi.) **[7]**. This will prevent backtracking from the completion of the loop, which is a short distance ahead. It will also avoid a steep climb at the end. About 100 feet after turning right, you will see a developed area ahead. This is the parking area where you began the hike. Your return to the kiosk trailhead completes a hike of 1.7 mi. **[1]**.

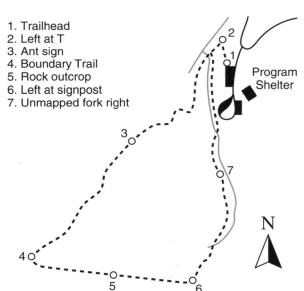

1. Trailhead
2. Left at T
3. Ant sign
4. Boundary Trail
5. Rock outcrop
6. Left at signpost
7. Unmapped fork right

Woodland Ecology Trail 👢👢

Distance Round-Trip: .56 mile

Estimated Hiking Time: 20 minutes

Caution: Be on the alert for copperhead snakes, which are poisonous. A few rocks protrude through the trail.

Trail Directions: The trailhead for Woodland Ecology Trail is on the left side of Kings Gap Road just before the loop through the Mansion Day-Use Area. A trail location map kiosk here also marks the trailheads for Maple Hollow Trail and Scenic Vista Trail [1]. Woodland Ecology Trail begins to the left of this kiosk. Follow purple trail blazes.

This trail was constructed in 1977 by the Youth Conservation Corps, which also wrote interpretive signs along the trail. This is one of the best interpretive trails in the state. It is an easy walk on a trail that is easy to follow. You will be exploring a chestnut oak forest. A member of the white oak group, chestnut oak acorns are less bitter than acorns from the red oak group. They are a preferred food for many wildlife species and were eaten by Native Americans.

Turn left at a fork just 175 feet into the trail. This is the point where the trail forms a loop. The first interpretive stations will explain how rotting stumps contribute to the soil, that blueberries, huckleberries, and mountain laurel thrive because they are not eaten by deer, and how animals use dead hollow trees as dens. An interesting sight is an unusually large chestnut oak that apparently was missed by loggers and forest fires.

The trail varies from sand to gravel and moss. Where moss covers the trail, it is like walking on a thick felt carpet. Moss and the dead leaves that accumulate on the forest floor hold moisture.

Follow the purple trail blazes and turn right at a four-way intersection (.3 mi.) [2]. This intersection is also marked with a sign. Maple Hollow Trail is both straight and to the left. Look for lichens in this area. Lichens are light green patches that are composed of algae and fungus. The forest canopy is dense, blocking so much of the sunlight that very few smaller plants can grow. One that does is mountain laurel, the Pennsylvania state flower. It blooms in late June.

Watch closely for signs of a charcoal hearth. It will appear as a black circular area about 20 feet across. The discolored soil was caused by the extreme heat of the hearth. Wood was stacked in a tight circle and burned slowly, for as long as two weeks, to produce the charcoal, which was then transported to the Cumberland Furnace. That iron furnace operated from 1794 to 1854.

In addition to chestnut oak, you will also observe red maple, sassafras, and pitch pine. Sassafras roots were used to make tea. Pitch from pitch pine was used to waterproof boats and buildings.

The loop is completed after .53 mi. Turn left to return to the trailhead (.56 mi) [1].

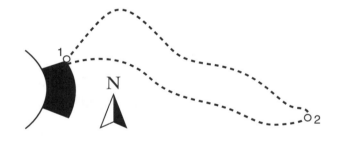

1. Trailhead
2. Maple Hollow Trail intersection

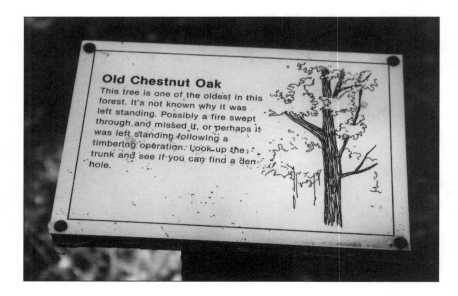

Old Chestnut Oak
This tree is one of the oldest in this forest. It's not known why it was left standing. Possibly a fire swept through and missed it, or perhaps it was left standing following a timbering operation. Look up the trunk and see if you can find a den hole.

34. Pine Grove Furnace State Park

- Tour a community built around an 18th-century iron furnace.
- Swim in an iron ore quarry.
- Visit the halfway point on the 2,000-mile Appalachian Trail.

Area Information

Pine Grove Furnace State Park is best known to serious hikers as the halfway point on the Appalachian Trail. Eating a half gallon of ice cream is a tradition when you get here. The food concession, located in an historic building, stays well stocked in that commodity.

This 696-acre park is located at the site of the Pine Grove Iron Furnace. A mill built in 1762 to cut the great pine forest into lumber was the first industry in the area. The iron furnace began operating in 1764, and for more than 100 years it manufactured stoves, kettles, and military supplies. Slate and brick operations occupied the area after that. Several old structures have been preserved, including the iron furnace. Fuller Lake, 1.7 acres, was an iron ore quarry. Laurel Lake supplied water for Laurel Forge, which reheated cast iron ingots from Pine Grove Furnace to produce wrought iron. This is one of the better examples of an iron furnace community, but it has relatively little development and less crowding than some others.

The iron company built the first recreational facilities. The land was purchased by the Commonwealth of Pennsylvania in 1913.

Directions: The park is located in southern Cumberland County, along Pennsylvania Route 233 between U.S. Route 30 and Interstate Route 81.

Hours Open: The park is open year-round. Day-use areas are open from 8:00 A.M. to sunset.

Facilities: The campground has 74 sites for tents or RVs. It has restrooms and drinking water but no showers. Sandy swimming beaches are located at both Fuller Lake and Laurel Lake. Anglers can catch trout, yellow perch, and chain pickerel at both of these lakes and trout in Mountain Creek. Biking is allowed only on service roads, highways, and the Hiker-Biker Trail.

Permits and Rules: Alcoholic beverages are prohibited. Boats must have either a state park launching permit, a state park mooring permit, or a current Pennsylvania Fish and Boat Commission registration. Only nonpowered and electric-powered boats are allowed. Outdoor recreational activities are restricted to locations where signs or physical improvements designate the appropriate use. Fires and the disposal of hot coals are restricted to provided facilities. Trash and litter must be placed in containers provided for this purpose, and disposal is limited to items accumulated during the use of the park. Pets must be leashed and controlled at all times, and they are not allowed at the swimming area or in overnight camping facilities. Soliciting and posting signs are prohibited.

Further Information: Department of Conservation and Natural Resources, Pine Grove Furnace State Park, RR 2, Box 399B, Gardners, PA 17324-9078; phone 717-486-7174.

Park Trails

Creek Trail 👢👢—.5 mile—Walk from the group camping area to the amphitheater.

Koppenhaver Trail 👢👢👢—1 mile—See mature stands of pine and hemlock along this loop.

Pole Steeple Trail 👢👢👢👢—.75 mile—Walk from Laurel Lake into the Michaux State Forest, up a very steep grade, to a quartzite outcrop with an excellent view of Pine Grove Furnace State Park.

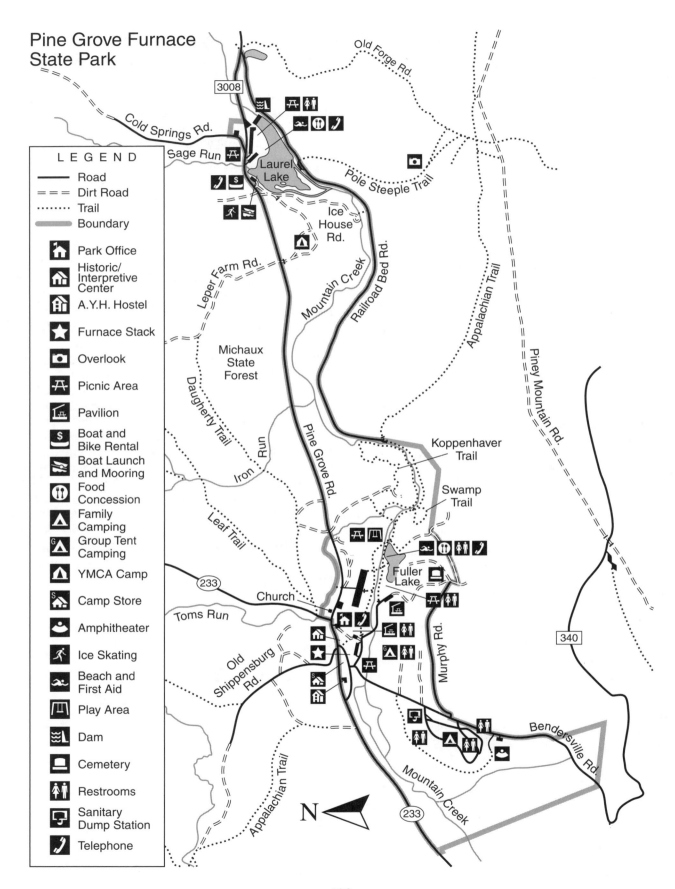

Pine Grove Furnace State Park

LEGEND

——	Road
= = =	Dirt Road
⋯⋯	Trail
▬▬	Boundary
🏠	Park Office
🏠	Historic/ Interpretive Center
🏠	A.Y.H. Hostel
★	Furnace Stack
📷	Overlook
⛱	Picnic Area
	Pavilion
$	Boat and Bike Rental
	Boat Launch and Mooring
🍴	Food Concession
▲	Family Camping
▲G	Group Tent Camping
▲	YMCA Camp
S	Camp Store
	Amphitheater
🏃	Ice Skating
	Beach and First Aid
	Play Area
	Dam
	Cemetery
🚻	Restrooms
	Sanitary Dump Station
☎	Telephone

3008

Cold Springs Rd.

Sage Run

Old Forge Rd.

Laurel Lake

Pole Steeple Trail

Ice House Rd.

Leper Farm Rd.

Michaux State Forest

Daugherty Trail

Iron Run

Leaf Trail

Mountain Creek

Railroad Bed Rd.

Appalachian Trail

Piney Mountain Rd.

Pine Grove Rd.

Koppenhaver Trail

Swamp Trail

Fuller Lake

Murphy Rd.

Church

233

Toms Run

Old Shippensburg Rd.

Appalachian Trail

Bendersville Rd.

340

Mountain Creek

233

N

A Walking Tour of the Pine Grove Furnace Iron Works 👢👢

Distance Round-Trip: .83 mile

Estimated Hiking Time: .5 hour

Caution: Watch for motor vehicles along most of this loop. Plan for considerably more than the estimated hiking time so you can examine the historic structures.

Trail Directions: Pick up a copy of the brochure "A Walking Tour of Pine Grove Furnace Iron Works" at the park office. Turn off Route 233 onto Hunter's Run Road at the park office, then turn right into the parking area by Fuller Lake. Use a trail at the left end of the parking area that leads to the swimming beach as your trailhead **[1].** You can see the swimming area from here. Fuller Lake was the largest iron ore quarry in the area. It is more than 90 feet deep. It filled with groundwater when it was abandoned. Walk toward the beach and turn right on a gravel road that follows Mountain Creek after crossing a footbridge (.05 mi.) **[2].**

As you walk this loop, try to imagine that all of the trees have been cut as far as you can see in every direction. The air is constantly filled with smoke that looks dull yellow due to flames from the iron furnace. There were several more buildings. You can visualize them by looking at those that remain. Busy workers were everywhere, hauling heavy loads and dying young from the unhealthy environment.

Follow the gravel road past a gate to a paved road (.2 mi.) **[3].** This is Quarry Road. Turn right to follow Quarry Road over a bridge, then leave Quarry Road where a dirt road forks right by the restrooms (.36 mi.) **[4].** The remains of the carpenter and blacksmith shops are across the dirt road from the restrooms. You can see the furnace to your left, but wait until later in this loop for a closer look.

Continue up a small hill to the park office, then left along Route 233 (.46 mi.) **[5].** The park office was once an inn. The Visitors Center, which you pass on your left, was a mill that ground grain grown on company land. It was powered by a waterwheel in the millrace that entered from the opposite side of Route 233. This community was mostly self-sufficient.

Turn left on the next road (.51 mi.) **[6].** To your right once stood the charcoal house. Charcoal was made in hearths in the surrounding area, then stored at the charcoal house. The old stable still stands and now houses the park store. Look at the iron bars on windows and the double doors at the far end. Turn left on the next road (.64 mi.) **[7].** To the right of this intersection stands "the big house," where the company owner lived. To the left stands the vine-covered company office, which is now a private residence.

This road splits after just a few paces. Follow Quarry Road left to the iron furnace. This cold-blast furnace was the heart of the community. The walls are eight feet thick with a core of fire brick. Workers loaded iron ore, charcoal, and limestone through the top of the stack. Blasts of air were forced into the bottom of the furnace by a waterwheel, and later by a steam engine, to increase the temperature of the fire. Once heated, the furnace would stay hot for days. The iron it produced was formed into bars or finished products such as decorative stove plates.

Continue along Quarry Road to complete the loop (.71 mi.) **[4],** then return to the trailhead at the parking area (.83 mi.) **[1].**

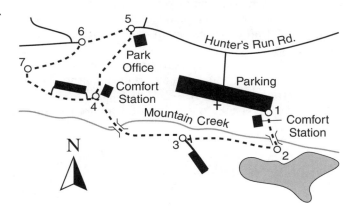

1. Trailhead
2. Footbridge
3. Paved road
4. Dirt road
5. Route 233
6. Leave Route 233
7. Left by company office

Swamp Trail 👢👢

Distance Round-Trip: 1 mile

Estimated Hiking Time: .5 hour

Caution: Swamp Trail is damp, and you will probably encounter biting insects during spring and early summer. Watch out for bicycles on the railroad grade.

Trail Directions: Wetlands are unusual in this part of Pennsylvania. This one is small but valuable. It is the only suitable habitat for several of its plant and animal inhabitants. You should carry a field guide to help identify some of the plants.

Park at the Fuller Lake parking area. At the far end of this parking area, a wide gravel trail goes past a dressing stockade and across a wooden footbridge. Use this trail at the edge of the parking area as your trailhead **[1]**.

Walk across the footbridge and turn left along the sandy swimming beach between Fuller Lake and Mountain Creek. The trail splits at the outlet of this small lake (.15 mi.) **[2]**. Both forks cross footbridges. Take the right fork, over the shorter footbridge, as directed by a sign. This is a wide, level bicycle path on an old railroad grade. It is marked by white trail blazes. Though you are not yet on Swamp Trail, examine the narrow bands of wetland on either side of the trail. Can you see how the raised railroad bed increased the wetland?

Several spur trails cut away from the bike trail. Ignore these until you reach a sign designating Swamp Trail (.42 mi.) **[3]**. The sign is small and blends into the background. Look for it after passing a pond on the right. Turn right onto Swamp Trail, crossing a ditch on a small footbridge, then turn right following yellow trail blazes. The trail is narrow, overgrown by mountain laurel, and you are constantly stepping on roots. But it is a short loop and an interesting study of a mountain marsh.

The swamp is to your right as you make this short loop. Try to identify submergent, floating, and emergent plants. Watch for frogs and insects. It is unlikely that you will see any of the larger mammals that visit the swamp to feed, such as raccoons and mink.

You complete the loop at the same place where you left the bike trail (.57 mi.) **[3]**. Turn left to return to the trailhead (1 mi.) **[1]**.

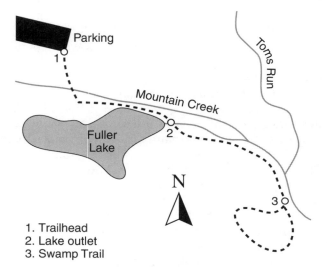

1. Trailhead
2. Lake outlet
3. Swamp Trail

35. Cowans Gap State Park

- Fish for trout, bass, and panfish in Cowans Gap Lake.
- Visit the site of a recent landslide.
- Enjoy Tuscarora Mountain scenery.

Area Information

Cowans Gap State Park is 1,085 acres nestled in a wooded valley of the Tuscarora Mountains, rising along the northwestern border to the spine of Cove Mountain with excellent panoramas. It is bordered on three sides by the Buchanan State Forest, which adds to the "big woods" atmosphere.

The park is named for Major Samuel Cowan, a British officer during the American Revolution who fell in love with the daughter of a Boston merchant. After the war they eloped, and when their wagon broke down he traded it to a Native American chief for this land. The first park facilities were constructed by the CCC. The park opened in 1937.

In addition to the fine trails in the park, Tuscarora Trail, a 105-mile trail that extends into Maryland, passes through Cowans Gap.

Directions: From U.S. Route 30 between McConnellsburg and Chambersburg, take Pennsylvania Route 75 north to Richmond Furnace, then follow the signs to the park on Richmond Road. From the Pennsylvania Turnpike, take Exit 14 to Route 75 south, then follow the signs from Richmond Furnace on Richmond Road.

Hours Open: Day-use areas are open from 8:00 A.M. to sunset. The park is open year-round.

Facilities: Cowans Gap State Park offers a full range of facilities, including 233 campsites for tents or RVs,

showers, a sanitary dump station, 10 rustic cabins, a lake for swimming from Memorial Day weekend through Labor Day, a food concession, boating and fishing, more than 450 picnic tables, and picnic pavilions.

Permits and Rules: Alcoholic beverages are prohibited. Boats must have either a state park launching permit, a state park mooring permit, or a current Pennsylvania Fish and Boat Commission registration. Only nonpowered and electric-powered boats are allowed. Outdoor recreational activities are restricted to locations where signs or physical improvements designate the appropriate use. Fires and the disposal of hot coals are restricted to provided facilities. Trash and litter must be placed in containers provided for this purpose, and disposal is limited to items accumulated during the use of the park. Pets must be leashed and controlled at all times, and they are not allowed at the swimming area or in overnight camping facilities.

Further Information: Department of Conservation and Natural Resources, Cowans Gap State Park, HC 17266, Fort Loudon, PA 17224-9801; phone 717-485-3948.

Other Areas of Interest

The birthplace of **James Buchanan,** the only American president born in Pennsylvania, is located about 30 minutes south of Cowans Gap. For information on this and other area attractions, write to Fulton County Tourist Promotion Agency, P.O. Box 141, McConnellsburg, PA 17233; phone 717-485-4064.

Tuscarora State Forest borders the park. For information write to District Forester, RD 2, Box 3, McConnellsburg, PA 17233; phone 717-485-3148.

Park Trails

Plessinger Trail 👢👢—1 mile—This is an easy hike along South Branch Little Aughwick Creek to Cameron Trail.

One Mile Trail Loop 👢👢—.75 mile—Take a pleasant stroll through mountain laurel.

Three Mile Trail Loop 👢👢👢👢—1.8 miles—A forested trail with a lot of mountain laurel, this has a very steep, rocky section.

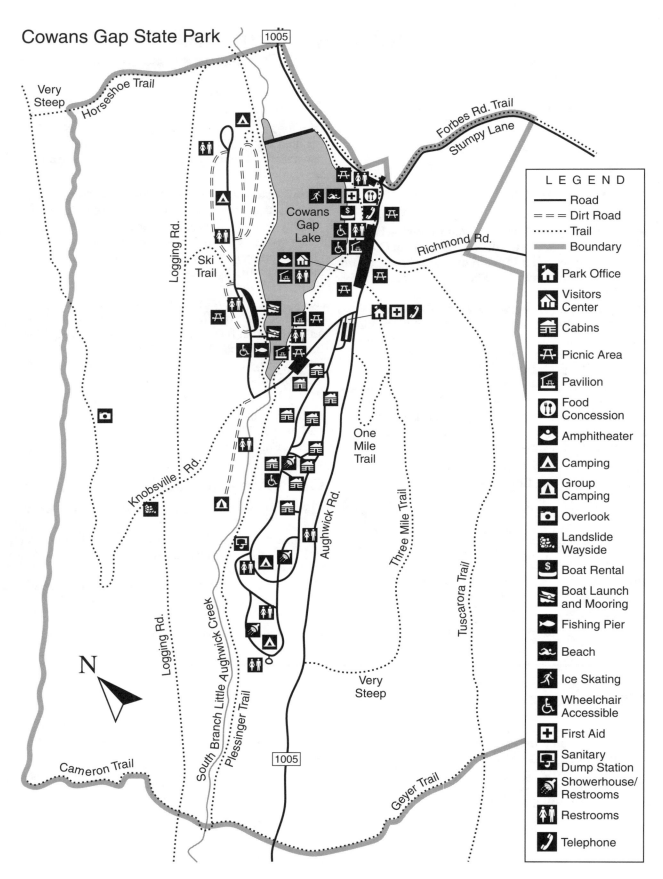

Cowans Gap State Park

1005

Very Steep

Horseshoe Trail

Forbes Rd. Trail

Stumpy Lane

Cowans Gap Lake

Richmond Rd.

Logging Rd.

Ski Trail

One Mile Trail

Knobsville Rd.

Aughwick Rd.

Three Mile Trail

Tuscarora Trail

Logging Rd.

South Branch Little Aughwick Creek

Plessinger Trail

Very Steep

N

Cameron Trail

1005

Geyer Trail

LEGEND

—— Road
=== Dirt Road
· · · Trail
—— Boundary

🏠 Park Office

🏠 Visitors Center

🏚 Cabins

🎪 Picnic Area

🏛 Pavilion

🍴 Food Concession

⛺ Amphitheater

⛺ Camping

⛺ Group Camping

📷 Overlook

🏔 Landslide Wayside

$ Boat Rental

🚤 Boat Launch and Mooring

🐟 Fishing Pier

🏊 Beach

⛸ Ice Skating

♿ Wheelchair Accessible

➕ First Aid

🚽 Sanitary Dump Station

🚿 Showerhouse/ Restrooms

🚻 Restrooms

📞 Telephone

Lakeside Trail 👢👢

Distance Round-Trip: 1.42 miles

Estimated Hiking Time: .75 hour

Caution: Insects might be a problem during spring and early summer.

Trail Directions: Lakeside Trail was chosen as the favorite trail of park visitors. It is a leisurely stroll that circles Cowans Gap Lake. Several places make good trailheads. We will use the footbridge over the outlet of Cowans Gap Lake, located at the end of Camping Area B **[1]**.

A sign at this trailhead points to Lakeside Trail crossing the bridge and along the lakeshore to the right. Start by walking across the bridge and over the earth and stone breastwork of the dam to a sharp right turn at the other end (.1 mi.) **[2]**. A sign here tells you that you are also following Tuscarora Trail. Trail blazes are blue and yellow. Do not let any changes in trail blaze colors fool you. This trail circles close to the lake, so you cannot get lost.

A gentle incline on a wide gravel trail leads into a wooded area with mountain ash, maple, hemlock, red oak, white oak, pine, and rhododendron, breaking out into the open by the swimming beach (.3 mi.) **[3]**. There are picnic tables here, restrooms, a food concession, and a parking area. You have already passed water fountains and will pass others.

Walk on a service road to a paved path past the back of the dressing stockade to some trees. Watch for yellow trail blazes, but spend more time looking at the reflections of the mountain in the lake, at large oak trees and squirrels. Turn right at the paved road

(.8 mi.) **[4]** and follow it across the lake inlet. You will pass a Lakeside Trail sign and a Plessinger Trail sign before crossing the inlet. Turn right after crossing the bridge on a narrow path. There is no trail sign here, but there are yellow trail blazes. This end of the lake is marshy right to the edge of the trail. Birds, frogs, and other wildlife prefer this area.

This side of the lake is a contrast from the other. It is not manicured. The only developments are the camping area, which does not extend to the lakeshore, and two boat-launching ramps. It is a very quiet, relaxing walk back to the trailhead at the outlet (1.42 mi.) **[1]**.

1. Trailhead
2. Cross dam
3. Beach
4. Paved road

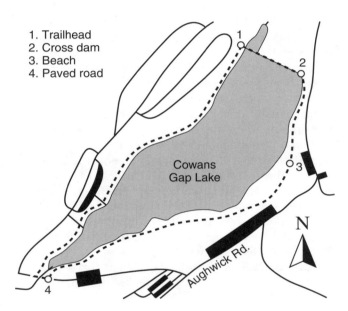

Knobsville Road

Distance Round-Trip: 3.2 miles

Estimated Hiking Time: 2 hours

Caution: One section of this trail is very steep. Do not walk out of the park onto private land.

Trail Directions: Though not a named trail for most of this loop, this is the best hike in the park. It gives you an unusual opportunity to walk through a landslide, and it passes two fine overlooks.

Knobsville Road is the main park road. Park headquarters is at the intersection of Knobsville Road and Aughwick Road. Drive past park headquarters and over the inlet to Cowans Gap Lake until a gate blocks the road. Park here and use the gate as your trailhead **[1].**

You immediately begin climbing on a gravel road through second-growth forest to the first point of interest, a landslide that occurred in 1996 (.3 mi.) **[2].** More than 40 inches of snow covered the mountain in mid-January of that year when a warm-weather system dropped 2 inches of rain. The bedrock on the mountain slopes 45 degrees, and Knobsville Road had cut through the topsoil. The rain and melting snow acted as a lubricant between the topsoil and the bedrock, and a 100-foot section above Knobsville Road broke loose. The road held, but the slide continued down the mountain. The landslide area is 50 feet wide by 1,600 feet long.

Knobsville Road makes a horseshoe curve to the right above the landslide to an overlook from a wooden platform (.9 mi.) **[3].** Below is an inspiring view of forest, Cowans Gap Lake, mountain ridges, and farms. Most hikers turn around at this point. The best of the trail has been accomplished. However, if you hike over the spine of Cove Mountain, there is an excellent panorama of Knobsville. To make a loop, continue to the intersection of Horseshoe Trail (1.6 mi.) **[4].** If you miss this turn, Knobsville Road passes into private land. Do not walk onto this private land.

Turn right on Horseshoe Trail to climb a very steep slope back up to the mountain crest, then down the side of the mountain on an easier slope. This is actually a firebreak and not a very good trail. Turn right at a grass-covered logging road (2.1 mi.) **[5].** Follow this back to Knobsville Road (3 mi.) **[6]** and turn left to return to the trailhead (3.2 mi.) **[1].**

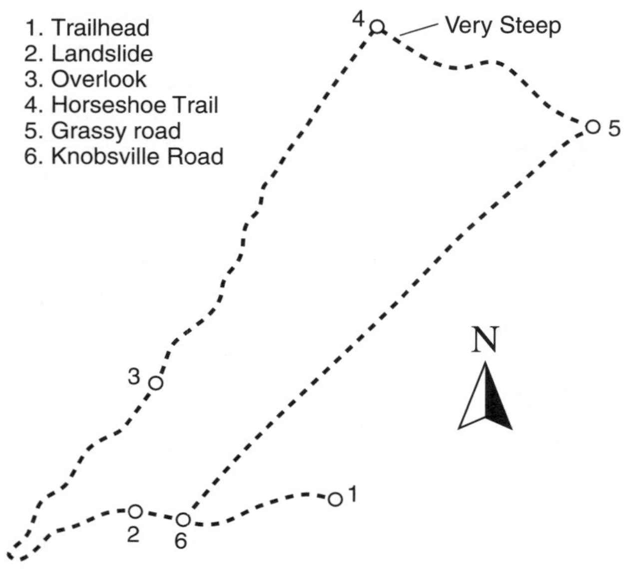

36. Caledonia State Park

- Bring your clubs to play the oldest golf course in south-central Pennsylvania.
- Swim in a large pool.
- Hike through one of the most beautiful forests in the state.

Area Information

Caledonia is one of the oldest state parks in Pennsylvania. It is named for an iron furnace owned by Thaddeus Stevens that began operating in 1837. Stevens, born in Caledonia County, Vermont, became a famous abolitionist and statesman. He is recognized as the father of the Pennsylvania public school system. In 1863, during the Civil War, Confederate troops under General Early destroyed the furnace. Today its only remnants are a reconstruction of the furnace, scars on the land left by charcoal hearths, and a canal that supplied water for a waterwheel that pumped air into the iron furnace.

Bird-watchers will find Caledonia State Park a rich area. Three distinctly different habitat types—hardwood forest, wet evergreen forest, and golf course—attract a great variety of birds. At least 120 species have been identified, of which 63 breed here. Visit the park during winter, when it is relatively quiet, for a chance of spotting the elusive northern goshawk.

The park is located on South Mountain, the northernmost ridge of the Blue Ridge Mountains. It contains surprisingly large eastern hemlock and white pine.

Directions: The main entrance is on U.S. Route 30 about halfway between Chambersburg and Gettysburg, on Pennsylvania Route 233.

Hours Open: Day-use areas are open from 8:00 A.M. to sunset. The park is open year-round.

Facilities: An 18-hole public golf course, built in the 1920s, makes this park very unusual. You can also enjoy swimming in a pool, tent or RV camping, biking, and fishing.

Permits and Rules: Alcoholic beverages are prohibited. Outdoor recreational activities are restricted to locations where signs or physical improvements designate the appropriate use. Fires and the disposal of hot coals are restricted to provided facilities. Trash and litter must be placed in containers provided for this purpose, and disposal is limited to items accumulated during the use of the park. Pets must be leashed and controlled at all times, and they are not allowed at the swimming area or in overnight camping facilities. Soliciting and posting signs are prohibited. Do not feed wildlife. Park only in designated areas.

Further Information: Department of Conservation and Natural Resources, Caledonia State Park, 40 Rocky Mountain Road, Fayetteville, PA 17222-9610; phone 717-352-2161.

Other Areas of Interest

The **Michaux State Forest** covers more than 85,000 acres near Pennsylvania's southern border. Write to District Forester, Michaux State Forest, 10099 Lincoln Way East, Fayetteville, PA 17222; phone 717-352-2211.

Park Trails

Blue Blaze Trail —.7 mile—Blue Blaze Trail connects Ramble Trail with the Appalachian Trail. It can be used to form a loop.

Thaddeus Stevens Historic Trail —.8 mile—Tour the historic sections of Caledonia State Park.

Midland Trail —.7 mile—This trail connects the major park facilities.

Charcoal Hearth Trail —2.7 miles—See five charcoal hearths, an old wagon road, and wildlife on the longest and most difficult trail in the park.

Trolley Trail —.7 mile—This short trail follows an old trolley grade. It is also used by bicycles.

Chambersburg Water Line —1.9 miles—Birds and wildflowers are abundant along this grassy trail.

Quarry Gap Road —1 mile—Connect this trail with sections of Greenwood Furnace Road and the Appalachian Trail to make a 3-mile loop.

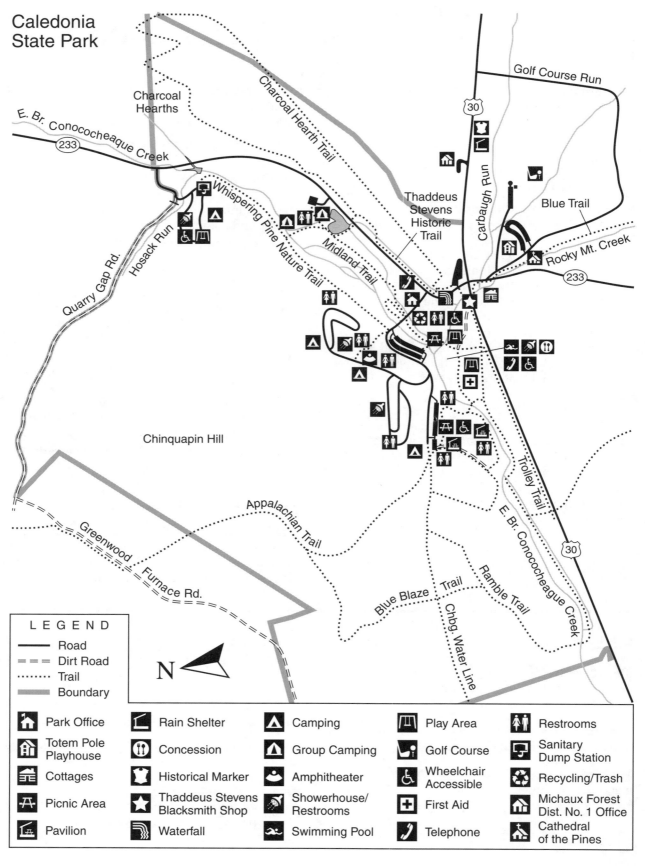

Caledonia State Park

Charcoal Hearths

E. Br. Conococheaque Creek

233

Quarry Gap Rd.

Hosack Run

Whispering Pine Nature Trail

Charcoal Hearth Trail

Midland Trail

Thaddeus Stevens Historic Trail

Carbaugh Run

30

Golf Course Run

Blue Trail

Rocky Mt. Creek

233

Chinquapin Hill

Appalachian Trail

Greenwood Furnace Rd.

Blue Blaze Trail

Chbg. Water Line

Ramble Trail

Trolley Trail

E. Br. Conococheaque Creek

30

LEGEND

— Road
=== Dirt Road
..... Trail
━━ Boundary

N

Park Office	Rain Shelter	Camping	Play Area	Restrooms
Totem Pole Playhouse	Concession	Group Camping	Golf Course	Sanitary Dump Station
Cottages	Historical Marker	Amphitheater	Wheelchair Accessible	Recycling/Trash
Picnic Area	Thaddeus Stevens Blacksmith Shop	Showerhouse/ Restrooms	First Aid	Michaux Forest Dist. No. 1 Office
Pavilion	Waterfall	Swimming Pool	Telephone	Cathedral of the Pines

Ramble Trail 👢👢

Distance Round-Trip: 2.1 miles

Estimated Hiking Time: 1 hour

Caution: This trail is quite level, but there are roots and rocks in a few places. Expect puddles and mud in rainy weather. Wear bright orange clothing during hunting season.

Trail Directions: A trailhead kiosk for Ramble Trail and other trails is located adjacent to Route 30. But since there is no parking near this kiosk, turn north on Route 233, turn left toward the swimming area, then turn left into the first parking area. Start the hike at the footbridge over East Branch Conococheague Creek **[1]**. Follow the Midland Trail sign across this and two more smaller footbridges, past the swimming pool on your right, then over a mowed field to a small log cabin. This is the Dock Memorial, which is the trailhead kiosk (.14 mi.) **[2]**.

Follow the Ramble Trail sign to the right, unless you have entered the Dock Memorial to look at the park map, in which case you turn left when you exit the cabin. Walk behind a larger cabin, following yellow trail blazes. After leaving the trees around these cabins, walk along the edge of a mowed field. Turn left by a Ramble Trail sign (.3 mi.) **[3]** at the end of the field. Ramble Trail is a loop that goes both right and left here.

You will see both yellow and white trail blazes in this area. The white blazes are for the Appalachian Trail, which shares the same course for a short distance. Ignore a left fork about 200 feet past the Ramble Trail sign. You will be following East Branch Conococheague Creek downstream through thick hemlock and rhododendron. You will also see scattered birch and hardwoods. After crossing a footbridge (.5 mi.) **[4]**, enjoy some unusually large white pine. This part of the trail follows a raised grade beside a small canal. Appalachian Trail and the white trail blazes cut to the left over a wooden footbridge (.6 mi.) **[5]**. Though polluted by the noise from Route 30, this is one of the prettiest pine/hemlock/rhododendron forests in the state. Watch for gray squirrels on the tree trunks and belted kingfishers perched over the creek.

Ramble Trail leaves the raised grade just before crossing an unusual stone footbridge (1 mi.) **[6]**. Stone posts at either end of the footbridge make good seats where you can ponder this scene. Water no longer runs under the stone bridge. When it did, it ran from the canal above the raised grade through a laid stone canal and cascaded over several human-made waterfalls. It its day, it was certainly beautiful. Now it is hauntingly beautiful.

A short drop after the stone footbridge leads over a small wooden footbridge to the edge of East Branch Conococheague Creek. Turn right, then cross the creek over a larger footbridge (1.1 mi.) **[7]**. This is the apex of the loop. Feel the cool air over the creek.

Ramble Trail is raised slightly and covered with wood chips as it winds back up the valley floor. The noise from Route 30 is more muffled. The forest, virtually all hemlock, rhododendron, and pine, has an almost Jurassic appearance; it is probably the only one of its kind you have seen in Pennsylvania.

Continue straight past the intersection with Blue Blaze Trail (1.38 mi.) **[8]**, following the yellow trail blazes. Turn right at a gravel road (1.47 mi.) **[9]**. Ignore a gravel road that forks acutely left. This road is not on the park map. It leads to the park dump. Ramble Trail forks right, away from the gravel road (1.71 mi.) **[10]**, at a trail sign. But instead of turning to stay on Ramble Trail, stay on the gravel road for a more direct route back to your vehicle. Along the way, you pass another intersection with the Appalachian Trail (1.77 mi.) **[11]**. Your road is paved past a yellow and black gate (1.86 mi.) **[12]**. Turn right past the swimming pool into the parking lot. The footbridge where you began this hike is at the near end of this parking lot (2.1 mi.) **[1]**.

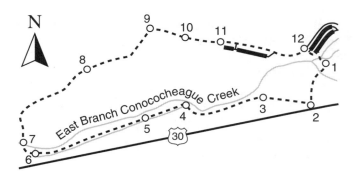

1. Trailhead
2. Dock Memorial
3. End of field
4. Footbridge
5. White blazes left
6. Stone footbridge
7. Cross creek
8. Blue Blaze Trail
9. Gravel road
10. Leave Ramble Trail
11. Appalachian Trail
12. Yellow and black gate

Whispering Pine Nature Trail 🥾

Distance Round-Trip: .3 mile

Estimated Hiking Time: .5 hour

Caution: The trail is shrouded with rhododendron and is hard to follow in places if you do not watch for the white trail blazes. Watch for briars.

Trail Directions: This was an interpretive trail with numbered posts at one time. While an interpretive brochure is still available at park headquarters, most numbers on posts are no longer visible. Nonetheless, this is a good study in forest habitat if you try to identify trees and plants along the way. Look for eastern hemlock, white pine, pitch pine, Virginia pine, black birch, tuliptree, red oak, white oak, sassafras, red maple, rhododendron, and mountain laurel.

The trail begins and ends on the park road between park headquarters and the swimming pool. Park in the first parking area after crossing two bridges over separate channels of East Branch Conococheague Creek, then walk back to the trailhead, which is between the two bridges **[1]**. A sign marks the trailhead, and the trail is marked by white trail blazes.

Turn left onto the trail. Look for skunk cabbage when you cross a footbridge. This area floods every spring and is generally wet, which promotes the growth of more plants than you would see on higher, drier ground. This type of wet forest habitat would have been quite common before the trees were cut to fuel iron furnaces and land was cleared for farming. Now it is critical to preserve places like this for wildlife habitat and to protect plants that can exist nowhere else.

Some trees are very large. One eastern hemlock stands out. Estimate its circumference at chest height. Then do the same to an exceptional white pine about 20 paces farther along the trail. A tulip tree about 25 more paces along is even bigger. Some huge trees have fallen in this area. Some have been cut to make way for the trail. Can you count the growth rings on these old trees? Each ring expresses a year of growth.

Rhododendron is very thick. This is a fabulous wildflower garden when it blossoms in early summer.

Turn left at a T that does not appear on the trail map, following the white blazes. Look for a huge oak near the T and identify the precise species. A white pine past here is about seven feet in diameter, one of the largest you will ever see. Its twin trunks tower above all surrounding trees.

You return to the paved road about 20 feet to the right from where you entered the forest (.3 mi.) **[2]**. Turn right to return to the parking lot

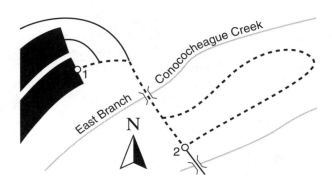

1. Trailhead
2. Road

37. Gettysburg

- Tour the most famous battle site in American history.
- See where Lincoln spoke the words that defined the Civil War and changed America.
- Enjoy one of the world's largest collections of outdoor sculpture.
- Walk under the shade of some of the oldest and most unusual trees in the state.

Area Information

On June 30, 1863, advance units of the Army of Northern Virginia under General Robert E. Lee and the Army of the Potomac under General George Meade met at the small southern Pennsylvania town of Gettysburg. By the next day, the confrontation exploded into the largest, bloodiest, and most famous battle of the Civil War. Following Pickett's Charge on July 3, when more than 5,000 of General Pickett's 12,000 men fell, General Lee withdrew his army. The Battle of Gettysburg had cost more than 51,000 men killed, wounded, or captured. From that point, the war became a defensive struggle by the Confederacy.

The defining moment of the Civil War came on November 19, 1863, when President Abraham Lincoln delivered the Gettysburg Address, perhaps the most famous speech in American history, at the Gettysburg National Cemetery.

Gettysburg National Military Park preserves the Gettysburg battlefield much as it was at the time of the great battle, with the addition of a cemetery and more than 1,400 monuments. Established by 1895 by an act of Congress, the park covers 6,000 acres. Licensed guides are available for auto tours of the park.

Directions: Gettysburg is on U.S. Route 30, 3 miles west of the intersection with U.S. Route 15. To reach the Visitor Center, turn south from Route 30 onto Washington Street about .8 mile.

Hours Open: The park is open year-round, daily from 6:00 A.M. to 10:00 P.M. The Visitor Center is open from 8:00 A.M. to 5:00 P.M. and until 6:00 P.M. during the summer.

Facilities: Within the park are the Visitor Center, the Cyclorama Center, trails for hiking and biking, picnic tables, and restrooms. The Visitor Center displays a huge collection of Civil War items and the Electric Map, an orientation program to the battle. The Cyclorama Center contains a painting of Pickett's Charge, completed in 1884, that is 360 feet long. Fees are charges at the Cyclorama Center and the Electric Map.

Permits and Rules: Do not climb on monuments or disturb structures, exhibits, plants, animals, or minerals. Collecting relics is prohibited. Pets must be leashed and attended at all times, and they are not allowed at the Gettysburg National Cemetery, the Visitor Center, or the Cyclorama Center. Picnic only at designated areas.

Further Information: Superintendent, Gettysburg National Military Park, 97 Taneytown Road, Gettysburg, PA 17325; phone 717-334-1124.

Other Areas of Interest

There are no campgrounds in the park. For information about private campgrounds and other local services, write to **Gettysburg Convention and Visitors Bureau,** 35 Carlisle Street, Gettysburg, PA 17325; phone 717-334-6274.

The **Eisenhower National Historic Site,** which was the home and farm of President Dwight D. Eisenhower, is located at Gettysburg. For tour information write to Eisenhower National Historic Site, 97 Taneytown Road, Gettysburg, PA 17325; phone 717-334-4474.

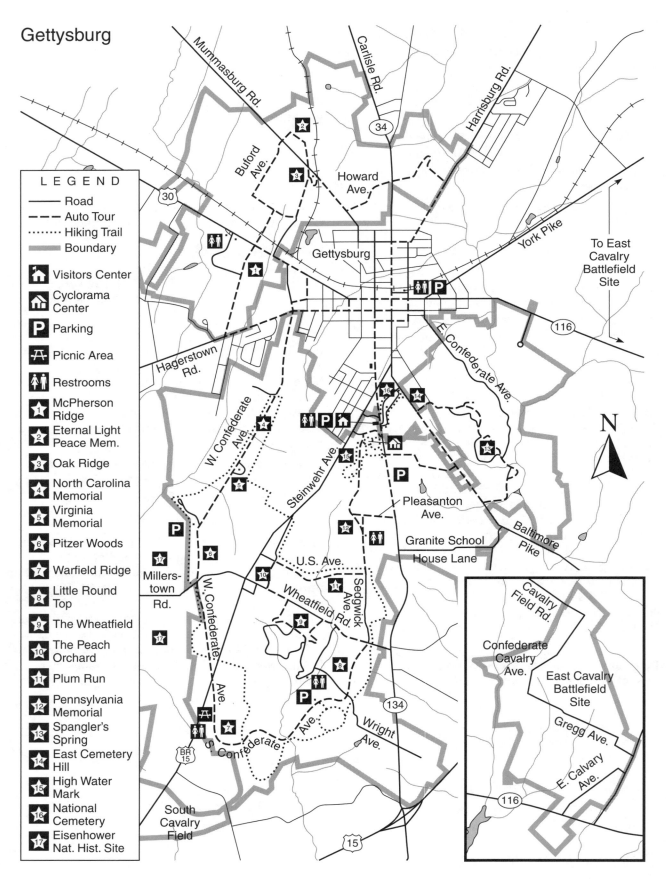

Gettysburg

LEGEND
— Road
- - - Auto Tour
····· Hiking Trail
▬ Boundary

🏠 Visitors Center
🏛 Cyclorama Center
P Parking
🅿 Picnic Area
🚻 Restrooms
1 McPherson Ridge
2 Eternal Light Peace Mem.
3 Oak Ridge
4 North Carolina Memorial
5 Virginia Memorial
6 Pitzer Woods
7 Warfield Ridge
8 Little Round Top
9 The Wheatfield
10 The Peach Orchard
11 Plum Run
12 Pennsylvania Memorial
13 Spangler's Spring
14 East Cemetery Hill
15 High Water Mark
16 National Cemetery
17 Eisenhower Nat. Hist. Site

The Gettysburg National Cemetery 🥾

Distance Round-Trip: .6 mile

Estimated Hiking Time: 20 minutes

Caution: The weather at Gettysburg gets very hot and muggy during the summer.

Trail Directions: This short paved loop through the Gettysburg National Cemetery should be a pilgrimage for all loyal Americans.

Park at the Visitor Center. Walk directly across Washington Street to the gate at the entrance to Gettysburg National Cemetery **[1]**. A paved walkway leads to an oval. Take the right side of the oval. The Lincoln Address Memorial is 140 feet from the gate. Read the Gettysburg Address before you go any farther, and reflect on what it has meant and continues to mean to this country. The actual spot where Lincoln delivered his Gettysburg Address during the dedication of the cemetery on November 19, 1863, is about 1,000 feet farther along the loop. Here he spoke 272 words that changed America. Think about how those words have redefined freedom.

As you pass thousands of small headstones, think about these young men who wanted to live just as much as you want to. They had hopes and dreams, families and friends, all of which they sacrificed for principles. They all stood bravely, facing a horrible barrage of lead and steel to preserve their vision of America.

Several states have erected monuments to their native sons who died at Gettysburg. One of the most impressive is the New York Monument, which rivals in height even the Soldiers National Monument. The Soldiers National Monument is the center of the semicircle of graves. The New York Monument is inside the apex of the loop, where you pass a monument to Major General John F. Reynolds (.3 mi.) **[2]**. Turn left by this monument.

You should have noticed that many of the trees in this cemetery are identified by signs. This is one of the finest tree preserves in the state. Many trees here are very old. Many are very unusual in Pennsylvania. Look for black locust, cucumber tree, bald cypress, sweet gum, purple beech, swamp cypress, Soulange's magnolia, tulip poplar, weeping beech, ginko, Norway spruce, sycamore maple, silver fir, Nordmann fir, golden plume cypress, oriental spruce, and basswood, along with more common Pennsylvania species such as eastern hemlock, silver maple, and white pine.

You complete the .6-mi. loop back at the gate **[1]**.

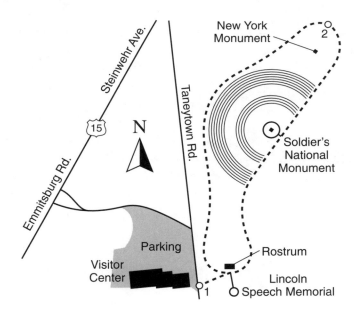

1. Gate
2. General Reynolds monument

Downtown Gettysburg Walking Tour 🥾

Distance Round-Trip: 1.5 miles

Estimated Hiking Time: 1 hour

Caution: Be cautious of traffic on the streets.

Trail Directions: Watch for plaques that identify buildings that stood during the Battle of Gettysburg. This is one of the best-preserved historical towns in the country of those that have been continually inhabited. While you walk the streets, try to block out the modern sights and imagine the streets filled with soldiers.

Start at the Gettysburg Travel Council and Information Center **[1]**. This building was built in 1858 as a railroad terminal. The exterior of this building is about the same as it appeared during the battle. Cross Carlisle Street and turn left, then turn right at Lincoln Square, which is actually a circle, onto Chambersburg Street. Chambersburg Street is U.S. Route 30, the first transcontinental highway in the United States. Route 30 spans the country from New York to Portland, Oregon. Christ Lutheran Church, across the street, served as a hospital during the battle.

Turn left at West Street (.3 mi.) **[2]**, which had fewer homes during the battle and was not paved but otherwise has not changed much since 1863. Turn left again at West Middle Street (.5 mi.) **[3]**, turn right onto South Washington Street (.6 mi.) **[4]**, then make a left onto West High Street (.7 mi.) **[5]**. Churches along this street serve as hospitals. The Gettysburg Municipal building, which is on your right after crossing Baltimore Street, was the county jail at the time of the battle.

Turn left at South Stratton Street (1 mi.) **[6]**, then left again onto York Street (1.2 mi.) **[7]**. Several homes here date back to the battle. Look for the historical marker at the former home of Samuel Gettys, who was the father of James Gettys, the founder of Gettysburg. The Gettysburg National Bank was a hotel during the battle. Confederate soldiers took a break here by looting whiskey. Try to spot a cannonball embedded under a second-floor window of a building near Lincoln Square.

Lincoln Square has changed in appearance. Storefronts on the ground floors of buildings have been modernized. However, several of the buildings are the same ones seen by the soldiers who marched along these streets. Turn right on Carlisle Street to return to the Travel Council and Information Center (1.5 mi.) **[1]**.

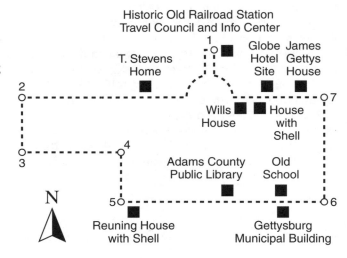

1. Travel Council
2. West Street
3. West Middle Street
4. South Washington Street
5. West High Street
6. South Stratton Street
7. York Street

West

Bordered on the north by New York and Ontario, on the west by Ohio and West Virginia, on the south by West Virginia and Maryland, and on the east by the Allegheny National Forest and the Appalachian Mountains, western Pennsylvania has contrasting areas of dense and sparse human population.

Topography

A narrow strip of Lake Erie Plains along the northwest corner of the state rises onto a glaciated area covering almost all of Erie, Crawford, Mercer, and Lawrence counties and parts of Warren and Venango counties. This glaciated area has more gently rolling hills than most of the state.

Most of the remainder of western Pennsylvania is in the Appalachian Plateau. Warren, Venango, and Forest counties are in a geographic area known as the Allegheny Plateau, more commonly called the Allegheny Highlands. To the south, it is called the Pittsburgh Plateau. Only a narrow strip along eastern Indiana, Westmoreland and Fayette counties, is in the Allegheny Mountains. This is some of the highest land in the state.

Major Rivers and Lakes

Pennsylvania has about 45 miles of shoreline on the north coast of the United States. Lake Erie is the 12th-largest lake in the world. One of the five Great Lakes, it connects the city of Erie with the Atlantic Ocean through the Welland Canal, Lake Ontario, and the St. Lawrence Seaway. Only a small portion of the lake is in Pennsylvania, but this 640,000 acres is the largest body of water in the state by a huge margin.

Conneaut Lake, in Crawford County, is the largest natural lake completely within Pennsylvania, though it is just 928 acres. Like several smaller lakes and ponds in the northwest corner of the state, it was created by Ice Age glaciers.

The Allegheny Reservoir and Pymatuning Reservoir are large human-made lakes. About a third of the 12,000-acre Allegheny Reservoir is in New York, and the Ohio border slices through Pymatuning Reservoir. Lake Arthur, in Butler County, is the largest state park lake in the state, at 3,225 acres.

Most of western Pennsylvania is drained by the Allegheny River, the northeastern headwaters of the Mississippi River. Originating in central Pennsylvania, then swinging through New York and reentering Pennsylvania through the Allegheny Reservoir, this river played a vital role in the westward expansion of the United States. It meets the Monongahela River, which flows north out of West Virginia, at Pittsburgh to form the mighty Ohio River. Some of the major tributaries, starting in the north, are Conewango Creek, Tionesta Creek, the Clarion River, and the Kiskiminetas River. The Beaver River, which flows into the Ohio River, drains the area along the Ohio border.

Common Plant Life

Allegheny hardwood forest, with large percentages of black cherry, red maple, sugar maple, red oak, northern white oak, and ash, covers much of Warren County and extends south to Interstate Route 80, and along the Allegheny Mountains south into West Virginia and Maryland. Silver maple, willow, and sycamore are abundant in the Allegheny River valley and along the major tributaries. Hemlock and white pine are also common. Mountain laurel is widespread on the Allegheny Highlands and is mixed with rhododendron through the Allegheny Mountains. Forest floors are generally covered by ferns. European grasses have replaced native grasses in most untended fields.

West of this forest is a checkerboard of woodlots, agriculture, and abandoned farms reverting to forest. Erie and Crawford counties are most intensively agricultural, with mostly dairy farms where corn, hay, clover, and other crops used for cattle feed are grown. Wetlands in the northwest corner are home to several rare and endangered plants.

Common Birds and Animals

White-tailed deer and eastern coyotes are abundant throughout western Pennsylvania, even into the suburbs of Pittsburgh and Erie. Black bears are most numerous in the Allegheny Highlands. Among the more common smaller mammals are raccoons, opossum, gray squirrels, red squirrels, chipmunks, red fox, gray fox, beavers, muskrats, and mink. River otters and fishers, both native species that were wiped out, have been reintroduced into the Allegheny Highlands.

The most striking increase in any bird population has been that of the Canada goose. Largely through the efforts of the Pennsylvania Game Commission, this species has spread so much that it is a nuisance in many areas. Mallards and wood ducks are abundant along lakes and streams. Red-tailed hawks, which perch along fields and soar the skies, are the most frequently seen raptor. Kestrels, red-shouldered hawks, turkey vultures, barred owls, and great horned owls are common. The varied habitat of forest, fields, and wetlands are home to a tremendous variety of songbirds. Among the most common are robins, red-winged blackbirds, and blue jays. Wild turkeys and ruffed grouse are common in the forests and farm edges.

Climate

Snowbelts stretching from Lake Erie into Erie, Crawford, and Warren counties dump large amounts of snow on this area. Snow cover lasts through most of the winter as far south as I-80. Average winter temperatures north of I-80 range from the mid-teens to the mid-30s. Average summer highs range from the low 50s to the low 80s.

The weather is similar south of I-80 because of high elevations. Snow cover does not tend to be as persistent. Winter temperatures range from the low 20s to the low 40s while summer temperatures range from the mid-50s to the mid-80s.

Best Features

- Lake Erie
- Presque Isle
- Allegheny National Forest
- Allegheny River
- Ohiopyle Falls
- Ohio River
- Allegheny Reservoir
- Pymatuning Reservoir

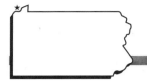

38. Presque Isle State Park

- Examine the only sand spit in Pennsylvania.
- Come during fall or spring to watch migrating birds seldom seen anywhere else in the state.
- Swim in the only surf in the state.
- Visit the most popular Pennsylvania state park.

Area Information

Presque Isle State Park is unique within Pennsylvania for several reasons. It is the state's only sand spit, a massive sandy peninsula created by the prevailing westerly wind, and due to that wind, it is constantly moving east at a rate of about half a mile per century. Several distinctly different ecological zones varying from recently deposited shoreline to climax forest are a result of this movement. Schedule a stop at Stull Interpretive Center early during your visit. Exhibits about the ecological succession of the sand spit and about the flora and fauna will make your hikes more meaningful.

This is a bird-watchers' paradise. At least 320 species have been observed in the park, including 45 species of special concern. It is a vital resting area for migratory birds, including unusual shorebirds that migrate from the Arctic to South America and numerous waterfowl. Many species nest here, some of which nest nowhere else in the state. Gull Point, the eastern tip of the peninsula, has been designated a nature area to protect the habitat of nesting and migrating shorebirds. It is closed to the public from April 1 to November 30.

The Perry Monument honors the Battle of Lake Erie, in which Commodore Oliver Hazard Perry's fleet defeated the British at Put-in-Bay, Ohio, during the War of 1812. Part of Perry's fleet was built in Presque Isle Bay. Perry's fleet returned to the Presque Isle Bay after the battle. His flagship, the *Niagara,* is on display across the bay in the city of Erie.

Directions: Pennsylvania Route 832, which intersects Pennsylvania Route 5, U.S. Route 20, and Interstate Route 90, leads to the park entrance.

Hours Open: The park is open year-round from 8:00 A.M. to sunset. Guarded beaches are open from Memorial Day weekend through Labor Day between 10:00 A.M. and 8:00 P.M.

Facilities: Presque Isle State Park facilities include guarded swimming beaches, beach houses, food concessions, picnic areas, pavilions, rest rooms, a marina, boat launch ramps, and an interpretive center.

Permits and Rules: Outdoor recreation is allowed only in areas where physical improvements or signs designate the appropriate purpose. Fires and disposal of hot coals are allowed only in provided facilities. All pets must be on a leash no more than six feet in length and under control at all times. Swimming is allowed only at guarded beaches while guards are on duty. Waterskiing is not allowed within 500 feet of shore except for takeoff and approach. Do not feed wildlife.

Further Information: Presque Isle State Park, P.O. Box 8510, Erie, PA 16505; phone 814-833-7424.

Other Areas of Interest

For information about Commodore Perry's flagship *Niagara* and other **Erie** attractions, contact Tourist and Convention Bureau, Greater Erie Chamber of Commerce, 1006 State Street, Erie, PA 16501; phone 814-454-7191.

Park Trails

Fox Trail 🥾—2.25 miles—Walk a weaving path through swamps and oak and maple forest.

Pine Tree Trail 🥾—.7 mile—A stand of pines grows along the edge of a sand plain community.

North Pier Trail 🥾🥾—.7 mile—Follow the shoreline between North Pier and Beach 11 on a sand ridge.

Grave Yard Pond Trail 🥾—.75 mile—This pond was the final resting place for many of Commodore Perry's men in the War of 1812.

Long Pond Trail 🥾—1 mile—Observe nesting or migrating waterfowl.

Multi-Purpose Trail 🥾—5.8 miles—A paved trail from the park entrance to the Perry Monument, this has been designated a national recreation trail.

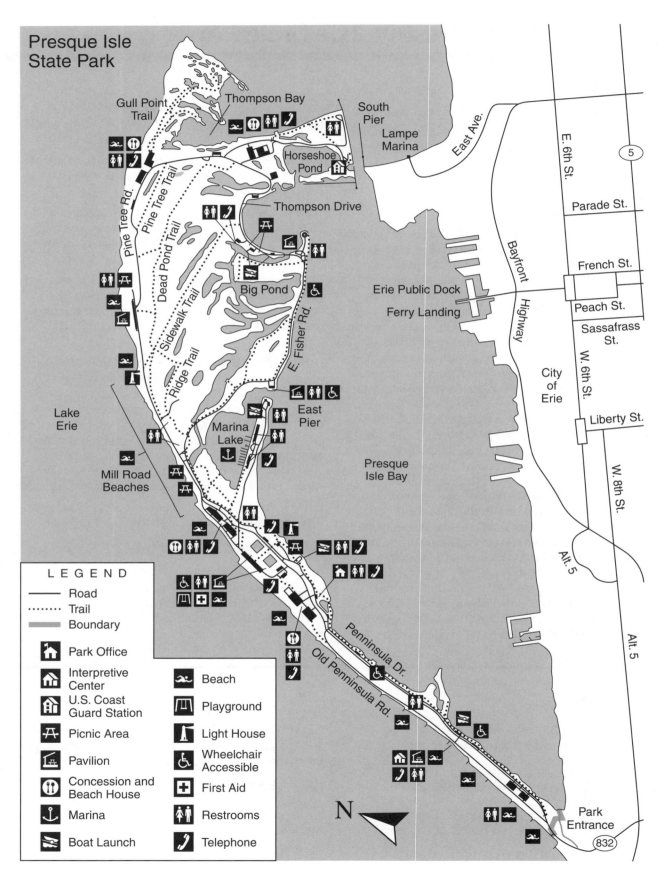

Presque Isle State Park

Thompson Bay

Gull Point Trail

South Pier

Lampe Marina

Horseshoe Pond

Pine Tree Rd.

Pine Tree Trail

Dead Pond Trail

Thompson Drive

Big Pond

Sidewalk Trail

Ridge Trail

East Fisher Rd.

Erie Public Dock

Ferry Landing

Lake Erie

East Pier

Marina Lake

Presque Isle Bay

Mill Road Beaches

Peninsula Dr.

Old Peninsula Rd.

Park Entrance

East Ave.

Bayfront Highway

City of Erie

E. 6th St.

Parade St.

French St.

Peach St.

Sassafrass St.

Liberty St.

W. 6th St.

W. 8th St.

Alt. 5

Alt. 5

5

832

LEGEND

—— Road

········ Trail

▬▬ Boundary

🏠 Park Office

🏛 Interpretive Center

🏠 U.S. Coast Guard Station

⛱ Picnic Area

⛺ Pavilion

🍴 Concession and Beach House

⚓ Marina

🚤 Boat Launch

🏊 Beach

🎠 Playground

🗼 Light House

♿ Wheelchair Accessible

➕ First Aid

🚻 Restrooms

📞 Telephone

150

Gull Point Trail 🥾

Distance Round-Trip: 1.9 miles

Estimated Hiking Time: 1 hour

Caution: A sign at the trailhead warns hikers that ticks are known to be in the area. Stay out of the brush, tuck in your pants cuffs, and consider wearing repellent. Do not bring pets on the trail. Though wide and level, this trail is sandy in most places. Walking on sand is more tiring than walking on firmer ground.

Trail Directions: The trailhead is located at the east end of the parking lot on the east side of Beach No. 10. You will see Lake Erie just a few yards to the north. A kiosk at the trailhead **[1]** outlines the unusual nature of Gull Point, one of the best bird-watching spots in the country. Bring high-powered binoculars or a spotting scope to identify unusual species. This most rapidly changing area of the park is like nowhere else in Pennsylvania, with unusual plants including American beach grass, brook lobelia, beach pea vine, and bushy cinquefoil.

This trail is a loop, with both sides joining at a trail sign just beyond the kiosk. Start on the right side of the loop. Several short trails cut between the sides of the loop, to your left as you walk toward Gull Point. Ignore these and walk straight ahead. The main trail is easy to follow, wide, and either sandy or short grass.

Watch for ducks and geese on a small pond on the right side of the trail. Overhead, you will probably see gulls, herons, and waterfowl. The first major fork in the trail **[2]** comes .2 mi. from the trailhead. A sign directs you to take the left fork to stay on Gull Point Trail. The right fork will take you onto a narrow point extending into Thompson Bay.

Another major fork at .5 mi. **[3]** is the loop of Gull Point Trail. You will take the left fork on the return trip, when it will be a right fork. But now, continue straight ahead. You will arrive at a split-rail fence **[4]** at .7 mi., on the edge of the beach in the back of a small bay. Here you will begin to see the wonderful variety of waterbirds. A light at the entrance to Presque Isle Bay can be seen across Thompson Bay, and beyond is Erie. Notice how sand is beginning to close off the mouth of the small bay directly in front of you. This is the process that formed some of the ponds in Presque Isle. The spot where you are standing did not even exist 100 years ago.

The major highlight of this trail is the observation platform (.9 mi.) **[5]** at the edge of the special management area. Bird-watchers should be able to add to their life lists here. Past the tower, an area well marked by signs is closed to all public use from April 1 through November 30 to protect migrating and nesting shorebirds including the sanderling, short-billed dowitcher, least sandpiper, ruddy turnstone, piping plover, common tern, and greater yellowlegs. Notice how the singularly annoying calls of the multitude of gulls blend to a melodic warble.

Backtrack from the observation tower until you reach the fork (1.4 mi.) **[3]** that begins the loop portion of the trail. Take the right fork toward Lake Erie. As you did on the other side of the loop, ignore several short trails that cut left. Walk roughly parallel to the lakeshore. As the trail passes very close to the beach, ahead you will see the kiosk at the trailhead. Stone structures in the lake were placed there to reduce sand erosion, the process that is building Gull Point.

The trail turns left away from the lake, then makes a right turn. A fork to the left in this turn goes to the other side of the loop. Take the right fork. You arrive back at the trailhead **[1]** after walking 1.9 mi.

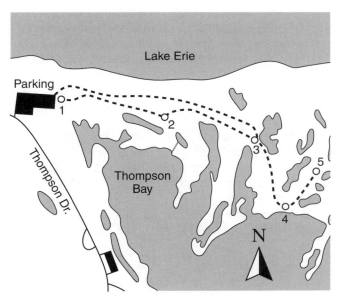

1. Trailhead
2. Fork
3. Loop fork
4. Split-rail fence
5. Observation platform

Sidewalk/Dead Pond Trails 🥾

Distance Round-Trip: 3.7 miles

Estimated Hiking Time: 2 hours

Caution: Between the end of Sidewalk Trail and the start of Dead Pond Trail you must walk along Thompson Drive. Watch for cars. Several stretches of Dead Pond Trail are sandy, which makes walking relatively difficult.

Trail Directions: The trailhead **[1]** for Sidewalk Trail is across the road from the lighthouse and Lighthouse Beach. There is a kiosk with a wooden map of the peninsula at the trailhead. However, this is an old map. Do not rely on it. Trails have been changed since it was erected.

Sidewalk Trail is a very straight, wide, level trail with a narrow concrete sidewalk running full length down the center. An intersection just 400 feet into the trail, the kiosk still visible behind, will not cause any confusion because you have the sidewalk to follow, and it is marked with signs. This is where you will complete the loop nearing the end of this hike. The loop circles an ecological reservation that includes three larger ponds. Waterfowl nest on these ponds, principally Canada geese, mallards, and wood ducks. Several other species might be spotted during spring and fall migrations. Ridge Pond is the first you will see inside the loop. Others will be visible to the right. You will also see several sand dunes that at one time were beach dunes.

Soon after making a sharp right turn, you arrive at Thompson Drive and the end of Sidewalk Trail (1.3 mi.) **[2]**. Turn left and walk along this hard surface road toward the head of Dead Pond Trail. Across Misery Bay to your right, you can see the Perry Monument, and farther across Presque Isle Bay, the Port of Erie Marine Terminal. Large ships are sometimes docked there.

After passing a sign at the turnoff to the Coast Guard station (1.9 mi.) **[3]**, start watching for the head of Dead Pond Trail (2 mi.) **[4]**. Dead Pond Trail starts straight toward Niagara Pond, then turns right, sweeping around the head of the pond. Ignore a right fork (2.1 mi.) **[5]** where the trail angles left, away from Thompson Drive.

B-Trail **[6]** intersects from the right at 2.8 mi. It is marked by a sign, as is A-Trail (3.3 mi.) **[7]**. Both of these trails are shortcuts out to Pine Tree Road. Note the climax pine forest in this area. White-tailed deer are common here, though due to human activity they probably will not be moving during the day.

Dead Pond Trail ends at Sidewalk Trail (3.6 mi.) **[8]**. Marsh Trail is straight ahead. This intersection is well marked. Turn right on Sidewalk Trail. The trailhead **[1]**, and end of this hike, is visible ahead, a total distance of 3.7 mi.

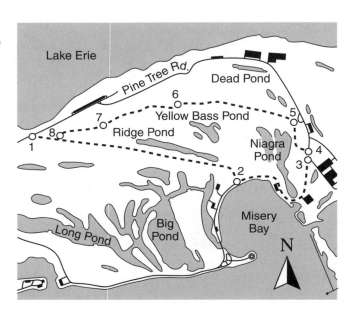

1. Trailhead
2. Thompson Drive
3. Coast Guard station
4. Dead Pond Trail
5. Fork
6. B-Trail
7. A-Trail
8. Intersection

39. Warren

- Canoe the route taken by French explorers on Conewango Creek and the Allegheny River.
- Fish for trout, bass, walleyes, muskellunge, northern pike, and catfish.
- Tour the historic district where homes recall the lumber and oil booms.

Area Information

In 1749, the French governor of Canada sent Celeron de Blainville on an expedition to reaffirm France's claim to the land west of the Appalachian Mountains. Celeron's party canoed down Conewango Creek and buried a lead plate where it emptied into the Allegheny River, which the French considered part of the Ohio River. At that time, the Senecas, one of the tribes in the Iroquois Confederacy, controlled this area. The Senecas had villages at the mouth of the Conewango and at several other level areas along the Allegheny River, where they cultivated corn and other crops. The Senecas made the unfortunate decision to ally with the British during the American Revolution. To punish them, Colonel Daniel Brodhead led a detachment from Fort Pitt up the Allegheny River valley and destroyed villages and crops in the area that is now Warren.

Warren was laid out in 1795, but the first settlers did not arrive until more than a decade later. The first structure was built by the Holland Land Company. Warren became one of the wealthiest towns in the United States during the lumber and oil booms of the 19th century. Great rafts of virgin pine tied up at Warren on their journeys downriver to Pittsburgh and Cincinnati. At one time, seven oil refineries were in the immediate vicinity of Warren. One remains a major employer. The timber industry also continues

to thrive. Numerous older homes from the boom era are preserved in an historic district.

Some of the finest fishing in Pennsylvania is within Warren city limits in the Allegheny River and Conewango Creek. Public access is allowed in several areas, including Betts Park, at the downriver end of Warren, and at "the Point."

Directions: Warren is located at the intersection of U.S. Routes 6 and 62.

Hours Open: Since Warren is not a park, this does not apply.

Facilities: Canoeing, boating, and fishing on the Allegheny River and Conewango Creek are a couple of the most popular activities inside city limits. A paved bike-and-hike trail follows Conewango Creek from Warren to North Warren. Picnic tables are located at Crescent Park, along the Crescent Park Tree Walk, and at "the Point," where Conewango Creek empties into the Allegheny River. Campgrounds are located nearby in the Allegheny National Forest and at Chapman State Park.

Permits and Rules: Bicycles may not be ridden on sidewalks.

Further Information: Northern Alleghenies Vacation Region, 315 Second Avenue, P.O. Box 804, Warren, PA 16365; phone 814-726-1222.

Other Areas of Interest

The **Pennsylvania State Championship Fishing Tournament** is held each fall on waterways in the Warren area. It is headquartered in Tidioute. Write to Pennsylvania State Championship Fishing Tournament, Inc., P.O. Box 242, Tidioute, PA 16351 (no phone).

Crescent Park Tree Walk 🥾

Distance Round-Trip: .7 mile

Estimated Hiking Time: 20 minutes

Caution: Ducks and geese are so numerous in this area that the ground can be slippery from their droppings. Feeding migratory waterfowl is illegal.

Trail Directions: Huge maples and oaks and unusual trees like the gingko make this one of the nicest tree walks in the state. Pick up an interpretive brochure at the Northern Alleghenies Vacation Region office at the corner of Second Avenue and Pennsylvania Avenue, a half block east from the Hickory Street Bridge. The brochure identifies and tells a little about 27 trees that are marked by numbered wooden posts. Note that these posts are not numbered sequentially along the trail.

Start at the south side of the Hickory Street Bridge in downtown Warren. Crossing from Warren to the south side, turn right at the end of the bridge. The trailhead is at the end of a cement sidewalk, where it splits into a brick path and a stone chip path **[1].** Take the left fork, the stone chip path. Continue past the four flags and monument, leaving the brick path by them for the return leg.

On the first leg of the trail, between the trailhead and the boat launch and heliport (.23 mi.) **[2],** you will see hawthorn, sugar maple, dawn redwood, redbud, red oak, swamp white oak, Virginia pine, scarlet oak, Norway spruce, silver maple, ginkgo, American elm, mountain ash, Norway maple, Austrian pine, sweet gum, black cherry, eastern white pine, bitternut hickory, and red maple. Ginkgo was preserved from extinction by Buddhist priests. American elm, once abundant in the eastern U.S., has nearly been wiped out by the Dutch elm fungus. The most impressive tree you see in this area, a towering, ancient white oak, is not in Crescent Park but across the street from Crescent Park on private property.

Several picnic tables and cooking grills are located near the trail past the heliport. On this second leg of the trail, you will see honey locust, crabapple, and several large silver maples on the riverbank. Crescent Park Tree Walk ends by a pavilion and a playground (.35 mi.) **[3].** Turn around and retrace your steps, then turn left onto the brick path (.68 mi.) **[4].**

The brick path passes four flags that commemorate the rich history of Warren. The Seneca Nation, France, Great Britain, and the United States all held sovereignty over this area. The beautiful Birdstone Monument depicts the Seneca chief Cornplanter, a Seneca Clan mother, and the three sisters—corn, beans, and squash. On this short brick loop you will also see serviceberry, dawn redwood, purpleleaf beech, northern white cedar, Japanese dogwood, and flowering dogwood trees.

The complete hike back to the trailhead is .7 mi. **[1].**

Crescent Park Tree Walk

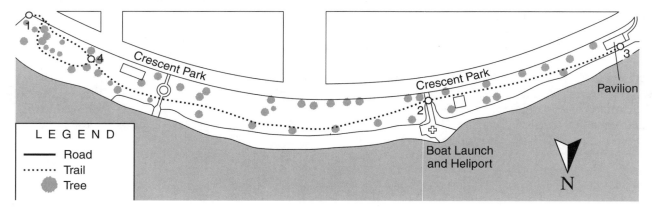

1. Trailhead
2. Heliport
3. Pavilion
4. Brick path

40. Chapman State Park

- Hike the rolling terrain atop the Allegheny Plateau.
- See a variety of wildlife, especially the abundant deer.
- Fish for trout, including native brook trout, in a lake and in streams.

Area Information

Chapman State Park shows a different view of the Allegheny Highlands than most other state parks in this physiographic region. The Allegheny Highlands is a plateau. While most state parks on this plateau are situated along the deeper valleys, Chapman State Park is on top of the plateau, at the headwaters of West Branch Tionesta Creek, where the terrain is more rolling, with smaller variations in elevation. The land in the park is heavily forested. But up the valley, on State Game Lands No. 29, the broad valley is a meadow with just a few scattered trees. A dense deer population and beavers help to keep it this way.

The area where the park is now was known as Buchers Mills. It was the site of a lumber mill from 1860 until 1904. Mostly white pine was cut here for about 20 years, until all of the pine in the area had been removed. Then the mill sawed hardwoods and hemlock. A hunting and fishing club bought the land before World War II. Soon after the war, the land was acquired for a state park.

Chapman Lake, rimmed by hemlock trees, is one of the most beautiful human-made lakes in the state. The present dam was constructed in 1949, near the site of the old earthen dam that supplied water for the sawmill. Trout fishing is excellent in the 68-acre lake. There are also a few largemouth bass. Nonpowered and electric-powered boats are allowed.

Directions: Turn off U.S. Route 6 at Clarendon, at the only traffic signal in town, onto Chapman Dam Road. The park is about 6 miles from Clarendon.

Hours Open: The park is open year-round. Day-use areas are open from 8:00 A.M. to sunset.

Facilities: The campground has 83 campsites for tents or RVs. Other park facilities are a sandy beach, a food concession, fishing, boating, a boat rental, picnic pavilions, and more than 200 picnic tables. Biking is allowed on park roads that connect with State Game Lands No. 29 and the Allegheny National Forest.

Permits and Rules: Alcoholic beverages are prohibited. Boats must have either a state park launching permit, a state park mooring permit, or a current Pennsylvania Fish and Boat Commission registration. Only nonpowered and electric-powered boats are allowed. Outdoor recreational activities are restricted to locations where signs or physical improvements designate the appropriate use. Fires and the disposal of hot coals are restricted to provided facilities. Trash and litter must be placed in containers provided for this purpose, and disposal is limited to items accumulated during the use of the park. Pets must be leashed and controlled at all times, and they are not allowed at the swimming area or in overnight camping facilities. Posting signs and soliciting are prohibited. All children age nine and under must be accompanied by a responsible adult at the swimming area.

Further Information: Department of Conservation and Natural Resources, Chapman State Park, RR 2, Box 1610, Clarendon, PA 16313-9607; phone 814-723-0250.

Park Trails

Hunters Ridge Trail 👢👢👢—2.8 miles—Look for fossils in rock formations along a rugged hillside.

Adams Run Trail 👢👢👢—2.9 miles—This is several trails that can be combined in various ways.

Lowlands Trail 👢—.2 mile—See a wetland area as you skirt the upper end of the lake.

Lumber Trail 👢👢—.4 mile—Follow a logging road to see evidence of logging activity.

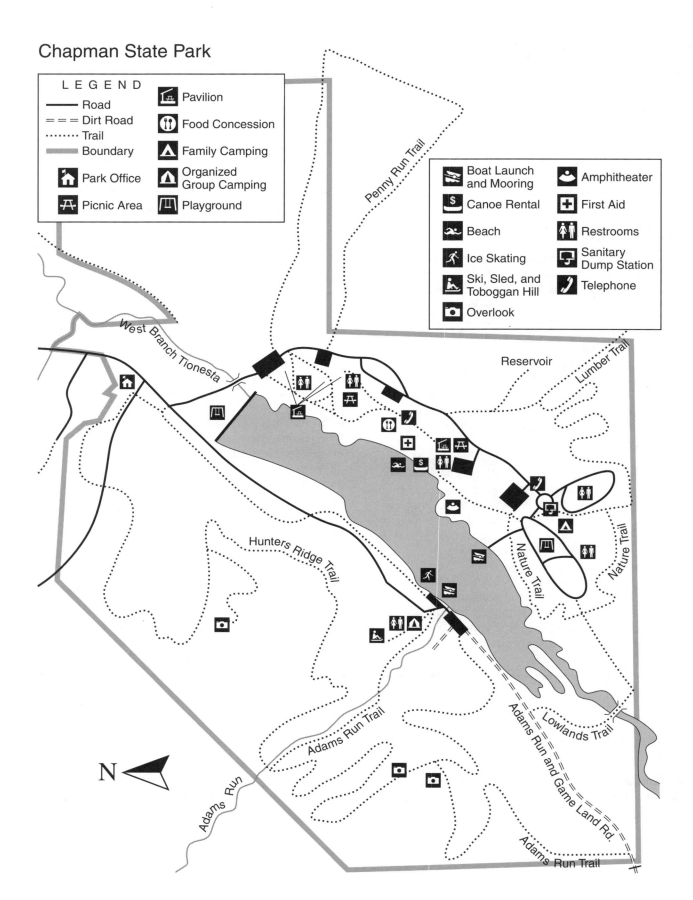

Chapman State Park

LEGEND

— Road
=== Dirt Road
····· Trail
▬▬ Boundary

Park Office
Picnic Area
Pavilion
Food Concession
Family Camping
Organized Group Camping
Playground

Boat Launch and Mooring
Canoe Rental
Beach
Ice Skating
Ski, Sled, and Toboggan Hill
Overlook
Amphitheater
First Aid
Restrooms
Sanitary Dump Station
Telephone

Penny Run Trail

West Branch Tionesta

Reservoir

Lumber Trail

Hunters Ridge Trail

Nature Trail

Nature Trail

Adams Run Trail

Adams Run

Lowlands Trail

Adams Run and Game Land Rd.

Adams Run Trail

N

Penny Run Trail 👢👢👢

Distance Round-Trip: 1.5 miles

Estimated Hiking Time: 40 minutes

Caution: A few roots protrude through this otherwise smooth trail.

Trail Directions: Drive into the park on Chapman Dam Road. Past park headquarters, stay on the paved road where it turns left and crosses West Branch Tionesta Creek immediately below Chapman Dam. Park in Parking Area No. 1, the first parking area past the creek. The trailhead is marked by a sign across the road from the upper end of the parking lot [1].

Walk around a gate and across a wooden footbridge. Follow blue trail blazes. The trail is wide and easy to follow. After a swing to the left, the trail turns right, through a hemlock stand into a beautiful hardwood forest. A large share of this forest is black cherry and red maple. In areas where the forest canopy is thin, you can pick blackberries along the trail during midsummer.

You are walking along the side of a hill. The land drops to your right toward Penny Run. Watch for deer in this area. Deer are abundant in and around the park. Black bears are also common, but they are elusive. When they are seen, it is usually at night while they are looking for food left out by humans.

You will realize that you are walking on an old woods road as you get farther from the trailhead. Logging activity was intensive here until the early 20th century. Logging is still a major industry on private land and the Allegheny National Forest around the park. You cross the border into the Allegheny National Forest .5 mi. from the trailhead

[2]. Watch for small yellow and black signs that mark the national forest boundary.

The climb is never terribly steep, but it is continuous until a sharp right turn near the head of the Penny Run valley (.6 mi.) [3]. From here, you cross five wooden footbridges in quick succession over a fairly level stretch. You can see all five footbridges while crossing the first bridge. The forest is mostly eastern hemlock, along with some birch, in this damp area.

At the next sharp right turn (.8 mi.) [4], you begin the descent back down the valley. Notice how bumpy the ground is. This is another sign of the early logging industry. Many of these bumps are the remains of tree stumps. Penny Run Trail ends at a paved road (1.4 mi.) [5]. Parking Area No. 2 is across the road. Turn right and follow the paved road to Parking Area No. 1, where you began this hike [1].

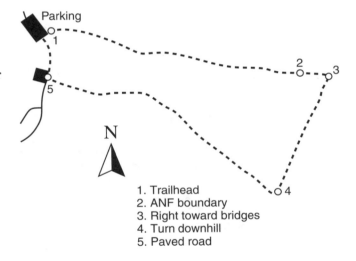

N

1. Trailhead
2. ANF boundary
3. Right toward bridges
4. Turn downhill
5. Paved road

Nature Trail 🥾🥾

Distance Round-Trip: 1 mile

Estimated Hiking Time: .5 hour

Caution: Remain on the trail to avoid poison ivy and several rare plants. Allow extra time to identify plants and animals.

Trail Directions: Stop at park headquarters for the self-guided trail booklet that explains numbered posts along the trail. Field guides for trees, shrubs, and birds will also be useful.

Drive into the park on Chapman Dam Road. Where this road splits past park headquarters, take the paved left fork across West Branch Tionesta Creek immediately below Chapman Dam. Continue on this road to Parking Area No. 4. Start your hike at the lower right corner of this parking area by two "Do Not Enter" signs [1]. Turn left past these signs onto a gravel service road, through a thick stand of hemlocks to the trailhead marked "Self Guiding Nature Trail" (.14 mi.) [2]. Turn right at the sign, following white trail blazes.

The interpretive stations are square posts with numbers. As you face the numbers, you face the feature described in the interpretive booklet.

Hemlock trees grow on top of long, low mounds by station 1. Hemlock bark was used to extract chemicals used at area tanneries. Though hemlock wood was used sometimes, these long mounds are the remains of rotted hemlock trunks. The trail is groomed with wood chips after you cross a wooden footbridge by this station.

Examine black cherry trees at station 2. Black cherry is used to make fine furniture and veneer. Most of the black cherry in the world grows on the Allegheny Highlands. It is abundant at Chapman State Park and in the surrounding area.

Identify American hornbeam trees by station 3. This small tree has little or no commercial value and only modest value as food for wildlife. The trail turns right along a service road for a short distance past this station, toward the campground boat mooring area, then turns left from the road across a wooden footbridge (.23 mi.) [3].

Club mosses by station 4 have been around for more than 3 million years. Also called ground pine, they are used as holiday decorations. Turn around to admire one of the largest eastern hemlock trees along this trail.

Station 5 is between two wooden footbridges. Examine the wetland area here very closely. It is valuable as a filter to keep sediments from the park from flowing into the lake, which you can see clearly from here.

Look at dead trees by station 6 and think of ways they contribute to the forest community. Trees near station 7 have been girdled by porcupines. Removing the bark all the way around a tree kills the tree. Porcupines are hated by many local residents for this habit and other destructive tendencies, such as chewing the sides of cabins and outhouses.

Stop and relax on a wooden bench at station 8. Study the great variety of plants and animals in the wetland.

Rushes and sedges growing in the wetland along the edge of the lake by station 9 are important foods for birds and other wildlife.

You can see several human-made wood duck nesting boxes from station 10. Wood ducks were killed to near extinction because their feathers were used by the women's fashion industry. Nesting boxes like these have helped to bring them back to common status. You are now at the inlet of the lake. Stop at a bench beside the water to watch for ducks, mink, and other animals that live near water.

You can see stages of forest succession at station 11. Station 12 is the last interpretive station. Pause here on the bench to identify three different fern species. Then continue to a grassy service road (.56 mi.) [4], where you turn left. This grassy road is an old railroad bed used to haul timber. Follow it to a gate, then onto a paved road through the campground, and finally onto the gravel service road that takes you back to Parking Area No. 4 where you began this hike (1 mi.) [1].

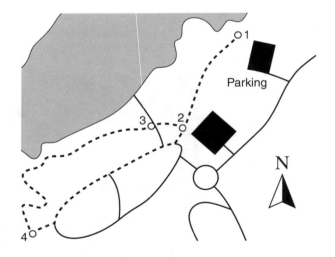

1. Trailhead
2. Self Guiding Nature Trail
3. Boat mooring area
4. Grassy road

41. Allegheny National Forest— Warren County

- Float the Allegheny River and camp on the smallest federally designated wilderness area.
- Fish for wild brook trout in hidden streams.
- Watch bald eagles soar.
- Explore unusual rock formations.

Area Information

The Allegheny National Forest covers more than 145,140 acres in Warren County. Nearly all of this is forested. Red oak and black cherry that grows here is considered the finest in the world for building furniture and other products. Wildlife is abundant, most notably white-tailed deer, black bears, and wild turkeys. Programs are under way to reestablish river otters and fishers. The Eastern coyote, a strain that sometimes weighs more than 65 pounds, has become established through migration. Bald eagles grace the skies around major waterways.

The 12,000-acre Allegheny Reservoir, in the northeast corner of the county, provides ample room for boaters and anglers, with less fishing and boating pressure than at most large lakes in the Northeast. The reservoir has given up state records for northern pike and walleye. Smallmouth bass are abundant, and muskellunge weighing more than 40 pounds are occasionally caught.

The Allegheny River below the reservoir is a National Wild and Scenic River. Several islands are part of the Allegheny River Islands Wilderness. Canoeists and other river voyagers can camp in primitive style on these islands. Trout fishing is outstanding between the dam and the city of Warren.

Smallmouth bass, walleyes, and muskellunge provide excellent sport throughout the 35 miles that the river flows through Warren County. There are more stocked and wild trout streams than an angler could fish in a year.

Directions: U.S. Route 6 between Warren and Kane passes through the heart of the Allegheny National Forest. U.S. Route 62 between Tionesta and Warren runs close to the western border.

Hours Open: Open year-round.

Facilities: There are numerous campgrounds; picnic areas; swimming beaches at the Allegheny Reservoir; trails for hiking, biking, cross-country skiing, snowmobiling, and ATVs; and boat access areas along the Allegheny Reservoir, Allegheny River, and Tionesta Creek.

Permits and Rules: Motor vehicles are not allowed off designated roads and trails. Do not carve, chop, cut, or damage any live trees. Do not damage or remove any historical or archaeological items. Extensive rules limit camping outside designated campgrounds. Watch for posted restrictions on fires.

Further Information: Allegheny National Forest, P.O. Box 847, Warren, PA 16365; phone 814-723-5150.

Other Areas of Interest

Warren and **Warren County** offer a variety of entertaining events throughout the year. Write to Travel Northern Alleghenies, 315 Second Avenue, Warren, PA 16365; phone 814-726-1222 or 800-624-7802.

Park Trails

Hickory Creek Wilderness Trail 👢👢👢—11.1 miles—Take a loop through the Hickory Creek Wilderness starting at Hearts Content National Scenic Area. While the terrain is not as rugged as in much of Warren County, this is a difficult one-day hike because of its length.

Allegheny National Forest

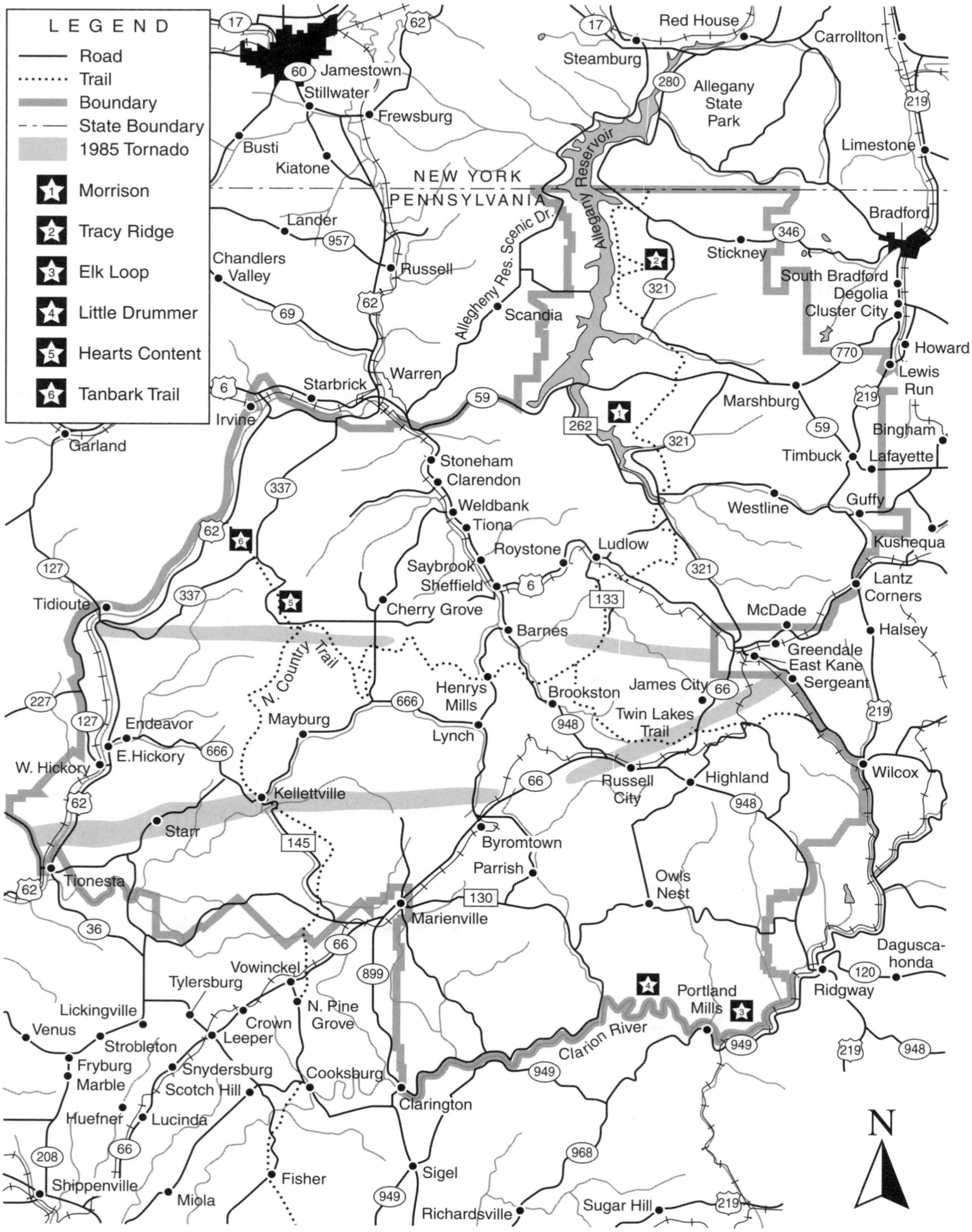

LEGEND

— Road
····· Trail
▬▬ Boundary
–·–·– State Boundary
▓ 1985 Tornado

⭐1 Morrison
⭐2 Tracy Ridge
⭐3 Elk Loop
⭐4 Little Drummer
⭐5 Hearts Content
⭐6 Tanbark Trail

NEW YORK
PENNSYLVANIA

Jamestown
Stillwater
Frewsburg
Busti
Kiatone
Lander
Chandlers Valley
Russell
Scandia
Warren
Starbrick
Irvine
Garland
Stoneham
Clarendon
Weldbank
Tiona
Royston
Saybrook
Sheffield
Cherry Grove
Barnes
Tidioute
Henrys Mills
Mayburg
Lynch
Endeavor
E. Hickory
W. Hickory
Kellettville
Starr
Tionesta
Byromtown
Parrish
Marienville
Vowinckel
Tylersburg
Lickingville
Venus
Strobleton
Fryburg
Marble
Snydersburg
Scotch Hill
Crown Leeper
N. Pine Grove
Cooksburg
Huefner
Lucinda
Shippenville
Miola
Fisher
Sigel
Clarington
Richardsville
Sugar Hill

Red House
Steamburg
Carrollton
Allegany State Park
Limestone
Bradford
Stickney
South Bradford
Degolia
Cluster City
Howard
Lewis Run
Marshburg
Bingham
Timbuck
Lafayette
Westline
Guffy
Kushequa
Ludlow
Lantz Corners
Halsey
McDade
Greendale
East Kane
Sergeant
James City
Brookston
Twin Lakes Trail
Russell City
Highland
Wilcox
Owls Nest
Dagusca-honda
Ridgway
Portland Mills

Allegany State Park
Allegheny Reservoir
Allegheny Res. Scenic Dr.
N. Country Trail
Clarion River

N

160

Hearts Content Scenic Area Interpretive Trail 🥾🥾

Distance Round-Trip: 1.1 mile

Estimated Hiking Time: .5 hour

Caution: Watch for falling limbs if you hike this trail in windy weather.

Trail Directions: Take Pleasant Drive south from Warren. About 9.5 miles from the city limits, as this road curves sharply right, turn left onto Hearts Content Road. The entrance to Hearts Content Scenic Area is a well-marked left turn about 4 miles farther. There is a large parking area on the left side of this road and a smaller parking area at the end where the road forms a small loop. The trailhead is at the end of this loop [1].

A kiosk at the head of the trail gives you an introduction to the area. Pick up a brochure about the trail here. This is one of few places where you can see a virgin forest, a forest much the same as it was before Europeans settled the area. Just past the kiosk is an information station that will teach you more about the differences between an old-growth forest and the trees you are accustomed to seeing. Your appreciation for Hearts Content will be enhanced by this information. Ignore a fork to the right here. This is where you will be returning to complete the loop.

As you continue along the trail, note that the tops are missing from several of the larger white pines. This is the work of lightning, and it serves as a reminder of why you should not stand under a pine tree, or any tall tree, during electrical storms. You pass another fork to the right [2] at .1 mi. A sign indicates that the right fork is the short loop and the straight path is the long loop. There is also an information station by a small fenced area. This is a demonstration of the effects that white-tailed deer have on the forest.

Continuing on the long loop, about 500 feet past the intersection, watch for a huge red maple with shaggy bark. Red maple is common in Pennsylvania, but you have probably never seen one with shaggy bark because they are usually cut long before they develop this condition. You might even mistake it for shagbark hickory, but look up at the leaves. About 700 feet past this tree is a plaque honoring owners of the Wheeler and Dusenbury Lumber Company, which saved this area from being cut during the great logging boom of the 19th century (.38 mi.) [3].

You arrive at the first of three wooden footbridges at .41 mi. [4]. The small spring stream that these bridges ford is the head of the West Branch Tionesta Creek. It is home to wild brook trout, the state fish, in its headwaters, and is stocked with trout downstream.

You have been walking generally downhill until you make a sharp right turn at .8 mi. [5]. This begins the third and final leg of the triangular hike, and a gentle climb. You might hear vehicles to your left on Hearts Content Road. If you are carrying a compass, you should see that you are walking generally north.

A couple of split-log benches in a cluster of very large hemlocks (.9 mi.) [6] is a good place to stop and reflect on what you have seen. Look at the narrow beams of sunlight peeking through the forest canopy. If you sit quietly and if there are few other people in the area, the chances are very good that you will see deer and other wildlife.

The end of the trail is near. You pass another small fenced area on your left, then reach a right fork almost exactly 1 mi. from the start of this trail [7]. Turn right, then left after a few steps at another fork where you see a sign marking the right fork as the short loop. This is the opposite end of the short loop leg that you passed earlier. If this is a bit confusing, do not worry. You will see the picnic area field through the trees. You can take any route to the field and turn right to the parking area. If you stay on the correct trail, you will arrive at the first information station to complete the loop, then turn left to the trailhead (1.1 mi.) [1].

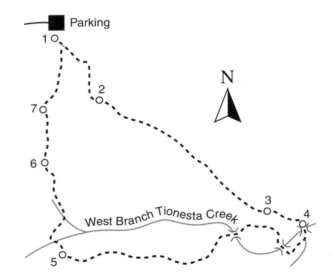

1. Trailhead
2. Short loop fork
3. Wheeler and Dusenbury plaque
4. Footbridge
5. Last leg
6. Split-log benches
7. Right fork

Tanbark Trail 🥾🥾🥾🥾

Distance Round-Trip: 9 miles

Estimated Hiking Time: 5 hours

Caution: This is a long hike for one day in hilly terrain. Rattlesnakes are rarely encountered, but they are present. You might get your feet wet at numerous spring seeps along the slope that drops to the Allegheny River.

Trail Directions: Tanbark Trail connects the Allegheny River and U.S. Route 62 with the North Country National Scenic Trail. These directions start at the intersection with the North Country Trail. Drive south from Warren or north from Tidioute on Pennsylvania Route 337 and turn onto Hearts Content Road. Turn right onto Forest Route 116 after 5.9 miles, then .4 mile down this road you reach the trailhead. A sign here marks North Country Trail and Tanbark Trail [1]. Tanbark Trail goes to the right.

Follow white diamond trail blazes, which are pieces of plastic nailed to trees. The trail is difficult to see in many places because it is covered with leaves and is not heavily used. Watch for changes in the makeup of the forest along the trail and try to figure out why it changes.

You come to Forest Route 119, a narrow dirt road, after just .3 mi. [2]. About 100 feet past the road a sign informs you that the Allegheny River is 8 miles ahead. Actually, it is a little farther than that. You also pass a sign marking the border of the Hickory Creek Wilderness, which you leave when you reach Hearts Content Road (.8 mi.) [3].

Across the road, you will begin to see blue diamond blazes along with the white diamond blazes. Ignore them and stick with the white blazes. You pass a marked intersection with Ironwood Trail, which cuts to the right, about 1,000 feet past Hearts Content Road. At the bottom of a shallow drainage, all within 65 feet, you cross a footbridge over a headwater of West Branch Tionesta Creek, take a sharp right turn onto an old road grade, then turn sharply left where the white blazes depart from the blue blazes (2.3 mi.) [4].

You begin climbing immediately. At 2.4 mi., you come to a T with Tom's Run Trail [5], where you again see blue blazes. Turn left to a sign, then turn right immediately, following the white blazes and continuing uphill.

Soon you begin dropping again toward Tom's Run. You reach another T with Tom's Run Trail at 3 mi. [6]. Do not let a sign confuse you. Turn left, following an old road grade for about 700 feet, then turn right to Hearts Content Road (3.3 mi.) [7].

Angle right across the road. After a short climb, you begin dropping. Feel the cool air when you pass through a narrow crevasse at a rock outcrop (3.7 mi.) [8]. Wait for your rest break, though, at a boulder just before you cross a footbridge over East Hickory Creek (3.9 mi.) [9]. Watch the pool under the footbridge and you will probably see a small brook trout, the state fish. Just across the pool is a mountain laurel bush, the state flower. And a hemlock, the state tree, is providing you with shade.

Across the creek, you climb through several large boulders, some larger than a big house, then reach the top of the plateau again. Though this area appears to be mountains, it is actually a highly eroded plateau. Do you know what the difference between the two is?

Ignore a single-track dirt road you pass just over a mile past East Hickory Creek. Walking is generally level, except for one shallow drainage, until the trail drops to Route 337 (6 mi.) [10], a blacktop road. Walk across this road, continuing along a level course on an old road for about 1,300 feet, then cut right at a trail sign.

Tanbark Trail dips down and across Slater Run, which began as Sandstone Springs, over a footbridge, then starts rising again. This is your last climb of the trail. After reaching the top of this rise you come to an unmarked T (7.4 mi.) [11]. Turn left. You are now on the slope to the Allegheny River. It becomes increasingly steep as you pass through large boulders and finally emerge onto Route 62 and the lower end of Tanbark Trail (9 mi.) [12].

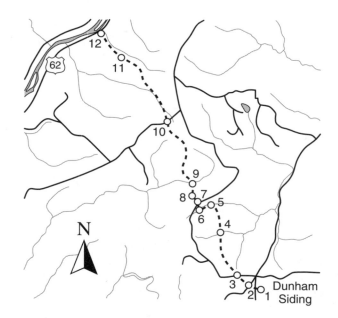

1. Trailhead
2. FR 119
3. Hearts Content Road
4. Leave blue blazes
5. Tom's Run Trail
6. Tom's Run Trail
7. Hearts Content Road
8. Crevasse
9. East Hickory Creek
10. Blacktop road
11. Unmarked T
12. Route 62

42. Erie National Wildlife Refuge

- Stroll through wooded wetlands.
- Observe nesting wood ducks, mallards, hooded mergansers, blue-winged teal, and Canada geese.
- Visit during spring and fall migrations to see a greater variety of waterfowl and shorebirds.

Area Information

Named for the Erie Indians who once inhabited the area, the Erie National Wildlife Refuge was established in 1959 to provide habitat for waterfowl and other wildlife. Erie is one of more than 500 national wildlife refuges nationwide purchased with funds from the sale of migratory bird hunting and conservation stamps. It is one of just two national wildlife refuges in Pennsylvania. This refuge consists of two divisions, Sugar Lake and Seneca, which are separated by about 10 miles.

Natural habitat of marshes, swamps, creeks, and beaver ponds has been enhanced by the construction of impoundments and dugout ponds providing more than 2,500 acres of wetland habitat. This is a bird-watcher's paradise, with 251 species identified. Waterfowl migrations occur March through early April and September through November.

Shorebirds are common on mudflats during summer and fall. The rare Henslow's sparrow is one of the 113 bird species that nest here. Many mammals are also abundant. White-tailed deer, eastern cottontails, mink, and red and gray fox are among the 47 mammal species present.

Directions: The Sugar Lake Division, 5,206 acres, is adjacent to the village of Guys Mills, about 10 miles east of Meadville on Pennsylvania Route 27. The Seneca Division, 3,571 acres, is about 10 miles north and 4 miles southeast of Cambridge Springs. The visitors center is located three quarters of a mile east of Guys Mills off Pennsylvania Route 198.

Hours Open: The refuge is open year-round. Cross-country skiing is allowed on trails during winter. Facilities are open daily from a half hour before sunrise until sunset unless posted otherwise. The visitors center is open Monday through Friday from 8:00 A.M. to 4:30 P.M.

Facilities: The visitors center has displays and provides information to visitors. A blind for observation and photography overlooks Reitz's Pond. An overlook above pool 9 is a good place to observe bald eagles.

Permits and Rules: Certain areas are closed for various reasons, including research. Watch for signs and check at the visitors center for current restrictions.

Further Information: Erie National Wildlife Refuge, 11296 Wood Duck Lane, Guys Mills, PA 16327; phone 814-789-3585.

Other Areas of Interest

Woodcock Creek Lake, which offers swimming, boating, picnic facilities, and camping, is about 12 miles north on Route 198. Write to Resource Manager, Woodcock Creek Lake, Box 629, Saegertown, PA 16433; phone 814-763-4422 or 814-763-4477.

Park Trails

Beaver Run Trail 👢👢—1 mile—A half-mile loop and a half-mile spur provide good opportunities to observe plants and wildlife in the Sugar Lake Division.

Deer Run Trail 👢👢—3 miles—See wetlands and forest with a good overlook in the Sugar Lake Division.

Muddy Creek Holly Trail 👢👢—1 mile—See winterberry holly in the Seneca Division.

Tsuga Nature Trail 👢👢

Distance Round-Trip: 1.2 miles

Estimated Hiking Time: 1 hour

Caution: If you hike during hunting season, wear bright orange clothing. Biting insects are common during spring and summer.

Trail Directions: The trailhead is adjacent to the visitors center, about a mile east of Guys Mills on Route 198. A kiosk at the trailhead [1] describes features of the refuge.

Level and surfaced with wood chips, Tsuga Trail descends gently from the trailhead to the first numbered post (.1 mi.) [2] by an area that has been replanted with native prairie grasses. Just past this interpretive station, the trail forks. Take the right fork, ignoring the left fork, which crosses a small footbridge.

Interpretive station 3 is just under .3 mi. from the trailhead at the dike of a small human-made impoundment [3]. The water level in the pond is controlled to keep it at an ideal depth for waterfowl. Interpretive station 4 is at the far end of this dike [4] at slightly more than .3 mi.

The trail turns sharply left past the dike, entering a brushy area. Interpretive station 5 is at a footbridge [5] that crosses a dugout pond .4 mi. from the trailhead. This type of human-made pond quickly assumes the characteristics of a natural pond. Like other human-made structures on the refuge, dugout ponds greatly increase the waterfowl habitat.

Interpretive station 6 at .5 mi. [6] is not as scenic as the other interpretive stations, but it is just as important. In appropriate areas, cooperative farmers plant specific crops under an agreement in which some of the crops are left standing for wildlife, another critical means of increasing the wildlife-holding capacity of the refuge.

A wood bench gives you the opportunity to relax just before a long footbridge over a beaver pond. Early mornings or late evenings are the most likely times to watch wood ducks winging between the hemlocks that ring this secluded pond. Interpretive station 7 is at this bridge [7] at .6 mi.

Interpretive station 8 at .8 mi. is in a wooded area [8]. The area had been logged just before the refuge was established. Trees here are in the pole timber stage, which generally makes for poor wildlife habitat.

Though this trail passes through wetlands, it is quite dry because it is raised and uses footbridges to cross ponds. It begins a gentle climb here through the woodlands. Interpretive station 9 at .9 mi. is surrounded by mature hemlock trees [9]. This trail is named for the hemlock, Pennsylvania's state tree, which has the scientific name Tsuga canadensis.

The trail forks at just under a mile. A sign indicates that the left fork is the short loop and the right fork is the long loop. The left fork returns to the trailhead [1] for a total distance of 1.2 mi. Interpretive station 10 is actually a few paces before the trailhead, but the trailhead is within view.

The right fork is the longer loop of this trail and is not shown on the map. It ends behind the visitor center with a total distance of 1.6 mi. This extended loop is rougher than the short loop, with protruding roots, numerous short but steep inclines and declines, and wet patches.

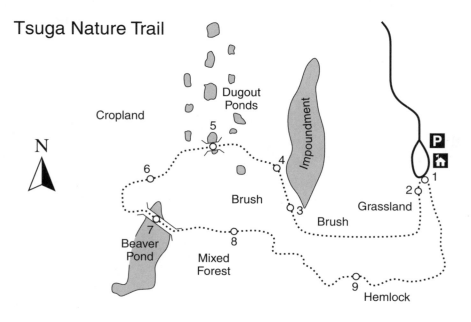

Tsuga Nature Trail

1. Trailhead
2. Grassland
3. Impoundment
4. Interpretive station 4
5. Dugout pond
6. Co-op farming
7. Beaver pond
8. Woodland
9. Hemlock trees

LEGEND

—— Road

········· Trail

🏠 Visitors Center

P Parking

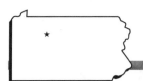

43. Allegheny National Forest—
Beaver Meadows Recreation Area

- Fish for bass and panfish in Beaver Meadows Lake.
- Hike through a beautiful red pine forest.
- Watch wild turkeys, deer, beavers, and other abundant wildlife in a remote setting.

Area Information

Forest County is the only county in Pennsylvania with no traffic lights, no four-lane highways, no shopping malls, and more deer than people. There are as many people in seasonal camps as there are permanent residents. Beaver Meadows Recreation Area is even out of the way for Forest County.

Beaver Meadows is on top of the Allegheny Plateau, at the headwaters of Salmon Creek. The terrain is more gently rolling than most of the plateau. A red pine and spruce forest surrounding the lake and savannah gives it a more northerly appearance. Wildlife, especially white-tailed deer, wild turkeys, beavers, waterfowl, and dozens of songbird species, are abundant.

The U.S. government acquired the Allegheny National Forest after the lumber industry had stripped the land by the early 20th century. Government work programs during the Great Depression created many of the recreational facilities, including the Beaver Meadows Lake Dam in 1936. Anglers catch largemouth bass and panfish in the lake and trout in nearby streams.

The campground and a boat launch were built during the 1960s by youths from the Blue Jay Job Corps Center. Trails were built during the 1980s by the Youth Conservation Corps.

Directions: Beaver Meadows Recreation Area is in Forest County. From Pennsylvania Route 66 in Marienville, turn north onto North Forest Street, which becomes Forest Road 128. Drive 3.8 miles, then turn right onto Forest Road 282. This intersection is marked with a large Beaver Meadows sign.

Hours Open: This area is open year-round.

Facilities: Beaver Meadows Lake was recently drained to control aquatic weeds. It will be restocked with largemouth bass and sunfish. The 37-site campground is suitable for tents or RVs. Sites can be reserved by phoning 877-444-6777. Numerous forest roads in the national forest are ideal for biking.

Permits and Rules: Boat motors are not allowed on Beaver Meadows Lake. Quiet time at the campground is from 10:00 P.M. to 6:00 A.M. Fires must be built in designated fireplaces. Do not cut or damage living trees or other plants. Do not pound nails into trees, picnic tables, or other government property. Pets must be on leashes, and they are not allowed in the water. Camping is not allowed in picnic areas. Motorized vehicles and saddle, pack, or draft animals are not allowed on hiking trails or cross-country skiing trails.

Further Information: Marienville Ranger Station, HC 2, Box 130, Marienville, PA 16239; phone 814-927-6628.

Other Areas of Interest

For information about the **Marienville Annual Oktoberfest** and numerous outdoor opportunities, write to Marienville Chamber of Commerce, P.O. Box 542, Marienville, PA 16239 (no phone).

Park Trails

Beaver Meadows Loop 👢👢—3 miles—Walk around a savannah and across a floating footbridge at the head of Beaver Meadows Lake.

Lakeside Loop 👢👢—.5 mile—This is a short loop that takes you closer to the lake from the Beaver Meadows Loop.

Penoke Path 👢👢—1.1 miles—Follow an old railroad grade through a savannah.

Beaver Meadows Recreation Area

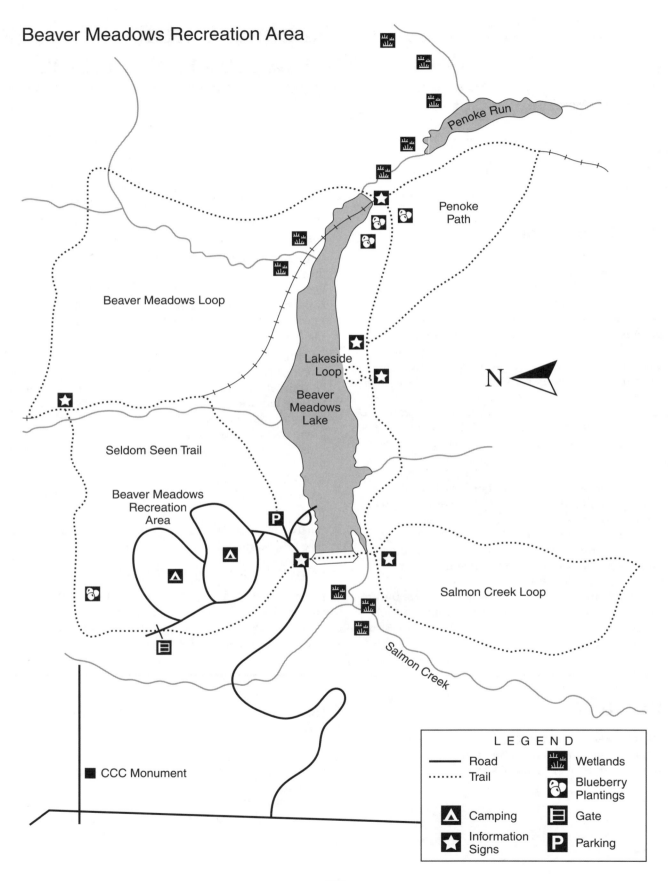

Penoke Run

Penoke Path

Beaver Meadows Loop

Lakeside Loop

Beaver Meadows Lake

Seldom Seen Trail

Beaver Meadows Recreation Area

Salmon Creek Loop

Salmon Creek

N

■ CCC Monument

LEGEND

—— Road		Wetlands
······ Trail		Blueberry Plantings
▲ Camping		Gate
★ Information Signs	P	Parking

Salmon Creek Loop 👢👢

Distance Round-Trip: 1.7 miles

Estimated Hiking Time: 1 hour

Caution: Numerous roots interfere with footing.

Trail Directions: Turn off Forest Road 128 and drive .8 mi. on FR 282 to the dam, which creates Beaver Meadows Lake. Start the hike at a sign that points across the dam to hiking trails **[1]**. Walk across the earthen breastwork and a footbridge over the outflow, then up a set of wooden steps to a trail sign (.1 mi.) **[2]**. You will also see a metallic trail map here and at all other major intersections. The trail splits three ways—two trails to the left and one to the right. Take the right fork onto the Salmon Creek Loop.

Follow blue diamond trail blazes on this narrow dirt path. While walking through a plantation of red pines you might be startled by the loud flush of a ruffed grouse. You can see a relatively long distance through the forest. A thick canopy and dense deer population do not allow for much undergrowth. Ferns are the dominant ground vegetation.

The trail curves right, down to the bank of Salmon Creek. This shallow valley floor is an unusual environment in Pennsylvania, a grassy savannah with only a few scattered trees. Poor soil, beavers, and deer prevent trees from maturing. Look for small dams and other evidence of the beavers for which this area is named.

An unmapped intersection is marked only by a small sign that says the trail behind you is for hiking only. Turn left here, staying with the blue diamonds, and begin a gentle climb. Watch for animal droppings on the trail that prove that animals, too, prefer to travel the easiest route. You may be able to determine what the animals were eating if you examine the droppings. The droppings were probably made by foxes, raccoons, or coyotes. All are abundant but seldom seen because they roam mostly at night.

Salmon Creek Loop makes an acute left turn near the top of the hill (.9 mi.) **[3]**. This is marked by white arrows in two blue diamonds on a wooden post. This is the apex of the loop, and you are at the edge of the red pine plantation. To your right is a small forest opening that separates you from a hardwood forest. Examine the opening for two very important trees that stand side by side. One is an apple tree, the other is dead. Why are they important? Also compare the ground vegetation in the opening with the ground vegetation under the dense forest canopy. How and why are they different? These openings are very valuable to wildlife because more sunlight reaches the ground, providing more low plant growth.

Your trail turns back into the pines. The terrain is fairly level. Numerous black cherry and sugar maple trees are mixed with the pines. You pass through a thick stand of spruce before beginning the descent, which completes the loop by the wooden steps (1.5 mi.) **[2]**. Walk across the dam to complete the hike (1.7 mi.) **[1]**.

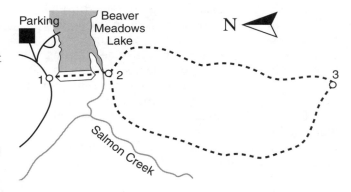

1. Dam
2. Top of steps
3. Acute left

Seldom Seen Trail 👢👢

Distance Round-Trip: 1.7 miles

Estimated Hiking Time: 1 hour

Caution: Watch for roots in the trail. Expect the ground to be wet in some places.

Trail Directions: Seldom Seen Trail begins across the road from the Beaver Meadows Lake Dam. The trailhead is marked by a sign and a metallic trail map **[1]**. The trail begins as a mowed path but soon narrows to a dirt path strewn with roots before entering a spruce plantation. It is blazed with blue diamonds.

Moss along the trail is an indication of dampness retained by the dense coniferous canopy. As you continue uphill, you leave the spruce and enter a mature hardwood forest. Black cherry and sugar maple are the predominant trees, with a mix of white pines.

Just as you enter a red pine plantation, Seldom Seen Trail passes a water pump at the intersection with a spur off the campground loop (.4 mi.) **[2]**. Walk across the loop at the end of this spur and turn left, as indicated by a trail sign, past a gate onto a service road. Follow this road around a right turn into an overgrown apple orchard. If you hike here during fall when apples are falling from the trees, do not be surprised by the sounds of deer or black bears running through the thick brush. Apples are a favorite food for both. You might even be able to determine which animal it is by the noise it makes. You can usually hear deer hooves hitting the ground. If the thought of meeting a bear frightens you, make some noise while walking.

Toward the end of this orchard, on your right, is a half-acre area where 550 highbush blueberry bushes have been planted inside a high fence that protects them from deer. You can get inside the fence through a gate that is hinged at the top (.5 mi.) **[3]**. These blueberries make the best pies in the world. Yes, even better than apple. But if you want to make a scientific comparison, apples are abundant along this trail, though most do not ripen until a couple of weeks after the blueberries.

The service road ends at the blueberry patch gate. Follow a grassy path to the edge of the red pine plantation, where the trail is dirt. As you walk down a gentle slope, look inside one of the plastic tubes on your left. Can you guess the purpose of these tubes?

About 150 feet after crossing a small stream on stepping stones, you reach a T intersection with Beaver Meadows Loop (1 mi.) **[4]**. This is the end of Seldom Seen Trail. Turn right here to complete a loop back to your trailhead. This trail is blazed with gray diamonds. You are now following a long-abandoned railroad bed that was used to haul logs. It can be recognized because it is very level and raised above the surrounding land. In some places you can see shallow depressions across the bed. What created those depressions?

Watch for a black arrow inside a gray diamond trail blaze that is mounted on a post. It marks a sharp right turn where you leave the railroad bed (1.2 mi.) **[5]**. You cross several small wooden footbridges through a forest wetland before reaching the trailhead of the Beaver Meadows Loop at a gravel road (1.6 mi.) **[6]**. Turn left, then left again at a stop sign to complete your loop back to the head of Seldom Seen Trail (1.7 mi.) **[1]**.

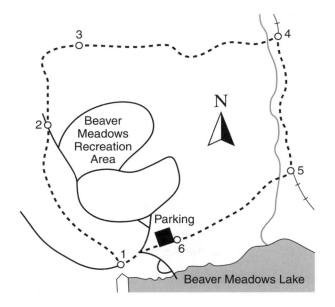

1. Trailhead
2. Water pump
3. Blueberry patch
4. Beaver Meadows Loop
5. Leave railroad bed
6. Gravel road

44. Buzzard Swamp

- Tour an area designed for waterfowl propagation.
- Fish for bluegills and largemouth bass in remote human-made ponds.
- See one of the few places where the Allegheny Plateau, also called the Allegheny Highlands, actually looks like a plateau.

Area Information

Buzzard Swamp is situated on top of the Allegheny Plateau, more commonly called the Allegheny Highlands, on the border of Forest and Elk counties. This is rolling terrain at the top of the Millstone Creek drainage. Farther down this drainage system, close to the Clarion River, the valley is cut deeper, creating the more rugged terrain that is more characteristic of the Allegheny Highlands. Also unlike the common image of the area, large fields surround the ponds at Buzzard Swamp. This is maintained for the benefit of wildlife, especially geese and ducks.

Buzzard Swamp is a poorly drained area that has been developed for wildlife management in a joint effort by the Allegheny National Forest and the Pennsylvania Game Commission. Fifteen ponds were built during the 1960s for waterfowl propagation. Many Canada geese, wood ducks, and other waterfowl nest here. This is also a critical stopover for many migrating waterfowl. Wetlands are being lost to development at an alarming rate. Human-made wetland areas like this have been vital in restoring waterfowl populations during the latter half of the 1900s.

The ponds also provide excellent angling for bass, bluegills, and catfish. Boats are allowed on the ponds outside the posted propagation area; however, boats must be carried or wheeled at least a mile to the pond closest to the gate at the trailhead.

Directions: From Pennsylvania Route 66 at Marienville, turn south on Pennsylvania Route 3002. About 1.3 miles south of Route 66, turn left at a sign, onto Forest Route 157. Follow this road 2.3 miles to a gate and a kiosk.

Hours Open: The area is open year-round.

Facilities: Buzzard Swamp is primarily a game-propagation area. Other than trails for hiking, biking, and cross-country skiing and fishing in the ponds, there are no recreational facilities. Boats are allowed on the ponds. Campgrounds and other facilities are available nearby in the Allegheny National Forest.

Permits and Rules: Do not enter the propagation area, which is well marked by signs. Do not disturb waterfowl nests or young animals. Motorized vehicles are prohibited. Motorized boats are not allowed on any of the ponds.

Further Information: Allegheny National Forest, P.O. Box 847, Warren, PA 16365; phone 814-723-5150. Or contact the Marienville Ranger Station, HC 2, Box 130, Marienville, PA 16239; phone 814-927-6628. The Marienville Ranger Station is located along Pennsylvania Route 66 about 2.5 miles north of Marienville.

Park Trails

The **Buzzard Swamp Trail System** consists of 11 miles of connecting trails, including the loop hike described on page 171.

Buzzard Swamp

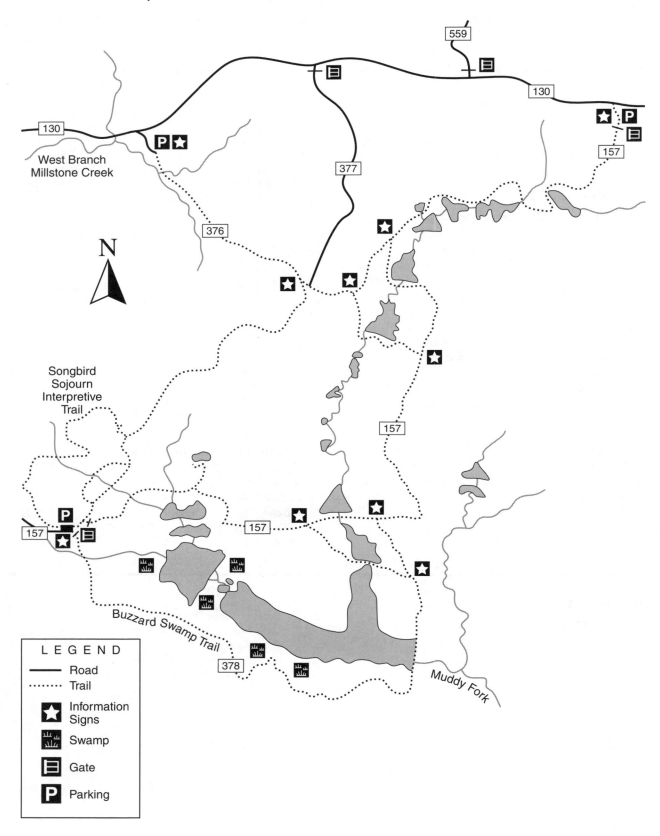

Buzzard Swamp Trail 🥾🥾

Distance Round-Trip: 3.5 miles

Estimated Hiking Time: 2 hours

Caution: There are no trail blazes. Several roads that are not on the map intersect with this trail. Look at the area map for landmarks and at trail signs at key intersections to keep you on the correct roads. There is very little shade along the first half of this hike. Wear bright orange clothing if you hike during fall or spring hunting seasons. Be careful and watch children when you cross the dam at Pond 6. A fall could result in serious injury. Mosquitoes and other biting insects are abundant. Be sure to carry water on this hike. None of the local water is fit to drink.

Trail Directions: Carry good binoculars or a spotting scope and a field guide to waterfowl on this hike. Canada geese, wood ducks, mallards, common mergansers, and perhaps other waterfowl species breed here. Goldeneyes, ring-necked ducks, hooded mergansers, ruddy ducks, green-winged teal, blue-winged teal, American wigeon, black ducks, and other waterfowl species, wading birds, and shore-birds stop here to rest and feed during their long spring and fall migrations. You might also see bald eagles, ospreys, red-tailed hawks, northern harriers, and other raptors soaring above the ponds and fields. Unusual birds including the American bittern and northern shoveler may be seen here occasionally. At night, great horned owls rule the sky. Deer, coyotes, mink, and other mammals are numerous.

The trailhead is at a kiosk by a small parking area **[1]**. A gate blocks vehicle access beyond the kiosk. Walk past the gate on a gravel road. This entire trail follows service roads that are blocked to public use. There are no trail blazes.

Thick brush and small trees surround the trail at the beginning, giving way to fields as you approach the ponds. A 40-acre propagation area is to your right, well marked by signs. Do not enter this area. Ponds 1,

2, and 3 are in the propagation area. You will need binoculars or a spotting scope with high magnification to identify waterfowl on these ponds from the trail. Turn right where the road forks by a trail sign (1 mi.) **[2]**. This takes you over a dike between Pond 4 and Pond 6. Examine the water-control device between these ponds (1.2 mi.) **[3]**. Controlling water depth in the ponds can increase or decrease aquatic vegetation.

Turn right again at the next fork (1.4 mi.) **[4]**. This takes you across the dam that creates Pond 6. This is the largest pond in Buzzard Swamp. Fishing for largemouth bass and bluegills is very good from the dam. You can see several dead trees rising out of this pond. These trees provide nesting dens for tree swallows and wood ducks, although human-made wood duck nesting boxes have also been placed in the area.

Make a sharp right turn after crossing the dam (1.8 mi.) **[5]**. Follow this road along the wooded hillside and Pond 6, past the propagation area. Turn right when you intersect with another gravel road to return to the trailhead (3.5 mi.) **[1]**.

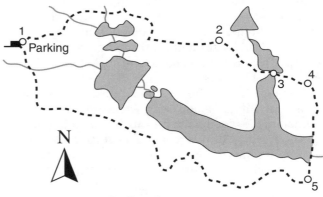

1. Trailhead
2. First fork
3. Water-control device
4. Right to dam
5. Right after dam

Songbird Sojourn Interpretive Trail 👢👢

Distance Round-Trip: 1.6 miles

Estimated Hiking Time: 1 hour

Caution: The ground is wet in several places, and there are no bridges over all but one of the stream crossings. However, streams are tiny. Many roots grow across the trail.

Trail Directions: Stop at the Marienville ranger station and pick up a copy of the Songbird Sojourn Interpretive Trail booklet, which explains the things you will see at 17 numbered posts along this trail.

Start this hike at the kiosk by the parking area **[1]**. Walk past the kiosk on the gravel road to the gate. The trailhead for Songbird Sojourn is to your left, marked by a sign (.02 mi.) **[2]**. A wide grass path begins by the sign. You will see white, blue, and gray diamond trail blazes. Follow the gray diamonds. Metallic maps of the area have been placed at strategic locations along the trail.

The trail forks near the first numbered post by a Norway spruce (.1 mi.) **[3]**. Take the left fork. The trail is narrower past this intersection and covered with leaves and other natural material, but the gray diamond trail blazes will keep you on course to see interpretive posts by a beech tree, an American beech tree, and a black birch tree.

The next intersection is at the fifth numbered post by a small human-made pond where you see a human-made wood duck nesting box (.4 mi.) **[4]**. Turn left onto a woods road and begin a mild climb. You see an interpretive post by a sugar maple tree before reaching the next intersection (.5 mi.) **[5]**. Notice how porcupines have chewed the edges of the metallic trail map at this intersection. Sheet metal

wrapped around the base of the post is supposed to prevent porcupines from climbing the post. Turn left here, onto a narrower section of the trail.

This is the steepest part of Songbird Sojourn Trail, passing a post by a tree growing from the top of a boulder. The climb ends close to the eighth post, by a black cherry tree. A forest opening that is maintained for the benefit of wildlife is on top of the hill. You begin a gentle descent before the tenth post by club moss, which is also called ground pine, a popular material for making Christmas wreaths. You will see a spring seep, a bigtooth aspen tree, an old railroad grade, apple trees, a human-made bluebird nesting box, a section of young forest, and a downy serviceberry tree before the trail ends at the parking area (1.56 mi.) **[6]**. A sign here recognizes the Youth Conservation Corps for building this trail in 1979. The complete loop back to the kiosk is 1.6 miles **[1]**.

1. Kiosk
2. Trailhead
3. Fork left
4. Wood duck nesting box
5. Intersection
6. Parking area

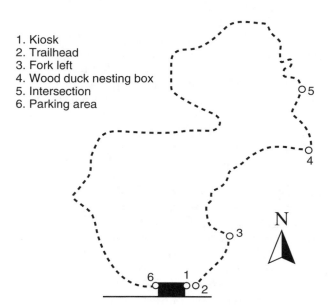

45. Cook Forest State Park

- Hike through stands of virgin timber that earned designation as a national natural landmark.
- Canoe on the Clarion River, suitable for novices during normal summer flow.
- Glimpse into the history of the great logging era at the Log Cabin Inn Visitor Center.
- Feast your eyes on splendid fall foliage, which peaks about the second week of October.

Area Information

In 1826, John Cook was the first permanent white settler in this area near the western end of the Allegheny Highlands. He and his family prospered in the timber industry. The Cook Forest Association was formed in 1920 to save what little virgin timber remained. In 1927, with money raised by that association, 6,055 acres were purchased from A. Cook Sons Company to form the first Pennsylvania state park acquired to preserve a natural landmark.

Today, Cook Forest is one of the most popular state parks. Thousands come to see the virgin hemlocks and pines, many about 350 years old and 200 feet tall. Abundant white-tailed deer are also a major attraction. There are 16 marked trails.

Directions: From the east, take Exit 13 off Interstate Route 80 onto Pennsylvania Route 36 north into Cooksburg. From the west, take Exit 8 off I-80 onto Pennsylvania Route 66 north to Leeper, then take Pennsylvania Route 36 south into the park.

Hours Open: The park is open year-round. Day-use areas, including trails, are open from 8:00 A.M. to sunset.

Facilities: The park contains 226 tent and trailer sites and two organized group tenting areas. Washhouses with hot and cold running water are open from late May to early October. From the second Friday in April to the end of antlerless deer season in early December, 24 family cabins are available. A swimming pool is open between 11:00 A.M. and 7:00 P.M. from Memorial Day weekend to Labor Day. The Clarion River provides fair trout and smallmouth bass fishing, Toms Run is stocked with trout, and there is a stocked trout pond for kids 12 and under and for handicapped anglers. Winter activities include 20 miles of snowmobile trails, a lighted ice-skating pond, 10 acres of sledding slopes, and three cross-country ski trails. Ski rentals are available. Log Cabin Inn Visitor Center, where a modest museum of area history is displayed, is open Sunday through Thursday from 10:00 A.M. to 5:00 P.M. and Friday and Saturday from 10:00 A.M. to dusk.

Permits and Rules: Park in designated areas and obey speed limits. Control pets at all times. Build fires and dispose of hot coals only in designated facilities. Alcoholic beverages are not allowed. Restrict your activities to designated areas.

Further Information: Cook Forest State Park, P.O. Box 120, Cooksburg, PA 16217; phone 814-744-8407.

Other Areas of Interest

Several **recreational businesses** are located near Cook Forest, including golf, water slides, horse rides, and canoe rentals. For details contact Cook Forest Vacation Bureau, Box 50, Cooksburg, PA 16217.

Park Trails

Liggett Trail —2 miles—This is a good trail for hikers with small children. It begins at Breezemont Drive and meets Toms Run Trail just before reaching Toms Run Road.

River Trail —1.5 miles—Second in popularity to Longfellow Trail, this begins at the Observation Tower, follows the Clarion River, then circles back to Fire Tower Road.

Cook Forest State Park

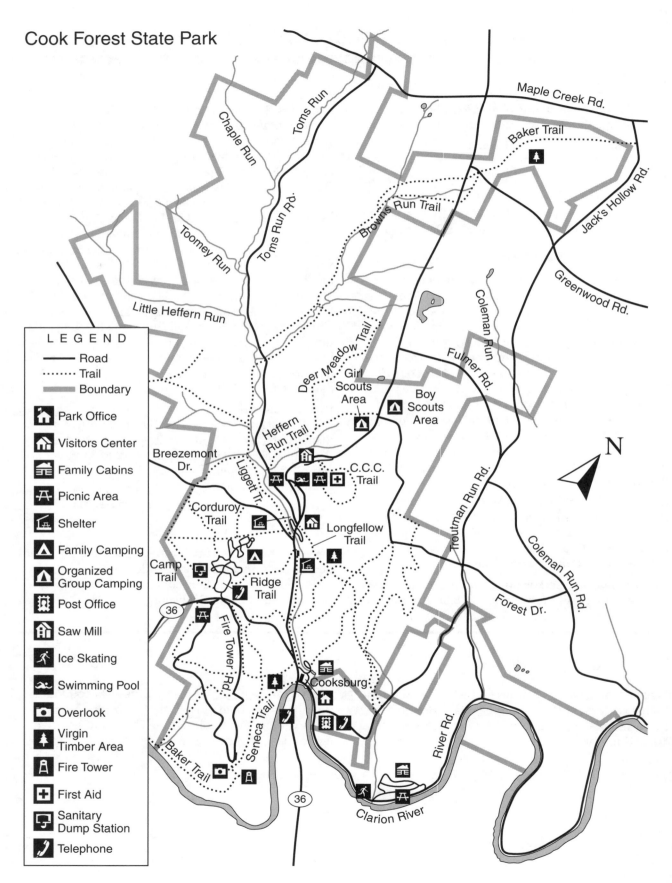

LEGEND

— Road
···· Trail
▬▬ Boundary

🏠 Park Office
🏠 Visitors Center
🏢 Family Cabins
🎪 Picnic Area
🏠 Shelter
⛺ Family Camping
⛺ Organized Group Camping
🏫 Post Office
🏠 Saw Mill
⛸ Ice Skating
🏊 Swimming Pool
📷 Overlook
🌲 Virgin Timber Area
🏛 Fire Tower
✚ First Aid
🚿 Sanitary Dump Station
📞 Telephone

Seneca Trail 🥾🥾🥾🥾🥾

Distance One-Way: .92 mile

Estimated Hiking Time: 40 minutes

Caution: There are numerous roots and rocks on this trail. Most of the trail is very steep, and a fall from the trail, while not a sheer drop, could result in a long slide stopped only by a tree or boulder.

Trail Directions: Seneca Trail takes you through a dense stand of rhododendron and along a hillside covered by ancient hemlocks, pitch pines, and white pines so steep the trail seems to hang over the Clarion River. To reach the trailhead, take Pennsylvania Route 36 north from Cooksburg to Fire Tower Road, a one-way loop, then drive to the parking lot near the fire tower at the apex of the loop. Note that a gate at the end of this loop closes at sunset.

Take the trail toward the fire tower and Seneca Point, as indicated by a sign. Before you begin the hike, take detours to the 70-foot fire tower, where you get a panoramic view of the Allegheny Highlands forest, and to Seneca Point, overlooking the narrow Clarion River valley. Stay inside the fenced area, avoiding hazardous ledges.

Seneca Trail, marked by a sign **[1]**, begins opposite Seneca Point with a short, steep descent, then becomes very level as it passes behind the restrooms, which are located by the parking area. The restrooms disappear from sight as the trail is swallowed by dense rhododendrons. During late spring, accented pink blossoms make this area a giant flower bed. After about a quarter mile, the trail starts to descend and becomes a trench for a short distance. A little more than 100 feet farther, you squeeze through a narrow gap between two large boulders. To the right, you can see the rim of the Clarion River valley.

At .4 mi., the trail forks **[2]**. The left fork is Deer Park Trail. Take the right fork, as indicated by a sign, to stay on Seneca Trail. You begin to descend into the Clarion River valley just a short distance farther. Watch for many rocks and roots that can either trip you or be used as steps in the trail through this area. Rhododendron thins out, and hemlock becomes the predominant forest component. These trees are small near the crest, then become larger as you descend. You are now in virgin forest, just as Native Americans saw it.

Note that the ground is wet, even in dry weather, as is typical of soils where hemlocks grow. Numerous small springs seep from the hillside. Small landslides demonstrate how fragile these hillsides are. Only the vegetation holds the soil in place. When other hillsides were logged, much of their soil was washed into the previously pristine Clarion River.

You will begin to see the river below to your right through the trees. At .69 mi. **[3]**, you are almost right over the river, which is now clearly in sight. Just ahead you will see a small footbridge followed by wood steps. Without the trail, because the hillside is so steep, few people would ever get this view of the river or of this steep habitat. At .71 mi. **[4]**, you encounter another footbridge and wood steps, this time over a slide area. Buildings and a highway are visible across the river, and a short distance farther you will see the Route 36 bridge and park headquarters.

Seneca Trail ends at Route 36 **[5]**, near the valley floor, after a distance of .92 mi. There is a parking lot at park headquarters, straight across the highway and down a paved road past the Cook homestead bed-and-breakfast. The total distance from the parking lot at the top of the trail to the parking lot at the bottom of the trail is just slightly more than a mile. Water and restrooms are adjacent to both parking lots.

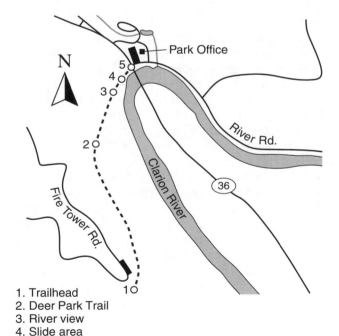

1. Trailhead
2. Deer Park Trail
3. River view
4. Slide area
5. Route 36

Longfellow Trail 👢👢👢👢

Distance Round-Trip: 1.83 miles

Estimated Hiking Time: 1 hour

Caution: Rocks and roots make footing hazardous in several areas. Watch for falling limbs in windy weather. Be cautious of vehicle traffic along Route 36 between the end of Birch Trail and the completion of the loop to the head of Longfellow Trail.

Trail Directions: Longfellow Trail passes through Forest Cathedral, the most popular tract of virgin hemlock and white pine in the park. Begin at Log Cabin Inn Visitor Center near the center of the park on Route 36. There is a sign indicating Longfellow Trail by this building **[1]**. As you are looking at the front of the cabin, the trail begins along the right side. Just past the cabin, you will see a wooden sign confirming that you are on the correct trail. About 400 feet farther, after the trail turns to the right, you will pass a memorial fountain recognizing the Cook Forest Association.

The trail begins a long, gradual climb that will become steeper as you rise in elevation. Immediately you are in a forest of mostly hemlock. After walking .26 mi., you will come to a fork in the trail **[2]**. Take the left fork. The right fork is B Trail, one of several trails, designated by capital letters, that provide optional routes through Forest Cathedral. There are trail-marker signs at each intersection. By this point you have seen many of the magnificent old-growth trees.

At .38 mi. you reach the intersection with D Trail **[3]**, and again take the left fork. Cathedral Area Windthrow is designated by a sign at .43 mi. **[4]**. Relax on the bench and read about a 1956 storm that blew down many trees in the area. This is a good place to reflect on the age of these trees, many of which were here while William Penn was governor of the Pennsylvania colony. Within sight a few feet ahead is another fork, this time with G Trail. Take the right fork where Longfellow Trail makes a sharp turn to the right. This ends the steepest part of the climb.

Indian Trail intersects at .52 mi. **[5]**. Take the right fork, as indicated by the sign, to stay on Longfellow Trail. A marker on a dead tree notes that this area is a national natural landmark. Within sight of this intersection, up Indian Trail, is an intersection with Joyce Kilmer Trail. You made a wrong turn if you hit that sign.

Still among huge hemlocks, the trail begins to descend. D Trail is met again at .76 mi. **[6]**. You can make a hard right onto D Trail to loop back to the trailhead or continue left on Longfellow Trail for a longer loop as described here. Longfellow Trail gets steeper just after D Trail and makes a turn to the right.

The forest floor is wet in some areas even during dry weather. Longfellow Trail meets C Trail at a T after .88 mi. **[7]**. Turn left. The trail takes a short turn uphill before continuing toward the bottom of the valley. This is a relatively difficult part of the trail, with very steep sections and many foot obstacles. To your right, through the trees, you will begin to see Toms Run below.

A footbridge crosses Toms Run at the bottom of the narrow valley **[8]**. Distance to this crossing is 1.08 mi. (Note an unmapped trail before crossing Toms Run. You can avoid walking along Route 36 by following this trail up Toms Run to the parking area at the Longfellow Trail head.) Across the bridge, the trail goes up steps to a small parking lot and the end of Longfellow Trail **[9]**. Total distance traveled on Longfellow Trail is 1.15 mi. Turn right, up the valley on Birch Trail, to complete the loop. This easy trail follows between Toms Run and Route 36.

Birch Trail ends at a parking lot by a picnic pavilion **[10]** after 1.57 mi. From here, walk through the parking lot and up the driveway to Route 36. Follow Route 36 back to the Longfellow Trail head at Log Cabin Inn Visitor Center **[1]**. Traffic on Route 36 is heavy during summer and fall weekends. Total distance of the loop is 1.83 mi.

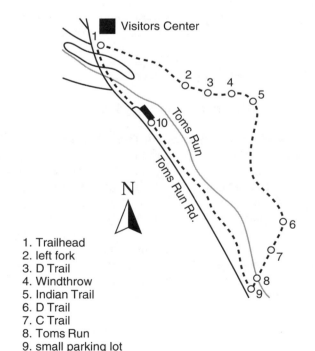

1. Trailhead
2. left fork
3. D Trail
4. Windthrow
5. Indian Trail
6. D Trail
7. C Trail
8. Toms Run
9. small parking lot
10. Picnic pavilion

46. Clear Creek State Park

- Launch canoes on the scenic Clarion River.
- Fish for native and stocked trout in Clear Creek and for trout and smallmouth bass in the Clarion River.
- Camp in cabins built by the CCC.

Area Information

Public campsites here opened in 1922. From 1933 to 1938, the CCC occupied the area and built cabins and several other facilities still used in what is now Clear Creek State Park. Recreational facilities include a small guarded beach, a disc golf course, and a basketball court. A small museum commemorates the CCC.

From the entrance to Clear Creek State Park on Pennsylvania Route 949, the park follows the steep valley of Clear Creek as it flows toward the Clarion River. It is hard to imagine a lovlier valley, especially during early summer while the laurel is in bloom.

Directions: From Pennsylvania Route 36 at Sigel, take Pennsylvania Route 949 east three miles to the park entrance.

Hours Open: Tent and trailer campsites and family cabins are open from the second Friday in April through the third Friday in December, depending on weather conditions. The swimming beach is open between 11:00 A.M. and 7:00 P.M. daily from Memorial Day weekend through Labor Day unless posted otherwise. The park is open year-round. Day-use areas are open from 8:00 A.M. to sunset.

Facilities: A playground, restrooms, a shower house, food concessions, picnic tables and picnic pavilions, a nature center, cabins, campsites for tents and trailers, a swimming beach, numerous hiking trails, and an amphitheater are available in Clear Creek State Park.

Permits and Rules: Outdoor recreational activities are restricted to locations where physical improvements or postings designate the appropriate purpose. Fires and disposal of hot coals are limited to provided facilities. Trash and other litter receptacles are provided, and disposal is limited to items accumulated during the use of state recreation areas.

Further Information: Department of Conservation and Natural Resources, Clear Creek State Park, RR 1, Box 82, Sigel, PA 15860-9502; phone 814-752-2368.

Other Areas of Interest

Allegheny National Forest borders the park along the Clarion River. Write to Allegheny National Forest, P.O. Box 847, Warren, PA 16365; phone 814-723-5150.

Cook Forest State Park, which contains virgin forest, is 11 miles west. Write to Cook Forest State Park, P.O. Box 120, Cooksburg, PA 16217-0120; phone 814-744-8407.

Park Trails

Clear Creek Trail —1.5 miles—An old logging trail, this follows the south side of Clear Creek from the swimming area to the camping area.

Frazier Trail —1.2 miles—Another old logging road, this goes from the Phyllis Run Trail to the National Fuel Pipeline.

Ox Shoe Trail —.8 mile—This is a self-guided educational trail. A pamphlet describing it is available at the museum, near the trailhead.

Phyllis Run Trail —1.2 miles—Starting from the Phyllis Run Picnic Area, the trail climbs toward the south following an old logging trail to the south boundary of the park and Zerby Trail.

Phyllis Run Loop —1.3 miles—One of the most scenic areas of the park, the loop runs up one side of Phyllis Run and down the other, beginning at the Phyllis Run Picnic Area.

Radcliffe Trail —.8 mile—Radcliffe Trail passes through hardwood and evergreen forest between the National Fuel Pipeline and the Phyllis Run Loop.

Ridge Trail —1.8 miles—Beginning at Clear Creek Trail, Ridge Trail takes you through a hardwood forest, then follows a valley of thick evergreen and rhododendron to the National Fuel Pipeline.

Sawmill Trail/Truby Trail —1 mile—Two of the more gentle park trails, they can be combined with part of Clear Creek Trail to form a loop.

River Trail 👢👢

Distance Round-Trip: .9 mile

Estimated Hiking Time: .5 hour

Caution: This part of the park is open to hunting, so wear bright orange clothing if you hike during hunting season.

Trail Directions: From the park entrance, follow the main park road down to the turnoff toward the canoe launching area. The trailhead **[1]** is between a small parking area at the apex of this loop and a small restroom building. The trail loop begins and ends at this point, with a sign pointing to River Trail in two directions. Start with the right fork, along the hillside, which is also part of Irish Rock Trail, an old road used by river rafters who tied their rafts to Irish Rock for the night.

Numerous rocks and roots protrude through the trail as you make your way along the hillside. Following the narrow trail as it turns and twists constantly around boulders and rhododendron patches could be difficult if not for yellow paint blazes on trees. But getting lost should not be a threat since the Clarion River is visible through most of this hike.

A sign by a wild grapevine cautions hikers not to disturb the vines because grapes are important wildlife forage. Oak and white pine are also significant forest components. You will also pass cucumber trees. Hike quietly, especially early or late in the day, and your chances of spotting wildlife are good. White-tailed deer, black bears, wild turkeys, and gray squirrels are common. Chances are good that you will see the black-color-phase gray squirrels in this area.

After walking about .2 mi., you arrive at a bench **[2]**. It faces uphill toward a thick rhododendron patch that limits your viewing range to a few yards. While this is certainly a beautiful sight while the rhododendron is in bloom, at any other time the view of the Clarion River in the other direction is much better.

Shortly after the trail turns left and begins dropping toward the river, you arrive at another bench (.4 mi.) **[3]**. Ahead you can see a sign noting that you are on River Trail. Then, as you get to the narrow river floodplain, the trail splits (.5 mi.) **[4]**. A sign shows Irish Rock Trail continuing upriver and River Trail turning downriver.

Most of the remainder of River Trail is over the narrow, sandy riverbank. Ignore a trail that forks uphill about 250 feet from the Irish Rock Trail fork. Though this trail is wider, paint blazes make it clear that you stay on the riverbank. A bench **[5]** at .54 mi. is a good place to stare at the river and, if you are lucky, watch common mergansers dive for fish. The land you see across the river is the Allegheny National Forest.

The trail leaves the riverbank for a short distance just below that bench; then where the trail drops back to the bank there is another bench. A sign by this bench, intended for canoeists, warns that camping is not allowed here. Below this bench, you walk the narrow bank under a thick canopy of hemlock and rhododendron.

You are near the end of the trail when you climb a set of steps away from the river (.9 mi.) **[6]**. You can see the trailhead at the top of these steps.

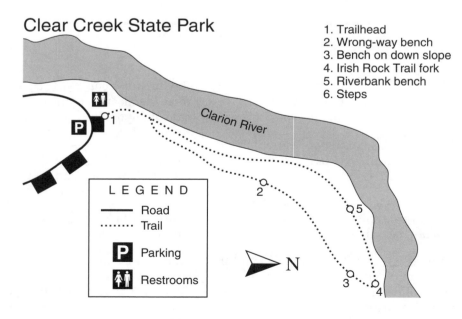

Clear Creek State Park

1. Trailhead
2. Wrong-way bench
3. Bench on down slope
4. Irish Rock Trail fork
5. Riverbank bench
6. Steps

Clarion River

LEGEND
—— Road
.... Trail
P Parking
🚻 Restrooms

N

47. Jennings Environmental Education Center

- Hike easy trails through a prairie, one of the most unusual habitats in Pennsylvania.
- See one of the most unusual reptiles in the United States, the massasauga rattlesnake.
- Revel in the beauty of the blazing star.

Area Information

The Jennings Environmental Education Center was established in the late 1950s by the Western Pennsylvania Conservancy for the primary purpose of protecting the blazing star. This striking wildflower is a prairie inhabitant. It is common in the Midwest but rare in Pennsylvania. Early August is the peak of the blooming season for the blazing star and several other wildflowers in the area. The park covers 352 acres, about 220 acres of which is forest habitat.

A relict prairie, one of few remaining areas of a greater eastward extension of the prairie that extended from the Rocky Mountains to the Appalachian Mountains, was discovered here by botanist Otto Emery Jennings, for whom this park is named. The Jennings Environmental Education Center was the first reserve established in Pennsylvania to protect one plant species and is now the only public relict prairie in the Commonwealth. At least 386 plant species, 134 bird species, and many other animals can be observed here. Take only photographs. It is illegal to molest any plant or animal.

The prairie exists here because of the soil conditions caused by the Wisconsin Ice Age about 17,000 years ago. It was once part of an extension of the Midwest prairie. But changing weather conditions, specifically more rainfall, allowed forest to grow over most of this extension. Thin topsoil prevented trees from growing in this area.

This unusual habitat is one of the few remaining strongholds for the massasauga rattlesnake. A timid reptile, it reaches a maximum length of only about 17 inches. Though it can inflict a poisonous bite, there are no reported cases of anyone dying from it. The massasauga and other snakes are strictly protected. Give them a wide berth and report sightings to the park office.

Directions: Jennings Environmental Education Center is bisected by Pennsylvania Route 528 south from the intersection with Pennsylvania Route 8, about 11 miles northwest of Butler.

Hours Open: The grounds are open year-round from 8:00 A.M. to sunset. The office is open from 8:00 A.M. to 4:00 P.M. Monday through Friday.

Facilities: Recreation is not the primary purpose of this area. There are several trails for hiking only, restrooms, a picnic pavilion, and picnic tables.

Permits and Rules: Alcoholic beverages are prohibited. Outdoor recreational activities are restricted to locations where signs or physical improvements designate the appropriate use. Fires and the disposal of hot coals are restricted to provided facilities. Trash and litter must be placed in containers provided for this purpose, and disposal is limited to items accumulated during the use of the park. Pets must be leashed and controlled at all times. Posting signs and soliciting are prohibited. Do not disturb or molest plants or animals.

Further Information: Department of Conservation and Natural Resources, Jennings Environmental Education Center, RR 1, Box 281, Slippery Rock, PA 16057-8701; phone 724-794-6011.

Park Trails

Massasauga Trail —.4 mile—Tour the habitat of the smallest and rarest of the three poisonous Pennsylvania snakes.

Oakwoods Trail —1.4 miles—The longest trail in the park loops through forest habitat.

Glacier Ridge Trail —.5 mile—See how glaciers formed the land.

Black Cherry Trail —.6 mile—Black cherry, one of the most beautiful woods for making furniture, is a major component of this hardwood forest.

Ridge Trail —.8 mile—Watch the habitat change from creek bottom to low ridge.

Jennings Environmental Education Center

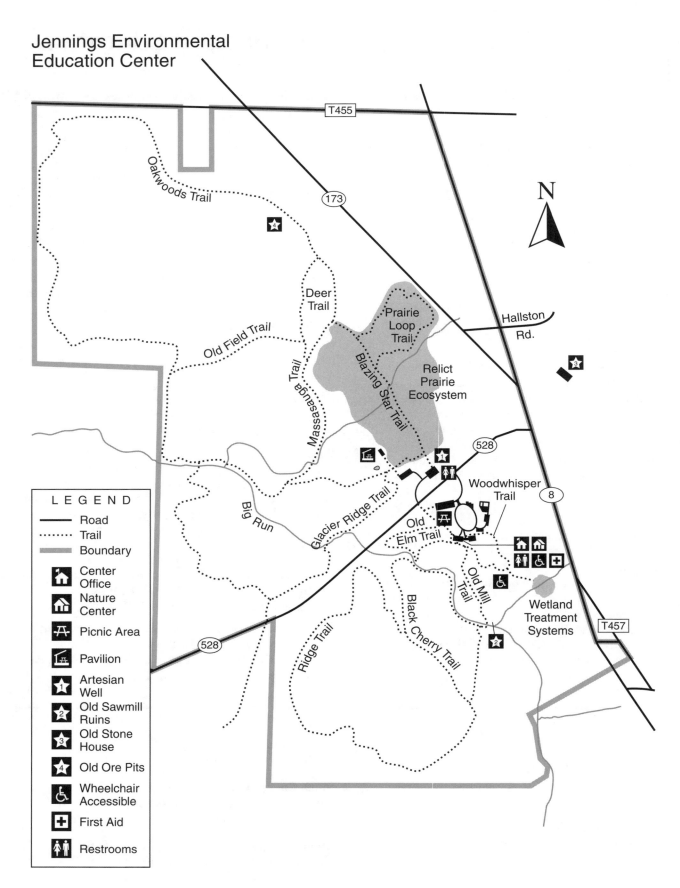

LEGEND
Road
Trail
Boundary

Center Office
Nature Center
Picnic Area
Pavilion
Artesian Well
Old Sawmill Ruins
Old Stone House
Old Ore Pits
Wheelchair Accessible
First Aid
Restrooms

Blazing Star Prairie Self-Guided Trail 🥾🥾

Distance Round-Trip: .6 mile

Estimated Hiking Time: .5 hour

Caution: Do not approach massasauga rattlesnakes. Their bite is poisonous. Stay on the trail. It is illegal to disturb plants or animals in any way.

Trail Directions: From Route 528, turn into the Relict Prairie Ecosystem, which is marked by a sign. Drive to the parking area adjacent to the restrooms. The trailhead is between two stone posts **[1].** The post on the right is inscribed in memory of Otto Emery Jennings, botanist, 1877–1964.

Walk between the posts. You will be walking on a wide, mowed grass trail. There are no trail blazes, but intersections are marked by trail signs. Interpretive signs explain this prairie ecosystem that is unusual in Pennsylvania. Prairie is a French word that means meadow. A prairie was a welcome sight to settlers since most of the state was covered by dense forest.

Massasauga Trail forks left 194 feet from the trailhead. Keep straight, as directed by a sign, on Blazing Star Trail. This is a prairie because glaciers left just 4 to 6 inches of soil over a 20-foot layer of clay, which is not suitable for most trees. One of the few trees that can grow here is the shingle oak, with leaves that look more like mountain laurel than oak. Watch along the edges of the trail for invading trees such as aspen and poplar. The poor soil will prevent them from maturing.

Turn right at the next intersection onto Prairie Loop Trail (.1 mi.) **[2].** Fire played a major part in maintaining this area as a prairie. But today, instead of natural fires, controlled fires are set intentionally. Our ability to put out natural fires has had a great impact on all habitats. It is a major reason that our forests do not return to their virgin state.

This is the precise edge of a glacier that was three quarters of a mile thick. The ridge to the south of the prairie is a lateral moraine, a mound that was pushed to the side of a glacier.

This prairie is home to several animals that are uncommon or nonexistent elsewhere in the state. Most, like the massasauga rattlesnake, are small and elusive. But if you carry binoculars and watch carefully, you might add one or more species to your life list of birds.

Turn left at the next intersection (.4 mi.) **[3]** to complete the loop and return to the trailhead (.6 mi.) **[1].**

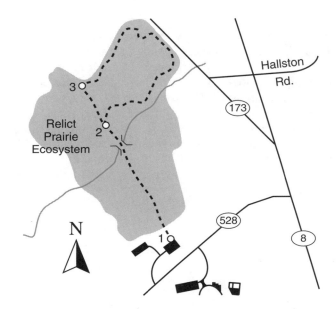

1. Trailhead
2. Prairie Loop Trail
3. Left turn

Woodwhisper Trail 👢

Distance Round-Trip: .36 mile

Estimated Hiking Time: 20 minutes

Caution: This trail is accessible to wheelchairs; however, there are mild ups and downs and gravel in a few places.

Trail Directions: From Route 8, turn onto Route 528, then turn left into the Jennings Environmental Education Center main complex. Turn right into the parking area. From the kiosk [1] at this parking area, turn right toward the education center building. It is 104 feet to a gravel trail that leads past picnic tables to the back of the building. If the offices are open, wheelchairs will have an easier route through the building. Cross a long, curved boardwalk directly behind the middle of the building. A trail sign identifies this as Old Mill Trail. Your trail is blacktop paved past the bridge.

Old Mill Trail forks to the right .1 mi. from the parking area kiosk [2]. Go straight past this intersection about 125 feet, up a mild rise, and pause on a bench. Sit quietly and listen to the sounds in this young hardwood forest. Try to identify different songbirds on the forest floor, in the lower vegetation, and in the canopy of black cherry, white oak, and maple.

Take a short detour on a gravel trail that forks right (.15 mi.) [3]. This leads to a wooden pavilion that overlooks the wetland treatment system (.2 mi.) [4].

This is an experiment in treating acid mine drainage with a passive treatment system. The prime concern is leeching metals, especially iron, out of the drainage. Drainage from a deep coal mine located a short distance from the park is being treated here.

Return to the paved trail and turn right. Two more benches offer chances to relax and enjoy the woods before the trail makes a hard right turn onto gravel. You are now within sight of the main building. Follow the gravel path to the road, then back to the parking area (.36 mi.) [1].

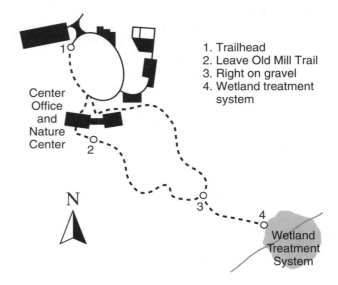

1. Trailhead
2. Leave Old Mill Trail
3. Right on gravel
4. Wetland treatment system

Center Office and Nature Center

N

Wetland Treatment System

48. Moraine State Park

- Fish the most productive trophy largemouth bass lake in Pennsylvania.
- Learn about continental glaciers.
- Visit one of the finest examples of reclaimed land.

Area Information

Moraine State Park is one of the finest and largest playgrounds in western Pennsylvania. One of its greatest claims to fame is that Lake Arthur, which covers 3,225 acres, is the best trophy largemouth bass water in the state. Fishing is also very good for channel catfish, crappies, bluegills, northern pike, muskellunge, and hybrid stripers. Ask at the park office or the marina office for a map that shows the locations of artificial fish-attracting structures.

Lake Arthur is a smaller re-creation of a natural lake that was created by Ice Age glaciers at about the same location. Glaciers played a major role in the formation of the Moraine State Park landscape. Moraine is soil, rocks, and debris that accumulate beneath and along the sides of glaciers. At least four great glaciers reached their southern terminus near Moraine State Park, leaving behind gently rolling hills and wetlands in the broad valleys.

Virtually all of the land in this area was disrupted in some way by humans. Coal mining, farming, logging, and other industries all contributed to the destruction. The Western Pennsylvania Conservancy was formed to purchase and reclaim the land that is now Moraine State Park. The dam that creates Lake Arthur was completed in 1968, and the park was dedicated two years later.

Directions: Moraine State Park is close to the intersection of Interstate Route 79 and U.S. Route 422. Route 422 passes through the park east to west. Pennsylvania Route 528 passes through the park north to south between Route 422 and Pennsylvania Route 8.

Hours Open: The park is open year-round. Day-use areas are open from 7:00 A.M. to sunset.

Facilities: Picnic tables and picnic pavilions are scattered throughout the park. At Lake Arthur, swimming is permitted at two beaches, there are 10 boat launch areas, a variety of boats can be rented, windsurfing is popular near Barber Point, and fishing is very popular year-round. There are trails for both mountain and road bikes, and bikes can be rented. Eleven cabins are available to rent. There is no camping, but private campgrounds are nearby.

Permits and Rules: Alcoholic beverages are prohibited. Boats must have either a state park launching permit, a state park mooring permit, or a current Pennsylvania Fish and Boat Commission registration. Boat motors are limited to a maximum of 10 hp. Outdoor recreational activities are restricted to locations where signs or physical improvements designate the appropriate use. Fires and the disposal of hot coals are restricted to provided facilities. Trash and litter must be placed in containers provided for this purpose, and disposal is limited to items accumulated during the use of the park. Pets must be leashed and controlled at all times, and they are not allowed at the swimming area or in overnight camping facilities. Posting signs and soliciting are prohibited. All children age nine and under must be accompanied by a responsible adult at the swimming area.

Further Information: Department of Conservation and Natural Resources, Moraine State Park, 225 Pleasant Valley Road, Portersville, PA 16051-9650; phone 724-368-8811.

Other Areas of Interest

For information about private campgrounds and other area services, write to **Butler County Tourist Promotion Agency,** P.O. Box 1082, Butler, PA 16003-1082; phone 888-741-6772 or 724-283-2222.

Park Trails

Hilltop Trail 🥾🥾🥾—1.1 miles or 3 miles—Take your choice of two loops to see different stages of forest regeneration.

Pleasant Valley Trail 🥾🥾—2.6 miles—Walk along the south shore of Lake Arthur.

Glacier Ridge Trail 🥾🥾🥾—14 miles—This is part of the North Country National Scenic Trail.

Five Points Trail 🥾🥾—1.5 miles—This is a pleasant forest hike for people staying in one of the rental cabins.

Moraine State Park

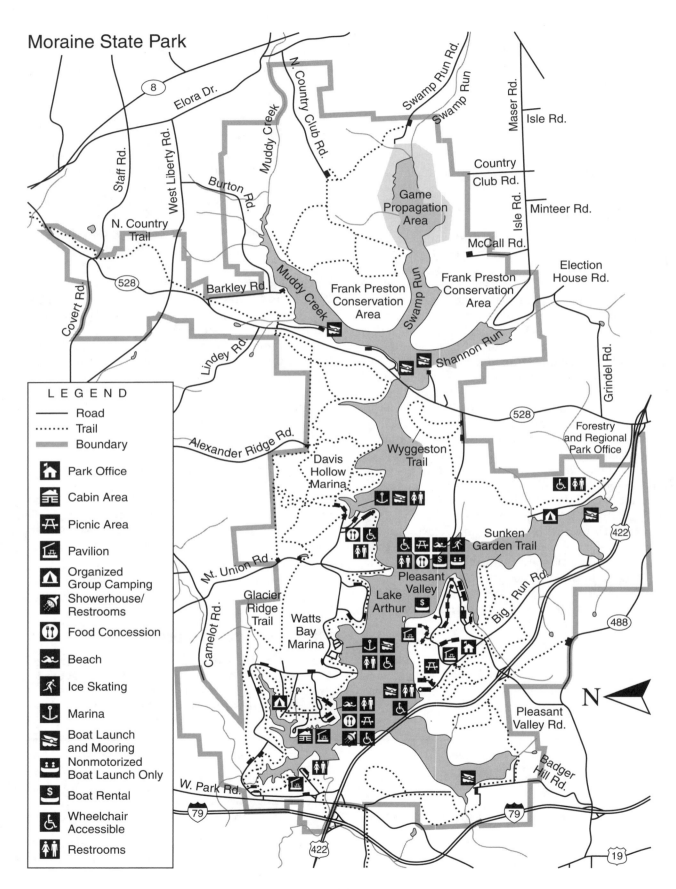

LEGEND

— Road
···· Trail
▬ Boundary

🏠 Park Office
🏘 Cabin Area
🏕 Picnic Area
⛱ Pavilion
⛺ Organized Group Camping
🚿 Showerhouse/Restrooms
🍴 Food Concession
🏊 Beach
⛸ Ice Skating
⚓ Marina
🚤 Boat Launch and Mooring
🚣 Nonmotorized Boat Launch Only
💲 Boat Rental
♿ Wheelchair Accessible
🚻 Restrooms

Wyggeston Trail Loop 👢👢

Distance Round-Trip: 1.6 miles

Estimated Hiking Time: 1 hour

Caution: This trail is narrow and nearly overgrown in places. But following it is not difficult because, in contrast to so many trails in heavily used parks, there are no confusing, unofficial spur trails.

Trail Directions: If you live in an urban or suburban area and want a pretty trail to escape civilization, this is perfect. This is not a heavily used trail. It traverses one of the quietest, most peaceful areas of Moraine State Park through a beautiful hardwood forest.

To reach this trailhead, turn west off Route 528 onto Christley Road. This turn is marked by a Wyggeston Trail sign on the opposite side of Route 528. About .1 mile along Christley Road, turn right into a shady parking area. You cannot see the parking area from Christley Road, but the gravel driveway is marked by a sign. A sign at the trailhead explains that this land was donated to the Western Pennsylvania Conservancy by the Frank W. Preston family and was named for a school Preston attended in England **[1]**.

Follow orange trail blazes from the trailhead into young hardwood forest. You will see some blue trail blazes. Though they appear to be newer than the weathered orange trail blazes, if you closely examine a few of the orange blazes, you can see that some, at least, were painted over blue blazes. You will see a lot of sassafras saplings beside the trail. The fragrant roots of these trees have been used to make tea since settlers learned about it from Native Americans. But do not harvest any roots in the state park. Most of the larger trees, which are only 8 to 10 inches in diameter, are cherry, maple, and tulip trees.

Farther along the trail, where it is apparent that you are walking on top of a narrow ridge, trees are larger. Some are more than 20 inches in diameter. You are witnessing various stages of forest succes-

sion. Virtually all of the virgin trees on the Pittsburgh Plateau were cut during the 19th century. Some of the land became farms, and a lot of it was ripped apart to mine coal, shale, and other rocks and minerals. Now, with the help of humans, nature is reclaiming the land.

Wyggeston Trail is fairly level until it drops off the right side of the ridge (.5 mi.) **[2]**. Some red oaks along this hillside are very large. After a few switchbacks, the trail bends left around the end of the ridge, then begins a gentle climb up a small valley to a fork where Wyggeston Trail splits (1.4 mi.) **[3]**. The right fork is not part of the loop. It is the most rugged trail in the park, passing a couple of historic sites before ending near the park office. Take the left fork to complete the Wyggeston Trail Loop at the parking area where you began (1.6 mi.) **[1]**.

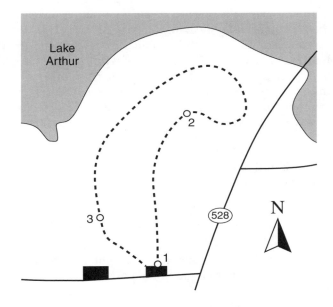

1. Trailhead
2. Drop off ridge
3. Wyggeston splits

Sunken Garden Trail 🥾

Distance Round-Trip: 1.6 miles

Estimated Hiking Time: 1 hour

Caution: Watch out for a few roots growing out of the trail; some uneven ground; and numerous unmapped, mowed trails that frequently cause confusion. Watch for thorny crabapple and multiflora rose on the sides of the trail.

Trail Directions: This is a great trail for flower lovers. You will see a wide variety of wildflowers in three distinctly different types of habitat—in woods, in meadows, and in the littoral zone of Lake Arthur. Also, bring your binoculars and field guide to birds.

Exit Route 422 onto Pleasant Valley Road. Drive north past the park office and turn right into the Pleasant Valley Boat Launch parking area. The trailhead, which is marked by a sign, is across from the restrooms at the head of the parking area **[1].**

You begin this hike through an area overgrown with berry bushes and a rainbow of wildflowers. Trail blazes are pink. Turn left at the first marked fork, as indicated by the Sunken Garden Trail sign and a pink trail blaze on a post (.1 mi.) **[2].** Cross a footbridge over a slow-moving stream on the way to the next major fork, where the short loop of Sunken Garden Trail splits (.16 mi.) **[3].** Take the right fork, where you can see pink trail blazes ahead. The forest is a mix of hardwoods and conifers, but the canopy allows enough light to reach the forest floor to support many wildflowers. About 50 feet after breaking into another flowery meadow, the trail splits three ways (.23 mi.) **[4].** The trail farthest to the right is marked private. The middle trail is not marked. Turn left, onto the trail marked by a pink trail blaze on a post.

You cross an overgrown ditch on a concrete bridge and leave the meadow. Watch the pink trail blazes through an unmapped intersection, then break into another colorful meadow. Try to count all of the colors. Turn left toward the lake and Sunken Garden at the next fork, which is also unmapped (.8 mi.) **[5],** and leave the pink trail blazes. This takes you along the edge of the lake, where you can see boats, anglers, and swimmers across the bay. Hike here during March–April and October–December to see an interesting variety of waterfowl during migrations. Most beautiful in this relaxing scene, though, is a long band of water lilies in the shallow water near shore. The trail slopes toward the lake here, which can be slippery when wet. Trees grow almost to the water. The largest are sugar maples.

Soon after the trail bends away from the lake, you complete the small loop (1.4 mi.) **[3].** Turn right and backtrack to the trailhead (1.6 mi.) **[1].**

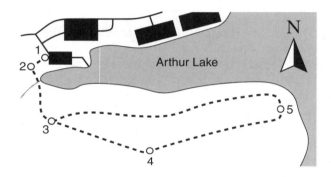

1. Trailhead
2. First marked fork
3. Small loop split
4. Private split
5. Turn toward lake

49. McConnell's Mill State Park

- Hike through the steep gorge of Slippery Rock Creek.
- Drive between and under massive boulders.
- Tour an old mill and a lime kiln.

Area Information

Stretched along the scenic gorge of Slippery Rock Creek, McConnell's Mill State Park is the natural gem of the Pittsburgh Plateau. It is also rich in human history and prehistory.

Slippery Rock Creek is the central feature of the 2,529-acre park. Its deep gorge originated when a huge glacier blocked the northward flow of water, and then water from the melting glacier eroded the gorge to more than 400 feet. This gorge is a national natural landmark.

You might assume that Slippery Rock Creek got its name from the countless rounded, slippery rocks in the streambed and along the sides of the gorge. But the real story is more interesting. A Native American trail crossed the creek by an oil seep. It was one particular oil-covered rock at this crossing that gave the creek its name.

The park is named for a gristmill on Slippery Rock Creek, built in 1868, that was purchased in 1875 by Thomas McConnell. This became one of the first rolling mills in the United States when McConnell replaced the waterwheel with a water turbine. The mill processed corn, oats, wheat, and buckwheat. It closed in 1928.

The land was conveyed to the Western Pennsylvania Conservancy, which has been instrumental in preserving some of the finest natural areas in western Pennsylvania. It became a state park in 1957. While you are in this park, be sure to tour the mill, where you will also see a covered bridge built in 1874. Drive north from the mill on a one-way road where you pass through a field of huge boulders, some of which hang over the road.

Directions: The park is about 40 miles north of Pittsburgh. Exit Interstate Route 79 onto U.S. Route 422 west, then turn left, at the park sign, onto McConnell's Mill Road.

Hours Open: The park is open year-round. Day-use areas are open from 8:00 A.M. to sunset.

Facilities: White-water boating is allowed on two sections of Slippery Rock Creek. Two areas are reserved for climbing and rappelling. There are 11 miles of trails, and two picnic areas with charcoal grills, more than 150 shaded tables, and restrooms. You can find good fishing for trout and smallmouth bass in Slippery Rock Creek. A section of the creek is under special "delayed harvest, fly-fishing only" regulations.

Permits and Rules: Alcoholic beverages are prohibited. Outdoor recreational activities are restricted to locations where signs or physical improvements designate the appropriate use. Fires and the disposal of hot coals are restricted to provided facilities. Trash and litter must be placed in containers provided for this purpose, and disposal is limited to items accumulated during the use of the park. Posting signs and soliciting are prohibited.

Further Information: Department of Conservation and Natural Resources, McConnell's Mill State Park, RR 2, Box 16, Portersville, PA 16051-9401; phone 724-368-8091 or 724-368-8811.

Other Areas of Interest

For information about the surrounding area, write to **Lawrence County Tourist Promotion Agency,** Cilli Central Station, 229 South Jefferson Street, New Castle, PA 16101; phone 724-654-8408.

Park Trails

Slippery Rock Gorge Trail 🥾🥾🥾—6 miles—This is the longest trail in the park, beginning in Hell Hollow and ending at McConnell's Mill. It is a segment of the North Country National Scenic Trail.

Alpha Pass Trail 🥾🥾🥾—.5 mile—Alpha Pass is one of the most scenic parts of the Slippery Rock Gorge.

McConnell's Mill State Park

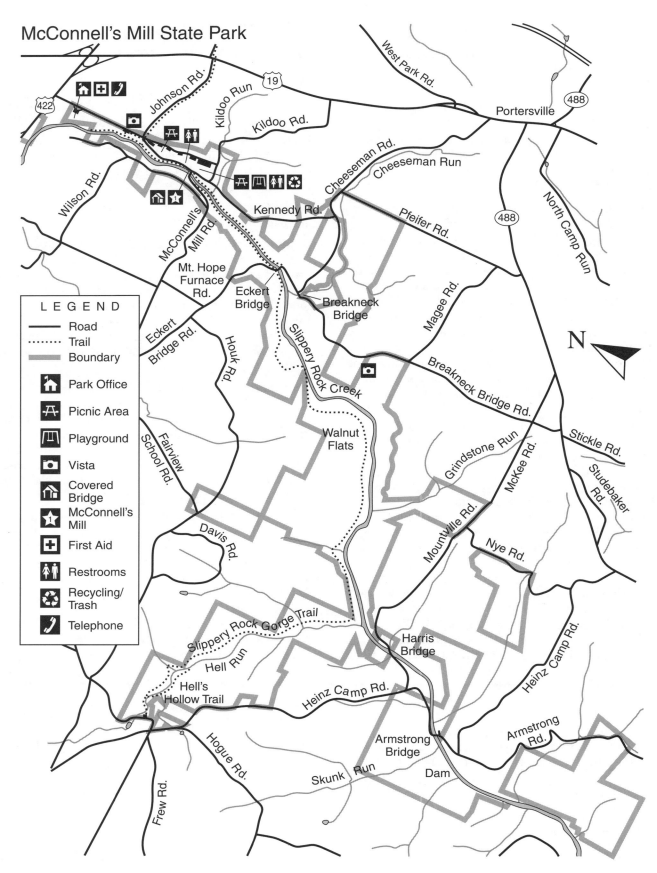

Kildoo Trail 👢👢👢

Distance Round-Trip: 2.1 miles

Estimated Hiking Time: 2 hours

Caution: Wear hiking boots with nonslip treads. Stay on the trail for your own safety and to preserve the fragile environment. You will be walking on rocks over most of the trail and over roots in other areas. Several springs seep across the trail. There are no trail blazes.

Trail Directions: Drive to the McConnell's Mill Historic Site. From the north, turn off Route 422 onto McConnell's Mill Road. From the south, turn off U.S. Route 19 onto Kildoo Road. The trailhead, which is marked by a sign, is located by the east side of the covered bridge **[1]**. Parking is limited to just a few cars here. On any busy day, the nearest parking might be at a nearby playing field or picnic area. Small parking areas at either end of Eckert Bridge can also be used to start this trail at the midway point.

Kildoo Trail begins as a blacktop path between huge boulders and under the shade of thick hemlocks. You are following Slippery Rock Creek downstream. Do not disturb any of the water-rescue devices that have been placed along the trail. Lives could depend on them. Slippery Rock Creek is a favorite destination for white-water boaters when the flow is right. Its churning course tumbles around and over huge boulders.

Study the unusual habitat in the gorge. Because the walls are so steep and the hemlock canopy is so thick, very little sunlight strikes this side of the gorge. Erosion prevents most soil buildup. Many of the plants that grow here are specialized for this environment. Try to identify lichens, American yew, common polypody, marginal woodfern, and wood sorrel. Look at spur trails and other places where people have wandered off the path and see how this has adversely affected the habitat.

The paved portion of this trail ends at a wooden footbridge over Kildoo Run (.2 mi.) **[2]**. The dirt and rock trail beyond the footbridge is far more difficult. Look up the cut to your left. This should give you a good impression of how boulders slipped down the sides of the gorge and into Slippery Rock Creek.

Kildoo Trail begins its steepest climb toward the top of Eckert Bridge (1 mi.) **[3]**. Turn right and cross the bridge. At the other end, turn right at a sign that points toward Old Mill (1.05 mi.) **[4]**. This is a section of Slippery Rock Gorge Trail and the North Country National Scenic Trail. You will be following blue trail blazes.

Stop at a bench about 550 feet past the bridge to listen to the sounds of the gorge. Hear songbirds, cicadas, and Slippery Rock Creek tumbling over boulders. Look around. This side of the gorge is different from the other side. The hillside is steep, but not as steep. There are fewer boulders. The forest is different. There is still a lot of hemlock, but it is mixed with birch, beech, sugar maple, and tulip trees. There are many more wildflowers, especially close to the creek, where more sunlight reaches the ground. Try to imagine the reasons for these differences between the sides of the gorge.

Watch for double blue slashes where the trail forks (1.2 mi.) **[5]**. Take the left fork, which climbs the hillside. The sandy right fork is a trail used by anglers. Pause to enjoy the wildflowers in this area.

Turn right where the trail meets a paved road, across the covered bridge to the trailhead (2.1 mi.) **[1]**.

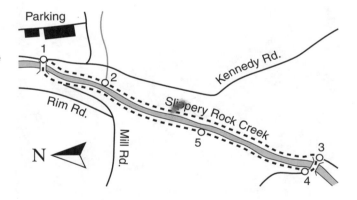

1. Trailhead
2. Kildoo Run
3. Eckert Bridge
4. Old Mill sign
5. Double blue slashes

Hell's Hollow Trail 👢👢

Distance Round-Trip: 1 mile

Estimated Hiking Time: .5 hour

Caution: Wear hiking boots with nonskid soles. Footing is slippery along much of the trail, especially where the thick forest canopy causes the trail to retain moisture. You will be walking along ledges in some places. There is a very steep descent at the end of the trail.

Trail Directions: Try to time this hike for spring, or after a good rain so there is a lot of water coming over Hell's Hollow Falls. This stream is barely more than a trickle during a dry midsummer. Bring a field guide to identify a good assortment of wildflowers.

The trailhead for Hell's Hollow Trail is at the southwest tip of the park. From the park office, follow McConnell's Mill Road south across the covered bridge by McConnell's Mill. You will begin to follow signs to Hell's Hollow before turning left onto Fairview School Road, then left onto Shaffer Road. The trailhead is on the left side of Shaffer Road

[1]. There is a parking area large enough for about a dozen cars and one picnic table.

The trail begins at the edge of the parking area by a blue trail blaze. You cross a long footbridge over Hell Run about 50 paces from the trailhead. Follow the wide path through a mixed hardwood forest to a Y intersection (.1 mi.) **[2]**. A sign directs you onto the right fork to Hell's Run Falls. The left fork is Slippery Rock Gorge Trail, which leads to Slippery Rock Creek, Walnut Flats, Eckert Bridge, Old Mill, and Alpha Pass. If you take the wrong fork, it is more than 6 miles to the next road.

The right fork crosses another footbridge over Hell Run, then a footbridge over a small tributary stream. Several spur trails lead to the stream. Benches have been placed alongside the trail at strategic locations where you can pause and enjoy the forest. The next major trail fork is very close to Hell's Hollow Falls. Take the left fork to the falls. This section of the trail is a very steep descent with a handrail to help your balance on slippery footing. Next come 21 steps, which finally reach the bottom of the waterfall (.5 mi.) **[3]**. Some water drops all the way over this 8-foot waterfall, some cascades over boulders.

Retrace your steps back up to the Y intersection and turn left about 100 feet to the top of an old lime kiln. Lime was a critical ingredient in the early iron industry. A fence has been placed around the hole at the top of the kiln. Do not walk around the fence because there are steep ledges.

Backtrack from here to the trailhead for a total hike of about 1 mi. **[1]**.

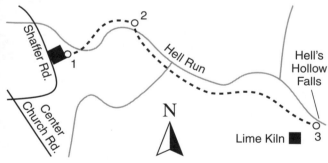

1. Trailhead
2. Sign at Y
3. Hell's Hollow Falls

50. Yellow Creek State Park

- Visit during fall and spring to see migrating waterfowl.
- Swim, boat, and fish in a 720-acre lake.
- Learn about the environment with special programs from Memorial Day to Labor Day.

Area Information

Yellow Creek State Park might be described as a typical Pennsylvania state park. The land, 2,981 acres, was purchased in 1963 through the Project 70 park-expansion program. Yellow Creek Lake was completed in 1969, and the park opened in 1976. But also like most state parks, it is a gem. The reverting farmland from which it was created is now a richly varied wildlife habitat. The lake has been stocked with bass, muskellunge, walleyes, northern pike, channel catfish, and several panfish species. Special big bass regulations are designed to give anglers access to trophy-size bass. The lake also provides outstanding waterfowl habitat. Several species nest here. More use it as a migration stopover, including perhaps the state's most beautiful duck, the blue-winged teal.

While there are no camping facilities, you can do just about any other normal outdoor activity here. Fish, picnic, boat, hike, or swim during summer. Try ice fishing, snowmobiling, sledding, skating, snowshoeing, or cross-country skiing during winter.

Directions: The entrance to the park is at the intersection of U.S. Route 422 and Pennsylvania Route 259, between Indiana and Ebensburg.

Hours Open: The park is open year-round. Day-use areas, which include the swimming beach, the picnic pavilions and major picnic areas, access to Ridge Top Trail, and the waterfowl observatory, are open from 8:00 A.M. to sunset. The swimming beach is open between 11:00 A.M. and 7:00 P.M. daily from Memorial Day weekend to Labor Day, unless otherwise posted.

Facilities: Visitors here can enjoy an 800-foot guarded swimming beach, hiking trails, snowmobile trails, picnic tables and cooking grills, picnic pavilions, a handicapped/children's fishing area, a waterfowl observatory, boat launch ramps, restrooms, a food concession, boat rentals, a playground, a sledding and tobogganing hill, and a classroom building.

Permits and Rules: Open ground fires are not permitted. Boats may only use motors of 10 hp or less. Boats must display either a current Pennsylvania boat registration, a state park launching permit, or a state park mooring permit. The mooring permit is required to moor boats overnight. Pets are not permitted on the beach, but they are allowed in the day-use area if kept on a leash of no more than six feet, and they must be attended at all times. Fishing is not permitted at the swimming beach, in the boat mooring area, from boat launching docks, or from the dam.

Further Information: Department of Conservation and Natural Resources, Yellow Creek State Park, 170 Route 259 Highway, Penn Run, PA 15765-9612; phone 724-357-7913.

Other Areas of Interest

Indiana County Tourist Bureau, 1019 Philadelphia Street, Indiana, PA 15701; phone 724-463-7505.

Park Trails

Damsite Trail —2.5 miles—Hike to the Yellow Creek Dam.

Yellow Creek State Park

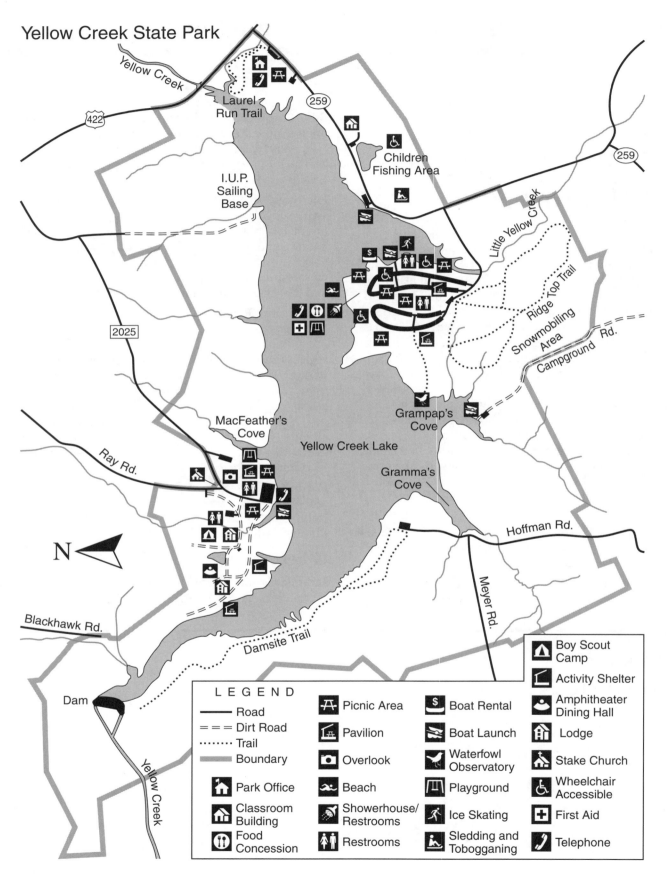

Yellow Creek

US 422

259

Laurel
Run Trail

I.U.P.
Sailing
Base

Children
Fishing Area

2025

Little Yellow Creek

Ridge Top Trail

Snowmobiling
Area

Campground Rd.

MacFeather's
Cove

Yellow Creek Lake

Grampap's
Cove

Gramma's
Cove

Ray Rd.

Hoffman Rd.

Meyer Rd.

N

Blackhawk Rd.

Damsite Trail

Dam

Yellow Creek

LEGEND

- Road
- = = = Dirt Road
- .... Trail
- Boundary

- Park Office
- Classroom Building
- Food Concession
- Picnic Area
- Pavilion
- Overlook
- Beach
- Showerhouse/ Restrooms
- Restrooms
- Boat Rental
- Boat Launch
- Waterfowl Observatory
- Playground
- Ice Skating
- Sledding and Tobogganing
- Boy Scout Camp
- Activity Shelter
- Amphitheater Dining Hall
- Lodge
- Stake Church
- Wheelchair Accessible
- First Aid
- Telephone

Laurel Run Trail 👢👢

Distance Round-Trip: .77 mile

Estimated Hiking Time: .75 hour

Caution: During wet weather, there will be numerous muddy places along this trail. Bring insect repellent. Stinging or biting insects can be annoying.

Trail Directions: Just after entering the park on Route 259, turn right into the park headquarters parking lot. Bring your flower field guide on this short hike. From the rich yellow daffodils and delicate wood anemones of early spring to the brilliant red bee balm and pink sweet william of summer, wildflowers paint the moist bottom land this trail traverses.

The trailhead is to the right of the parking lot as you face the headquarters building. It is simply marked "trailhead" **[1]**. The trail splits after 133 feet at a sign reaffirming this as Laurel Run Trail, with an arrow pointing to the right fork. You will hear the babbling of Laurel Run before arriving at its bank a short distance down this right fork. A wooden bench **[2]** almost .1 mi. from the trailhead gives you the opportunity to pause and take in the atmosphere. Is that mountain laurel or great rhododendron growing beneath the hemlocks on the other side of the creek? Both grow in this park.

Farther along, the trail crosses a narrow wooden footbridge. Wildflowers are abundant in this area. The second wooden bench **[3]** is .2 mi. from the trailhead. Highway traffic is visible across the creek, so this is not where I would choose to pause. Yellow arrows on brown wood posts mark the trail. Footing is good, and there are no significant elevation changes. It is easy to imagine trout waiting for a meal to drop from laurel that hangs over the creek in several places.

After crossing another narrow footbridge, the trail bends left away from the creek. Ahead you can start to see Yellow Creek Lake. A fork in the trail at .39 mi.

is not shown on the map. But a sign indicates Lake Trail to the right and Main Trail to the left. Lake Trail is a very short detour to the edge of the lake, where Laurel Run joins. Larger trees in this area include cucumber tree, cherry, and oaks.

A third bench (.4 mi.) **[4]** is the apex of the trail loop. Stop here to look for waterfowl and plants that grow along the edge of the lake. The best time to see a variety of waterfowl species is during spring or fall migrations. During summer, you are most likely to see Canada geese, mallards, or wood ducks. On the opposite shore, you can see a human-made wood duck nesting box.

As you return with the lake at your back, flowers continue to grace the trail. Undergrowth beneath pines, spruce, oaks, and other trees is thick, excellent wildlife habitat, as demonstrated by deer tracks across the trail. The journey is completed, a distance of .77 mi., back at the trailhead. The parking lot is only about 100 feet farther.

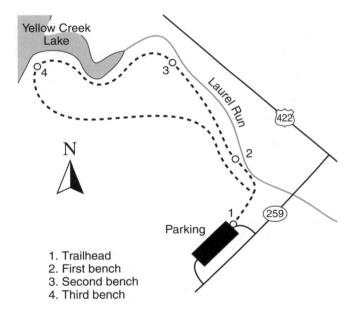

1. Trailhead
2. First bench
3. Second bench
4. Third bench

Ridge Top Trail 🥾🥾🥾

Distance Round-Trip: 2.3 miles

Estimated Hiking Time: 1.5 hours

Caution: Roots protrude through this trail in several areas. An intersection on the back half of the trail can be confusing.

Trail Directions: Enter the day-use area from Route 259. The trailhead **[1]** is on the left, marked with a sign, just before you reach a loop at the end of the road. There is a six-car parking area and a picnic table opposite the trailhead. Ridge Top Trail crosses a wooden footbridge and begins a moderate climb immediately at the trailhead, turning left through a stand of red pine along the side of the ridge until it reaches nearly to the top. It takes you on a journey through several stages of reverting farmland, from maturing forest to fields overgrown with brush and thorns, from ridge tops to creek bottoms. Wildlife-viewing opportunities are excellent, depending on your timing and stealth.

Soon after the trail levels out near the top of the ridge, a bench (.1 mi.) **[2]** offers a relaxing view of Yellow Creek Lake. Ignore a trail that intersects from the right about another 10th of a mile along the trail. Watch for white paint blazes on trees marking Ridge Top Trail.

A few steps after crossing a footbridge, you arrive at a bench (.4 mi.) **[3]**. You can see a stone foundation across the trail. Take time to examine all that remains of settlers' dreams.

The trail turns right over the top of the ridge, then arrives at a signpost (.5 mi.) **[4]** indicating that the beach is to the right and the trail is to the left. Ridge Top Trail begins dropping into a narrow valley here, across a wooden footbridge, then back up the ridge on the opposite side. Soon Little Yellow Creek comes into view in a larger valley. After passing a bench, the trail drops rather steeply into this valley.

As posted signs come into sight, the trail turns right, back up the ridge, roughly following the property boundary. A bench at the top of this ridge **[5]**, almost 1.1 mi. from the start of the trail, is the apex of this loop. Thick brush and thorns surround the trail, an indication that this is the edge of an overgrown field. Ignore a small trail that forks to the right.

The trail is wide and relatively level where it turns away from the posted land and through the field.

Forest surrounds the trail again just before it drops into a small valley. At the bottom of this valley is a bench (1.4 mi.) **[6]** beside a small stream that flows through a concrete tube covered with dirt. You are back in overgrown field at the top of this slope.

A rather confusing intersection **[7]** greets you at 1.6 mi. A sign points right to the beach just before you cross a wide trail. Across that trail you can see another signpost that shows Ridge Top Trail continuing straight ahead. From this point on, snowmobiles use the trail during winter.

Ridge Top Trail makes a sharp left, then a sharp right, crossing another pair of trails. But another signpost is visible ahead to keep you on the right trail. You are now walking between a spruce plantation on your left, and what was once a windrow on your right.

Almost .2 mi. farther, the trail begins dropping off the ridge top and away from the overgrown field toward Yellow Creek Lake. Ignore a small trail that forks to the left at the bottom of a particularly steep slope. Turn right at a T (2 mi.) **[8]**. You can see the lake straight over a signpost at this T.

You are now in the homestretch, first through a spruce plantation so thick it forms a complete canopy in places, then left at another T just before you complete a 2.3-mi. loop at the trailhead.

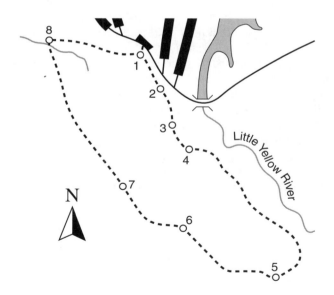

1. Trailhead
2. Lake-view bench
3. Bench by foundation
4. Beach signpost
5. Bench at apex
6. Bench by stream
7. Confusing intersection
8. T

51. Raccoon Creek State Park

- Visit the site of a 19th-century resort.
- Rent a cabin for a family vacation.
- Fish on a quiet lake for bass, walleyes, and panfish.

Area Information

Raccoon Creek State Park has a long history as a recreational area. More than 200 years ago, Frankfort Mineral Springs was a famous health spa. People from all over the country came here for the healing powers of mineral water.

The land that is now a state park, including the mineral springs, was purchased by the National Park Service during the 1930s to provide recreational land close to Pittsburgh. Before U.S. involvement in World War II, the CCC and the WPA, two federal programs that employed jobless workers during the Great Depression, built a recreation demonstration area here. It was transferred to the Commonwealth of Pennsylvania in 1945. The 101-acre lake was built in 1948, followed by other improvements.

This is one of the larger Pennsylvania state parks. It covers 7,323 acres on the Pittsburgh Plateau, a segment of the Appalachian Plateau characterized by rolling hills. Raccoon Creek State Park is a forest oasis surrounded by a patchwork of farms, reverting farmland, and suburban sprawl. This park serves very well as a place to escape the fast pace of urban and suburban life in the Pittsburgh area.

Directions: The park is 25 miles west of Pittsburgh in southern Beaver County by way of U.S. Route 30. Coming from Pittsburgh, turn left into the park at the park sign. Approaching from the north or south, exit Interstate Route 79 onto U.S. Routes 22 and 30, or enter via Pennsylvania Route 18, which bisects the park.

Hours Open: The park is open year-round. Day-use areas are open from 8:00 A.M. to sunset.

Facilities: Fish for bass, walleyes, catfish, and panfish in Raccoon Creek Lake. Camp in tents or RVs in the 176-site campground with hot showers and a sanitary dump station. Ten family cabins are available for rent; contact the park office. Nonpowered and electric-powered boats may be used on the lake. There are picnic pavilions and more than 600 picnic tables. A swimming beach is open from Memorial Day weekend through Labor Day.

Permits and Rules: Alcoholic beverages are prohibited. Boats must have either a state park launching permit, a state park mooring permit, or a current Pennsylvania Fish and Boat Commission registration. Only nonpowered and electric-powered boats are allowed. Outdoor recreational activities are restricted to locations where signs or physical improvements designate the appropriate use. Fires and the disposal of hot coals are restricted to provided facilities. Trash and litter must be placed in containers provided for this purpose, and disposal is limited to items accumulated during the use of the park. Pets must be leashed and controlled at all times, and they are not allowed at the swimming area or in overnight camping facilities. Posting signs and soliciting are prohibited. All children age nine and under must be accompanied by a responsible adult at the swimming area.

Further Information: Department of Conservation and Natural Resources, Raccoon Creek State Park, 3000 State Route 18, Hookstown, PA 15050-1605; phone 412-899-2200.

Other Areas of Interest

Hillman State Park is a large but undeveloped area less than 5 miles south of Raccoon Creek State Park. Park maps are not available. For information, contact Raccoon Creek State Park.

Raccoon Creek State Park

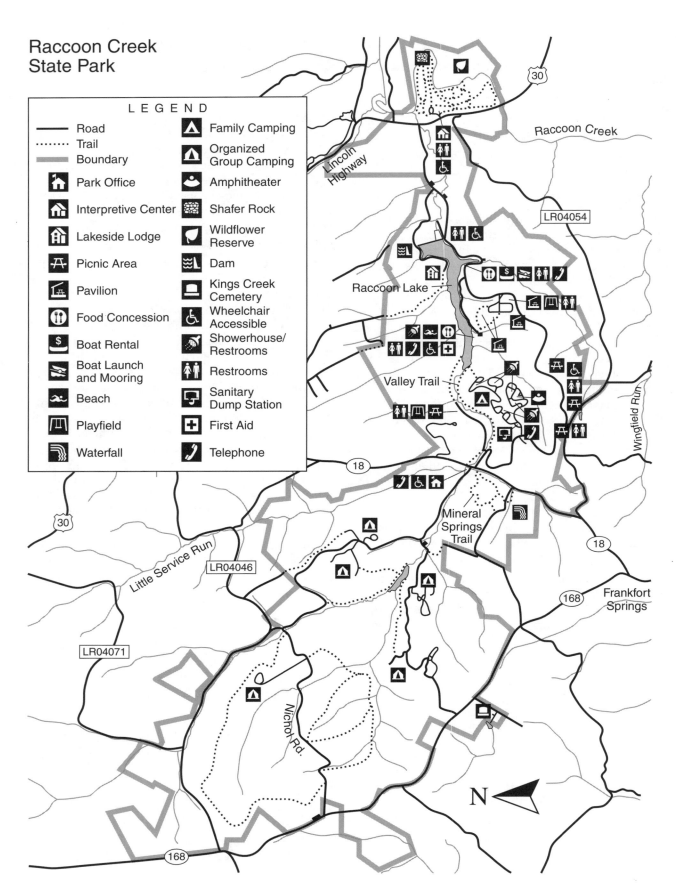

LEGEND

—— Road	▲ Family Camping
···· Trail	▲ Organized Group Camping
▬▬ Boundary	Amphitheater
Park Office	Shafer Rock
Interpretive Center	Wildflower Reserve
Lakeside Lodge	Dam
Picnic Area	Kings Creek Cemetery
Pavilion	Wheelchair Accessible
Food Concession	Showerhouse/ Restrooms
Boat Rental	Restrooms
Boat Launch and Mooring	Sanitary Dump Station
Beach	First Aid
Playfield	Telephone
Waterfall	

Mineral Springs Trail 👢👢👢

Distance Round-Trip: 1.5 miles

Estimated Hiking Time: 1.5 hours

Caution: Most of the trails marked on the park map as Mineral Springs Trail and Upland Meadow Trail are overgrown and for practical purposes no longer exist. However, the Mineral Springs Trail does exist to the Frankfort Mineral Springs and to the restored spa. A section of this trail is along the edge of a cliff.

Trail Directions: Drive south past the park office on Route 18, then pull into a small parking area by the Frankfort Mineral Springs sign on the right side of the highway. Use the footbridge beside this parking area as your trailhead **[1]**.

Walk across the bridge onto a dirt road, then turn left onto a dirt path. A sign by a bench on the opposite side of the road points toward Frankfort Springs. This path is surfaced with gravel. It takes you across the spring stream, then up a cool, narrow valley to the source of the spring at Falling Rock (.2 mi.) **[2]**. Falling Rock is an overhanging bedrock outcrop. During wet periods, water falls over the rock. In times of drought, the springs seep out of the rock in orange streams, dripping into two stone cisterns, where the water can be collected. People began coming here to a health spa during the 1790s. The water contained 15 minerals that were believed to have medicinal properties. This spa continued operating until 1912.

More than a few people still come here for the water. The belief that the water has curative powers persists. Pause here on a bench to enjoy the cool air and the beautiful rock outcrop. Because of the constant dampness, moss, wildflowers, hemlock trees, and other plants grow from the sides of the rock, framing the scene in many colors and shades.

The trail makes a sharp right turn at the springs, then ascends a crumbling paved path and a set of steps to the road you left near the beginning of the hike (.25 mi.) **[3]**. Here, the road is grassy. A stone building across the road is a restoration of the Frank-

fort House health spa, which served customers during summers until 1912. Look for other signs of the health spa around this building.

According to the park map, Mineral Springs Trail should form a loop with Upland Meadow Trail above the restored spa. But these trails are overgrown. Instead, take a left from the top of the steps, up the grassy road. You will see orange trail blazes. Watch closely alongside the trail to find intersecting game trails. Turn right at the first major fork (.5 mi.) **[4]**. This wide, grassy trail makes a gentle descent through thick multiflora rose, then rises again through a plantation of pine and spruce. Follow this trail to the top of a knob, where you will see a metal tower beside a small cement block building (.8 mi.) **[5]**. This is a radio communications tower for the park. See if you can identify white oak, red maple, sassafras, and red pine on this knob.

Turn around here and backtrack to the restored spa. Instead of going down the steps to the mineral spring, stay on the road back to the trailhead (1.5 mi.) **[1]**. Be careful, especially with children, between the spa and the trailhead. There is a sheer cliff to the right of the road.

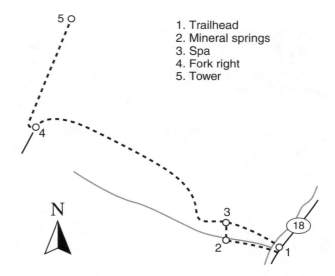

1. Trailhead
2. Mineral springs
3. Spa
4. Fork right
5. Tower

Valley Trail 👢👢👢

Distance Round-Trip: 2.4 miles

Estimated Hiking Time: 1.5 hours

Caution: Several fallen trees block this trail. There are no trail blazes. Watch for poison ivy.

Trail Directions: Turn east off Route 18, near the park office, toward the camping area, then park in the first small parking area on the right, about .1 mile past the intersection. Begin the hike here **[1]**. Walk up the road, around a curve to the right, to the trailhead on your left, which is marked by a sign (.1 mi.) **[2]**.

If you are staying in the campground, you will probably want to hike this trail in the opposite direction or have someone drop you off at this trailhead and hike one-way back to the campground.

Turn left through a gap in the guardrail onto a narrow dirt path by this sign. The trail descends into the valley of Traverse Creek. Though this park is named for Racoon Creek, it is laid out along the valley of Traverse Creek. Raccoon Creek flows just a short distance through the Wildflower Reserve at the eastern tip of the park.

Valley Trail takes you along a steep hillside overlooking the bottom of the Traverse Creek valley. Watch the valley floor for beautiful wildflowers. Near the beginning of the trail, there are some exceptionally large sycamore trees. Closer to the trail, both above and below, you will see equally large white oaks. Farther along the trail you will see impressive sugar maples and red oaks. Pause at a standing dead pine and try to determine how it is contributing to the forest community. Examine the tree closely to see what inhabits it.

As you hike this trail, look for signs that this park was laid out differently in the past. Uphill to the right you will see a barricade that was the end of a road. Look to the left while crossing a footbridge at a broken-down shack that still houses a large tank. Farther along you will see a broken-down outhouse. What other signs can you find? There are natural terraces on the steep hillside to your right. How do you imagine they formed?

Valley Trail goes into a steep climb at about the same point where Raccoon Creek Lake is coming into view. If you are hiking during spring or fall, outside the busy tourist season, you will probably see waterfowl on the water.

Valley Trail ends at a T (1.2 mi.) **[3]**. You can recognize this intersection by several timbers that have been placed across the trail you are intersecting to divert water runoff and prevent erosion on this steep slope. To your right, this trail leads to the camping area. To your left, though it is not shown on the park map, it leads to the lake and the swimming beach. Turn around here and retrace your steps back to the parking area (2.4 mi.) **[1]**. Though it appears on the park map that the first half of this hike should have been easier because it followed Traverse Creek downstream, actually the return trip is easier.

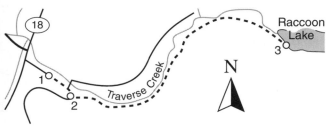

1. Parking area
2. Trailhead
3. Turn around

52. Wildflower Reserve—Raccoon Creek State Park

- See one of the finest displays of wildflowers in the state.
- Walk a combination of easy and moderately difficult trails.
- Learn about local plants and animals at the nature center.

Area Information

The 314-acre Wildflower Reserve at Raccoon Creek State Park is considered one of the finest and most distinctive wildflower displays in western Pennsylvania. It was purchased in 1962 by the Western Pennsylvania Conservancy. More than 500 species of flowering plants can be viewed along 5 miles of trails. This is accomplished through maintenance of a variety of habitats including abandoned fields, floodplain forest, pine plantations, and oak/hickory hardwood forest.

Learn about the plants and animals of the Pittsburgh Plateau at the nature center. Note that this is also referred to as the interpretive center. Start with the plants displayed around the outside of this tasteful building that blends peacefully into the natural surroundings. Each plant is identified by a small sign. Inside you will find extensive photos of wildflowers and wild animals. Several mounted animals are on display. A favorite of kids is a touching table, where you can feel snakeskins, furs, and animal bones.

Peak wildflower blooms occur from late April through mid-May. The first flowers to bloom, in mid-April, are snow trillium, skunk cabbage, coltsfoot,

and trailing arbutus. The last to bloom are closed gentian in September and witch hazel in October.

Directions: The park is 25 miles west of Pittsburgh in southern Beaver County by way of U.S. Route 30. Coming from Pittsburgh, turn right at the Wildflower Reserve sign. Watch for this sign after you see a sign at the entrance to Raccoon Creek State Park. Approaching from the north or south, exit Interstate Route 79 onto U.S. Routes 22 and 30. If you start from the park, take the main park road past Raccoon Creek Lake to the intersection with Route 30. Turn right after .2 mile to the entrance on the left.

Hours Open: This is a day-use area, open from 8:00 A.M. to sunset.

Facilities: The nature center, restrooms, and hiking trails are the only facilities at theWildflower Reserve. Many other facilities, including camping and picnicking, are available elsewhere in Raccoon Creek State Park.

Permits and Rules: Do not disturb plants or wildlife in any way. Collecting natural materials is not allowed. Pets are not allowed. Smoking is not allowed on the trails. Trails are for walking only. Bicycles, horses, or motorized vehicles are not allowed.

Further Information: For information about the Wildflower Reserve, phone the nature center, 412-899-3611. You can also get information from Raccoon Creek State Park, 3000 State Route 18, Hookstown, PA 15050; phone 412-899-2200.

Park Trails

This area is a maze of interconnecting trails. Some of these trails are not shown on the area map. Most hikes involve several trails.

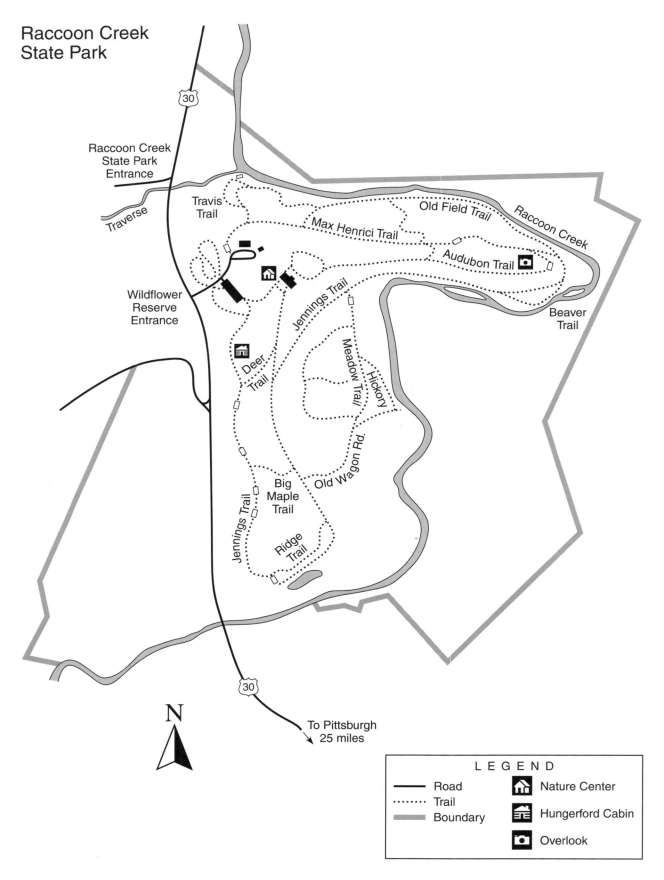

Raccoon Creek State Park

Raccoon Creek State Park Entrance

Traverse

Travis Trail

Max Henrici Trail

Old Field Trail

Raccoon Creek

Audubon Trail

Beaver Trail

Wildflower Reserve Entrance

Jennings Trail

Deer Trail

Meadow Trail

Hickory

Jennings Trail

Big Maple Trail

Old Wagon Rd.

Ridge Trail

N

To Pittsburgh
25 miles

LEGEND

— Road

⋯ Trail

▬ Boundary

🏠 Nature Center

🏚 Hungerford Cabin

📷 Overlook

Jennings/Deer/Old Wagon Road Trails 👢👢

Distance Round-Trip: .5 mile

Estimated Hiking Time: .5 hour

Caution: Watch for poison ivy. Some sections are quite steep and narrow, with numerous roots that can trip careless walkers. Stay on the trails. Be especially cautious on Old Wagon Road, where a cliff-like slope drops to the right.

Trail Directions: This is a nice hike through mature trees with a lot of ground cover, including flowering plants.

Start this hike at the end of the parking area nearest the nature center **[1]**. Walk straight across a mowed lawn toward woods on what appears to be a seldom-used service road to a wooden sign on the right side of the path. This sign points straight ahead to Hungerford Cabin and Jennings. The wide, rising trail is surfaced with gravel beginning at the tree line. It gets steeper around a right turn. Trees and ground cover are dense. A large red maple with sprawling low branches is particularly impressive.

The road ends at Hungerford Cabin (.1 mi.) **[2]**. Examine the old stonework in the chimney. Proceed through a clearing by the cabin to a bench where a narrower dirt trail reenters the woods and descends a steep slope. Watch your footing. Numerous roots protrude into the path.

Turn left at a signpost that indicates this is the direction for Deer Trail (.2 mi.) **[3]**. From this intersection you can hear and see traffic on Route 30 to your right. Deer Trail is about the width of a natural deer trail and crossed by large roots. But it is fairly level. It ends at a T where it meets Old Wagon Road (.3 mi.) **[4]**. Turn left onto Old Wagon Road.

Old Wagon Road is a gravel trail about three feet wide. It climbs modestly toward the nature center. Supervise children carefully along this section of the trail, where there is a steep dropoff along the right side. You can see the worn surface of another trail at the bottom of this dropoff. Old Wagon Road splits just before you reach the nature center (.46 mi.) **[5]**. Take the right fork to visit the nature center. Take the left fork to return to the parking area where you began this hike. Turn left when you come to a sidewalk by a kiosk. You can see the parking area from here. The complete loop is .5 mi. **[1]**.

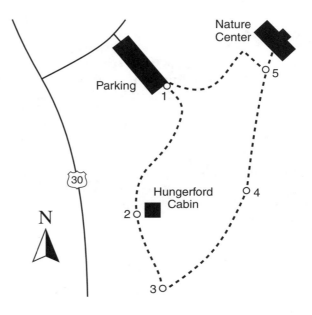

1. Trailhead
2. Hungerford Cabin
3. Deer Trail
4. Old Wagon Road
5. Nature center

Audubon Trail 👢👢👢

Distance Round-Trip: 1.1 miles

Estimated Hiking Time: 40 minutes

Caution: Watch for poison ivy. There are several steep areas as well as cliffs just to the side of the trail. Roots protrude through the trail in many areas. Be prepared for a variety of terrain.

Trail Directions: Start this hike where a paved sidewalk leaves the left corner of the parking area toward the nature center **[1]**. A sign in the lawn near the nature center points straight ahead to Audubon Trail and Henrici Trail. Proceed across the mowed lawn to another sign at the edge of the woods (.06 mi.) **[2]**. Turn right to stay on Audubon Trail. This section of the trail is part of an interpretive loop. A rope is strung on top of posts along the left side of the trail. Kids should hold onto this rope to avoid a ledge on the opposite side of the trail. A sign at the next trail fork directs you onto the right fork (.15 mi.) **[3]**. You are leaving the interpretive loop.

The trail is wide, but you must still be aware of the cliff to the right. Short spur trails lead to the edge of this cliff. It is temptingly impressive but very dangerous.

The sign is missing from the post at the next intersection (.3 mi.) **[4]**. Go straight. This begins the loop portion of the hike. You will be returning over that left fork.

Audubon Trail intersects with Jennings Trail 24 feet before it ends at a rock overhang at the point of the ridge (.47 mi.) **[5]**. The cliff is not as high as it is back along the trail, but it is still high enough to be very dangerous. Stay back and keep children under constant supervision. Turn left here onto Jennings Trail, or right if you have walked onto the rock overhang, down a steep slope over loose gravel and stone steps.

Rounding a sharp bend to the left, you will see Raccoon Creek below to the right, then arrive at a T intersection with Henrici Trail, which is marked by a signpost (.52 mi.) **[6]**. Turn left onto Henrici Trail. This trail is level for a short distance along the creek, then it begins rising up the hillside and across a weathered wooden footbridge.

Make a sharp left at the next intersection to cut back to Audubon Trail (.7 mi.) **[7]**. You can see another intersection and a sign about 50 feet ahead on Henrici Trail from this turn.

After a steep climb you arrive at Audubon Trail to complete the loop portion of this hike (.77 mi.) **[4]**. Turn right and retrace your steps back to the parking area (1.1 mi.) **[1]**.

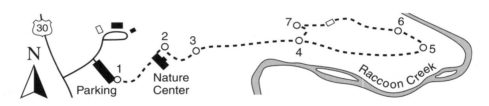

1. Trailhead
2. Audubon/Henrici split
3. Leave loop
4. Missing sign

5. Jennings Trail
6. Henrici Trail
7. Cutback trail

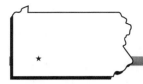

53. Point State Park

- Visit one of the most significant historic sites in American history, where numerous conflicts occurred between the French, the British, Native Americans, and American colonists.
- Straddle the formation of one of the world's great rivers.
- View the majestic Pittsburgh skyline.
- Watch huge commercial river barges.

Area Information

It was only natural that the confluence of the Allegheny and Monongahela Rivers that forms the mighty Ohio River would play a pivotal role in the colonization of America. This was the gateway to the west. Control of this area meant control of the major route into the area west of the Appalachian Mountains. The first European explorer to pass through here was René-Robert Cavelier Sieur de La Salle, in 1679. Many others followed.

The Virginia Colony, which laid claim to the area, started building Fort Prince George here in 1754, but it was never completed. That same year it was captured by the French, who built Fort Duquesne. They used it as a base for raids on the western frontier.

General John Forbes commanded an army of British and Colonials that captured Fort Duquesne from the French in 1758, though the French burned the fort before it fell into British hands. A small installation here was called Mercer's Fort for the next two years, then the more formidable Fort Pitt was constructed by the British. This was a five-sided structure, .5 mile around the perimeter, with a bastion at each corner. It was named to honor a British prime minister.

Under Virginian, French, British, and finally American control, the point between the Allegheny and Monongahela was a center for settlement and the jumping-off point for the settlement of all points west. Fort Pitt was abandoned in 1792. By the 1950s, the area had become a commercial slum. Governor David L. Lawrence, 1959–63, a pioneer of urban renewal, was instrumental in the development of Point State Park. A spectacular fountain is located at the tip of the point. The Fort Pitt Museum is located in one of the five original bastions of Fort Pitt.

Directions: You can reach the park via Interstate Routes 376 and 279, from the north via Pennsylvania Route 8, and from the south via Pennsylvania Route 51.

Hours Open: The park is open from 8:00 A.M. to 11:00 P.M. Fort Pitt Museum is open from 9:00 A.M. to 5:00 P.M. Tuesday through Saturday, and noon to 5:00 P.M. on Sunday.

Facilities: The park has numerous benches, restrooms, and paved paths.

Permits and Rules: Alcohol, skateboarding, bicycles, in-line skating, and unauthorized vehicles are prohibited.

Further Information: Department of Conservation and Natural Resources, Point State Park, 101 Commonwealth Place, Pittsburgh, PA 15222; phone 412-471-0235.

Other Areas of Interest

The **Pittsburgh Zoo** is a leader in the conservation of endangered species. For information write to Pittsburgh Zoo, One Hill Road, Pittsburgh, PA 15206; phone 800-474-4966.

For more information about places to see and things to do in **Pittsburgh,** write to Greater Pittsburgh Convention and Visitors Bureau, Four Gateway Center, Pittsburgh, PA 15222; phone 800-366-0093 or 412-644-5512.

Fort Pitt 🥾

Distance Round-Trip: .8 mile

Estimated Hiking Time: .5 hour

Caution: This hike is accessible to wheelchairs except for the steps to the fountain, which can be avoided.

Trail Directions: Start this hike on a wide brick path at the entrance to Point State Park near the corner of Commonwealth Place and Liberty Avenue **[1].** To your right is a grass-covered structure shaped like an arrowhead. This is the lower remnant of the original rampart walls of the Music Bastion and the Curtain Wall, one of five bastions of Fort Pitt. The drawbridge was located here.

Walk under the highway overpass (.1 mi.) **[2],** then turn right, following a sign that points to River Walk. There are two trails here. The right fork goes uphill. Take the left fork, which is a brick path. This path merges with a brick sidewalk loop that splits almost immediately. Take the left fork by the Pittsburgh Symphony Stage (.2 mi.) **[3].**

To your right, across the Allegheny River, you can see Three Rivers Stadium, the home of the Pittsburgh Pirates and the Pittsburgh Steelers. Two stadiums are currently under construction to replace Three Rivers Stadium. The Allegheny River drains most of northwest Pennsylvania. It was a major route used by the French when they began exploring the Mississippi River region.

After a 90-degree left turn around stone-block restrooms, turn right, down a set of steps, and walk around the magnificent fountain. Three pumps force the water into a 150-foot column. Halfway around the fountain, look downstream at the Ohio River. The Allegheny River is to your right, the Monongahela River to your left (.4 mi.) **[4].** Pleasure boat traffic is heavy. You might also see huge commercial barges pushed by tugboats. You can see an old submarine moored by shore downriver to the right.

Look at the high bluffs across the Monongahela River. These have caused transportation problems throughout Pittsburgh's history. One partial solution is Fort Pitt Tunnel, which you can plainly see emerging from the bluff.

Continue around the fountain and back up the steps, where you face the imposing Pittsburgh skyline. Turn right at the top of the steps, then make a 90-degree turn to begin walking upriver along the Monongahela. Trains run up and down this valley, on the opposite side of the river, almost continually. Turn left at the first fork onto the inner loop (.5 mi.) **[5].** The outline you have observed inside this loop is the outline of Fort Duquesne, the French fort that preceded Fort Pitt. If you have read the history of this region, you probably imagined that such an important fort was much larger.

Turn right at the fork just before the blockhouse (.6 mi.) **[6].** This blockhouse is the only surviving structure from Fort Pitt. It was built in 1764 under the supervision of Colonel Henry Bouquet. Past the blockhouse on the right is the Fort Pitt Museum. It was built into a restored section of the wall of Fort Pitt. After you walk out of the museum, turn right under the highway overpass to return to the trailhead (.8 mi.) **[1].**

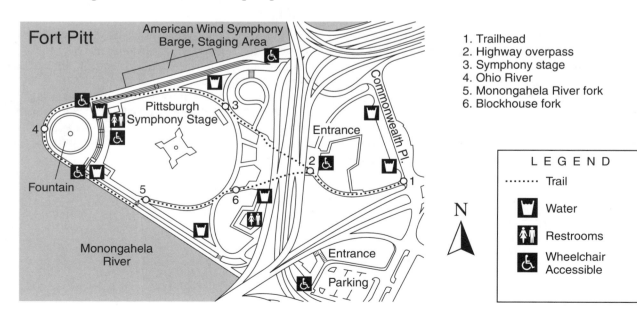

1. Trailhead
2. Highway overpass
3. Symphony stage
4. Ohio River
5. Monongahela River fork
6. Blockhouse fork

LEGEND
...... Trail
Water
Restrooms
Wheelchair Accessible

N

54. Ryerson Station State Park

- Get off the beaten path in a location only an hour south of Pittsburgh.
- Fish for trout, panfish, and bass in R.J. Duke Lake.
- Learn about nature from campfire programs, an interpretive center, and guided hikes.
- Swim at a guarded pool.

Area Information

Ryerson Station State Park is located in the southwest corner of the state, less than 5 miles from the West Virginia border. Its name commemorates Fort Ryerson, which was constructed nearby in 1792 on the order of Virginia authorities to be used as a refuge from Indian attacks. This area was once under the jurisdiction of the Virginia Colony, and later the state of Virginia, and was on the route to the western frontier.

Two years after the land was acquired in 1958, Ronald J. Duke Lake was formed by damming the north fork of the Dunkard Fork of Wheeling Creek. Ronald J. Duke was a manager of Ryerson Station State Park. This lake covers 62 of the park's 1,164 acres. It is stocked several times each year with trout by the Pennsylvania Fish and Boat Commission.

Directions: From Interstate Route 79 in Greene County, turn west onto Pennsylvania Route 21. Turn left onto Bristoria Road between Graysville and the West Virginia border. A sign marks this turn. Bristoria Road passes through the park and past the park office.

Hours Open: The park is open year-round. Day-use areas are open from 8:00 A.M. to sunset. A guarded swimming pool is open between 11:00 A.M. and 7:00 P.M. from Memorial Day weekend to Labor Day, unless otherwise posted.

Facilities: A family campground for tents or trailers has 50 sites, including 16 with electrical hookups. There are pit toilets and a sanitary dump station. A primitive organized group camping area can accommodate 80 people. This area has toilet facilities, fire rings, picnic tables, and drinking water. A boat launch area is located near park headquarters. Grills, drinking water, comfort facilities, and more than 300 picnic tables are scattered around the park. A children's play area is located at the main picnic area. A food concession is located by the guarded swimming pool. Three of five picnic pavilions can be reserved.

Permits and Rules: Boats used on R.J. Duke Lake must have either a state park launching permit, a state park mooring permit, or a current registration from the Pennsylvania Fish and Boat Commission. Advance reservations are required for the group camping area. Pets must be leashed and controlled at all times and may not be taken into swimming or overnight camping areas. Alcoholic beverages are prohibited. Outdoor recreational activity is restricted to locations where physical improvements or postings designate the appropriate purpose. Dispose of coals only in facilities that are provided for that purpose.

Further Information: Department of Conservation and Natural Resources, Ryerson Station State Park, RR 1, Box 77, Wind Ridge, PA 15380; phone 412-428-4254.

Park Trails

Three Mitten Trail —1.4 miles—Shaped like a mitten, this trail is open to snowmobiles during winter.

Polly Hollow Trail —.9 mile—This trail connects Three Mitten Trail with Deer Trail.

Iron Bridge Trail —.8 mile—This trail connects Deer Trail with Pine Box Trail.

Fox Feather Trail —1.3 miles—A self-guiding loop, this is connected with Iron Bridge Trail and Lazear Trail.

Lazear Trail —2.4 miles—Named for the family that once owned this land, this is the longest trail in the park.

Orchard Trail —.3 mile—This trail connects Lazear Trail with Tiffany Ridge Trail.

Tiffany Ridge Trail —.8 mile—Check out Solitude Hollow.

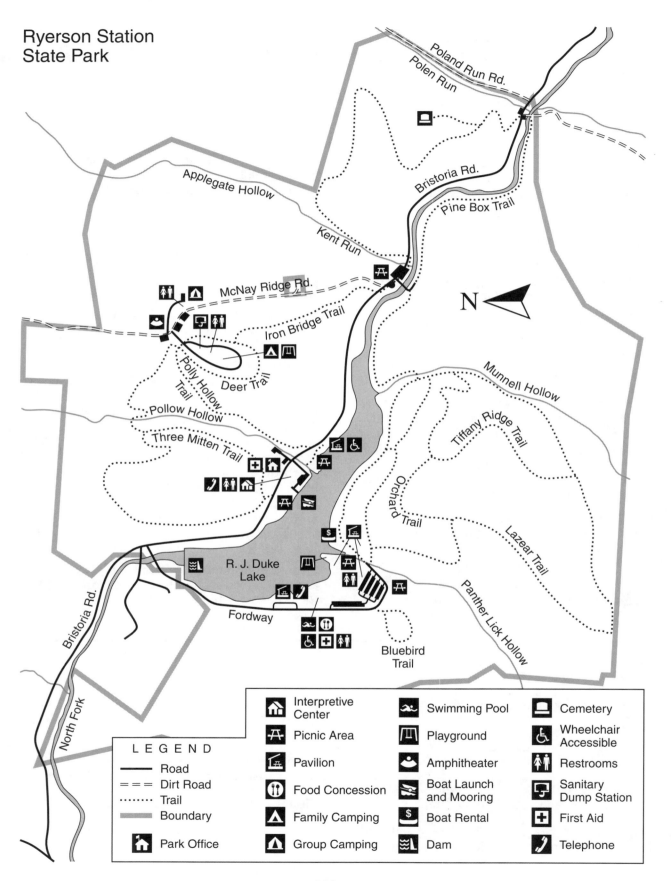

Ryerson Station State Park

N

LEGEND
— Road
=== Dirt Road
···· Trail
▬ Boundary
🏠 Park Office

🏠 Interpretive Center
🏕 Picnic Area
⛺ Pavilion
🍴 Food Concession
🏕 Family Camping
🏕 Group Camping

🏊 Swimming Pool
🎠 Playground
⛱ Amphitheater
🚤 Boat Launch and Mooring
$ Boat Rental
🌊 Dam

💻 Cemetery
♿ Wheelchair Accessible
🚻 Restrooms
♻ Sanitary Dump Station
✚ First Aid
📞 Telephone

Poland Run Rd.
Polen Run
Bristoria Rd.
Pine Box Trail
Applegate Hollow
Kent Run
McNay Ridge Rd.
Iron Bridge Trail
Polly Hollow Trail
Deer Trail
Pollow Hollow
Three Mitten Trail
Munnell Hollow
Tiffany Ridge Trail
Orchard Trail
Lazear Trail
R. J. Duke Lake
Fordway
Panther Lick Hollow
Bluebird Trail
Bristoria Rd.
North Fork

Pine Box Trail 👢👢👢👢

Distance Round-Trip: 2 miles

Estimated Hiking Time: 1.25 hours

Caution: Several portions of this trail are very steep, with loose footing. Protect yourself from ticks.

Trail Directions: Stay on Bristoria Road past R.J. Duke Lake to the Iron Bridge Picnic Area, on the right, across from the entrance to McNay Road. The trailhead **[1]** is at a picnic area sign that also notes Pine Box Trail. Begin by crossing Iron Bridge, then immediately turn left, upstream. This first level stretch passes through an open area, following North Fork. Walk quietly and watch ahead for great blue herons. Numerous red-winged blackbirds will be more tolerant of your presence.

Pine Box Trail becomes about as narrow as a game trail and begins to climb the steep hillside at .2 mi. **[2]**. Here the valley also is narrower and the steep hillside rises immediately from the side of the creek. Look at an unusually large sycamore tree here, and note the composition of the forest on and near the valley floor. Compare it with the forest you will encounter farther along the trail at higher elevations. Even along this section of the trail on the steep hillside above the creek, the trees below you are different than the trees above on the right.

You cross a wooden footbridge **[3]** below a rock outcrop at .4 mi. Below is a beautiful pool in the creek. When trout are feeding, you can see them swirling at the surface. During May, trillium blossoms in the moist soil by the trail. Soon the trail drops back to the valley floor, then turns left across a bridge (.7 mi.) **[4]** on Riggs Road. Pine Box Trail then crosses Bristoria Road and begins to climb to the left. Trail signs direct you through this area. There is also a larger sign marking the park border to your right.

This portion of the trail appears to be an old farm or logging road. Hardwoods, including numerous white oaks, dominate the forest as the riverine forest disappears. During spring, clusters of fire pink add brilliant color to the forest floor. These red wildflowers are abundant in several areas along the trail ahead. A fork at a switchback could be confusing if not for a sign directing Pine Box Trail uphill to the right.

Under the shade of several spruces, a spur trail **[5]** to historic Stahl Cemetery that cuts to the right is the 1-mi. mark. To this point, the trail has been climbing since crossing Bristoria Road. Past the cemetery spur, the trail follows the side of the hill, close to the top, with mild undulations.

After crossing a spring stream, which flows under the trail through a pipe (1.4 mi.) **[6]**, the trail turns left into a steep decline. The stream cuts an increasingly deep gorge. In places, the trail is so steep that footing is tricky. At 1.7 mi., the trail forks **[7]**. It appears that Pine Box Trail should go straight, but a yellow arrow directs you to turn left. The narrow gorge changes to a broader ditch in this area, and soon the stream empties into Kent Run. Follow this downstream to Bristoria Road (2 mi.) **[8]**. Here you can see the trailhead a short distance to the right.

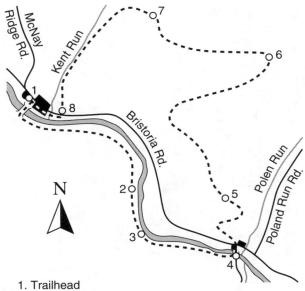

1. Trailhead
2. Narrow climb
3. Footbridge
4. Riggs Road bridge
5. Cemetery spur
6. Pipe
7. Fork
8. Bristoria Road

Deer Trail 👢👢

Distance Round-Trip: .8 mile

Estimated Hiking Time: .5 hour

Caution: Though this trail is relatively level, there are a couple very short, steep areas, one at the start of the trail and the other at the end.

Trail Directions: From Bristoria Road, turn onto McNay Ridge Road. About a half mile up this road, turn into the Polly Hill camping area. Deer Trail circles this camping area, which is situated on top of a knob. It is a fine area for bird watching, especially for birds that inhabit the forest canopy. Because of the steep slope below the trail, you can look into the canopy at eye level. Right where the campground drive becomes a loop, look to the left for a sign indicating the direction to Iron Bridge Trail and Deer Trail **[1].** Deer Trail begins with a

steep but short drop over the edge of the hill, then a left turn. After just 200 feet the trail forks **[2].** Take the right fork, angling downhill. The left fork, as you can see at this point, crosses McNay Ridge Road.

From here, Deer Trail begins its circle around the knob, through a beautiful mixed forest with only gentle ups and downs. You can see shagbark hickory, sycamore, red oak, and wild grapevine, among others. Iron Bridge Trail forks to the left at .3 mi. **[3].** Wild grapevine is abundant around the end of the knob in an area with relatively little undergrowth. This is an important food for several species of wildlife.

Ignore several minor forks to the right. These have been made by people walking from the campground, which is not far away from the trail at any point. You will observe several unusually large red oak trees along this latter third of Deer Trail.

Polly Hollow Trail forks left at .8 mi. **[4].** This is marked by a sign that also indicates that Three Mitten Trail is to the left. You are now very near the end of Deer Trail, just 100 feet to the right at this fork and up a short climb.

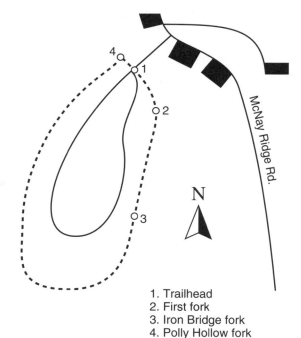

1. Trailhead
2. First fork
3. Iron Bridge fork
4. Polly Hollow fork

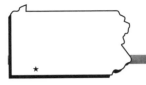

55. Ohiopyle State Park

- Ride a raft down the thundering Ohiopyle Rapids.
- Catch trout from the beautiful Youghiogheny River.
- Tour Frank Lloyd Wright's famous Fallingwater.

Area Information

Ohiopyle is one of the more highly developed and most popular parks in the state. It is nationally known for white-water rafting and for its bike trails. This 19,052-acre park surrounds the 1,700-foot-deep Youghiogheny River Gorge, where the Youghiogheny River cuts through Laurel Ridge, some of the highest land in the state. Approximately at its center are the magnificent Ohiopyle Falls and the small community of Ohiopyle. The Lower Yough (pronounced Yock), beginning below the falls, contains several class III and class IV rapids. The Middle Yough, above the falls, has class I and class II water. The Youghiogheny River Bike/Hike Trail follows the river on abandoned railroad grades for 28 miles. Raft, kayak, and bike rentals and guide services are available in the park.

In vivid contrast to the activity and development area near Ohiopyle Falls, most of this park is wild. Whether you are floating, biking, or hiking in the gorge, the only motor vehicle you will hear is the echo of a train.

Directions: Ohiopyle State Park can be reached via Pennsylvania Route 381, four miles north of U.S. Route 40 at Farmington.

Hours Open: The park is open year-round. Access is not guaranteed during winter. Day-use areas close at sunset.

Facilities: Food, gas, inflatable boat and kayak rentals, and bicycle rentals are available in the Ohiopyle village. The 237-site campground with tent and trailer sites has a washhouse with hot showers, flush toilets, a sanitary dump station, and play areas for children. Reserve campsites by phoning 888-PA-PARKS. Two picnic areas are equipped with tables, grills, rental pavilions, playing fields, and rest rooms.

Permits and Rules: Do not park in nondesignated areas. You must contact the park office in advance to leave a vehicle in a parking area overnight. All motor vehicles and equestrians are prohibited on the Youghiogheny River Bike/Hike Trail. Ask for a brochure about white-water boating regulations.

Further Information: Department of Conservation and Natural Resources, Ohiopyle State Park, P.O. Box 105, Ohiopyle, PA 15470-0105; phone 724-329-8591.

Other Areas of Interest

Pennsylvania's largest cave, **Laurel Caverns,** is off U.S. Route 40 between Uniontown and Farmington. Write to Laurel Caverns Geological Park, 200 Caverns Road Park, Farmington, PA 15437; phone 724-438-3003 or 800-515-4150.

Fallingwater, one of famed architect Frank Lloyd Wright's most widely acclaimed works, is between Ohiopyle and Mill Run off Pennsylvania Route 381. For a schedule of tours and for reservations, write to Fallingwater, P.O. Box R, Mill Run, PA 15464; phone 724-329-8501.

Park Trails

Great Gorge Trail —2.6 miles—See Cucumber Falls and wildflowers in season.

Meadow Run Trail —3 miles—Get wet in cool, natural water slides.

Sugarloaf Trail —3.8 miles—Climb 800 feet in elevation.

Baughman Trail —3.1 miles—Climb 900 feet with a spectacular overlook midway.

Kentuck Trail —3.9 miles—Hike up and down forested terrain.

Jonathan Run Trail —1.6 miles—See several waterfalls and blooming rhododendron from late June to early July.

Beech Trail —2.4 miles—Walk through large stands of beech as you drop down the Youghiogheny River Gorge.

Laurel Highlands Trail —70 miles—Ohiopyle State Park is the southern terminus of this trail. Reservations must be made to camp overnight through Laurel Ridge State Park; phone 724-455-3744.

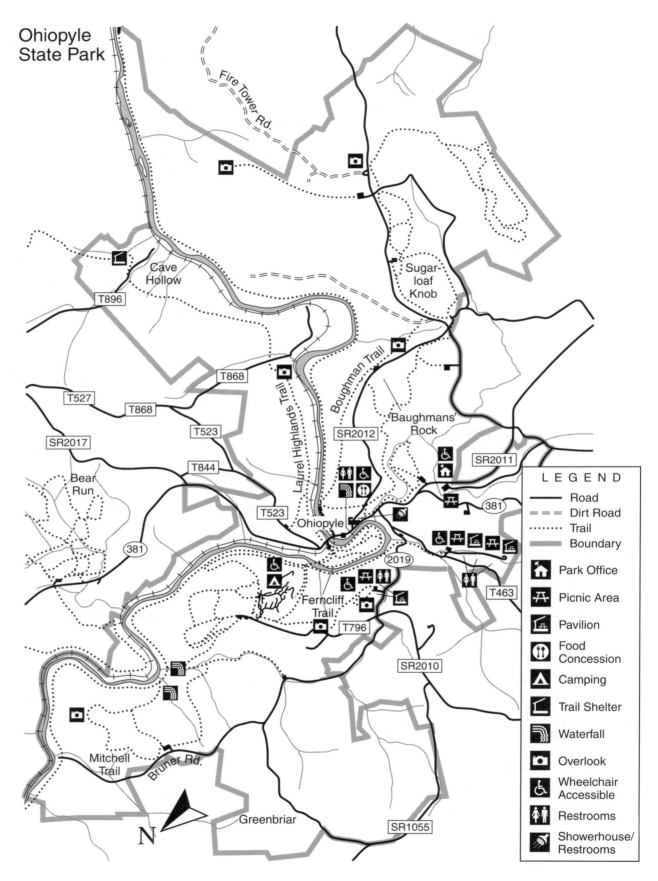

Ohiopyle
State Park

Fire Tower Rd.

Cave
Hollow

T896

T868

T527

T868

T523

SR2017

T844

T523

Bear
Run

381

Ohiopyle

Laurel Highlands Trail

Boughman Trail

SR2012

Sugar-
loaf
Knob

Baughmans'
Rock

SR2011

381

2019

Ferncliff
Trail

T463

T796

SR2010

Mitchell
Trail

Bruner Rd.

Greenbriar

SR1055

N

L E G E N D

———	Road
= = =	Dirt Road
··········	Trail
▬▬▬	Boundary
🏠	Park Office
⚷	Picnic Area
⌂	Pavilion
🍴	Food Concession
⛺	Camping
⌐	Trail Shelter
🌊	Waterfall
📷	Overlook
♿	Wheelchair Accessible
🚻	Restrooms
🚿	Showerhouse/ Restrooms

Ferncliff Trail 👢👢👢

Distance Round-Trip: 1.9 miles

Estimated Hiking Time: 1.5 hours

Caution: Rocks along the river can be very slippery, especially when wet. There are several places just off the trail where you could fall over rock ledges.

Trail Directions: Leaving the village of Ohiopyle heading north on Pennsylvania Route 381, turn left onto Ferncliff Drive and into a parking area just after crossing the Youghiogheny River. Just as you enter the parking area, there is a wide trail on your left that is blocked to motor vehicles by wood posts **[1]**. From here you begin a hike through one of the most spectacular and unspoiled natural areas in the state.

Just after you start down this trail, you will see a kiosk ahead that describes the Ferncliff Peninsula National Natural Landmark. Continue past the kiosk and under a railroad bridge. You are now very close to the Youghiogheny River, heading downriver. The trail forks at .1 mi. **[2]**. Take the left fork, as indicated by the first Ferncliff Trail sign. Take a moment here to examine a huge white oak tree. Because this area was once a popular resort, a virgin forest was preserved.

An information station entitled Ferncliff Fossils **[3]** at .2 mi. describes lepidodendron and cordaite fossils you see as you walk across boulders along the edge of the river. These were ancient trees. This is a favorite area for sunbathers. The trail is indistinct since the footing is bedrock, but you will have no trouble staying on course because the river is on your immediate left, and to your right is a steep bank shrouded in rhododendron. The roar of the falls becomes louder until you are standing on the brink **[4]**, .4 mi. from the parking lot. You will certainly want to pause. Be very cautious. There are sheer drops onto the rocks. Here, just as the trail angles uphill and away from the river through a rhododendron tunnel, an information station describes how the falls were formed.

Less than 100 feet past the falls, a spur trail leads downhill to an overlook. This provides the best view of the falls, from a wooden bench on a boulder, crowded on three sides by rhododendron, which hangs over the riverbed.

Past the overlook, Ferncliff Trail continues to climb through mature hemlock, white pine, and rhododendron. To your left is a beautiful view of the river and of river voyagers beginning their wild ride through the Middle Yough.

An information station describes the Youghiogheny Gorge **[5]** at .5 mi. Buffalo Nut Trail forks hard to the right here. This is another spectacular view of the river. Ferncliff Trail continues to follow the river as it meanders to form the Ferncliff Peninsula, though the river is out of view much of the time. The forest here, on top of the peninsula, is mature hardwood.

Oakwoods Trail forks to the right **[6]** at .7 mi. Ignore that fork, staying to the left. An unmarked trail forks toward the river after another 500 feet. Ignore that and other less-distinct unmarked trails that lead down to the river. You will also pass the fork with Fernwood Trail **[7]** at 1 mi. Do not let the similarity of names confuse you. Stay to the left on Ferncliff Trail. When in doubt, follow the rectangular black paint blazes on trees and boulders.

Not far from the Fernwood Trail Fork, the trail starts a gentle descent, and you will get glimpses of the river through the trees to your left. An information station entitled Eastern Hemlock (1.3 mi.) **[8]** explains that the hemlock is the state tree. This is one of the better views of the river on the latter half of this trail.

Ferncliff Trail pulls away from the river at an unmarked fork **[9]** at 1.6 mi. Stones have been placed along the left side of Ferncliff Trail, directing you uphill to the right. Another unmarked intersection with several trails could be confusing if not for the parking area visible to your left. Depending on where you parked, you might want to leave the trail here. Go straight through this intersection to complete the loop at **[2]** 1.8 mi., then turn left past the kiosk to the edge of the parking lot **[1]** for a total distance of 1.9 mi.

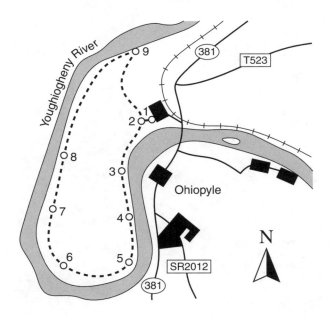

1. Trailhead
2. Fork
3. Ferncliff Fossils
4. Ohiopyle Falls
5. Youghiogheny Gorge
6. Oakwoods Trail
7. Fernwood Trail
8. Eastern Hemlock
9. Unmarked fork

Mitchell Trail 👢👢

Distance Round-Trip: 2.3 miles

Estimated Hiking Time: 1.25 hours

Caution: Wear bright orange clothing during hunting season.

Trail Directions: From Pennsylvania Route 381 just south of the Ohiopyle village and the bridge over Meadow Run, turn west onto Pennsylvania Route 2019, past Cucumber Falls, onto Bruner Road, about 4.5 miles to the Old Mitchell Place Parking Area. The Mitchell Trail trailhead [1] is on the higher side of the parking area, to the right.

Mitchell Trail begins in a gentle decline through an overgrown field, a remnant of the Old Mitchell Place. Nature is reclaiming the field with maple, tulip tree, cherry, and thorn apple, though heavy browsing by deer has disrupted the process. Three wood posts intended to prevent vehicles from using the trail (.1 mi.) [2] mark your entry into mature timber. This is an excellent area for bird watching during the spring migration. The trail is wide, smooth, and grassy.

During the white-water boating season, you will see numerous vehicles back in the parking area. A takeout area for Middle Yough floats is located a short dis-

tance down Bruner Road. However, once away from the parking area, this lightly used trail gets you away from most human activity. The only sounds along the trail are from birds and wind rustling through the trees. Though this trail lacks the spectacular scenery seen elsewhere in the park, it offers serenity.

The trail soon turns back through overgrown fields. Watch for wild turkeys feeding on the abundant grasshoppers in the tall grass during late spring and early summer. A T at .5 mi. is an intersection with Kentuck Trail [3]. Turn left, through a dip and into more mature timber, in and out of another overgrown field, and back into mature timber again at .6 mi. [4].

The remainder of Mitchell Trail follows the contour of the ridge top through mature hardwood timber. Walk quietly and you might see white-tailed deer, turkeys, and an assortment of songbirds. The trail is marked with painted red blazes; however, the trail is easy to follow without them. The land always descends to your right until you return to the parking area. If you wander away from the trail to the right, you will see that the slope becomes much steeper. At about 1.2 mi. the trail turns sharply left [5], pulling away from the Youghiogheny Gorge and up the Bruner Run valley.

The one potentially confusing unmarked trail fork [6] is at 2 mi., very close to the end of Mitchell Trail. Stay to the left, following the red blazes uphill. The right fork is apparently an old farm trail or logging trail. At this point you might hear vehicles on Bruner Road, or even see them through the dense forest.

You will see the parking lot to your right before completing the loop [1] after hiking 2.3 mi.

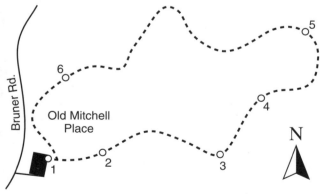

1. Trailhead
2. No vehicle posts
3. Kentuck Trail
4. Leave overgown field
5. Bruner Run valley
6. Unmarked fork